Handbook of Cross-Cultural Psychology

SOCIAL PSYCHOLOGY

VOLUME 5

EDITED BY

Harry C. Triandis
University of Illinois at Urbana-Champaign, USA

Richard W. Brislin
Culture Learning Institute, East-West Center, Hawaii, USA

ALLYN AND BACON, INC.
Boston   London   Sydney   Toronto

Library of Congress Cataloging in Publication Data

Main entry under title:

Handbook of cross-cultural psychology.

Includes bibliographies and index.
CONTENTS: v. 1. Triandis, H. C. and Lambert, W. W., editor. Perspectives.—v. 2. Triandis, H. C. and Berry, J. W., editors. Methodology.—v. 3. Triandis, H. C. and Lonner, W. Basic processes.— [etc.]
1. Ethnopsychology—Collected works. I. Triandis, Harry Charalambos, 1926—
GN502.H36   155.8   79-15905
ISBN 0-205-06501-5 (v. 5)

Printed in the United States of America.

Contents

Volume 3.   BASIC PROCESSES

Volume 4. DEVELOPMENTAL PSYCHOLOGY   (in press)

Preface

Cross-cultural psychology has been expanding in the past twenty years[1] to the point that there is now a need for a source book more advanced than a textbook and more focused than the periodical literature. This is the first handbook of cross-cultural psychology. It is an attempt to assemble in one place the key findings of cross-cultural psychologists. In addition to serving the needs of graduate instruction, the *Handbook* will be useful to advanced undergraduates and to professional social and behavioral scientists.

This *Handbook* will do more than summarize the state of cross-cultural psychology in the 1970s. It should provide a bridge that will allow more traffic in the direction of a new kind of psychology. One of the key facts about psychology is that most of the psychologists who have ever lived and who are now living can be found in the United States. About 50,000 psychologists live in the United States and several thousand more graduate each year. The rest of the world has only about 20 percent of the psychologists that are now or have ever been alive. Moreover, psychology as a science is so overwhelmingly the product of German, French, British, Russian, and North American efforts that it is fair to consider it an entirely European-based enterprise (with American culture considered the child of European culture). Yet, science aspires to be universal. Cross-cultural psychologists try to discover laws that will be stable over time and across cultures, but the data base excludes the great majority of mankind who live in Asia and the Southern Hemisphere. Are so-called "psychological laws" really universal? Are theories merely parochial generalizations, based on ethnocentric constructions of reality? This *Handbook* assembles reports of the methods, procedures, and findings that ultimately will give definitive answers to such questions, answers that are crucial for the development of psychology. If psychology must be changed to understand the behavior and experience of the majority of mankind, then this is a fact of profound importance. If not, it is still good to know that no changes are needed. The reality probably lies between these two extremes, and different psychological laws can be held as "true" with varying degrees of confidence.

We engage in cross-cultural psychology for many reasons, which are enumerated in the Introduction to Volume 1. Volume 1 examines the field in broad perspective and examines how it relates to some other fields. Volume 2 focuses on methodology, since the cross-cultural enterprise poses formidable methodological difficulties. The remaining volumes concentrate on basic psychological processes such as learning, motivation, and perception (Volume 3); developmental processes (Volume 4); social psychological (Volume 5); and psychopathological (Volume 6) phenomena.

One key policy decision for a handbook is whether to cover the material exhaustively, saying a word or two about every study, or in depth, saying rather more about a few key studies. Our decision for greater depth resulted in incomplete coverage. However, much of the work in cross-cultural psychology is methodologically weak. Rather than attacking such studies, we decided to de-emphasize them in favor of those studies that are methodologically defensible. However, this was not a decision that was applicable to all the methodologically weak areas. In some areas of cross-cultural psychology, there has been so *much* weak work that any student starting to work on related problems is likely to find dozens of studies and hence get the impression that this is a respectable area of inquiry. In such cases we could not ignore the weak studies. But while we had to quote them and criticize them, we could not sacrifice much space in this effort. For instance, most of the work using versions of the prisoner dilemma game in different cultures results in uninterpretable findings. In Volume 5 Leon Mann and Gergen, Morse, and Gergen discuss this work and show why it is weak.

Some work was left out simply because space limitations did not allow complete coverage. Other work was omitted on the grounds that it really is not cross-cultural psychology, and may more appropriately be included in comparative sociology, cultural anthropology, or some other field. Some of these decisions are inevitably arbitrary. Obviously, a *Handbook* like this one is likely to *define* the field, both by what it includes and by what it excludes. We are distinctly uncomfortable about some of the exclusions. For instance, our coverage of Freudian, neopsychoanalytic, and related cross-cultural studies is extremely limited. However, other theoretical systems, such as a "liberated cognitive behaviorism" (Triandis, 1977) will encompass the insights derived from this tradition. We have very little discussion of ethnoscience, ethnomusicology, and ethnolinguistics; we believe these materials now belong to other neighboring disciplines. It is of course obvious that this judgment may be wrong. A revision of this *Handbook*, which may be necessary in a decade or two, could well give a central position to one of these topics.

In writing this *Handbook* we have been very much aware of the probability that psychologists from non-European-derived cultures will find it among the most useful books that they may obtain from European-derived cultures. Much of what psychologists teach in their own cultures is based on studies done with subjects from European-derived cultures. They cannot be sure that such information is culture-general. This *Handbook* faces this question and could become a companion volume of any European-derived psychology book. Since many psychologists do not have English as their first language, we have tried to keep the language as concise as possible. If the style appears telegraphic at times, it is intentional.

We allowed the authors of the chapters considerable freedom in expressing themselves. We felt that an international enterprise such as this *Handbook*, should not impose narrow, possibly ethnocentric standards. Thus, authors have been allowed to use the style and spelling that is more appropriate in their own country. English now exists in many versions; the language of Scotland is not identical to Indian English. Rather than obliterate such differences with a heavy editorial hand, we have preserved them.

Volume 1 includes background material that any serious student of cross-cultural psychology would want to know. It examines the history, the major theoretical frameworks, and the relationship between cross-cultural psychology and some other closely related disciplines.

Volume 2 concentrates on methodological problems. Cross-cultural psychology has all the methodological problems of research done by psychologists in a homogeneous culture, plus additional ones that arise because it is cross-cultural. The authors describe the particular technique and emphasize the special difficulties—the particular methodological dilemmas that one faces in cross-cultural work—stressing those strategies developed to deal with those dilemmas. For example, since the reader is assumed to know about experimental methods, the chapters on experiments deal only with special concerns of cross-cultural psychologists doing experiments.

Volume 3 focuses on basic psychological processes—perception, learning, motivation, and so on. Here we tried to give the experimental psychologists who investigate such processes a chance to expand their perspective. We focused on what appears to be universal, but also emphasized ways in which cultural factors may intrude and change some of the processes.

Volume 4 examines developmental perspectives. Some of the key areas discussed are the development of language, personality, and cognition. Since the major effort in the past twenty years in cross-cultural developmental psychology has been on testing aspects of Piaget's theoretical system, a major focus is on this topic.

Volume 5 deals with cross-cultural social psychology. It examines the major traditional topics—attitudes, values, groups, social change—and some of the newer topics—environmental psychology and organizational psychology.

Volume 6, the last one, is of greatest interest to clinical psychologists or psychiatrists. The focus is on variations of psychopathology, on methods of clinical work, as well as on the cultural and family antecedents of psychopathology.

Our expectation is that the committed student of cross-cultural psychology will want to own all six volumes. However, in this age of specialization and high costs we know that many will buy only Volume 1 plus one other. Finally, certain specialists will want a single volume to enlarge their perspective on their own discipline, by examining the related cross-cultural work. These different patterns of acquisition produce a serious policy problem concerning coverage. A key theory or key cross-cultural finding may have to be mentioned in each volume for those who purchase only one volume, which may create considerable overlap across volumes. However, the authors have cross-referenced chapters in other volumes. Also, we have allowed minimum coverage of a particular topic that has been covered extensively in another volume, so that purchasers of only one volume will acquire some superficial familiarity with that topic.

In some cases, the topics are sufficiently large and diffuse that coverage by two different authors does not result in redundancy. When this was the case, I simply sent copies of the relevant sections of other chapters to these authors and asked them, when revising, to be fully aware of coverage in other chapters.

The idea to publish a *Handbook of Cross-Cultural Psychology* originated with Jack Peters of Allyn and Bacon, Inc. He asked me at the 1972 meetings of the American Psychological Association, in Hawaii, whether I would be interested in editing such a handbook. The idea appealed to me, but I was not sure of the need. We wrote to a sample of distinguished psychologists for their opinions. They were almost unanimous in thinking that such a handbook would be worth publishing. At the conference on "The Interface between Culture and Learning," held by the East-West Center, in Hawaii, in January 1973 we asked a distinguished, international sample of cross-cultural psychologists for their opinion. They were also supportive. By the summer of 1973 a first outline of a handbook was available, but it also became very clear that I alone could not handle the editing. The handbook should reflect all of psychology; I was not competent to deal with such a vast subject. Hence the idea emerged of having several Associate Editors, who would cover different aspects of the topic.

The Society for Cross-Cultural Research, at its 1975 Chicago meetings, heard a symposium in which G. Kelly, G. Guthrie, W. Lambert, J. Tapp, W. Goodenough, H. Barry, R. Naroll, and I presented our ideas about the shape of the *Handbook*, and we heard criticism from both anthropologists and psychologists in the audience about our plans.

In January 1976 we were fortunate to be able to hold a conference sponsored by the East-West Center, Hawaii, in which about two-thirds of the chapters were thoroughly discussed. We are most grateful to the Center for this support. The East-West Center held a course for post-doctoral level, young social scientists from Asia, the Pacific, and the United States, using the drafts of the *Handbook* chapters as a textbook. Richard Brislin, Stephen Bochner, and George Guthrie were the faculty. Fifteen outstanding young social scientists[2] were thus able to give us feedback from the point of view of the consumer, but even more important, they pointed out statements that may have been ethnocentric, incorrect, confusing, and outdated.

From the very beginning, we were committed to producing a handbook with authors from every continent. This was not possible. However, the *Handbook* includes chapters by authors from nine countries. To avoid as much ethnocentrism as possible, I appointed a board of twenty Regional Editors. These editors were asked to supply abstracts of publications not generally available in European and North American libraries. These abstracts were sent to those chapter authors who might find them useful. Thus, we increased the chapter authors' exposure to the non-English international literature. By summer 1975, fourteen of these twenty Regional Editors had supplied abstracts listed by cultural region. They were:

Africa

R. Ogbonna Ohuche (University of Liberia, Monrovia, Liberia)
The late M. O. Okonji (University of Lagos, Nigeria)
Christopher Orpen (University of Cape Town, South Africa)
Robert Serpell (University of Zambia, Lusaka, Zambia)

Circum-Mediterranean

Yehuda Amir (Bar-Ilan University, Israel)
Terry Prothro (American University, Beirut, Lebanon)

East-Eurasia

S. Anandalakshmy (Lady Irwin College, New Delhi, India)
John L. M. Dawson (University of Hong Kong)
Wong Fong Tong (Jamaah Nazir Sekolah, Kuala Lumpur, Malaysia)
S. M. Hafeez Zaidi (University of Karachi, Pakistan)

Insular Pacific
Subhas Chandra (University of South Pacific, Fiji)

South America

Eduardo Almeida (Mexico City)
Gerardo Marin (Universidad de los Andes, Bogotá, Colombia)
Jose Miguel Salazar (Universidad Central de Venezuela, Caracas, Venezuela)

It should be mentioned that with such an international group of authors, chapters required particularly skillful editing of the style so that all chapters would be excellent not only in content but in language. My wife, Pola, and Doris S. Bartle supplied this expertise and were among those who contributed to the realization of a truly international undertaking.

A number of colleagues functioned as special reviewers for individual chapters. Thanks are due to S. M. Berger, Charles Eriksen, Lucia French, Lloyd Humphreys, and Fred Lehman for their critical comments. In addition, the final version of each volume was read by a scholar, and I would also like to acknowledge their valuable suggestions and comments: Volume 1, Daniel Katz; Volume 2, Uriel Foa; Volume 3, Lee Sechrest; Volume 4, Barbara Lloyd and Sylvia Scribner; Volume 5, Albert Pepitone; and Volume 6, Ihsan Al-Issa.

Harry C. Triandis

NOTES

1. Documentation of this point would include noting that several journals (the *International Journal of Psychology*, the *Journal of Social Psychology* and the *Journal of Cross-Cultural Psychology*) publish almost exclusively cross-cultural papers; there is a *Newsletter*, first published in 1967, that is largely concerned with this area; there are *Directories* of the membership of cross-cultural psychologists, first published by Berry in the *International Journal of Psychology* in 1969, then revised and extended and published as a booklet by Berry and Lonner (1970) and Berry, Lonner, and Leroux (1973); and finally, there is the International Association for Cross-Cultural Psychology, which has held meetings in Hong Kong (1972), Kingston, Canada (1974), Tilburg, Holland (1976), Munich, West Germany (1978), which now has a membership of about 350 active researchers from about fifty countries. Psychology has been an international enterprise for almost a century, and the Union of Scientific Psychology, and the International Association of Applied Psychology have been meeting every two or so years, since the turn of the century. But the emphasis on collecting *comparable* data in several cultures is relatively new, and has expanded particularly after the mid 1960s. A number of regional international organizations, such as the Interamerican Society of Psychology, and the Mediterranean Society of Psychology, have become active in the last twenty years.

2. Listed by country the participants were:
   Australia: Brian Bishop (Perth, Institute of Technology), Margaret M. Brandl (Darwin, Department of Education), Betty A. Drinkwater (Townsville, James Cook University), Michael P. O'Driscoll (Adelaide, Flinders University).
   Fiji: Lavenia Kaurasi (Suva, Malhala High School)
   Indonesia: Suwarsih Warnaen (Jakarta, University of Indonesia)
   Japan: Yuriko Oshimo (University of Tokyo) and Toshio Osako (Tokyo, Sophia University)
   Pakistan: Sabeeha Hafeez (Karachi University), Abdul Haque (Hyderabad, University of Sind)

Philippines: Liwayway N. Angeles (Rizal, Teacher Education)
Thailand: Jirawat Wongswadiwat (Chaingmai University)
United States: Angela B. Ginorio (New York, Fordham University), Howard Higginbotham (University of Hawaii), Caroline F. Keating (Syracuse University), and James M. Orvik (Fairbanks, University of Alaska)

At the conference, the following authors and editors, in addition to Brislin, Bochner, and Guthrie, were also present: Altman, Barry, Berry, Ciborowski, Davidson, Deregowski, Draguns, Heron, Holtzman, Hsu, Jahoda, Kiineberg, Lambert, Longabaugh, Lonner, R. and R. Munroe, Michik, Pareek, Price-Williams, Prince, Sanua, Sutton-Smith, E. Thompson, Tseng, Triandis, Warwick, Zavalloni.

Biographical Statements

HARRY C. TRIANDIS, the General Editor, was born in Greece, in 1926. During childhood he received several cross-cultural influences: German and French governesses, French and Italian high school years. After three years of engineering studies at the Polytechnic Institute of Athens, he attended McGill University in Montreal, Canada, where he graduated in Engineering. He worked in industry for three years, during which he obtained a master's degree from the University of Toronto. But engineering was not as interesting to him as studying people. He returned to McGill to learn basic psychology, and studied with Wallace E. Lambert and Don Hebb. From there he went to Cornell University, where he studied with W. W. Lambert, W. F. Whyte, T. A. Ryan, Alexander Leighton, and others. From Cornell in 1958 he went to the University of Illinois, where he is now Professor of Psychology. He conducted cross-cultural studies in Greece, Germany, Japan, and India, and worked in collaboration with black psychologists on the perceptions of the social environment among blacks and whites. His books include *Attitude and Attitude Change* (1971), *The Analysis of Subjective Culture* (1972), *Variations in Black and White Perceptions of the Social Environment* (1975), and *Interpersonal Behavior* (1977). He was Chairman of the Society of Experimental Social Psychology (1973–74), President of the International Association of Cross-Cultural Psychology (1974–76), President of the Society for the Psychological Study of Social Issues (1975–76), President of the Society of Personality and Social Psychology (1976–77), and Vice-President of the Interamerican Society of Psychology (1975–77).

RICHARD W. BRISLIN was born in Barre, Vermont and lived in New England until his family moved to Alaska, where he graduated from high school. He accompanied his family on its next move to Guam, and he received a B.A. degree there in English and American literature. Guam provided extensive cross-cultural experience since other students came there from various Pacific islands (especially Palau, Truk, Ponape, and the Marshalls) to pursue a higher education. He received his Ph.D. from the Pennsylvania State University, with a dissertation involving a trip back to Guam to study translation problems. He is now a research associate at the Culture Learning Institute, East-West Center in Honolulu, Hawaii where he continues his interests in cross-cultural methodology and social psychology. He is director of a yearly program, "Cross-cultural research for behavioral and social scientists" that attracts approximately twenty participants each year from Asia, the Pacific, and North America. He is coauthor or editor of four books: *Cross-Cultural Research Methods* (1973); *Cross-Cul-*

tural Perspectives on Learning (1975); *Cross-Cultural Orientation Program* (1976); and *Translation, Applications and Research* (1976). Since 1973 he has edited a yearly volume, *Topics in Culture Learning.*

ANDREW R. DAVIDSON became interested in cultural influences on behavior during a peripatetic undergraduate career that included studies at the American University of Beirut, University of the West Indies, and Sterling College, Kansas, United States. This interest increased during his graduate work in psychology at the University of Illinois where he studied with Harry Triandis, Roy Malpass, and Martin Fishbein. While at Illinois he coauthored review chapters on cross-cultural psychology for the *Annual Review of Psychology* and the *Biennial Review of Anthropology.* After receiving his Ph.D. in 1974 he moved to Seattle where he initially worked as a research scientist at Battelle Human Affairs Research Centers. He presently teaches psychology at the University of Washington. He has investigated the interrelation of beliefs, attitudes, and behavior and coordinated a survey research project in India, Korea, Fiji, Iran, Mexico, and the United States that compared the validity of a number of decision-making models for predicting family planning decisions and behavior.

ELIZABETH THOMSON is a member of the research staff at Battelle Human Affairs Research Centers. Her research is on population growth and family planning in developing countries. Her academic background is in mathematical statistics (B.S., 1967), sociology (M.A., 1976), and psychology at the University of Washington. She has worked extensively with Arthur Lumsdaine of the University of Washington on research ranging from the development of computer-assisted instructional programs to the evaluation of family planning communication activities in the developing world.

MARISA ZAVALLONI was born in Milano (Italy) in 1929. Her cross-cultural experience began as a university student at the Sorbonne (Paris, France) where she obtained a licence in psychology, then in London and New York where she obtained her Ph.D. from Columbia University. Since then, she has taught at the University of Santiago de Chile, Paris, Geneva, and Brussels before joining the University of Montreal in 1975. Her cross-cultural research included the West Indies, several African countries, Europe, and the United States. She has been for almost a decade the Associate Director of the Research Center for the Study of Intergroup Relations, a joint unit of the École des Hautes études en Science Sociale, and of International Social Sciences Council (UNESCO).

KENNETH J. GERGEN received the B.A. degree in 1957 from Yale University, and after two years of travel in the U.S. Navy, entered the Ph.D. program at Duke University. He joined the teaching staff at Harvard

University after obtaining the degree in 1963. With a grant from the Ford Foundation he carried out cross-cultural research in Sweden in 1966. He moved to Swarthmore College in 1967, and spent 1968–69 in Rome, Italy, and in North Africa as a Guggenheim Fellow. In 1971 he became a Professor of Psychology at Swarthmore College and with a grant from the National Science Foundation, carried out cross-cultural research in Japan and other Asian countries in 1972–73. In 1976 he received a Fulbright Research Fellowship to carry out studies in France. His primary interests have been in social perception, the self-concept, social exchange, and theory development within the social sciences. He has authored or edited seven books, including *The Concept of Self, The Psychology of Behavior Exchange, The Study of Policy Formation* (with R. Bauer), and *Social Psychology in Transition* (with L. Strickland and F. Aboud).

STANLEY J. MORSE is currently Lecturer in Psychology at the Flinders University of South Australia. He received his B.A. in sociology from Antioch College in 1965 and his Ph.D. in social psychology from the University of Michigan in 1971. In 1973 he went to Brazil as a Fulbright-Hays Fellow to help establish the country's first graduate level program in social psychology. Then he worked as Coordinator of Social Research at Brazil's Institute for Space Research, evaluating the impact of a large-scale educational TV and radio project in the northeast of Brazil and teaching research methods to graduate students in educational technology. Morse has also been a Lecturer in Psychology at the University of Cape Town (South Africa), a research fellow at the National Institute of Psychology in Rome, Italy and Visiting Associate Professor of Psychology at the University of Saskatchewan (Canada), as well as Assistant Professor of Psychology at New York University. Morse has published numerous articles on such topics as interpersonal attraction, social exchange, and psychological factors in political behavior and is the author of the chapter on collective behavior in *Social Psychology: Explorations in Understanding* (1974). He also coedited the book, *Contemporary South Africa: Social Psychological Perspectives* (1975). Morse is currently involved in cross-cultural research on national identity and on patterns of social interaction.

MARY M. GERGEN took her B.S. and M.A. degrees from the University of Minnesota, graduating Phi Beta Kappa. She was a research assistant at Harvard University's Department of Social Relations from 1965–67, working primarily on cross-cultural reactions to foreign aid. With a grant from the McNeill Foundation, she conducted field interviews in North Africa, Greece, and Italy on the problem of aid. Further cross-cultural research was carried out in Japan in 1972–73 as Research Associate under a grant from the National Science Foundation. She is currently a Ph.D. candidate at Temple University, and an instructor in social psychology at Swarthmore College. She has coauthored papers on reactions to aid, women's liberation, drug usage, and political activism, and is currently co-authoring a text in social psychology.

LEON MANN is Professor of Psychology (since 1972) at Flinders University of South Australia. An Australian, he attended the University of Melbourne, receiving his B.A. (1961) and M.A. (1962) in the field of social psychology. His doctoral work at Yale University in the United States was carried out as a member of the Communication and Attitude Change project. After receiving his Ph.D. (1965) he returned to Australia to teach at his alma mater. From 1968–70 he taught in the Department of Social Relations at Harvard University, and from 1971–72 at the University of Sydney. Dr. Mann, who is a Fellow of the Australian Academy of the Social Sciences, has held visiting professorships at Stanford University and the Hebrew University of Jerusalem. His interest in cross-cultural research includes comparisons between various forms of crowd behavior in Australia, the United States, and Israel. He is the author of *Social Psychology* (1969), *Collective Behavior* (forthcoming), and, with Irving Janis, *Decision Making: A Psychological Analysis of Conflict, Choice and Commitment* (1977).

JOHN W. BERRY was born in Montreal, in 1939. He grew up in rural Québec, completed high school in Montreal, and then spent three years working as a merchant seaman. He graduated from Sir George Williams University (Montreal) in 1963, and obtained a Ph.D. from the University of Edinburgh in 1966. His research hau been directed toward the study of the development of behaviour in differing ecological and cultural settings, toward the psychological effects of acculturation and the study of intergroup attitudes and relations. He has conducted field studies in Arctic Canada (Eskimo, Cree) and the mid-north (Ojibway, Carrier and Tsimshian), in Africa (the Temne of Sierra Leone and the Pygmy of the Central African Republic), in Australia (the Arunta, the Koongangi, and the Illawara) and in New Guinea (the highland Telefol and the coastal Motu). His books include *Social Psychology: The Canadian Context* (edited with G.J.S. Wilde, 1972), *Culture and Cognition* (edited with P. Dasen, 1974), *Applied Cross-Cultural Psychology* (edited with W. Lonner, 1975), *Multiculturalism and Ethnic Attitudes in Canada* (with R. Kalin and D. Taylor, 1976), and *Ecology of Cognitive Style: Comparative Studies in Cultural and Psychological Adaptation* (1976).

ARNOLD S. TANNENBAUM is a Program Director in the Organizational Behavior Program at the Survey Research Center, Institute for Social Research, and Professor in the Department of Psychology at the University of Michigan. He holds a degree in electrical engineering from Purdue University (1945), and Ph.D. degrees in psychology from Syracuse University (1954) and Göteborg University (1976, honorary). He has been on the staff of the Organizational Behavior Program since 1949, directing a series of studies concerning industrial and other kinds of organizations. During 1958–59 he served with the Organization for European Economic Cooperation as consultant in the Human Factors Division of the European Productivity Agency. He has also taught abroad under a Fulbright Fellowship, and has lectured widely in Europe. He served as consulting editor for the journal, *Modern Organizations*, published in Yugoslavia, and is the author and coauthor of several books including *Social Psychology of the Work Organizations, Control in Organizations,* and *Hierarchy in Organizations.* The latter describes research undertaken in a number of countries.

IRWIN ALTMAN was born in 1930 and raised in New York City where he attended public schools and New York University. He did graduate work in social psychology at the University of Maryland and received a Ph.D. in 1957. He has had a varied professional career, having worked in a private contract research organization, a university research office, and a U.S. Navy laboratory. Since 1969 he has served as a Professor and Chairman of the Psychology Department at the University of Utah. He also taught at the American University, Washington, D. C. and at the University of Maryland. His books include *Small Group Research* (1966) with J. E. McGrath, *Social Penetration* (1973) with D. A. Taylor, and *The Environment and Social Behavior* (1975). He and Martin Chemers are currently writing a book on *Culture and Environment.* Altman has been Chairman of the Society of Experimental Social Psychology (1975–76), Chairman of the American Psychological Association Task Force on Environment and Behavior (1973–76), Division 8 (Personality and Social Psychology) representative to the American Psychological Association Council of Representatives, and a member of the Board of Directors of the Association for the Study of Man-Environment Relations (1968–71).

MARTIN M. CHEMERS received his Ph.D. in social psychology from the University of Illinois in 1968. Research for his doctoral dissertation involved an analysis of interpersonal conflict between Iranians and Americans and the development of training materials designed to alleviate intercultural conflict. That work followed earlier studies in communication and conflict between American students and foreign students studying in America. More recently Chemers has studied the role of cultural differences on perception and communication among subcultural groups within the United States. Dr. Chemers has lived for extended periods in Iran and Germany and has traveled in Europe, Asia and North America. He is a Professor of Psychology at the University of Utah, at Salt Lake City.

1

Introduction to *Social Psychology*

~~~~~~~~~~~~~~~~~~~~~~~~~~~~~~~~
Richard W. Brislin
~~~~~~~~~~~~~~~~~~~~~~~~~~~~~~~~

Extending the basic definition of psychology as "the scientific study of behavior and experiences," social psychology studies behavior and experience with respect to social stimuli, especially stimuli associated with people's interaction with other people. Core topic areas such as affiliation, attraction, socialization, conformity, resource exchange, intergroup interaction, and organizational behavior follow closely from the basic definition. Other core topic areas such as attitudes and values are central to social psychology since people acquire attitudes and values through interaction with others.

The majority of social psychological studies are based on methods, approaches, assumptions, and models developed in North America and Western Europe. Some cross-cultural investigators in the field of social psychology have followed this tradition while others have attempted to develop new methods, approaches, assumptions, or models because the traditional approach limited progress toward explaining social behavior in other cultures.

In recent years social psychology has experienced a crisis that includes dissatisfaction with past accomplishments and an absence of widely accepted guidelines for future efforts (Triandis, 1975b). Numerous critics have recommended various directions for more profitable research (e.g., see McGuire, 1973; Gergen, 1973; Helmreich, 1975; Elms, 1975; Lewin, 1977). Since some of these recommendations involve cross-cultural research, it is important to understand the recent history of social psychology that the critics are reacting to. Certain approaches to social psychology became very influential in the 1950s and 1960s, and these traditional approaches were a core part of the curricula for graduate students. After studying these approaches, some students rejected the tradition and embraced newer developments, including cross-cultural studies.

The basic assumption of the tradition is that experimental control is necessary. This central goal of control means that researchers (experimenters) have to choose independent variables to which people in their studies are exposed and that the researchers must examine the nature of the independent variables by manipulating them. As a function of the independent variable's manipulation, certain dependent variables would be affected that the researcher would measure. Relationships between independent and dependent variables would be explained by theoretical concepts that supposedly summarized the findings of various studies. Independent variables most often involved some sort of manipulation of the social environment (e.g., pressures to conform, as reviewed in Chapter 5 of this volume by Mann; or various communications, as reviewed in Chapter 2 by Davidson & Thomson). Dependent variables most often involved measures of behavior (e.g., response to group pressure; attitude change) that were either independently observed or reported by the people themselves. Most often, such studies were carried out in university laboratories in which the experimenter had control over (a) the presence, absence, or level of the independent variables, and (b) possible extraneous sources of influence that might affect the dependent variables.

There were certainly other sorts of research done. For example, certain investigators chose to look at natural variations (as found in the real world) as independent variables rather than to manipulate them. Examples might be a person's position in an organizational hierarchy (see Chapter 7 by Tannenbaum); or a major change in a person's lifestyle (see Chapter 6 by Berry). Measures gathered from people who had experienced one or more of these natural variations would then be treated as dependent variables (e.g., job satisfaction; interpersonal stress). Functional relationships between independent and dependent variables would then be suggested. But when field studies of this sort were done, the standards used by other professional researchers in judging them were often the same that applied to laboratory studies in which the experimenter had more opportunities to achieve control. Laboratory studies became favored by many influential social psychologists. Researchers attempting field research ran the risk of not being able to publish their work, since referees considered "control" a major factor in judging research articles submitted to them.

The value placed on control forced investigators to create experimental situations in which independent variables could be more and more precisely defined. This precision led to studies that investigated a *very* small part of the wide repertoire of social behavior. This latter point will be explored later when the "culture of social psychology" is discussed. Unfortunately, space does not permit a thorough examination of another major research tradition in social psychology: survey research. However, the arguments for the importance of "control" are similar in this research approach to those in the choice of topic areas for investigation, measures of people's background characteristics (e.g., socioeconomic status), and precision in the wording of questionnaires. Similar, also, are arguments related to the linking of independent and dependent measures, and judgments by professional colleagues. Most studies of the values and value systems held by people have used the survey approach. (These are reviewed in Chapter 3 by Zavalloni.)

Some investigators have used the traditional approach in cross-cultural research. The studies on the social psychology of groups reviewed by Mann are the clearest examples of the direct application of standard laboratory social psychological methods in other cultures. But other investigators have questioned such direct application, raising the same sorts of issues covered by Berry in his Introduction and by the various contributors to Volume 2 of this *Handbook*. Researchers questioning tradition have wondered whether or not the older approaches allow investigators to document important, central aspects of human behavior in cultures other than the ones in which a certain research tradition developed.

Cross-cultural researchers have rarely been clear about their objections to standard social psychological methods. The following points, however, seem to be implied in introductions to their research articles and in their comments (after research papers have been presented) during professional meetings. The best way to present these ideas is to reexamine traditional social psychology's basic assumptions, as presented earlier, and to ask whether or not the assumptions are sensible in the case of cross-cultural research.

(a) "Researchers have to choose independent variables. . . ." This most crucial research step carries the assumption that the investigator knows enough about the behavior under study to choose important independent variables. A point often forgotten is that in most social psychological research investigators are members of the culture being studied. The investigators, then, can make good guesses regarding important independent variables, based on their own backgrounds, since they can reflect on how *they* would react to the independent variables. But this knowledge is rarely present when an investigator enters another culture. Hence, when a researcher imports a standardized social psychological procedure that determines the independent variables to be studied, there is no assurance that the independent variables will include behavior or stimulus conditions considered central and important in other cultures. Examples of standardized procedures that may be culture bound include the Asch conformity situation (see Chapter 5 by Mann), a game in which cooperative or competitive behavior is possible (see Chapter 4 by Gergen, Morse, &

Gergen), or one-sided versus two-sided communications (see Chapter 2 by Davidson & Thomson).

When the hard, preliminary work of understanding which antecedents of behavior are important in a culture has not been completed, standardized procedures are inappropriate and often nonsensical. Many cultural anthropologists reject such work because the procedures social psychologists use are often alien to other cultures. Further, the anthropologists charge that social psychologists would come to the same conclusion if they would do the preliminary field work necessary to determine the appropriateness of various independent variables.

(b) "... researchers must examine the nature of independent variables by manipulating them." Assuming that independent variables have been wisely chosen, methods for manipulating them must be found. Manipulation can take the form of an experimenter's arranging the presence or absence of an event, or it can take the form of presenting various levels of an independent variable to different people. Problems arise (a) in the actual administration of the manipulation, (b) in the measurement of whether or not the manipulation was successful, and (c) with the assumptions regarding metrics of various levels of the independent variable.

Administrative problems arise when people in a study do not understand how social psychologists do research. Of course, such a state of affairs is usual in cross-cultural research. People in many cultures view researchers as a novelty. Thus researchers often provide stimulation for conversation. Nance (1975), for instance, documented the tremendous impact that visitors had on the private conversation among members of the Filipino tribe, the Tasaday. People often discuss the fact that some people receive the independent variable (especially if it is a desired commodity), while others do not receive it. They may wonder why there is a difference, complain, and sometimes create so much extraneous activity as to "wash out" the effects of the independent variable. Studies using deception are even more prone to misunderstanding. Commonly used in North America, deception studies involve the manipulation of independent variables by misleading people. An example is Feldman's (1968) study in which trained accomplices pretended to need help in staged situations set up in Boston, Paris, and Athens. Naive passers-by then could help the accomplice if they chose to do so. Admittedly, valuable data were obtained in this study, but a price is paid when hard feelings are generated. Students from Asia and the Pacific often point out that such studies are emotionally rejected in their countries. They asked: "If experimenters deceive their subjects, why should the people of the culture believe *anything* that the researchers say?" This is a hard question to answer. Cross-cultural researchers will have to weigh the potential negative consequences of deception when deciding on which methods might be used in a cross-cultural investigation.

Another problem related to manipulation is the assessment of the manipulation itself. The experimenter has a goal in manipulating a variable; was the goal achieved? This question is answered through a formal assessment of the independent variable's manipulation, and the assessment is usually carried out by measuring subjects' reactions. For instance, Sinha (1968) wanted to manipulate cooperation versus competition motives among Indian subjects. He did so through a series of instructions, and he measured the success of the instructions by administering a Thematic Apperception Test (see the chapter by Holtzman in Volume 2 of this *Handbook*). As predicted, subjects gave cooperative or competitive themes according to the instructions they received. With this assurance that the independent variable was successfully manipulated, Sinha continued the experiment that was concerned with group productivity as a function of subjects' motives and the resources available to the subjects. When the independent variable is not assessed, explanation of results is often impossible. For instance, Frager (1970) found that Japanese college student subjects who were exposed to the Asch conformity situation behaved in a manner strikingly different from subjects in the United States (see Chapter 5 by Mann for a longer discussion of this study). But since the nature of the independent variable (the Asch situation) was not assessed, there is no way to explain the results. Does the manipulation *mean* exactly the same in all cultures?

A third problem occurs when experimenters want to investigate various levels of an independent variable, for instance, high, medium, and low levels of some motive. In such cases, researchers are dealing with ordinal and sometimes presumed-interval scales. The problems involving metrics and suggested solutions are the same as those discussed extensively in Volume 2 of this *Handbook*. The only addition here is the reminder that although almost all those discussions deal with metrics involving dependent variable development and measurement, the same arguments hold when researchers attempt to formulate various *levels* of independent variables.

(c) "As a function of the independent variable's manipulation, certain dependent variables would be affected and these would be measured by the researchers." The effects of independent variables are usually measured through observations of people's behavior or through their self-reports. Again, researchers have a good idea of what behavior or self-reports mean in their own culture. Since they also know the meaning of the independent variables, they can suggest theoretical links between them. But such understanding is not assured in other cultures. What exactly does it mean to check "agree" or "disagree" on a particular questionnaire item? The meaning could reflect true feelings about the subject matter under study or personality dispositions to answer in a certain way. Or to take another example, what does it mean to contribute to a group's productivity by working hard on an experimental task? The meaning could be a desire for achievement or it could be a desire for affiliation with other members of the group. What does it mean for a head-of-household to refuse to live in a certain type of neighborhood? The meaning could be rejection of the minority groups that live in that neighborhood or it could be a desire to increase the family's chances for various benefits that are valued in a certain culture. Without extensive preliminary investigation into the meaning of various behaviors and self-reports, cross-cultural social psychologists cannot interpret their data.

(d) "Relationships between independent and dependent variables would be explained by theoretical concepts. . . ." A researcher who works with theoretical concepts derived in one culture runs the risk of making mistakes if those concepts are put forth to explain data gathered in another culture. To use the technical term, the concepts become imposed etics if they are not modified according to information gathered in the other culture. A better method is to allow for the possibility that much more powerful explanatory mechanisms might come from concepts found to be important in the other culture (emics). The most effective researcher, then, is one who has a healthy scepticism of theories developed in one or two parts of the world (e.g., United States and Western Europe) since (s)he realizes that while the theories may explain certain behavior quite well, they may not explain other behavior patterns found in other cultures. The cross-cultural concepts of emics and etics are explained more fully in Volume 2 of this *Handbook,* and Chapter 2 by Davidson and Thomson in this volume.

What Can Cross-Cultural Social Psychology Do?

Given these problems, is cross-cultural social psychological research possible? Why do it? Can anything be done to make good research more likely? Suggested directions toward answers to these questions will be given in this and the next section.

There are benefits of cross-cultural research for all psychology (e.g., Strodtbeck, 1964; Whiting, 1968; Brislin, Lonner, & Thorndike, 1973). Certain general categories proposed by these researchers can be applied to the more specific case of social psychological research, and other categories can be added to that original list which are unique to cross-cultural studies of social psychological variables.

1. Cross-cultural studies force an examination of situational variables since such variables obviously differ from culture to culture. Just in travelling between cultures researchers can observe differences in such

variables as crowding, differential access to basic nutritional requirements, and bureaucratic structures that may affect social behavior.
Instead of focusing on only dispositional variables of people, cross-cultural researchers are more likely to study the interactions between dis-
position and situation; this approach should yield better data.

2. Certain theoretical concepts and frameworks are taken for granted in
the countries where they were developed; cross-cultural research can
lead to an expansion of these concepts and frameworks. Research investigations into certain areas carried out, for instance, in the United
States have been so numerous that concepts underlying the research
become reified. The concepts are then overused in research done in
other cultures. For instance, the literature on the relationship between
similarity and attraction is voluminous in the United States. Researchers
in other parts of the world (e.g., Eastern Europe, Africa) are surprised to
see so much emphasis on this topic and warn that the concepts may not
be as valuable in their countries. They point out that such variables as
kinship ties and length of relationships between people may be more
important determinants of interpersonal ties than whether or not the
people are like each other. Similarly, much attitude-change literature
from North America has been concerned with the *content* of communications from person to person. Researchers from Asia point out that in
their countries the *form* of the communication may be as important as
the content. In fact, they add that Asians often find it difficult to interact
with North Americans, since the latter emphasize content over form so
much in their interpersonal relationships. Good cross-cultural research
should lead to expansion of such concepts and the frameworks used to
link the concepts. For example, cross-cultural researchers have had an
impact on a major theoretical position through their studies of Piagetian
concepts (see the review in Volume 4 of this *Handbook*). There will be
similar expansions of frameworks in social psychology over the next
twenty years.

3. The study of certain theoretically important topics is impossible in certain cultures since key aspects necessary to the success of a research
study are unavailable to investigators. Such variables may be much
more accessible in other cultures. For instance, the very rich (defined by
position on a socioeconomic continuum within a given society) have
been notoriously unavailable to researchers in certain parts of the
world. In other parts, however, visiting researchers are assigned a good
deal of status and have easy access to the rich and powerful. Or, it is
difficult to gain access to children with nutritional problems in certain
cultures but much easier (unfortunately) in others. Such access, of
course, brings with it the sorts of special responsibilities and ethical
issues discussed by Warwick (Volume 1 of this *Handbook*), a point to be
reiterated later in this introduction.

4. Researchers who engage in cross-cultural studies may become more
sensitive to variation in human behavior because of the culture shock
they inevitably experience in travelling between cultures. The word

"may" is used (and this entire paragraph is placed last) because this potential benefit of cross-cultural research is not firmly established. However, it follows from recent discussions of culture shock (Adler, 1975; Harris, 1976) that emphasize the learning possibilities that occur when people move between cultures. The affective state generated by experiencing different behaviors can stimulate learning. For instance, researchers from the United States who work in Japan invariably comment on the importance of a person's position in a group and the seeming lack of emphasis on individuality. Such an experience can motivate analysis of such topics as the relationship between individuals and groups in various cultures. Ideally, people who have had intercultural experiences are less rigid in their thinking, more open to seeing alternative solutions to problems, less prone to stereotype behaviors not common in their own lives, and more sensitive to the fact that different behaviors may lead to the same desired consequences (Brislin & Pedersen, 1976; Triandis, 1976). Obviously, all of these qualities are beneficial to people in research.

Suggestions for Better Research and Theory Development

If researchers accept the view that cross-cultural studies have a valuable role, what can be done to insure better research? In general, the answer is that much data must be gathered on possibly important independent and dependent variables before any "final" study is carried out. Gone are the days when researchers could do research on what happened to interest *them*. There are at least two reasons: (1) If researchers pick topics that interest them, there is no assurance that they will be picking topic areas that are important in other cultures. (2) There are not enough research opportunities any more to allow the luxury of doing studies because they interest the researchers. Access to other cultures is "drying up" since fewer and fewer researchers are being given permission to do studies. Leaders in other cultures are simply saying "no" to research requests (documented in Bochner, Brislin, & Lonner, 1975, pp. 7–10; see also chapter by Warwick in Volume 1 of this *Handbook*). Further, the two reasons are related, since leaders are refusing requests partly because they see no relevance to much proposed research. Hence when the rare research opportunity arises, it is important to ensure that it will yield the greatest probability of success. Since a researcher may not have a second or third chance to follow up an original set of findings (in distinct contrast to laboratory or even field studies within a country where research facilities are well established), it is important to do the study only after one has extensively examined the context of the phenomena under investigation. This study of context is also important for theory development that is, of course, of central importance for cross-cultural contributions to social psychology.

This *Handbook* contains several treatments on the development of theory in cross-cultural psychology and on cross-cultural contributions to a more general theory of human behavior. Triandis treats this topic in his general introduction to all six volumes; Jahoda's major concern is to review the strengths and weaknesses of various theoretical approaches (Volume 1). In addition, Lonner treats theory in his discussion of cultural universals (Volume 1). His treatment of various categories of universals should help in conceptualizing types and scopes of theories. Berry's chapter (this volume) is specifically concerned with fitting data to a broad theory, and Mann has a very helpful explanation of hypothesis and theory testing in the appendix to his chapter (this volume).

The benefits of having a number of statements on theory spread throughout several chapters outweigh the disadvantages. The major benefit is that the multiple statements reflect the diversity, lack of agreement, but potentially helpful plurality of views among theoreticians. A single statement might give the impression of more homogeneity of thought than actually exists. An important concept that has not been sufficiently covered in any of these treatments, however, is the relation between theory and method in cross-cultural studies. Mann (appendix to Chapter 5 in this volume) is correct in pointing out that cross-cultural studies are most helpful when aspects of a culture are considered independent variables. Such studies are especially useful when the independent variables increase the range or type of "treatments" beyond that found in any one culture. Examples might be type of economy, type of preparation for seemingly disorganized events, or range of educational opportunities. Cultures, then, allow for a "panorama of possibilities" regarding selection of important variables for theory development. A practical outcome of this culture-theory link, however, is that social psychologists must be flexible in either (a) selecting theoretical positions for development, or (b) selecting cultures that provide good opportunities to test a certain theory. The former position is probably more realistic. Certain cultures, not all, will be willing to host a project designed by researchers. Leaders of these cultures will undoubtedly impose reasonable conditions, such as demands that data gathered have a practical return. Given these inevitable constraints, successful researchers will be those who can integrate the practical demands with an investigation of a theory. The theory finally chosen for development will often be in an area that is unfamiliar to the investigator.

The question then becomes, "How can investigators discover important variables and interrelationships, given that they may not be intimately familiar with certain cultures willing to host them?" Triandis (1975a, 1977b) has proposed a "loose" and wide-ranging theory designed to help identify important relationships that should lead to more "tight" theories after empirical research. Triandis (1977a, p. 144) also proposes the following classification of potentially important variables. (Some changes have been made for purposes of the present chapter.)

1. The *ecology:* the physical environment, resources, geography, climate, fauna and flora.
2. The *subsistence system:* methods of exploitation of the ecology to survive: agriculture, fishing, gathering, industrial work.
3. The *cultural system:* the man-made part of the environment; this includes both objective culture (roads, tools, factories) and external subjective culture (norms, roles, and values as they exist outside the individual).
4. The *social system:* patterns of interaction, such as formation of groups, roles, family structure, institutional behavior.
5. The *interindividual system* or *socialization system:* social behaviors (e.g., conformity, helping, aggression, intimacy, covertness), particularly methods of child rearing.
6. The *projective system:* myths, dreams, fantasies, folklore.
7. The *individual system:* perceptions, learning, motivational patterns, individual attitudes; *perceived* norms, roles, values, and other aspects of the subjective culture that connect the individual system with the cultural system.

Most often (certainly not always), social psychologists are concerned with the effects of variables in categories 1 through 6 on variables in category 7, or with the interrelationships among variables within category 7. These concerns are just part of a "division of labor" since behavioral and social sciences in other disciplines are concerned with relationships between and among other categories. Social psychologists who become involved in interdisciplinary work will undoubtedly engage in research outside the typical pattern suggested above (Dinges, 1977).

Triandis (1975a, 1977b) has also suggested methods that researchers can use to identify key variables within the categories. Data collection should be based on a wide-ranging nomological network of concepts that have possible significance to a general topic area chosen by the researcher. The wider the net that is cast, the greater the chance of collecting key data. Triandis's specific research interests concern interpersonal relations, so his system must be modified by others who wish to study other areas. He has always been quick to recommend that researchers should be willing to modify concepts and methods to measure the concepts, based on facts the researchers discover in other cultures. A few examples, however, should be given to show how the wide-ranging data collection procedure might occur. Triandis (1975a) posits that the probability of an act being performed by a person is a function of the *habits* of the person, the *behavioral intention* to emit the act, and the *facilitating conditions* relevant to the performance of the act. Behavioral intentions, in turn, are posited to be a function of the *social determinants* (norms, roles, socially shaped self-concepts, and interpersonal contracts), the *affect* attached to the behavior, and the value of the *perceived consequences* of the behavior. There are other concepts in this complex system, but those already presented are enough to serve as examples. For each concept, Triandis suggests different methods of measurement. If the behavior under study is how people from the so-called "majority culture" behave toward members of minority groups, measures might be as follows. (Only one item per concept is presented here; in actual use, there would be multiple items.) For social determinants, the basic question is "What *should* people do?" Various items would be written to measure people's perceptions of norms, such as:

People in my country

should ____ ____ ____ ____ ____ should not

be friendly toward members of group X.

For the value of perceived consequences, people might react to a variety of outcomes that follow from the behavior under study:

People who are friendly toward group X members are likely to be asked for help by members of group X.

strongly disagree ____ ____ ____ ____ ____ strongly agree

There is no intention to reify these concepts or measurement methods. Additional modification should be frequently made, depending upon the nature of a specific research project. In models like those of Triandis, for instance, Brislin and Olmstead (1973) have urged that more attention be given to the measurement of extraneous events (Wicker, 1971) that may cause competition leading to a lower probability of a certain behavior. Such measurement, in the present example, might deal with questions about people's willingness to pay additional taxes for minority group programs. There are also other ways to operationalize the concepts than the semantic-differential type of measurement presented above. The point is that a complete analysis must be made of the variables that may be related to a researcher's topic area, and that the analysis will be easier if a wide ranging inventory such as that suggested by Triandis is used as a starting point. Other frameworks from the behavioral/social sciences may be tapped, such as a functional analysis of the various perceived antecedents and consequences of a certain behavior in a certain culture. With this extensive data set as background, researchers can intelligently choose independent and dependent variables for more thorough analysis. Combined with extensive study of the ethnographic literature and cooperation, when possible, with indigenous researchers and leaders, research has a good chance of yielding valuable results.

Just one example of the benefits from these efforts should be mentioned since previous lack of analysis has caused problems. Difficulties in data interpretation stem from the confounding of "culture" with other categories. In many studies "culture" means "nationality;" in others it means "culture within a nation," or "subculture;" or "local population." In other studies, "social class" would be much more accurate and descriptive. If the type of analysis suggested previously was done, independent variables would be specified and thus the global term "culture" would not be used as an explanatory concept.

Another analysis of the relation between theory and method in cross-cultural research was done by Malpass (1977). He points out that many methodological problems actually have theoretical importance. For instance, such methodological issues as (a) gaining cooperation, (b) eliciting answers to questions, and (c) designing experimental conditions that bear similarity to real-life situations demand that researchers learn a great deal about another culture. Much of this learning can then contribute to theory development, for instance, on the conditions under which people cooperate or refuse to cooperate (point [a], above). Malpass suggests a number of well-established theoretical areas, such as "instrumentality" and "signal detectability," as a *starting point* in determining what participants in other cultures mean when they present the researcher with a response to some stimulus. These theories demand that the researcher know what may be going on "in the participant's head." All possible reasons for classes of responses have to be identified, and identification of these reasons will lead to concepts that are appropriate for theory development.

Acceptance of Social Psychological Research

The future of cross-cultural psychology is completely dependent upon the good will of people in other cultures (insiders) who play host to visiting investigators (outsiders). If potential hosts become upset with some investigators, they may refuse permission for all future research. Social psychologists have a special responsibility for the future of cross-cultural research. This responsibility stems from the fact that social psychologists (developmental psychologists run a close second) deal with variables that are familiar to many people, and thus the people can comment on the final research project. Such potential commentary on social psychological research stands in sharp contrast to such arcane areas as perception (reviewed by Deregowski in Volume 3, this *Handbook*). Knowledge of insiders' opinions about past research, then, would be valuable since such knowledge can guide investigators into choosing research areas considered important by insiders. This step in the research process, assuring acceptability by insiders, constitutes another difference between single-country and cross-cultural research.

Brislin (1977) gathered opinions on research from insiders and some of the results provide guidelines for future research. In this project, 105 insiders from twenty-four countries in Asia and the Pacific read research reports from the behavioral/social sciences that were written about their countries. They then commented on the research following a prepared set of questions. In general, their input was insightful, a finding that reinforces previous recommendations that visiting researchers engage the talents of indigenous colleagues. For instance, insiders were sensitive to the emic-etic distinction even though they might not have known the technical terms. The following are comments by insiders.

> The class structure as shown by the author represents an example of imposing Western concepts to the Thai social structure. Other, more careful observers have documented that Thai social structure can be best described in terms of a superior-subordinate society, rather than in terms of Western categories of class structure (Brislin, 1977, p. 194).

> My experience in the past has been that the scholars on Indian culture, or should I call them "intellectuals," having studied the cultural patterns of Indians in India go down to the colonies and try to relate all their hypotheses upon the people of ethnic Indian background. They go there with some preconceived notions and try to search for these elements or they come across some similar notions or gestures, get highly excited and jump to sweeping generalizations such as those put forth by the author in this article (Brislin, 1977, p. 195).

Other insiders accepted the general observation a researcher made, but then expanded on it.

> I agree that Western observers complain about our indirect response to things. We consider it polite, Westerners consider it not frank but you have to bear in mind that among Laotians these are not problems. Being in that kind of society with these values, we have learned to understand the message that other people are sending without it being stated in words. It is not so much what you say but the way you say it that counts (Brislin, 1977, p. 193).

> (After a description of a situation in which two Pakistani women, who previously used first names to address each other, entered into marriages that put them into a more formal relationship): The formality is factual but "appeared ill at ease when in each other's company" is too general a statement. It would vary from individual to individual rather than [be] a rule (Brislin, 1977, p. 194).

Other categories of response included corrections of certain observations, comments about the writer, suggestions for uses of the writings, and updatings of the material.

In various places throughout their commentary, insiders gave specific advice for doing better research that is likely to be useful in the cultures from which they come. These guidelines would also be applicable to a methodological analysis, as in Volume 2 of this *Handbook*. They are covered here because they deal with relations between insiders and outsiders who do research; thus the principles have a strong social psychological component. In summary form, insiders advise:

1. Learn the language spoken in the culture being studied. People in the culture will be grateful that outsiders have taken the trouble. More information will be accessible to an ethnographer who has learned the language.

2. Talk to a wide variety of people, not just to those at the top of the status hierarchy, and not just to one informant.

3. Specify the exact place within a culture where the data was gathered. Do not generalize beyond this place unless there is evidence that such generalization is justified. Include this specificity in the title of the ethnography, e.g., "Kin and culture in Majuro, Marshall Islands," rather than "Kin and culture in the Marshalls."

4. Provide good evidence for generalizations. Gather data using such techniques as surveys. Avoid generalizations based only on impressions.

5. Avoid the journalistic-like technique of describing specific situations when these can be misinterpreted as being *typical* of the culture. Such descriptions may catch reader interest, but there are dangers involved. A specific example is a description like, "A sad-looking young child was walking down the street, crying, but nearby adults paid no attention." Such statements lead to careless generalizations, such as "adult lack of concern" from readers.

6. Be careful in interpreting motives from behavior. Many times ethnographers are accurate in describing behavior, but are inaccurate in diagnosing the motives or reasons for the behavior. To describe motives, ethnographers must learn the point of view of people in the culture. One insider was explicit on this point: "The author was sensitive, but he has not researched deeply enough to understand the causes for some of the behavior he observed" (Brislin, 1977, p. 199).

7. For those cultures that are changing, and whose people have to learn new ways, the ethnographers can improve their performance by reading and studying the same sorts of materials (newspapers, technical reports, production figures, projections) that insiders must read. If an outsider just talks to insiders and writes up the conversations, the insiders are not helped because the product is only what the insiders already know. But if outsiders study the same material as insiders, then the outsider's independent opinion may be helpful. A specific comment: "We ourselves value those writings whose authors have read the same material that we have to know to make decisions" (Brislin, 1977, p. 199).

Many of these points have been recently discussed by social scientists in efforts to improve research; some of these discussions can be found in this *Handbook*. It is easy, however, to ignore the advice of other social scientists. But it would be unwise to ignore the advice of insiders.

Orientation to the Chapters in This Volume

The chapters by John Berry (Chapter 6) on social and cultural change, and by Andrew Davidson and Elizabeth Thomson (Chapter 2) on attitudes and beliefs, deal clearly with the concepts of emics and etics. Both chapters also contribute to theory development by suggesting concepts that can unify the many and diverse studies which they review. Berry begins his chapter by outlining why psychological antecedents and consequences of social/cultural change are important topics for study. After pointing out similarities and differences in the study of social change as practiced by anthropologists, sociologists, political scientists, and economists, Berry analyzes such conceptual problems as the value-laden nature of processes, the universality of processes and states, and the linearity of change. Focusing specifically on psychological variables, Berry organizes his treatment according to proposed antecedents and consequences of social change. Antecedents include attitudes and beliefs, achievement orientation, authoritarian socialization, behaviors acquired through operant conditioning, and modal personality. Consequences include behavioral shifts and acculturative stress. Throughout the chapter, theoretical concepts such as psychological differentiation are proposed which may eventually account for the diverse findings in the area of social/cultural change.

This chapter will become a major resource for any researcher contemplating work in this area. Since he presents the material so well, Berry's greatest service is likely to be that others can disagree on certain points and thus further the development of certain concepts. There are certainly areas in which further work is needed. Just two are (1) the relation between antecedents and consequences, and (2) the analysis of the power of certain explanatory concepts. Related to the first area, Berry discusses five sets of variables as antecedents to change (listed in the previous paragraph). These, however, could just as well have been placed in the section on the consequences of change. Future research will undoubtedly involve designs that allow the consideration of interactions and feedback loops among variables that are presumed to be antecedent and consequent to social/cultural change.

More research is needed on the power of explanatory concepts. For instance, Berry reviews his own work (see Chapter 6; see also Berry, 1976) involving variables analyzed across various American Indian tribes. Relationships are statistically significant, but the figures being correlated are *means* of samples, not measures taken from individuals. In practice, an individual from a certain tribe is assessed, the score averaged into a mean, and the mean is then analyzed along with the means of scores from other tribes. The individual is not the unit of analysis in this procedure. Thus the results of such research say little or nothing about how well the concepts explain *individual* behavior. More attention is needed on statistics that measure the "percent of variance accounted for" when assessing the importance of different independent variables. Unfortunately, the resulting figures will probably show far less explanatory power than would be presumed from reading Berry's presentation of research on these variables.

Davidson and Thomson begin Chapter 2 with a review of methodological problems that have plagued progress in the study of attitudes and beliefs. They then review a wide body of literature, focusing on studies that best exemplify their view of the relation between attitudes and beliefs. The review is divided into three sections. In the first, certain life experiences such as education, age, sex, residence, occupation and social class are related to the attitudes and beliefs held by people. There is an emphasis on the processes by which attitudes and beliefs are formed. In the second section, various theoretical concepts designed to explain interrelations between beliefs and attitudes are reviewed. These concepts are analyzed as they apply to three well-developed research areas: family socialization, attitude and belief change, and intergroup stereotypes. In the third section, studies relating attitudes and beliefs to actual behavior are reviewed. Emphasis is placed on various formal models and on the cross-cultural validity of the components within each model. The authors conclude by noting that the lack of theory, rather than the lack of adequate methods, has been the greater hindrance to progress.

Although Davidson and Thomson present excellent advice for future research, one possible underemphasis is the need for a willingness to modify existent theoretical positions when doing cross-cultural research. Social psychologists such as Fishbein have presented models for integrating attitudes, beliefs, and behavioral intentions. The models include detailed guidelines for measuring all of the concepts involved. Davidson and Thomson review the cross-cultural research on such models, but they do not emphasize enough the need for revision that might involve a change, addition, or subtraction of a major concept. Too often, well established models like Fishbein's overdirect research activities so that the models may become imposed etics that invalidate the research.

Zavalloni (Chapter 3) begins her review of the literature on values by analyzing reasons for lack of development in the field. She feels that too much past research has been concerned with describing clusters of responses (labeled "values") *across* individuals rather than with developing an understanding of psychological processes *within* individuals. She thus reanalyzes the nomothetic versus ideographic controversy as it applies to values research. In building up to a statement about her recommendations for the future, Zavalloni reviews the most influential approaches. She analyzes early developments in anthropology and sociology that include the culture-personality approach, abstract classification schemes for the comparison of cultures, an interdisciplinary approach by Kluckhohn and Strodtbeck that included empirical scales, and a functional analysis from sociological investigators. Large-scale cross-national surveys of values are reviewed, with emphasis placed on methodological problems and various ways of explaining the data that are obtained. Another major tradition, psychometric approaches, is also covered with emphasis placed on a number of widely used scales. Zavalloni then groups a number of research endeavors under the heading "cognitive measures" since the various approaches all deal with the relation between individuals and their active involvement with their subjective worlds. She finally reviews her own work with the "Multistages Social Identity Inquirer" which represents an attempt to integrate the nomothetic and ideographic approaches.

A number of factors have contributed to the underdevelopment of research on values. In addition to the conceptual problems reviewed by Zavalloni, two other reasons can be suggested. First, because values is a concept used by many disciplines, the tensions associated with deciding among different disciplinary viewpoints hampers development in the area. Specifically, whenever research of interdisciplinary interest is done, any one individual (trained in only one of the disciplines) cannot satisfy readers in all disciplines. Each academic tradition has its preferred approaches and no one investigator can follow them all. The individual investigator, no matter what methods are chosen, is then likely to be attacked by parochial critics. Consequently, the researcher is motivated to do future research in an area more closely aligned with just one discipline. A partial solution to the problem is for potential critics to become more sensitive to the problems of interdisciplinary research (Sherif & Sherif, 1969; Dinges, 1977) and to familiarize themselves with the approaches of various disciplines, not just their own. A second reason for the lack of development in values research is the paucity of studies that have focused on validation with outside criteria. Previous research has been overly concerned with paper and pencil measures and not concerned enough with independent criteria to validate the measures.

Examples of good independent criteria for research on values can be found in Chapter 5 by Leon Mann on small groups. Beginning with evidence concerning the universality of groups among human beings, Mann analyzes the group as an agent of socialization with special emphasis placed on the family and the peer group. Well-developed research topics

from North America and Europe are reviewed in relation to their manifestations in various cultures in all parts of the world. These include conformity, obedience, group pressure on the deviate, conflict resolution,
group discussion, and the risky shift. The optimal and preferred structures
for work, learning, and communication are then reviewed with the treatment centering on leadership style and communication networks. The
processes of cooperation and competition among group members and between different groups are analyzed with suggestions made for increasing
the limited knowledge now available concerning these processes. The
final topic area covered concerns collective behavior such as riots, panic,
rumor transmission, and crowd formation. Mann concludes by pointing
out that too much research has depended upon North American and European models that are imposed on other cultures.

Researchers in the area of small groups, for better or worse, have used
standard social psychological experiments in a variety of cultures and
have excluded emiclike experiments designed differently for each culture
under study. They have found interesting results, as Mann points out, but
the weakness is a lack of theoretical focus to integrate the diverse data.
This is not Mann's fault since attempts at theoretical integration at the
present time may be premature, or even damaging. Several directions for
the future can be suggested, however. First, emic-type studies should be
employed in addition to etic-type studies which use standard, well known,
experimental techniques. Second, better theory can be developed by
combining values research with the kinds of behavioral measures reviewed by Mann. For instance, Mann reviews studies on conformity, leadership, and collective behavior. For each of these behaviors, a variety of
measures is available for their assessment. These behaviors can then be
linked to values, measured by available techniques, in the form of hypotheses for research. The antecedent-consequent technique (specifically
reviewed by Zavalloni) may prove very fruitful. For instance, it might be
suggested that preferred leadership style (e.g., authoritarian versus democratic) would follow from certain measurable values (e.g., collective versus
individualistic orientation), and these would lead to predictable styles of
collective behavior in various cultures (e.g., carefully planned versus on-
the-spot contagious demonstrations). More effort should be placed on developing hypotheses which integrate findings that are now widely scattered throughout the literature.

Arnold Tannenbaum (Chapter 7) begins his treatment of organizational psychology by reviewing several classic theories that have guided
empirical research. Studies of managers and managerial roles are analyzed
emphasizing the values, perception of norms, needs, attitudes, and cognitive styles that differentiate managers in various countries. Supervisors
and the supervisory role receive attention with the review focusing on

leadership and effectiveness. Research on organization members is reviewed with the treatment centering on workers' reaction to their jobs and to their organizations, as well as reactions to policies like pay and seniority systems. Recent research on workers' response to job enlargement programs is then analyzed, including programs in which workers have some control over policy in their organizations. Finally, Tannenbaum reviews difficulties related to translating principles from organizational research into action programs.

Tannenbaum's review differs significantly in tone from the others in this volume. For the most part, the chapter reviews work done in other countries following research models developed largely in the United States. The chapter is little concerned with such central cross-cultural concepts as emics and etics. This emphasis is inevitable given the state of research on organizational psychology. Few researchers in this area have familiarized themselves with the literature on cross-cultural methodology or with the various integrative concepts reviewed throughout these volumes. The present state of the field involves the examination of etics in various countries, an approach that has led to some worthwhile research since the organizations studied in the various countries have similar goals (e.g., profit, service). A major limitation, as Tannenbaum wisely reminds the reader in the last pages of his chapter, is a lack of knowledge concerning how the etics (e.g., close versus general supervision of workers; Protestant ethic rationality) manifest themselves in specific countries. Finding answers to this question will undoubtedly provide a good deal of focus to future research. Another limitation is that etic-oriented treatments lead to research in which the lower incidence of a presumably beneficial etic is labelled "harmful." For instance, in reviewing individual-level correlates of a country's economic development, field independence is presented in such a way that the absence of it seems debilitating. Such conclusions, presented in such firm wording, would not be reached if both emics and etics were considered. Berry considers both in reviewing the concept of field independence in his chapter.

In analyzing the relation between cross-cultural and environmental psychology, Irwin Altman and Martin Chemers (Chapter 8) take a broad systems approach which posits complex interdependence among variables, feedback loops, and multiple causation. After presenting a historical background and a conceptual framework, the authors analyze various world views that people hold concerning the environment. Various approaches to the study of environmental perception and cognition are reviewed with emphasis placed on people's subjective representational systems that relate them to their culture. Various overt social behaviors are analyzed; the treatment of empirical studies is organized around the themes of privacy, personal space, territory, and crowding. Finally, the authors analyze outcomes or products of behavior in the form of cities, communities, houses, interiors of homes, and other man-made modifications of the natural environment.

Altman and Chemers were faced with the task of writing the first review covering the relation between cross-cultural studies and environmental psychology. The choices they were faced with typify the difficulties of doing such an original review, and Altman recommended that these difficulties be discussed here. Given space limitations and the research approaches that they were most familiar with, Altman and Chemers decided to start with the current field of environmental psychology and to build outwards into the possible contributions cross-cultural studies can make. But as a consequence of this decision they did not take an alternate path: to start with cross-cultural studies to determine their contribution to environmental psychology. However, other chapters written by more active cross-cultural researchers touch on issues in environmental psychology.

One such contribution is Berry's review of the effects of ecology on psychological adjustment, and on the relation between past and present ecologies in response to social change. Davidson and Thomson treat certain environmental conditions as independent variables in their review of research on climate, residence, and population density. In other volumes of this *Handbook*, Deregowski (Volume 3) reviews the research on the relation between physical environment and basic perceptual processes. Dasen and Heron (Volume 4) point out the importance of environmental differences on the acquisition of cognitive functioning as assessed by Piagetian tasks. To obtain a more complete picture of the relation between environmental psychology and cross-cultural studies, readers will have to consult all these chapters.

Gergen, Morse, and Gergen (Chapter 4) feel that the concept of behavior exchange may be important in the development of a broad theoretical framework for the integration of many social psychological studies. They review a number of topic areas that have been subjected to empirical investigation, including reciprocity and equity in social exchange. As part of the latter review, the authors analyze the work of the Foas who posit six classes of resources and suggest interrelations among them: love, services, goods, money, information, and status. The authors explicitly examine how principles developed from research in one part of the world hold up in various cultures. They also critically examine the empirical research on behavior exchange and make suggestions for a reorientation of the field.

Gergen et al. were faced with the difficult task of reviewing a research area whose promise has not been fulfilled. As reviewed in the beginning of their chapter, the concept of behavior exchange has the potential of becoming an integrative concept in cross-cultural social psychology. Weaknesses of research endeavors to date, however, have prevented progress toward findings of any consequence. The ill-advised use of investigative techniques developed largely in the United States is probably responsible. Early in this introduction, the trend toward investigations that center on a very small range of human behavior was reviewed. One such small range was cooperative/competitive behavior as measured by experimental games and tasks. It is not too far-fetched to argue that a "culture" was established in which investigations of minute behaviors associated with these games and tasks became publishable. A major reason behind this development was convenience: the tasks could be studied in university laboratories easily available to investigators. Even within the United States, it is debatable whether or not much has been learned through these studies (Helmreich, Bakeman, & Scherwitz, 1973, pp. 343–44).

These games and tasks were used cross-culturally, but little was learned as the authors admit in reviewing both their own empirical work and that of others. The major reason was that researchers gave insufficient thought to the meaning of these experiments in cultures other than university laboratories in North America. In fact, there is a danger that young researchers might continue in this tradition since the literature is given so much coverage in this *Handbook* (Mann also reviews some of these studies). It is necessary in the future to study a much wider range of behaviors involving exchange. For instance, Gergen et al. review work on perception of foreign aid, an approach that sounds promising. Multiple methods must be used to determine what is cooperative and competitive, and what constitutes exchange within each culture. A complete analysis of exchange behaviors should be carried out, focusing on both independent and dependent variables, according to inclusive frameworks, such as the one by Triandis (1975a) mentioned earlier. The research mistakes reviewed by Gergen et al. must not be repeated if cross-cultural investigations of social psychological concepts are to assume a position of importance.

References

ADLER, P. The transnational experience: an alternative view of culture shock. *Journal of Humanistic Psychology*, 1975, *15*(4), 11–23.

BERRY, J. *Human ecology and cognitive style.* New York: Wiley/Halsted, 1976.

BOCHNER, S., BRISLIN, R., & LONNER, W. Introduction. In R. Brislin, S. Bochner, & W. Lonner (Eds.), *Cross-cultural perspectives on learning.* New York: Wiley/Halsted, 1975, pp. 3–36.

BRISLIN, R. Ethical issues influencing the acceptance and rejection of researchers who visit various countries. In L. Loeb-Adler (Ed.), *Conference on issues in cross-*

cultural research. New York: New York Academy of Sciences, 1977, Vol. 285, pp. 185–202.

BRISLIN, R., LONNER, W., & THORNDIKE, R. *Cross-cultural research methods.* New York: Wiley, 1973.

BRISLIN, R., & OLMSTEAD, K. An examination of two models designed to predict behavior from attitude and other verbal measures. *Proceedings of the 81st Annual Convention of the American Psychological Association,* 1973, pp. 259–60.

BRISLIN, R., & PEDERSEN, P. *Cross-cultural orientation programs.* New York: Wiley/Halsted, 1976.

DINGES, N. Interdisciplinary collaboration in cross-cultural social science research. In R. Brislin & M. Hamnett (Eds.), *Topics in culture learning,* Vol. 5. Honolulu, Hawaii: East-West Culture Learning Institute, 1977, pp. 136–43.

ELMS, A. The crisis of confidence in social psychology. *American Psychologist,* 1975, *30,* 967–76.

FELDMAN, R. Response to compatriot and foreigner who seek assistance. *Journal of Personality and Social Psychology,* 1968, *10,* 202–14.

FRAGER, R. Conformity and anticonformity in Japan. *Journal of Personality and Social Psychology,* 1973, *26,* 309–20.

GERGEN, K. J. Social psychology as history. *Journal of Personality and Social Psychology,* 1973, *26,* 309–20.

HARRIS, J. Culture shock: the experience and the behavior in diverse settings. Paper delivered at the meetings of the American Psychological Association, Washington, D.C., 1976.

HELMREICH, R. Applied social psychology: the unfulfilled promise. *Personality and Social Psychology Bulletin,* 1975, *1,* 548–60.

HELMREICH, R., BAKEMAN, R., & SCHERWITZ, L. The study of small groups. *Annual Review of Psychology,* 1973, *24,* 337–54.

LEWIN, M. Kurt Lewin's view of social psychology: the crisis of 1927 and the crisis of 1977. *Personality and Social Psychology Bulletin,* 1977, *3,* 159–72.

MALPASS, R. Theory and method in cross-cultural psychology. *American Psychologist,* 1977, *32,* 1069–79.

McGUIRE, W. The yin and yang of progress in social psychology. *Journal of Personality and Social Psychology,* 1973, *26,* 446–56.

NANCE, J. *The gentle Tasaday.* New York: Harper & Row, 1975.

SHERIF, M., & SHERIF, C. (Eds.), *Interdisciplinary relationships in the social sciences.* Chicago: Aldine, 1969.

SINHA, J. The n-Ach/n-Cooperation under limited/unlimited resource conditions. *Journal of Experimental Social Psychology,* 1968, *4,* 223–46.

STRODTBECK, F. Considerations of meta-method in cross-cultural studies. *American Anthropologist,* 1964, *66,* 223–29.

TRIANDIS, H. Culture training, cognitive complexity, and interpersonal attitudes. In R. Brislin, S. Bochner, & W. Lonner (Eds.), *Cross-cultural perspectives on learning.* New York: Wiley/Halsted, 1975a, pp. 39–77.

———. Social psychology and cultural analysis. *Journal for the Theory of Social Behavior,* 1975b, *5,* 81–106.

———. The future of pluralism. *Journal of Social Issues,* 1976, *32*(4), 179–208.

————. Cross-cultural social and personality psychology. *Personality and Social Psychology Bulletin*, 1977a, *3*, 143–58.

————. *Interpersonal behavior*. Monterey, Calif.: Brooks-Cole, 1977b.

WHITING, J. Methods and problems in cross-cultural research. In G. Lindzey & E. Aronson (Eds.), *Handbook of social psychology* (2nd ed., Vol. 2). Reading, Mass.: Addison-Wesley, 1968.

WICKER, A. An examination of the "other variables" explanation of attitude-behavior inconsistency. *Journal of Personality and Social Psychology*, 1971, *19*, 18–30.

2

Cross-Cultural Studies of Attitudes and Beliefs[1]

*Andrew R. Davidson
and Elizabeth Thomson*

Contents

Abstract

The following conceptual framework was utilized to organize the relevant literature: A person acquires beliefs about an object on the basis of life experiences. The affective value of these beliefs influences the person's attitude in a positive or negative direction. The attitude, in turn, is related to the favorableness of the individual's set of behaviors concerning the object. Based on this framework, the literature review was divided into three sections: (1) belief and attitude formation; (2) the interrelation of beliefs and attitudes; and (3) the relation of attitudes to behavior. Prior to the literature review, a number of methodological problems pertinent to the cross-cultural study of attitudes and beliefs are discussed.

In the methodology section two idealized objectives that motivate the attitude researcher to obtain data from more than one culture are outlined.

The first objective is to establish boundary conditions for attitudinal models and theories. In the most obvious case, a researcher would test an attitudinal model that previously had been validated for one cultural group in at least one other culture. The second motivation for doing comparative research is to study the effects of cultural and ecological factors on attitudes and behavior. In studies of this type, the researcher gathers data from more than one culture to obtain variance on at least one of the variables (e.g., climate) in the model or hypothesis. Although this is the most easily conceptualized form of transcultural study, it introduces sampling (cultures, not individuals, are the sampling units) and equivalence of measurement problems (both functional and score equivalence are required) that are more difficult to solve than the problems encountered in research that tests the generality of psychological theories.

The first portion of the literature review that examines the relation between life experiences and attitude and belief formation organized the literature into studies that were designed to either (a) obtain cultural variance or environmental experiences that were similar for all members of a culture (e.g., political structure, social and economic organization, population density), or (b) establish boundary conditions for theories of attitude and belief acquisition. Among the latter studies, the primary research areas include family socialization, intergroup stereotypes, and the relation of personal characteristics (e.g., age, gender) to attitudes. The evidence cited demonstrates that a number of life experiences that are common across cultures do, in fact, transcend unique cultural experience in leading to the formation of beliefs and attitudes.

The second section of the literature review examines cross-cultural research on attitude and belief structure and the interrelation of beliefs and attitudes. There is considerable support for the cross-cultural generality of a core set of dimensions of attitude and belief structure. In addition, the evidence cited suggests that basic cognitive processes, such as inferential belief formation, cue utilization, and attitude formation are relatively invariant across cultures. What does vary from culture to culture is the belief content of these structures and processes.

The final section of the literature review focuses on the relation between attitudes and behavior. Although very little cross-cultural research has been done on this topic, there is some indication that by assessing both attitudinal and behavioral variables at corresponding levels of specificity, i.e., measuring attitude toward a specific behavior for the prediction of a specific behavior or measuring a global attitude toward an object for the prediction of a multiple-act behavioral criterion, a reasonable degree of accuracy can be obtained. If variables are not measured at correspondent levels of specificity, weak and nonsignificant correlations are usually observed.

In the conclusion, it is noted that the greatest hindrance to the development of an integrated and cumulative cross-cultural body of knowledge related to attitudes and beliefs is not the lack of application of adequate methodology, but the lack of application of adequate theory.

Introduction

In the course of preparing this review, over 400 articles relevant to the cross-cultural study of attitudes and beliefs were identified. Given space limitations, a complete survey of these research findings is impossible. Even if adequate space were provided, such an endeavor would be of limited value since many of the published studies contain such serious methodological inadequacies that their findings are of questionable validity. Accordingly, this review focuses on the theoretical and methodological problems in cross-cultural attitude research. Articles that illustrate these problems have a higher probability of being cited. Research that does not compare data from two or more cultural or national groups has usually been excluded.

The organization of the relevant literature is based on (a) the definition of attitude and belief, and (b) the conceptualization of the relations between life experiences, beliefs, attitudes, and behaviors. Despite the abundance of attitude definitions, there appears to be general consensus that an attitude is a learned predisposition to respond in an evaluative (from extremely favorable to extremely unfavorable) manner toward some attitude object. A measure of attitude should, therefore, index an individual's position along a favorable-unfavorable dimension with regard to the object. The standard attitude scaling procedures (Thurstone, Likert, and Guttman scaling and the evaluative dimension of the Semantic Differential) each provide such a measure.

The second variable of interest in this review, belief, is considered the cognitive element of a person's attitude. Each belief represents a piece of information that a person has about some object. As Fishbein and Ajzen (1975) have indicated, this information is frequently in the form of an association between an object and an attribute. For example, the belief that "Albanians are friendly" links the object "Albanians" to the attribute "friendly." This association is conceptualized in terms of a subjective probability. A belief measure should, therefore, index a respondent's position along a subjective probability dimension with regard to the degree of association between an object and an attribute. If the respondent were presented with the statement that Albanians are friendly he might, for example, be asked to judge the statement on one of the following scales: agree-disagree, likely-unlikely, true-false, probable-improbable, or yes-no.

Those familiar with attitude research will recognize that belief statements are the items most frequently scaled to obtain a measure of attitude. This procedure is most apparent in Likert and Thurstone scaling. Traditionally, the scaling of belief statements to measure attitudes can be traced in part to the recognition by some early attitude theorists (see, for example, Thurstone, 1928; Doob, 1947) that a relation exists between one's attitude toward an object and one's beliefs about that object. An attitude toward an object is some function of the affective value of the attributes associated with that object.

This view of the relation between attitudes and beliefs forms the basis for the conceptual framework that will be used to structure the chapter. This framework can be stated as follows: A person acquires beliefs about an object on the basis of his life experiences. Each attribute associated with the object has some degree of affect (even if it is of neutral or zero intensity). Depending on the affective value of the attributes associated with the object, the person's attitude toward the object is influenced in a positive or negative direction. The attitude, because it predisposes the individual to respond in an evaluative manner toward the object, will be related to the favorableness of the individual's set of behaviors concerning the object. The consequences of performing the behavior will, in turn, influence the formation of new beliefs. This framework is not presented as an attitudinal theory that has achieved cross-cultural validation. Rather it is presented as an organizing principle whose usefulness and accuracy will continually be reassessed as the relevant literature is reviewed.

Based on this conceptual framework, the literature review is divided into three sections. The first section examines the relation of life experiences to attitudes and beliefs and examines the process by which attitudes and beliefs are formed. The second section reviews the interrelation of beliefs and attitudes and evaluates the cross-cultural validity of current theories of cognitive and affective organization. The final section of the review examines the relation of attitudes and beliefs to behavior. The cross-cultural evidence regarding the attitude-behavior relation is considered and an attempt to isolate variables that influence the magnitude of that relation is made.

A number of methodological problems that are especially relevant to the cross-cultural study of attitudes and beliefs are discussed prior to the literature survey. The discussion is presented both as an aid to the reader in evaluating the material that is reviewed and as a guide (as opposed to a discouragement) to the researcher in designing cross-cultural investigations.

Methodological Issues

The choice of methodology should, of course, be determined by the objectives of the research. Accordingly this section opens with a brief discussion of the two idealized types of objectives that would cause the attitude researcher to obtain data from more than one culture. These are described as idealized types because they are theoretically and methodologically defensible.

The first reason to obtain cross-cultural data is to establish the boundary conditions (Willer, 1967) for attitudinal models and theories. In the most obvious case, a researcher would test a model or hypothesis that previously has been supported for one cultural group in at least one other culture. Following such a study the research could designate, among the cultural groups studied, those for whom the model is valid and those for whom it is not. If appropriate individual level information has been obtained in each cultural group it is frequently possible to do much more. Depending on the diversity of the groups studied and the individual variables that were measured, the researcher should be able to begin to specify the variables defining the populations for which the model is not valid (e.g., the model is not valid for illiterates). With this information it is possible to improve the model by incorporating these boundary conditions in the model.

The second reason for doing comparative research is to study the effects of cultural and ecological factors on behavior. In studies of this type, the researcher gathers data from more than one culture to obtain variance on at least one of the variables (e.g., climate, sociocultural system, etc.) in the model or hypothesis. Although this is the most easily conceptualized form of transcultural study (Strodtbeck, 1964), it introduces sampling and equivalence of measurement problems that are more difficult to solve than does the type of research that tests the generality of psychological theories. The following section presents a discussion of some of these problems in cross-cultural research.

Sampling

Attitudes and beliefs are acquired by individuals; therefore, study of the relation of other variables (including culture variables) to attitudinal variables requires that the basis (actual or implicit) of the attitudinal variable be individual measurement. Other variables, however, may be measured at any of three different levels:

1. global (e.g., type of government)
2. aggregates of individuals (e.g., percent literate)
3. individual (e.g., education)

Independent variables measured at the individual level pose no unique theoretical or methodological problems for cross-cultural attitude research. However, the relations of global and aggregate variables to individual attitudes raise the problems that are discussed below.

Global variables.   Global variables are those variables on which there is no variance (or very little variance) among individuals within a cultural group. For example, take a culture located along some continuum of centralization of government; any two individuals in the culture would be subject to the same degree of centralization of government (i.e., there would be no individual-level variance on this measure). Therefore, analysis of the effects of global variables on attitudes and beliefs must necessarily utilize cultural groups as cases and aggregated attitude and belief measures as dependent variables.

Each cultural group can be defined by its position in a hypothetical space in which the dimensions are global variables (e.g., climate, political system, language). In order to isolate analytically the effects of any one global variable from the effects of other global variables defining the culture, it would be desirable to sample a relatively large number of cultures, in the same manner as individuals are usually sampled. Then adequate nonsystematic variance will be introduced in the global variables not being studied to allow for an analysis of the effect of the global variable of interest on the attitudinal variable. If the global variables are intercorrelated, then the global variables not being studied should also be measured so that their effect on attitudes and beliefs can be controlled either statistically or by sampling procedures.

Of course, the incremental cost of each cultural unit in an investigation of attitudes or beliefs usually precludes the selection of more than a few cultures for analysis. However, even under less than ideal conditions, greater confidence can be placed in findings where more than one culture is selected to represent each value of the global variable of interest, and where the cultures at each value differ on other relevant global dimensions. For example, Berry (1973) used a 2 × 3 factorial design to investigate the effects of food accumulation (low, medium, high) and acculturation to the larger society (traditional, acculturated) on attitudes of Amerindian (Canada) communities toward relations with Euro-Canadian society. At least two communities were sampled at each level of each global variable, so that within each level a crude estimate could be made of "error variance." However, within each cell of the 2 × 3 design, only one community was sampled; the combined effects therefore cannot be separated from the effects of the other (unmeasured) global characteristics defining each culture.

In one sense, investigations of attitudinal differences and similarities between cultures can be viewed as attempts to study the effects of the global variable, "culture," or "national group," on the aggregate attitudes or beliefs of the individuals categorized as belonging to each group. However, since the "independent variable" is identical with case, no statements can be made about its effects. That is, it is not possible to determine the attitudinal and belief consequences of being German versus being Malaysian, since there is no variability in "German-ness" or "Malaysian-ness" that can be separated from the German/non-German or Malaysian/non-Malaysian differences on other variables. It may be possible, however, to determine the consequences of living in an industrialized versus nonindustrialized society by comparing such sets of aggregate responses as Germany/United States/Japan versus West Malaysia/Tanzania/Ecuador. In this example, there is variability on other variables at both levels of industrialization, so there is less likelihood of confounding differences in attitudinal response due to global variables that are not being studied with that due to industrialization.

The best examples of culture/case sampling are studies utilizing anthropological data on beliefs from the Human Relations Area Files (Murdock, 1957). Gathering data from these accumulated files is, of course, much simpler and less costly than conducting surveys in a similar number of cultures. However, the cultural groups for which data are available are primarily isolated and nonliterate cultures, and not representative of the cultures in which the majority of people live today. Further, many psychological variables of interest are not included in these data.

Aggregate variables.   Aggregate variables are those that are measured at the group level, but are based on actual or implicit individual variables. For example, per capita income is the average of individual incomes; percent literate can be thought of as the average of individual literacy scores (1=literate; 0=illiterate). In cross-cultural attitudinal research, aggregate measures may be utilized for one of two reasons:

(1) The theory behind the relationship of interest is based on individual variables that were not measured. In this case, aggregate variable relationships are poor substitutes for individual variable relationships and should be used primarily to generate hypotheses rather than to make conclusions (e.g., Buchanan & Cantril's, 1953, finding of a positive relation between per capita calorie supply and "personal security").

(2) The aggregate measure is theoretically a "global" variable. For example, the fact that 60 percent of the work force is employed in agricul-

ture represents a social and economic organization that may have psychological impact on all individuals in a society. In such cases, aggregate variable relationships are as acceptable as global variable relationships and are subject to the sampling concerns mentioned.

Prior to using aggregate independent variables in cross-cultural research, the investigator should examine the theoretical link between the aggregated independent variable and the individual responses that comprise the aggregate attitude or belief, and modify the study design and/or conclusions appropriately.

Cross-Cultural Equivalence of Attitude and Belief Measures

Demonstrating the equivalence of measures is probably the most difficult methodological problem in comparative research. In his excellent discussion of this topic, Poortinga (1975) has distinguished between two types of test equivalence—functional and score equivalence. Functional equivalence indicates that a test measures the same attribute in different groups of people. Score equivalence indicates that the test not only measures the same attribute in different groups but also that the quantitative scale is the same in each group. That is, if subjects from different cultural groups obtain an equal score on the test they have an equal amount of the attribute. In order for the scores of culturally different groups to be meaningfully compared, the test must satisfy both the conditions of functional and score equivalence.

Unfortunately, when tests are used cross-culturally, score equivalence is rarely achieved (cf. Cole & Bruner, 1971; Jahoda, 1969; Poortinga, 1975; Triandis, 1977b; Triandis, Malpass, & Davidson, 1973). The lack of equivalence can be caused by unequal familiarity with test materials, differences in the meaning of the test situation, unequal understanding of the test format and directions, differential susceptibility to response sets, differences in the connotative meaning of linguistically correct translated items, and a variety of other variables. The number of variables that might plausibly cause score nonequivalence is so great that it is probably not feasible to measure and control for all of them in any one study. Accordingly, in the absence of convincing evidence of score equivalence, comparisons of mean test score differences between cultural groups are of little value.

If mean differences between cultural groups on attitudinal variables usually cannot be compared, what kind of comparative analyses are possible? Methodologically, the most defensible comparative strategy is to test the universality of a psychological model or theory. This approach offers two important advantages; both arise from the fact that *within* each culture the researcher is looking at the relations between a *number* of variables. First, only the functional equivalence of measures is required. Second, cultural differences can often be meaningfully interpreted because they tend to appear as a difference in one relation in the presence of cultural similarities in other relations.

The development of measures that are functionally equivalent is always difficult. However, the difficulty decreases as the strength of the theory or model that one is testing increases. If the terms of the theory are at a high level of abstraction (i.e., not content- or method-bound) then culturally relevant measures of the theoretical constructs can be constructed (cf. Brislin, Volume 2 of this *Handbook*; Davidson, 1977; Malpass, 1977; Pike, 1966; Triandis, 1977b). The construct validity of these measures can, in turn, be investigated within each culture psychometrically to determine their functional equivalence (Berrien, 1967). Here again, a strong theoretical framework is a help because it indicates how the newly constructed measure should relate to other variables in the framework. (For a discussion of the logic of construct validity in cross-cultural research, see Irvine & Carroll's chapter in Volume 2 of this *Handbook*.)

On the basis of a general pattern of similarity, one can begin to investigate specific cultural differences in the relations between variables. As Campbell (1964) observed, differences between cultural groups are only interpretable against a background of considerable similarity. In the absence of demonstrations of similarity it is impossible to distinguish cultural differences from a large number of alternative explanations that could plausibly account for the difference (e.g., failure to communicate, inadequacy of measures, subject motivation, etc.). In the presence of demonstrations of similarity the plausibility of most of the alternative explanations is markedly decreased.

An application of this approach in the attitude area can be found in Davidson, Jaccard, Triandis, Morales, and Diaz-Guerrero (1976). They tested a model for the prediction of behavior from attitudinal and belief variables (Triandis, 1975) in Mexico and the United States. The elements of the model are at an adequate level of abstraction (e.g., perceived consequences, affect toward the behavior). The measures for the elements were constructed within each culture (e.g., the perceived consequences of performing the behavior were elicited separately for each cultural group). The predictive utility of the model was similar for each cultural group. Once this cross-cultural similarity was established it was possible to investigate between-group differences. In this regard, it was found that the relative influence of the components in predicting intentions varied as a function of the cultural group studied; specifically, the Mexican and American upper-middle class samples emphasized the person's attitude toward the act while the Mexican lower class samples emphasized the person's perceived moral obligations.

The Relation of Life Experiences to
Attitudes and Beliefs

As explained in the introductory section of this chapter, the assumption is made that beliefs and attitudes are learned, and that they reflect the individual's experience with his/her environment. This section of the chapter is therefore devoted to examining those relationships between life experience and attitudes/beliefs that have been investigated cross-culturally. However, before specific cross-cultural studies are examined, some brief notes on the theoretical and methodological perspectives around which this discussion is organized are provided.

First of all, investigations of the relation of attitudes/beliefs to life experiences should be justified on the basis of a theoretical link between the particular experiences and attitudes/beliefs that the research has selected to examine. It is not scientifically meaningful merely to determine that Experience E and Attitude A are related, unless one has some theoretical notion about, or can in fact demonstrate, how Experience E leads to the acquisition of information that has relevance for Attitude A. One would think that such a guideline is so obvious that there is little reason to state it. However, investigations in this area (both single culture and cross-cultural) have often neglected to specify such theoretical links. This neglect causes difficulty in evaluation of both the study's rationale and the value of the data.

Secondly, the unique difficulties of cross-cultural research raise the further question of the cross-cultural equivalence of measurements of experience. The researcher must theoretically explain or empirically demonstrate that the independent variables actually represent functionally equivalent experiences in each culture studied. As was pointed out before in relation to the functional equivalence of attitude measures, it may be necessary to use different operationalizations in different cultures in order to classify experience in similar ways across cultures. This is particularly important with regard to such comprehensive measures of "experience" as gender, age, climate, etc.

Finally, alluding to the discussion in the previous section, there are two primary reasons to investigate cross-culturally the relation between experiences and attitudes or beliefs. The first is to establish boundary conditions for theories of attitude and belief acquisition. The second is to obtain variance on environmental experiences that are the same or nearly the same for all members of a particular cultural group. (Note, again, that the effects of the totality of cultural experience cannot be examined since the "variable" would be synonymous with case.) Therefore the remainder of this section is organized around studies that have been directed primarily toward one of these two purposes.

Experiences Common to Individuals within Cultures

Experiences that are identical or nearly identical within groups of individuals and that vary significantly only across groups are referred to as *global* experiences. As indicated in the methodology discussion, groups (e.g., cultures) are the unit of sampling. The limitations of the small number of cultural units sampled are responsible for the scarce and relatively weak findings examined below on the effects of the physical environment and social/economic structure on attitudes and beliefs.

Physical aspects of the environment are a large part of an individual's experience and should therefore affect his/her attitudes and beliefs not only directly but also indirectly through their impact on the social and economic organization of the society in which the individual lives. The only aspect of the physical environment that has been examined in a systematic way is population density. Population density appears to have negative effects on feelings of personal security (Buchanan & Cantril, 1953) and affiliative and other social responses to individuals or groups (Bass & Franke, 1972; Munroe & Munroe, 1972). Unfortunately, the number of cultures sampled in each of the studies mentioned was too small for definitive conclusions to be drawn. Additionally, it is highly likely that population density has only an indirect impact on individual attitudes and beliefs through the social and economic structures that are developed to deal with it. In any case, the rationale behind the empirical relations is weak unless one can hypothesize what experiences related to population density lead to the acquisition of particular beliefs (e.g., the number of people one must speak to in a given period of time, the volume of noise one is exposed to, etc.).

The hypothesis that climate affects attitudes was not supported in research in Africa by Doob (1968). Similarly, Lambert, Triandis, and Wolf (1959), using HRAF data, found no relation between temperature level and attribution of malevolence or benevolence to deities. Note that the implied theory behind these investigations is that somehow direct physiological perception of the environment might lead to the acquisition of certain beliefs and attitudes (e.g., physical comfort leads to psychological comfort, or a set of "happy" attitudes).

The social and economic organization of societies may also shape, at least in part, some aspects of individual attitudes and beliefs. Due to the difficulties of sampling societies, rather than individuals, there is little evidence to support this assertion, except among subsistence-level cultures. Differences in sex role attitudes (Barry, Bacon, & Child, 1957), intragroup

attitudes (Edgerton, 1965), outgroup attitudes (Berry, 1973), tradi-
tional/modern attitudes (Dawson, 1974), and child-training beliefs and
practices (Barry, Child, & Bacon, 1959) have been attributed to differences
in the primary economic base of cultures. Swanson (1960)—who, like
Barry et al. (1957), made use of data from the Human Relations Area
Files—found the social organization of such societies to be related to the
structure of deistic beliefs. Both Barry et al.'s (1957) and Swanson's (1960)
findings appear to have a plausible theoretical base. In the former case, the
sex role differences appear where the economic functions of males and
females have been separated. In the latter instance, beliefs about the "organization" of deities appears to parallel the actual organization of the societies (see Durkheim, 1954). It is relatively easy in these studies to
understand how the different social experiences might lead to the acquisition of certain types of beliefs.

Among industrial societies, the extent of social class divisions has
been related to management belief "styles" in industry (Bass & Franke,
1972) and to satisfaction with the societal environment (Buchanan & Cantril, 1953). The theoretical bases of these relationships are, however, relatively obscure. Diaz-Guerrero (1973) reported that increases in industrial
production were greater among countries whose adolescents scored more
"actively" (in a "male" manner) on "coping style;" the "active syndrome"
is apparently considered to have positive utility for industrial economic
activity. Muller (1970) distinguished between two sets of countries on the
basis of patterns of political beliefs. In the United States, Great Britain,
and West Germany, beliefs in the responsiveness of government to citizen
influence encourage individuals to acquire the skills and dispositions necessary for the exercise of influence, which in turn affects the degree to
which individuals feel confident of their *personal* ability to influence government. In Mexico and Italy, those who are confident of personal influence have not developed beliefs in their government's general
responsiveness. It is suggested that these differences are due to the difference in political structures and that the latter pattern of beliefs is a source
of stress on democratic organization.

The influence of social organization and other "global" experiences
on attitudes and beliefs appears to need a great deal of further study. Implicit in the vast number of studies of cultural differences in attitudes and
beliefs is a legitimate interest in the effects of "culture" on these psychological variables. However, as indicated in the methodology section, it is
virtually impossible to differentiate the effects of "culture" from the effects of functional nonequivalence in the measuring instrument. Further, it
would seem of greater importance to discover the relationships between
specific aspects of culture and sets of attitudes/beliefs. It is somewhat dis-
tressing that the number of cross-cultural studies falling into this category
is so limited and that those reviewed are characterized either by small

samples or by samples unrepresentative of the industrial societies of today and tomorrow. Perhaps the lack of research in this area is due to a disciplinary gap—social organization is generally considered in the realm of sociology, and attitudes in that of psychology. Whatever the reason for the scarcity of research, however, further attention is needed in this area.

Boundary Conditions for Theories of Attitude and Belief Acquisition

The methodologically strongest and scientifically most meaningful research on the relation of experiences to attitudes and beliefs is found among studies that attempt to establish boundary conditions for theories or models of attitude/belief acquisition that have been well established in at least one culture. The major research areas in which such studies have been undertaken are family socialization, attitude or belief change, and intergroup stereotypes. In addition, the large number of cross-cultural studies on the relation of personal characteristics (age, gender, occupation, etc.) to attitudes and beliefs suggests that some transcultural experiences have effects on the formation of attitudes and beliefs that are independent of the effects of culturally specific experiences.

Family socialization.   Investigations of the effects of family socialization or parental behavior on attitudes and beliefs are dominated by research using HRAF data. Lambert et al. (1959) and Spiro and D'Andrade (1958) investigated specific hypotheses based on the theory that parental behavior is the model for an adult's beliefs about supernatural beings. For example, deities were believed to be aggressive in societies in which high pain and low indulgence were used in infant care, and in which child training emphasized self-reliance, independence, responsibility, and rigidity (Lambert et al., 1959). Beliefs regarding the contingent nature of supernatural nurturance and punitiveness were related to early dependence satisfaction and later dependence anxiety (Spiro & D'Andrade, 1958). These findings were consistent with the theoretical notion that, since deities are seen as supernatural parents, their behavior should be seen as consistent with the behavior of one's human parents.

Rosenblatt (1966) used HRAF data to show that early frustration of oral needs and prolonged socialization away from those needs leads to greater concern for affection in adulthood (i.e., importance of romantic love in marriage). Stephens (1961) reported that sexuality-specific child-training practices (e.g., punishment for masturbation) were related to the severity of menstrual taboos, while more general harshness such as aggression training and obedience pressure were not. Both of these studies make a clear theoretical link between particular socialization experiences and the relevant adult attitudes/beliefs.

While the HRAF studies appear to be relatively well grounded in theory, they do have the methodological difficulties inherent in the use of aggregate independent variables (see Ford, 1967). Each of these studies relates an aggregate socialization variable (i.e., some anthropological equivalent of modal behavior) to an aggregate (modal) belief variable. Further, the modal belief variable was not necessarily systematically measured but may have been asserted by the anthropologist with minimal evidence. Prior to making a definitive statement about the effects of certain childhood experiences on adult beliefs and attitudes, it is necessary to examine *individual* variation on each of these types of variables within different cultures.

Although there has been considerable cross-cultural research at the individual level devoted to the developmental aspects of cognition, personality, and psychopathology (see *Handbook* chapters by Tapp in Volume 4 and Sanua in Volume 6), much less evidence is available on the development of attitudes and beliefs. (The discussion of the relation of age to certain attitudes or beliefs will provide some insight into this area.) The best (and perhaps only) example we found of the type of research needed is provided by Triandis and Triandis (1962). They hypothesized that individual insecurity would be positively related to social distance toward outgroups and that, therefore, child-training practices that produce insecure adults would be reported more frequently by individuals showing high social distance than among individuals showing low social distance. Although the insecurity hypothesis was not clearly supported by their data on Greek and American subjects, the following relationships were found between childhood experiences and social distance: (a) high social distance was associated with greater paternal influence; low social distance, with greater maternal influence; (b) social distance was negatively related to the clarity of explanation of norms in the home; (c) there were no consistent relations between social distance and punishment or warmth in the home. These results are consistent with the findings of Triandis and Triandis (1960) with United States subjects of varying ethnic backgrounds and with those of Martin and Westie (1959) and Saarbourg (1958), who investigated the relation of child-training practices and tolerance.

McClelland (1961) utilized a somewhat different methodological approach in assessing the familial antecedents of achievement motivation in adolescent boys. Rather than utilizing the boys' reports as an indicator of parental behavior, he questioned the mothers of the boys directly regarding their expectations for their sons' behavior. In each of the three countries studied, a different relationship was found between "achievement training" (the lower the age at which mothers expect certain behaviors, the higher the achievement training) and achievement motivation in boys (Brazil—negative; Germany—positive; Japan—no relation). Similarly, no clear relation was found between mothers' "caretaking pressure" (age at which caretaking behaviors were expected) and the boys' scores on "optimism."

Intergroup stereotypes. The cross-cultural study of intergroup stereotypic beliefs and evaluations has become increasingly popular during the last three decades. In particular, there has been a great deal of interest in various "contact hypotheses"; that is, how are intergroup stereotypes affected by direct or indirect contact (familiarity) with other groups? The largest body of research in this area deals with ethnic group relations. (For a review of the contact hypothesis in the area of ethnic relations, see Amir, 1969.) Such studies are a special case of intergroup stereotypes in that attitudes and beliefs of the groups studied are affected not only by the minority status of at least one of the groups, but also by a long history of already established inequalities, physical differences, etc. Further, in the majority of cases, the groups share a geographical location and a larger, usually national, cultural heritage. These conditions may or may not be present in cross-national or other cross-cultural research, depending on the groups involved.

Campbell (1967) provided a general theoretical framework that can encompass both the situation of ethnic minority stereotypes and stereotypes between other, more general, types of cultural groups. He regards a stereotypic belief as a perceptual response to a stimulus (the stereotyped person or group). As such, it is a function of the stimulus intensity, drive, value, and habitualization. Drive, value, and habitualization are intrapsychic characteristics of the observer, while stimulus intensity is a function of the degree of exposure to the stimulus and its contrast to the observer's adaptation level (i.e., the nature of the environment prior to the presentation of the stimulus). In terms of a particular stereotypic belief, habitualization is the frequency with which the respondent has used the stereotype in the past. Value is the utility of liking or not liking the stereotyped person or group. (Campbell implies that there is always a positive utility in disliking an outgroup, but there would seem to be situations in which liking an outgroup could have positive utility such as relations between two groups allied in a conflict with other outgroups.) The stereotype-relevant component corresponding to drive is not clearly stated by Campbell; in any event, since this element of the response is not clearly related to any of the research reviewed, any potential effects of drive on the stereotypic response will be ignored. The intensity of the stereotype stimulus (person or group) is a function of the *actual* contrasts between members of the observer's group (ingroup) and the person or group members being stereotyped (outgroup), as well as the amount of contact (frequency of exposure) the observer has with them.

From his theory, Campbell derives several hypotheses regarding the determinants of a stereotypic response. His *contact hypothesis* is stated thus:

The more opportunities for observation and the longer the exposure to the outgroup, the larger the role of real differences in the stereotypes. This implies that the nearer outgroups will be more accurately stereotyped, and that outgroups with which most interchange of persons and interaction occurs will be most accurately stereotyped (1967, p. 821).

Note, however, that the value and habitualization components do not disappear with increased contact and are capable of wiping out entirely or even changing the direction of the contact effects. For example, where groups are of unequal status, increased contact might increase the value of maintaining appropriate social distance through negative stereotypes.

While Campbell's theory focuses on the independent variables, Vassiliou's (Vassiliou et al., 1972) theory deals with the dependent variable, the stereotypic response. They point out that stereotypes can vary on a number of dimensions, including:

1. *Complexity.* The number of traits assigned to the other group.
2. *Clarity.* (a) *Polarization* of the judgments on each trait dimension; that is, the extent to which people from one group assign non-neutral value of the trait to people from another group. (b) *Consensus,* that is, agreement among people in assigning the trait to another group.
3. *Specificity-Vagueness.* The extent to which the traits are specific or vague (abstract).
4. *Validity.* The extent to which the stereotypes correspond to substantially realistic assignments of traits.
5. *Value.* The favorability of the assigned traits.
6. *Comparability.* The extent to which the framework of the perceiver is involved in the stereotyping so that a comparison is made between autostereotype (group looking at itself) and heterostereotype (one group looking at another) (pp. 90–91).

These dimensions, in turn, vary in their relative dependence on one or another of the independent variables. The example given above, in which contact and value interact to change a stereotype response, implicitly involves the evaluative dimension of the stereotype, but not necessarily any of the others.

Using the framework just described, it is possible to understand the cross-cultural evidence on the relation between stereotype responses and contact with the stereotyped group. Each finding must be examined in relation to (a) the dimension of the stereotype examined and (b) the intrapsychic characteristics of the respondents (value, habitualization) that must be regarded as a "given" at the time of response, even though they are undoubtedly the result of some past experience in which contact may have been involved.

First, the nonevaluative components of stereotypic responses will be considered. There is some evidence that familiarity with another culture may increase the accuracy of stereotypes (Berrien, 1969a; Brewer &

Campbell, 1976; Lindren & Vu, 1974; Vassiliou et al., 1972). Berry (1970) reported a greater consensus and complexity in stereotyping among those more familiar with the stereotyped group. Greater consensus would be the natural result of more accurate beliefs about the group as a whole, while complexity could be the result of greater variation in experience with individual group members. Triandis and Vassiliou (1967) and Vassiliou et al. (1972) report similar findings for Americans stereotyping Greeks, but not for Greeks stereotyping Americans. Since Greeks without contact had clearer stereotypes than Americans without contact, it may be that the habitualization level of Greeks for some responses was so high it could withstand the effects of new information gained from contact.

Brewer and Campbell (1976) report that, among their sample of East African tribes, group familiarity was *negatively* related to consensus on stereotypic beliefs. As they suggest, this may be due to the widespread reputation of the groups selected to be stereotyped. The highly habitualized responses of the low familiarity respondents would tend to be less diverse; the high familiarity respondents, having had a greater variety of experiences with individual members of a stereotyped group, would tend to provide more diverse responses. Brewer and Campbell also suggest that the relationship between contact and diversity in stereotypic beliefs may be curvilinear. No contact or information about a group could result in random responses—highly diverse and varying in accuracy. Limited contact should increase the stimulus intensity for the group as a whole, leading to more accurate and less diverse responses (which are easily habitualized). Extensive contact should increase the variety of experience with individual group members (greater stimulus intensity) and lead to more diverse (though not necessarily more accurate) stereotypic beliefs.

It should be noted that, of the studies referenced above, all but one use aggregate rather than individual measures of "familiarity" or "contact." That is, the relations between contact and stereotype responses are based on differences between groups who are assumed (via geographical proximity, "cultural" distance) to have varying amounts of information about the stereotyped group or are based on correlations between aggregate responses toward several groups. In the one study where an *individual* level of analysis was reported (Lindgren & Vu, 1974—years of residence in host country), respondents were from a single cultural group.

Prompted by the need to improve intergroup relations, the evaluative component of stereotypic responses has been the focus of research. The cross-cultural findings regarding the relationship of contact or familiarity with a group and evaluations of that group are not consistent. This should not be surprising if the Campbell theory of stereotypes is accepted. Contact should provide new information (beliefs) about a stereotyped group, but the degree to which the evaluation of the group is shifted may depend on one or all of the following:

1. evaluation by the observer of the new information
2. utility to the observer of liking or disliking the stereotyped group (which may change as a result of the contact)
3. consistency of the new information with other habitualized responses
4. strength of habitualization to consistent or inconsistent responses

These propositions allow reconciliation of apparently conflicting cross-cultural findings regarding the relationship between contact with and stereotypic evaluation of a cultural outgroup. Brewer (1968), Brewer and Campbell (1976) and Brislin (1971) reported more favorable evaluations between cultural groups of greater geographical proximity; in these studies the groups shared a larger cultural heritage (African and South Pacific, respectively) and there was no evidence of actual conflict between them (i.e., the value of denigrating the outgroup was neutral and the proximal status did not change it). The single exception noted by Brislin was a pair of groups between which there was a political conflict. Brewer and Campbell (1976) did find that more centrally located tribes had a higher degree of self-esteem relative to their evaluations of outgroups than did more remote tribes. The centrally located groups were in greater competition with the groups stereotyped, and thus there was positive value in denigrating the other groups relative to one's own.

Triandis and Vassiliou (1967) and Vassiliou et al. (1972) also report an interaction between value and contact in determining stereotype responses. In these studies, the utility of favorable versus unfavorable responses was due not to intergroup conflict, but to unequal status between the groups. In the hypothesized higher status (United States) group, contact was *negatively* related to evaluation of Greeks; in the hypothesized lower status group (Greeks), contact was *positively* related to evaluation of United States nationals. These results are consistent with the notion that contact increases the value of negative stereotypes for the high-status group, since they can be utilized to maintain the social distance appropriate to the inequality of status. On the other hand, contact increases the value of positive stereotypes for the lower status group, since they are consistent with aspirations to the higher status.

Brewer and Campbell (1976) report a clear positive relationship between familiarity with and evaluation of outgroups. Their measures of familiarity and evaluation are aggregated for each group and then correlated across stimulus and respondent group pairs. Using individual-level correlations, they generally found less strong relationships between contact and stereotypic beliefs. However, they suggest that the evaluation of outgroups is less affected by individual contact than by the degree of contact across the entire respondent group. This suggests that the reinforcements of one's group for habitualized stereotypic beliefs may be as important as information acquired from individual contact in determining stereotypic responses.

Again, all of the studies just cited have measured contact at the aggregate level; that is, all individuals in a group are assumed to be at the same level of contact or familiarity with a given stereotyped group, although they may vary in contact or familiarity with different groups. One study measured familiarity at the individual level, and found a positive relation between familiarity and evaluation of an outgroup (Loomis, Loomis, & Gullahorn, 1966). Since there was no reason to expect any interaction between contact and the value of negative stereotyping, these findings are consistent with the theoretical considerations and aggregate findings cited above.

An examination of the cross-cultural research on intergroup stereotypes reveals that the theoretical framework provided by Campbell (1967) is generally supported. A few specific hypotheses derived from Campbell's theory (some of them explicitly suggested by Campbell) that were evidenced in the cross-cultural literature were considered. However, the theory offers much more that has yet to be empirically examined, particularly at the cross-national level.

Vassiliou et al. (1972) provided a set of specific hypotheses regarding contact and stereotyping that deal with the different dimensions of stereotypic responses that are consistent with Campbell's theory, but make more explicit some of the implications of the theory. (Note that "normativeness" refers to the habituation level of a response, and "sociotype" refers to an *actual* group characteristic.)

1. The larger the difference between the sociotypes of Groups A and B, on characteristic X, the more likely it is that X will appear in the stereotypes of the two groups.
2. Contact has the effect of changing the stereotypes to match the sociotypes; that is, it increases the validity of stereotypes.
3. Non-normative stereotypes change very much with contact.
4. Normative stereotypes change very little with contact.
5. The greater the contact, the greater the clarity of non-normative stereotypes.
6. Contact has no effect on the clarity of normative stereotypes.
7. The greater the contact, the more contrastive the autostereotypes.
8. The greater the contact, the greater the complexity of stereotypes.
9. The greater the contact, the greater the specificity of stereotypes.
10. When $\bar{X}_A - \bar{X}_B$ is large, there will be a contrast phenomenon; that is, the two groups will see each other as more different than they really are.
11. When there is neither contact nor a normative stereotype, the nature of heterostereotypes will be purely projective. The greater the contact, the less projective the stereotype [and the more valid, as per (2) above].

12. When $\bar{X}_A - \bar{X}_B$ is small and contact is large, there will be no differences perceived between auto- and heterostereotypes.

13. Autostereotypes are coordinated with other self-percepts to maximize self-esteem (Vassiliou et al., 1972, p. 114).

It is clear from these statements that, at least in this particular research area, there exists a thoroughly explicated body of theory, for which there is some empirical support. Cross-cultural studies are badly needed to systematically test propositions such as those just listed in a wide variety of cultural contexts.

Attitude and belief change.   The generality of findings from the United States concerning attitude change has been examined by the number of cross-cultural investigators. As is frequently the case in the United States, these studies are limited to experimental laboratory situations, and in most cases used college students as subjects.

The effects of communicator credibility on attitudes and beliefs were investigated in a number of studies. Whittaker and Meade (1968) reported that high communicator credibility had immediate effects on beliefs; they did not, however, replicate the "sleeper" effect noted by Hovland and Weiss (1951) and Hovland, Lumsdaine, and Sheffield (1949), in which opinion change due to a low credibility source increased over time while opinion change due to a high credibility source decreased over time. In another study, Whittaker and Meade (1967) found that male communicators were perceived as more credible than female communicators; however, the male communicators had no greater effects on belief change than did female communicators.

McGinnies (1968) found that source credibility affected opinion on a highly salient international issue, and the effects were greatest when prior beliefs about the issue were not strongly held. He suggests that these findings support the assimilation-contrast theory formulated by Hovland, Harvey, and Sherif (1957) and Sherif and Hovland (1961). Stronger commitment to a position supposedly narrows the latitude of acceptance so that the *contrast effect* is more likely to occur. The contrast effect leads to derogation of messages that fall outside the latitude of acceptance; they are judged to be farther from the respondent's own position than they actually are. Diab (1965, 1966) examined the assimilation-contrast hypothesis more directly. His findings support the contrast effect. However, the *assimilation effect* was not supported—there was no tendency to perceive a greater-than-actual closeness of beliefs as the message and respondent belief become closer.

McGinnies (1966a) failed to find any effects of the primacy or recency of a communication on attitude or belief change in his study with Japanese subjects. He attributes the absence of such effects to the fact that the issue discussed was one on which the respondents had already obtained considerable information and formulated beliefs to which they were strongly committed. Evaluations of the communicator appeared, however, to be based on primacy rather than recency, i.e., they were determined by the first message communicated and were favorable when the first message was consonant with previously held beliefs and unfavorable when it was not; their initial evaluations were not changed when the communicator "switched sides." Since the respondents had no previous information about the communicator, these results are consistent with the conclusion of Hovland and Mandell (1957), that "the nearer one comes to achieving primacy in the sense of the first presentation of unfamiliar material, the more apt is one to obtain primacy effects" (p. 139).

McGinnies (1966b) was able to replicate the findings of Hovland, Janis, and Kelley (1953), regarding the greater effectiveness of two-sided versus one-sided communication on immediate attitude change among those initially opposed to the communication. The same effects were noted on convincingness ratings and impressions of the communicator. Less clear findings were reported regarding the superiority of one-sided communication in influencing individuals whose beliefs initially coincided with the content of the communication, but they were consistent with those of Hovland et al. (1953).

Implied social pressure on attitudes and beliefs has been investigated by Bronfenbrenner (1967). He reported that school-age respondents in the United States and the USSR committed themselves more strongly to socially approved behavior, if they thought adults would be aware of their intentions. In the absence of perceived adult monitoring, the USSR respondents showed commitment to socially approved behavior if the respondents thought their peers would be aware of their intentions; however, in the United States this perceived "peer pressure" was associated with greater commitment to (adult) socially *dis*approved behavior.

In summary, cross-cultural investigations of theories of attitude and belief change are isolated and few in number. They do not provide systematic evidence for the universality or boundary conditions of theories formulated in the United States. A few investigators (e.g., Diab 1965, 1966; McGinnies 1966a, 1966b, 1968) have attempted to set up series of investigations in order to systematically test some of the major hypotheses. It is unfortunate that their published research is not more extensive and that such investigators are not currently working in concert.

Relation of personal characteristics to attitudes/beliefs.   From a theoretical point of view, cross-cultural studies of the relation of personal characteristics to certain attitudes or beliefs can merely serve to support the original assumption—that beliefs and attitudes reflect life experience. In these studies personal characteristics such as gender, age, and education can be considered as indicators of a diverse set of experiences that are generally associated with each characteristic. The major focus of such studies is primarily to discover the content rather than the structure of the characteristics (experiences) and attitudes/beliefs that are linked in the same manner in several cultural contexts.

In many of the studies reviewed here, the examination of attitude/belief differences among individuals with different characteristics was incidental to the purpose of the study, and the use of the results relevant to this section should not reflect on the overall merits of the study. However, in some cases, the primary purpose of the study was to examine such differences, and much of this research is subject to criticism on both theoretical and methodological grounds. As will be pointed out more specifically, only a few such studies have (a) theoretically or empirically examined the functional equivalence of the personal characteristics as indicators of experience; or (b) provided a theoretical basis for the relevance of the experience to the attitudes/beliefs of interest. Personal characteristics that have been used in cross-cultural studies as indicators of life experience include gender, age, residence, education, occupation, and social class; each will be discussed in turn.

a. Gender. In almost every society there have been distinctions made between the societal functions and other behaviors prescribed for males and females. Since these distinctions have followed similar patterns in the majority of cultures (usually related to the different reproductive role of each sex), it is not surprising to find some attitudes and beliefs that exhibit consistent sex differences from culture to culture. Cross-cultural male/female differences have been reported in attitudes toward marriage roles (Arkoff, Meredith, & Iwahara, 1964; Kalish, Maloney, & Arkoff, 1966); occupational roles (Seward & Williamson, 1969); and beliefs about parental obedience (Smith, Ramsey, & Castillo, 1963). However, in situations where there is no clear theoretical link between male/female experience and beliefs (that is, no reason to expect differences), consistent cross-cultural differences were not found; such attitudinal measures include attitudes toward life-styles (Beg, 1966); other cultures (Berrien, 1969a; 1969b; Lindgren & Vu, 1974; Loomis et al., 1966); "human nature" (Buchanan & Cantril, 1953); and food (Babayan, Budayr, & Lindgren, 1966).

An important methodological point should be mentioned regarding cross-cultural studies of sex differences in attitudes and beliefs. Males and females selected for study may not be equally representative of males and females, respectively, in the larger culture. Arkoff et al. (1964) note that the strong egalitarian attitude of the Japanese females in their study may be due to the university experience (or family background that led to the university experience) of these women, which is unusual for Japanese females; the Japanese male university students, however, were relatively typical of middle and upper class males in Japan. Similarly, the absence of sex differences between two such samples could be a result of similarity of experience that is not duplicated in the general male and female populations. In none of the studies cited thus far were attempts explicitly made to control statistically or by sampling such experience variables as education, family background, work experience, etc., that could exaggerate or minimize experience differences between men and women, boys and girls.

   b. Age. Investigations of age differences in attitudes and beliefs suggest that, as individuals grow older, they acquire and retain more information which leads to a greater accuracy and/or diversity of beliefs (Johnson, Middleton, & Tajfel, 1970; Lambert & Klineberg, 1967; Middleton, Tajfel, & Johnson, 1970; Tajfel, Jahoda, Nemeth, Campbell, & Johnson, 1970; Tajfel, Jahoda, Nemeth, Rim, & Johnson, 1972). Age may also affect the salience of a particular attitude object. Among adults, some age differences are reported in managerial values (Bass & Eldridge, 1973) and fertility/family planning attitudes or beliefs (Elam, 1971; Miro, 1966). These differences can be reasonably attributed to changes in the importance of various occupational and/or fertility outcomes as one grows older. Katona, Strumpel, and Zahn (1971) reported that younger heads of household (under thirty-five) in Germany, Holland, Great Britain, and the United States had greater expectations of economic betterment, more unfulfilled desires for material goods, and a greater desire to work more hours than did older heads of household. These differences can probably be attributed to the differing economic situations, job skills, etc., that characterize the two groups.

   It is necessary to establish equivalence of meaning in the experience variable as well as the theoretical relevance of the experience to attitude or belief formation. Is a "generation gap" in years equivalent to the same type of gap in experience across cultures? Do the different experiences associated with age have theoretical relevance for the attitude or belief in question?

   c. Residence. Investigations of urban/rural differences in attitudes/beliefs have focused on lifestyle (Beg, 1966); fertility values (Fawcett, Arnold, Balatao, Buripakdi, Chung, Iritani, Lee, & Wu, 1974; Kahl, 1967; Miller & Inkeles, 1974); social distance and attitudes toward across-the-border nationals (Gullahorn & Loomis, 1966; Loomis et al., 1966); political beliefs (Muller, 1970; Searing, 1969); job and career satisfaction (Kahl, 1968); and modernity (Inkeles, 1977; Kahl, 1968; Miller & Inkeles, 1974; Portes, 1973). In most cases the relationships are weak and often disappear when such factors as education or occupation are controlled. The lack of relationships found in most of these studies is not surprising for two reasons: (1) the most frequently used measure, *current* residence, may not clearly differentiate groups according to experiences associated with longer-term versus shorter-term residence in a locale; and (2) rarely has a theoretical link been suggested between the experiences associated with a particular residential area and the attitudes/beliefs of interest. As an example of the latter concern, Fawcett et al. (1974) suggest that urban-rural differences in the values associated with children are due to the differential economic utility of children in urban versus rural areas. Such hypotheses are useful not only for clarifying expected relationships, but also for suggesting additional confirmatory research (e.g., examining the economic utility of children in rural versus urban areas).

d. *Education, occupation, and social class.* Education, occupational prestige, and social class are usually highly intercorrelated and they often represent similar experiences. Much of the literature regarding the attitudinal effects of these variables deals with the concept of "modernity." The fact that some strong empirical relations have been found between such experiences and modern attitudes may be due in part to the theoretical base from which the studies were designed. Inkeles (1969a; 1973) examines in some detail the particular experiences associated with formal education and/or factory work that he believes lead to modern beliefs and attitudes. For example, the logic of machinery and mechanical processes may be absorbed as a result of factory work and transferred to an individual's system of beliefs. Similarly, Schuman, Inkeles, and Smith (1967) suggest that literacy opens one's mind to new ideas, so that when social change occurs, "the more literate man will be quicker to perceive the change and will find it easier to redefine his beliefs in ways that fit his new needs and interests" (p. 11). Although such assumptions are not tested, they do provide some justification for investigating the relationship between such "modern" experiences and an individual's beliefs.

It has been firmly established that the strongest predictor of modern attitudes is education or literacy (Inkeles, 1969a; 1969b; 1974; 1977; Kahl, 1968; Miller & Inkeles, 1974; Portes, 1973; Schuman et al., 1967; Doob, 1957). This positive relation remains when controlling for age, factory experience, mass media exposure, urban or rural residence, length of urban residence, status of dwelling, urban or rural origin, agricultural or nonagricultural employment, and parental background. Dawson (1973) reports, however, that at the university level, "selective return" to more traditional beliefs occurs when students critically evaluate both traditional and modern beliefs. Whether this reevaluation and return to selected traditional beliefs is maintained through the adult life of a university graduate cannot be determined from Dawson's data.

Occupation is also positively related to modernity (Inkeles, 1969a; 1969b; 1974; Kahl, 1968; Miller & Inkeles, 1974; Portes, 1973; Schuman et al., 1967), but the relation diminishes in strength or disappears when education, urbanism, etc. are controlled (Inkeles, 1969a; Miller & Inkeles, 1974; Schuman et al., 1967). Similar zero-order findings have been reported for social class indices (Doob, 1957; Godwin, 1972; 1975; Inkeles,

1969a; Kahl, 1967; 1968; Miller & Inkeles, 1974; Portes, 1973). Where income or standard of living is the measure of social class, the relationship with modernity remains when controlling for urbanism or education in Brazil and Mexico (Kahl, 1968) and in Guatemala (Portes, 1973); these findings are not supported by Miller and Inkeles's (1974) work in Pakistan, India, Israel, and Nigeria.

One particular variant of modern attitudes that has been investigated cross-culturally is the set of beliefs related to fertility and its regulation. The weak or inconsistent relations between education or social class and fertility ideals or attitudes toward birth control (Godwin, 1972; 1975; Kahl, 1967; 1968; Elam, 1971; Miro, 1966) appear to support Miller and Inkeles's (1974) contention that fertility/family planning attitudes are not a direct result of modern experience, but are indirect results of a generalized modernity resulting from such experiences as education, urbanism, factory experience, etc.

Attitudes toward or beliefs about other groups have been investigated as a function of both education and social class. Education has been negatively related to social distance or prejudice (Gullahorn & Loomis, 1966; Pettigrew, 1958), and positively to attitudes toward a border country (Loomis et al., 1966), understanding another culture (Lindgren & Vu, 1974), and to feelings of commonality with foreigners (Buchanan & Cantril, 1953). Similar findings with regard to social class were reported by Buchanan and Cantril (1953) and Pettigrew (1958) but not by Loomis et al. (1966), and Doob (1957).

The major focus of cross-cultural research on attitudinal outcomes of occupational experience involves attitudes toward the occupation itself. Again, at the theoretical level, one would expect an individual with different occupational experiences to have different beliefs and attitudes about that particular set of experiences. Several investigators report that individuals at higher occupational levels are generally more satisfied with their jobs (Haire, Ghiselli, & Porter, 1966; Inkeles, 1960; Kahl, 1968). There also appear to be differences in the determinants of job satisfaction (Inkeles, 1960; Simonetti & Weitz, 1972) and in work goals (England & Lee, 1974; Bass, 1974) according to occupational level. However, other investigators have found little or no differences in job satisfaction (Slocum & Topichak, 1972) or its sources (Hines, 1973). The inconclusiveness of this set of research may be due primarily to the range of occupational level; in some cases the range is from unskilled laborer to professional, while in others high- and low-level managers or high- and low-skill manual workers comprise the variation. The more similar the actual occupational experience of the respondents, the less often attitudinal differences would be expected.

A final set of attitudinal variables that have been related to social class are beliefs (and practices) regarding the rearing of and instilling of values in children. Although the measures differ, the evidence appears consistent that working or lower class parents are more likely to emphasize obedience while middle class parents tend to be more permissive and encouraging of individual self-control in their children (Inkeles, 1960; Kohn, 1969; Pearlin & Kohn, 1966; Prothro, 1966; Rapp, 1961). The consistency of these findings is strengthened by a theoretical framework provided by Pearlin and Kohn (1966); their hypothesis that parents ". . . value for their children the characteristics that seem most appropriate to the conditions of the parents' lives . . . [e.g.] the characteristically different occupational experiences of middle- and working-class parents" (p. 466) is relatively well supported by their data.

   e. Summary. The evidence cited above appears to support the general assumption that experience even as grossly represented by such personal characteristics as gender, age, occupation, etc., is related to attitudes for which that experience is theoretically relevant and is *not* related to attitudes for which no relevancy is apparent. Further, those investigations that were based on theoretical assumptions about the attitudinal implications of the particular experiences examined provide by far the strongest and most conclusive evidence that some transcultural experiences do, in fact, transcend unique cultural experience in leading to the formation of beliefs and attitudes.

Attitude Formation and Structure

In contrast to the prior section that examined the relation of life experiences and attitudes/beliefs and the subsequent section that will review the relation of attitudes/beliefs and behavior, this section will be concerned primarily with the relation of variables within the "black box." That is, cross-cultural studies of the content, structure, and interrelation of beliefs and attitudes will be reviewed. As stated in the introduction, it is frequently assumed that an attitude toward an object is some function of the affective value of the attributes associated with that object. This section will review the cross-cultural evidence for this relation and will consider the implications of such a relation for the construction of cross-cultural attitude measures. However, before analyzing the relation between attitudes and beliefs the research examining the content and structure of attitudes and beliefs will be reviewed.

Belief Content

A belief has been defined as the perceived relation between an object and an attribute. One approach for measuring this relation is word association. A number of variants of this technique have been used cross-culturally.

These include free association (e.g., "list ten words that come to mind"; Schaffer, Sundberg, & Tyler, 1969), association to a stimulus word (Rosenzweig, 1961; Szalay & Bryson, 1973; Szalay & Lysne, 1970; Szalay, Windle, & Lysne, 1970), structured associations (e.g., "the———butterfly"; Jakobovits, 1966), and perceived antecedents or consequences of an object or behavior (Davidson, Jaccard, Triandis, Morales, & Diaz-Guerrero, 1976; Fawcett et al., 1974; Triandis, Kilty, Shanmugam, Tanaka, & Vassiliou, 1972b). The most general conclusion that can be drawn from the studies using this paradigm is that within groups with similar life experiences (including cultural experiences), there is a greater degree of similarity in content of associations than between groups with different life experiences. Although there is evidence (Jakobovits, 1966; Rosenzweig, 1961) that for some content domains cross-cultural similarity exists with regard to the most frequently mentioned associations, for the majority of content domains in each of the studies mentioned there were important group differences.

The existence of cultural differences in the content of beliefs about objects is, perhaps, an obvious and trivial finding. However, since beliefs are the items most frequently scaled to obtain a measure of attitude, this finding of cultural differences carries an important and frequently overlooked implication. Namely, the researcher who attempts to maintain linquistic equivalence by using an identical set of beliefs in different cultures to measure attitude toward some object is at considerable risk of employing a measure that is differentially salient or relevant for the cultural groups. As previously discussed, differential item relevance can preclude functional and test score equivalence.

An alternative approach would be to determine for each cultural group studied (perhaps using the association paradigm) the salient beliefs that are held about the attitude object. Identical methodologies (e.g., item analysis) could then be used to scale beliefs for the attitude measure in each culture. This approach would have two advantages. First, it would provide an emic measure of an etic variable (attitude). Second, since only salient beliefs are used for each population, an analysis of the beliefs not only indicates an individual's attitude but also suggests why he holds that attitude.

Belief Structure

The primary belief content area for which structure has been systematically investigated cross-culturally is that of behavioral intentions (see Triandis, 1977a). A behavioral intention measures the probabilistic relation between an individual (the object) and a behavior (the attribute); accordingly, it meets the definition of a belief. Triandis and his associates have attempted to establish etic factors of behavioral intentions based on judgments of emic behaviors. Triandis, Vassiliou, and Nassiakou (1968) independently elicited several thousand behaviors in Greece and the United States. Facet analysis was then employed to obtain a small ($N¿60$), maximally heterogeneous sample of behaviors for each group. Factor analyses yielded four etic dimensions—(1) Association-Dissociation, (2) Superordination-Subordination, (3) Intimacy-Formality, and (4) Hostility—and a number of emic factors. Osgood (1970) employed a logical analysis of interpersonal intentions and obtained similar etic factors. Additional studies (Triandis, Kilty, Shanmugam, Tanaka, 1972a) that obtained data from respondents in five very different cultures support the existence of these four etic factors.

Attitude Structure

The most extensive cross-cultural study of attitude structure to date was initiated in 1960 and probably will not be fully reported until 1980. Directed by C. E. Osgood (see Osgood, 1977; Osgood, May, & Miron, 1975), the aims of the project are (a) to test the cross-cultural generality of three factors of affective meaning—evaluation, potency, and activity (E, P, and A)—that had appeared regularly in their earlier studies with English-speaking Americans; if such generality could be demonstrated, (b) to construct comparable instruments (semantic differentials) for measuring the dimensions of affective meaning in diverse cultures; and (c) to utilize these instruments in the comparative study of the affective aspects of subjective cultures around the world. The researchers have made considerable progress in realizing their aims. They have demonstrated the generality of E, P, and A for twenty-one language/culture communities, constructed comparable semantic differentials for measuring aspects of subjective culture in each community, and utilized these instruments in measuring 620 diverse concepts in the twenty-one communities. When the final data are completely analyzed they will comprise a *World Atlas of Affective Meaning*.

As the researchers have carefully developed emic measures for the etic dimensions of E, P, and A, and since the items comprising the evaluative factor are coming to be the most widely used measures of attitude, their methodology merits special attention. The respondents in each culture were male, monolingual, high school students. They were asked to give the first qualifier (adjective) that occurred to them for each of 100 familiar concepts. The 10,000 responses obtained for each culture were then analyzed in terms of frequency and diversity of usage across the 100 concepts. Those qualifiers that were (a) most frequently mentioned, (b) highly diverse, and (c) relatively independent of each other in their use were utilized in the construction of semantic differential scales. A second sample of 200 respondents then rated 100 concepts against fifty such scales; subgroups of twenty respondents each rated a subset of ten concepts because the task is so time consuming. Within each culture, the mean ratings of twenty subjects on each scale for each concept were calculated and the scales were then correlated across the 100 concepts. This correlation matrix was submitted to principal components factor analysis, with an orthogonal varimax rotation if the unrotated solution was semantically obscure. Comparisons of the factor structures revealed considerable similarity. In all of the cultures an evaluative factor was present and dominant, and a dynamism factor (combination of potency and activity) was also observed.

Additional support for the generality of E, P, and A, was obtained from a pancultural factor analysis of the same data set. In this analysis, the mean on each scale, in each culture, for each concept was computed. The scales were then correlated across the 100 concepts and this matrix was submitted to principal components factor analysis. The first three factors are clearly recognized as E, P, and A, and every culture contributed to the definition of these dimensions. The results provide a preview of the overall pattern of findings that can be expected from the *World Atlas of Affective Meaning*. Since the items from all cultures were correlated across concepts, the finding that scales from each culture contributed to E, P, and A indicates that the concepts mean about the same thing in each culture. That is, the pan-cultural analysis strongly suggests that a concept that is good, potent, and active in one culture will tend to be good, potent, and active in other cultures. Thus, when the *World Atlas of Affective Meaning* is completed it will show a general pattern of cross-cultural similarity.

On the basis of the pan-cultural factor analysis, it was possible to select for each language/culture community, those descriptive scales that were functionally most equivalent in representing the underlying dimensions of meaning. However, in the *World Atlas of Affective Meaning*, where between-cultural-group mean comparisons of the meaning of concepts will be presented, the measures will require both functional and score equivalence. The semantic differential research team has not yet demonstrated the cross-cultural score equivalence of their measures.

Relation of Beliefs and Attitudes

The process of inferential belief formation.   It is assumed that individuals form beliefs on the basis of their life experiences, and these beliefs, in turn, influence the formation of new beliefs and attitudes. The process by which new beliefs are formed is frequently an inferential one. For example, if a subject is informed that a person he does not know is generous, sociable, and popular, and is then asked to state whether he believes the respondent is good-natured or not, he would probably be able to make such a judgment. This type of judgment would be based on inference.

Theorists have suggested that the formation of inferential beliefs may be based either on evaluative consistency (Heider, 1958) or descriptive (probabilistic) consistency (Peabody, 1967). That is, a person known to be friendly might also be judged as sociable either because the two traits have a common positive evaluation or because of their descriptive similarity with regard to interpersonal pleasantness. In an important study designed to investigate the relative importance of descriptive and evaluative similarity, Peabody (1967) orthogonally manipulated the evaluative and descriptive similarity of adjective pairs. The results of the study clearly indicated that for United States college students, inferences follow lines of descriptive similarity.

A number of cross-cultural studies have also investigated the process underlying inferential belief formation. Initial work in the area of stereotyping (e.g., Buchanan & Cantril, 1953) supported the notion of evaluative consistency. Berrien (1969a) summarized the hypothesizing of many stereotype researchers as follows:

> It has generally been held that the characteristics ascribed to persons or groups we dislike are not those of which we approve; and conversely we tend to ascribe favorable characteristics to persons or groups we admire ... (p. 173).

More recently Peabody (1968), in a cross-cultural extension of the work cited above, once again demonstrated that if descriptive and evaluative similarity are separated, traits assigned to national groups are based to a greater extent on descriptive similarity. In summary, if the effects of evaluative and descriptive consistency are not separate, belief formation may appear to be based on evaluative similarity. However, if the effects are separated, descriptive similarity appears to play the predominant role in inferential belief formation for the cultural groups studied.

Cue utilization.   In the review of the studies of inferential belief the primary concern was with the process of trait inference. In studies of cue utilization, the review will focus on the relative importance of information (cues) from a variety of content domains for responses to a separate content domain. For example, a subject might be asked to judge a person's IQ from information about his grade point average, aptitude test scores, and number of hours studied per week. Studies of cue utilization in the United States (see Slovic & Lichtenstein, 1971) demonstrated that a person's inferences are generally predictable with considerable accuracy on the basis of a weighted linear combination of cues.

Triandis and his associates (Triandis, 1963; Triandis, Davis, & Takezawa, 1965; Triandis, Tanaka, & Shanmugam, 1966; Triandis and Triandis, 1960; 1962; Triandis & Vassiliou, 1972) have conducted a large number of cross-cultural studies of cue utilization. Most of these studies have investigated the effects of such cues as sex, religion, race, and occupation on social distance, using a factorial design for the presentation of all possible combinations of cues. For example, Triandis et al. (1965) studied the effects of information about race, occupation, religion, and nationality in Germany, the United States, and Japan. Scales of social distance were first independently standardized for each national group. Subjects then gave social distance ratings for hypothetical stimulus persons created from all possible combinations of all levels (two or three) of the above cues. The order of importance of each cue for determining social distance in each culture was as follows:

(a) United States: race, occupation, religion, and nationality
(b) Germany: occupation, religion, race, and nationality
(c) Japan: occupation, race, nationality, and religion

Data from this study and similar studies by Triandis and Triandis (1960, 1962) suggest that the weights given to the four cues are also affected by the demographic characteristics of the subjects (e.g., social class, religion, ethnic background, sex).

It should be noted that this study stands as a good methodological example of many of the issues that have been discussed here. First, the social distance scale was independently validated in each culture. Second, cultural differences were examined in terms of differences in the relations among a number of variables. Third, the researchers, in addition to reporting global level (cultural) differences, attempted to determine the boundary conditions of the relations found using individual level variables (e.g., sex, social class, religion). The only weakness of the Triandis et al. (1965) study is the absence of a good theory on which to base predictions of the relative importance of the four cues in each cultural group. Such a theory, derived from prior research on subjective culture, was used in Triandis and Vassiliou (1972); the researchers accurately predicted that, in employee selection decisions, Greeks would give greater weight to recommendations by friends and relatives and lesser weight to recommendations by neighbors and unknown persons than would Americans.

While this programmatic research effort has indicated cultural differences in terms of the importance of different cues in the judgment process, it has also demonstrated many similarities. The most important may be that, although there is clearly some evidence for nonlinear combination of cues (interaction effects), most of the variance in judgment can be accounted for by a linear combination (main effects) rule.

The only cross-cultural study reviewed that used a multiple regression approach to cue utilization was reported by Cvetkovich and Lonner (1973). They asked college students in four countries to make birth planning decisions for hypothetical families that varied on each of eight familial characteristics. The median regression weights for each characteristic were quite similar across cultures. As in the Triandis cue utilization studies, a linear combination of the data yielded an adequate prediction of the subjects' responses.

In sum, cross-cultural research on cue utilization suggests that an individual's inferences are derived in a consistent and predictable manner from the information available. Regardless of methodological approach or content area, integration of diverse items of information is found to be well approximated by a weighted linear model. However, all of the studies cited used subjects of relatively high socioeconomic status (e.g., college students, managers). It remains to be demonstrated that these findings hold for groups of lower socioeconomic status.

Attitude formation. If attitude toward an object is some function of the affective value of attributes associated with that object, a model is needed to specify the exact nature of that relation. A number of models have been proposed, including the congruity principle (Osgood, Suci, & Tannenbaum, 1957), the summation model (Anderson & Fishbein, 1965) and the averaging model (Anderson, 1965). According to the congruity principle a subject weights the evaluation of the attributes that enter into the interaction by their relative polarization. In the summation model the subject is thought to weight the evaluation of each attribute by the probability of its association with the object. The averaging model hypothesizes that attitude is equal to the sum of the evaluation of each attribute weighted by the importance of the attribute and divided by the sum of the importance weights. Research in the United States has demonstrated the superiority of both the averaging model and the summation model over the congruity principle for predicting attitudes (Anderson, 1971; L. R. Anderson & Fishbein, 1965).

The adequacy of these three models for predicting attitudes has been compared in a number of cross-cultural investigations. Tanaka (1972) obtained evaluative ratings of a nationality component (e.g., America), a noun component (nuclear testing) and then a composite of two components (e.g., American nuclear testing) for Japanese and Finnish subjects. Using the congruity model and a variant of the averaging model, predictions concerning the attitude toward the composites were made from the evaluative ratings of the individual components. Both models provided accurate (r's ranged from .85 to .93) and similar predictions of composite evaluation. Two other studies (Triandis & Fishbein, 1963; Triandis et al., 1966) compared the predictive validity of congruity and summation models for the evaluation of the complex stimulus people using American, Greek, Indian, and Japanese students as subjects. In most comparisons of the models presented in these studies the summation principle provided the more accurate predictions.

In the above tests of the Fishbein additive model the subjective probability relating the person and attribute was assumed to be one. In a more recent study in Mexico (Jaccard, Davidson, Triandis, Morales, & Diaz-Guerrero, 1975), both probability and evaluation were measured for each attribute. Results indicated that the Fishbein model accounted for most of the nonerror variance in evaluation of the attitude object. Szalay, Windle, and Lysne (1970) found similar results testing the summation model using indirect methods (frequency of association) for measuring beliefs. In summary, for the populations and topics reviewed, there appear to be no culturally determined boundary conditions modifying the models of attitude formation.

Similarity and interpersonal attraction/social distance.   The research just reviewed has suggested that attitudes toward an object are based on information about that object. However, much of the research on interpersonal attitudes has dealt with the noninformational bases of attraction, especially that of similarity of beliefs, interests, or personality traits. A good proportion of this research is based on the theoretical work of Rokeach (1960) and Byrne (1971). Based on balance theories of interpersonal attraction (Heider, 1958), Rokeach hypothesized that the primary determinant of social distance is the degree of perceived similarity of belief between the respondent and the stimulus person. Byrne has produced a similar model with regard to interpersonal attraction. The model states that attraction is a linear function of the proportion of similar opinion items. The predictions of both Rokeach and Byrne have been supported by data from the United States.

A number of cross-cultural studies have also produced data relevant to these hypotheses. Brewer (1968) compared the utility of the predictions from a number of theories—including Rokeach's similarity theory—in accounting for the social distance between East African tribes. In support of Rokeach's theory, similarity accounted for the greatest proportion of nonerror variance in social distance. Further evidence for the similarity-liking relation can be found in studies by Buchanan and Cantril (1953), Lambert, Anisfeld, and Yeni-Komshian (1965), and Tajfel et al., (1970).

Byrne, Gouaux, Griffitt, Lamberth, Murakawa, Prasad, Prasad, and Ramirez (1971) experimentally tested his model in five cultural groups. In strong support of the model, attraction was found to be a linear function of the proportion of similar items. Although there was a main effect for culture on mean level of attraction, culture did not interact with the similarity effect.

Recently, Ajzen (1974) has presented evidence indicating that attraction is related to similarity because of the empirical association between similarity and evaluation. Ajzen separated the effects of similarity and evaluation in an orthogonal design and reported that while evaluation had a significant effect on attraction, similarity did not. Support for Ajzen's view can also be found in the cross-cultural literature. There is evidence, for example, of the empirical association between similarity ratings of traits and evaluative ratings of traits (Berrien, 1969b; Buchanan & Cantril, 1953; Lambert et al., 1965). In addition, there is evidence that subjects who negatively evaluate their own traits have a greater degree of liking for dissimilar than similar others (Tajfel et al., 1972).

In conclusion, there can be little doubt concerning the empirical association between similarity and attraction or social distance. However, the basis of this relationship is still unclear. From evidence presented in this and the preceding portions of this section, it appears that interpersonal attraction and social distance are a function of the evaluation of the attributes that one associates with the other person or group.

Attitudes, Beliefs, and Behaviors

Before examining cross-cultural investigations of the relation between attitudes and behavior, it is important to establish one major methodological guideline that should by now be familiar to the reader, i.e., the question of cross-cultural functional equivalence. This issue has been discussed in relation to the measurement of experiences, beliefs, and attitudes; it is just as important in the measurement of behavior. To what extent do the same behaviors have the same meaning in different cultures? Is writing a letter to a government a functionally equivalent measure of political participation in Chile and Israel, where different political processes operate (Inkeles, 1969b)? Sommer (1968) provides an example of this problem with identical dyadic seating arrangements that evoked different median ratings of intimacy in different cultures. In cross-cultural research, just as much care should be applied to the development of behavioral measures as is beginning to be applied to the development of attitudinal measures. It is unfortunately the case that in almost all of the studies referenced below the question of functional equivalence in observed behavior has not been raised, let alone satisfactorily answered.

The study of the relation between attitudes, beliefs, and behaviors can be viewed from two basic theoretical perspectives; the design of the empirical research necessarily depends on which perspective a particular investigator intends to take, i.e., whether the theoretical interest is in (1) behavioral responses as measures of attitudes or (2) causal relations between beliefs, attitudes, and behaviors. This review of cross-cultural investigations of beliefs, attitudes, and behaviors is organized according to the perspective that was explicitly or implicitly the basis of the research, noting instances where the study design and stated theoretical intent are inappropriately matched.

Behavior as a Measure of Attitude

The first perspective that may be taken is that behavioral responses toward an object are one of many possible indicators of a generalized attitude toward (evaluation of) that object. As such, any *single* behavioral act toward an object is analogous to a single belief or attitude response on a written questionnaire. Therefore, one should not expect a very high relation between that particular behavior and other measures of the generalized attitude. For example, it is not surprising that Godwin (1972; 1975) reports low correlations between Kahl's (1968) scale of "trusting" attitudes and beliefs and a single type of "trusting" behavior in a gaming situation; the relations are about as large as one would expect for an item-scale relation, and should be treated as such, not as an attitude-behavior causal link. Similar findings are reported by Inkeles (1969a) regarding the relation between "modernity" and each of five "modern" behaviors.

On the other hand, one should expect a high relation between a generalized nonbehavioral measure of attitude toward an object and a *multiple-act* behavioral measure that consists of a representative sample of possible favorable and unfavorable responses to the object. These multiple-act criteria are viewed as behavioral measures of the same underlying attitude toward the object (Fishbein & Ajzen, 1974). The findings of Loomis et al. (1966) that there is a high positive relation between a generalized attitude toward "linkage" with a neighboring country and a set of behavioral "linkages," could be interpreted as showing attitudinal consistency using both behavioral and belief measures.

Several investigators have included behaviors as well as beliefs in constructing attitude scales. For example, Inkeles' (1969a) "active citizenship" scale and Muller's (1970) "political involvement" scale (see also Almond & Verba, 1963) are combinations of beliefs, behavioral intentions, and self-reports of behavior. Gordon (1972) examined the interrelations of measures of political beliefs and participation in a political demonstration to show that attitudes can be assessed by measuring affective, cognitive, and/or behavioral components.

It should be emphasized that none of the referenced investigations mentioned can be interpreted as having established causal links between beliefs, attitudes, and behaviors. Further, the degree of association one should expect between such behavioral and nonbehavioral indicators of attitude depends on the degree to which each set of items has been subjected to scaling procedures. As Fishbein (1967) notes, investigations of the relation between nonbehavioral and behavioral measures of attitudes seldom, if ever, subject the behavioral items to the same rigorous analyses performed in the construction of verbal attitude measures.

Causal Relations between Beliefs, Attitudes, and Behavior

The second perspective on the relation between beliefs, attitudes, and behaviors views each of these variables as separate constructs rather than as different measures of the same underlying predisposition. As such, the investigator may wish to investigate causal relations among them. The theoretical organization discussed in the introductory section will be used to discuss two types of causal hypotheses that might be investigated and to provide guidelines for the appropriate empirical research.

First, hypotheses in which certain attitudes are seen as causally prior to the behaviors of interest will be examined. As already indicated, investigations attempting to predict specific behaviors from generalized attitude measures are methodologically inappropriate for tests of such hypotheses. Since the behavioral measure has been moved from a general to a specific level, the specificity of the nonbehavioral attitude to be investigated must also be increased. The most specific measure of attitude would be evaluation of the behavior itself or intention to perform the behavior. For example, a generalized attitude such as modernity may be behaviorally represented by any number of different "modern" behaviors; but a single behavior cannot adequately represent the cluster of behavioral responses that may be associated with such a generalized attitude. It is therefore not surprising to find a low relation between this generalized attitude and a single behavior selected from the larger set of behaviors (Inkeles, 1969a). However, one might expect a very strong relation between reading newspapers daily (e.g., Inkeles, 1969a) for a given period of time and previously measured favorability toward reading newspapers daily over that same period of time.

A few cross-cultural studies have attempted to relate generalized attitude measures to specific behaviors (Inkeles, 1969a; Godwin, 1972: 1975), or to make causal statements about the interrelations of nonbehavioral attitude measures and the nonspecific clusters of behavioral measures (Inkeles, 1969b; Loomis et al., 1966; Muller, 1970; Weigert & Thomas, 1970). In every instance, the relations found are inconsistent or weak, or can be theoretically interpreted only as a relation between behavioral and nonbehavioral indices of the same underlying predisposition. On the other hand, where measures of very specific attitudes or beliefs about the behavioral criterion or about the object of the behavior were obtained, they were strongly positively related to the performance of the behavior (Brislin, 1971; Dawson, 1963; Diab, 1965; Freedman, Hermalin, & Chang, 1975; Goldberg, Sharp, & Freedman, 1959; Kelley, Shure, Deutsch, Faucheux, Lanzetta, Moscovici, Nuttin, Rabbie, & Thibault, 1970; Lindgren, Silva, Faraco, & DaRocha, 1964). Only the Freedman et al.(1975) study utilized a measure of evaluation of the behavioral criterion itself; such an evaluation (attitude) is at the highest level of specificity with regard to the behavior.

Evidence provided by Jaccard et al. (1975) with behavioral intentions as the criterion variable, indicates that evaluation of the behavior may be able to more accurately predict behavior than other, less specific measures of attitude. The greater the correspondence between the specificity of the attitude and behavior measures, the greater should be the size of their relationship.

The second set of causal hypotheses about the relation of beliefs, attitudes, and behaviors involves the effects of behavioral outcomes on the formation of new attitudes or beliefs. The specificity problem has not often arisen in this area. Investigators rarely use multiple-act criteria as the independent variable, and almost always attempt to predict a highly specific belief or attitude. However, there do seem to be gaps in specifying the underlying process of the effects of behavioral outcomes on attitudes and beliefs, as well as in measuring all the relevant variables. From the chapter's theoretical perspective, the process would be as follows: while holding attitude A, an individual performs behavior B which is relevant to A. The subjective or perceived outcomes of performing B are new experiences E that may or may not be consistent with A and may or may not alter A. In order to examine causal hypotheses of this sort, the investigator would ideally want to examine the nature of E and its relation to A in order to discover how E might change A. However, most cross-cultural studies that include attitudinal and behavioral measures are cross-sectional in design. In such cases one cannot determine whether presently held beliefs and /or attitudes are based on outcomes of self-reported concurrent or previous behavior, or whether the attitudes and beliefs were also held prior to performing the behavior (e.g., Brislin, 1971; Dawson, 1963; Diab, 1965; Kelley et al., 1970). In order to establish and delineate the process of the attitudinal effects of behavior, one needs to know at least the nature of an attitude before and after performing a particular behavior. It would also be useful to know the nature of the subjective experience E arising from the behavior and to demonstrate that it does or does not lead to attitude change. None of the studies reviewed examined, either empirically or theoretically, the intervening variable of subjective experience in the behavior-attitude relation. Three cross-cultural investigations did establish a logical order in which behavior preceded the attitude measure (Barrett & Franke, 1969; Melikian & Prothro, 1954: Tong, 1967), but only the latter provided a prebehavior attitude measure so as to eliminate the possibility that the attitude of interest was also held prior to performing the behavior.

The reader will have noticed at this point that cross-cultural research on the relation between attitudes/beliefs and behavior has been minimal. Obviously, the difficulties of sorting out causal relations in what is generally considered to be a continual feedback process (attitude→ behavior→ experience→ attitude, etc.) are compounded by problems of functional equivalence of both attitudinal and behavioral measures (and, if measured, equivalence of subjective outcomes of behavior). There is at present, however, a substantial theoretical literature on several aspects of the attitude/behavior relation, much of it supported by empirical research in the United States. The scarcity of such data from other cultures suggests that this research area is in great need of cross-cultural extension.

Conclusion

This review of cross-cultural studies of attitudes and beliefs emphasized theoretical and methodological issues at the expense of substantive findings. An issue that was not anticipated at the outset became clear as the relevant literature was reviewed—there is a strong dependency of method on theory. Stated simply, it is very difficult to design a methodologically defensible cross-cultural attitude study; without a reasonable theory it is impossible. Theory is required to guide method in the selection and development of equivalent stimuli and response materials. The greatest hindrance to the development of an integrated and cumulative cross-cultural body of knowledge related to attitudes and beliefs is not the lack of application of good method, but the lack of application of good theory.

Evidence for the important role of theory can be seen in the relative advances discussed in each of the sections of the review. In the section which examined the interrelation of beliefs and attitudes researchers were able to draw on well-developed models of cognitive organization and demonstrate their cultural generality. In contrast, in the section relating life experiences to attitudes and beliefs, there existed very few well-articulated theories to draw on, and most researchers were reduced to testing vague and intuitive hypotheses.

The substantive findings reviewed here suggest that basic cognitive processes, such as information processing and cue utilization, are relatively invariant across cultures. What does vary from culture to culture is the belief content of these processes.

Note

1. Preparation of this paper was supported by a grant from the Battelle Institute Program in Behavioral and Social Sciences. The authors wish to thank Richard Brislin, R. Kenneth Godwin, Harry C. Triandis, and the participants of the East-West Conference "Cross-Cultural Research for Behavioral and Social Scientists" for their critical comments on earlier drafts of this paper.

References

AJZEN, I. Effects of information on interpersonal attraction: similarity versus affective value. *Journal of Personality and Social Psychology,* 1974, *29,* 374–80.

ALMOND, G. A., & VERBA, S. *The civic culture.* Princeton, N.J.: Princeton University Press, 1963.

AMIR, Y. Contact hypothesis in ethnic relations. *Psychological Bulletin,* 1969, *71,* 319–42.

ANDERSON, L. R., & FISHBEIN, M. Prediction of attitude from the number, strength, and evaluation aspects of beliefs about the attitude object: a comparison of summation and congruity theories. *Journal of Personality and Social Psychology,* 1965, *2,* 437–43.

ANDERSON, N. H. Averaging versus adding as a stimulus-combination rule in impression formation. *Journal of Experimental Psychology,* 1965, *70,* 394–400.

ARKOFF, A., MEREDITH, G., & IWAHARA, S. Male dominant and equalitarian attitudes in Japanese, Japanese-American, and Caucasian-American students. *Journal of Social Psychology,* 1964, *64* 225–29.

BABAYAN, S. Y., BUDAYR, B., & LINDGREN, H. C. Age, sex, and culture as variables in food aversion. *Journal of Social Psychology,* 1966, *68,* 15–17.

BARRETT, G. V., & FRANKE, R. H. Communication preference and performance: a cross-cultural comparison. In *Proceedings of the 77th Annual Convention of the American Psychological Association,* 1969, pp. 597–98.

BARRY, H., III, BACON, M. K., & CHILD, I. L. A cross-cultural survey of some sex differences in socialization. *Journal of Abnormal and Social Psychology,* 1957, *55,* 327. (Reprinted in I. Al-Issa & W. Dennis (Eds.), *Cross-cultural studies of behavior.* New York: Holt, Rinehart and Winston, 1970, pp. 275–85.)

BARRY, H., III, CHILD. I. L., & BACON, M. K. Relation of child training to subsistence economy. *American Anthropologist,* 1959, *61,* 51–63.

BASS, B. M. *European and American managers' life goals and career success* (IRGOM Technical Report 74-2). Rochester, N.Y.: Graduate School of Management, University of Rochester, 1974.

BASS, B. M., & ELDRIDGE, L. D. Accelerated managers' objectives in twelve countries. *Industrial Relations,* 1973, *12,* 158–71.

BASS, B. M., & FRANKE, R. H. Societal influences on student perceptions of how to succeed in organizations: a cross-national analysis. *Journal of Applied Psychology,* 1972, *56,* 312–18.

BEG, M. A. Value orientations of Indian and American students—a cross-cultural study. *Psychologia,* 1966, *9,* 111–19.

BERRIEN, F. K. Methodological and related problems in cross-cultural research. *International Journal of Psychology,* 1967, *2,* 33–43.

———. Familiarity, mirror imagining and social desirability in stereotypes: Japanese versus American. *International Journal of Psychology,* 1969a, *4,* 207–15. (Reprinted in W. W. Lambert & R. Weisbrod (Eds.), *Comparative perspectives on social psychology.* Boston: Little, Brown, 1971, pp. 141–51.)

————. Stereotype similarities and contrasts. *Journal of Social Psychology*, 1969b, *78*, 173–83.

BERRY, J. W. A functional approach to the relationship between stereotypes of familiarity. *Australian Journal of Psychology*, 1970, *22*, 29–33.

————. Ecology, cultural adaptation and psychological differentiation: traditional patterning and acculturative stress. Paper presented at the Seminar on the Interface between Culture and Learning, East-West Culture Learning Institute, Honolulu, Hawaii, 1973.

BREWER, M. B. Determinants of social distance among East African tribal groups. *Journal of Personality and Social Psychology*, 1968, *10*, 279–89.

BREWER, M. B., & CAMPBELL, D. T. *Ethnocentrism and intergroup attitudes: East African evidence.* New York: Wiley/Halsted, 1976.

BRISLIN, R. W. Interaction among members of nine ethnic groups and belief-similarity hypothesis, *Journal of Social Psychology*, 1971, *85*, 171–79.

BRONFENBRENNER, U. Response to pressure from peers versus adults among Soviet and American school children. *International Journal of Psychology*, 1967, *2*, 199–207.

BUCHANAN, W., & CANTRIL, H. *How nations see each other: a study in public opinion.* Urbana, Ill.: University of Illinois Press, 1953.

BYRNE, D. *The attraction paradigm.* New York: Academic Press, 1971.

BYRNE, D., GOUAUX, C., GRIFFITT, W., LAMBERTH, J., MURAKAWA, N., PRASAD, M., PRASAD, A., & RAMIREZ, M., III. The ubiquitous relationship: attitude similarity and attraction. *Human Relations*, 1971, *24*, 201–07.

CAMPBELL, D. T. Distinguishing differences of perception from failure of communication in cross-cultural studies. In F. Northrop & H. Livingston (Eds.), *Cross-cultural understandings: epistemology in anthropology.* New York: Harper & Row, 1964, pp. 308–36.

————. Stereotypes and the perception of group differences. *American Psychologist*, 1967, *22*, 817–829.

CHU, G. C. Culture, personality and persuasability. *Sociometry.* 1966, *29*, 169–74.

COLE, M., & BRUNER, J. S. Cultural differences and inferences about psychological processes. *American Psychologist*, 1971, *26*, 867–76.

CVETKOVICH, G., & LONNER, W. A transnational comparison of individual birth planning decisions for hypothetical families. *Journal of Cross-Cultural Psychology*, 1973, *4*, 470–80.

DAVIDSON, A. R. The etic-emic dilemma: can methodology provide a solution in the absence of theory? In Y. H. Poortinga (Ed.), *Basic problems in cross-cultural psychology.* Amsterdam: Swets and Zeitlinger, 1977, pp. 49–54.

DAVIDSON, A. R., JACCARD, J. J., TRIANDIS, H. C., MORALES, M. L., & DIAZ-GUERRERO, R. Cross-cultural model testing: toward a solution of the etic–emic dilemma. *International Journal of Psychology*, 1976, *11*, 1–13.

DAWSON, J. L. M. Traditional values and work efficiency in a West African mine labour force. *Occupational Psychology*, 1963, *37*, 209–18.

————. Adjustment problems encountered by individuals in the process of modernization in the resolution of traditional-modern attitudinal conflict. Paper presented at Seminar on the Interface between Culture and Learning, East-West Culture Learning Institute, Honolulu, Hawaii, 1973.

————. Theoretical and measurement problems in the study of individual modernity in Asia. Paper presented at the Second Congress of the International Association for Cross-Cultural Psychology, Kingston, Ontario, Canada. 6–10 August 1974.

DIAB, L. N. Studies in social attitudes: I. Variations in latitudes of acceptance and rejection as a function of varying positions on a controversial social issue. *Journal of Social Psychology,* 1965, *67,* 283–95.

————. Reaction to a communication as a function of attitude-communication discrepancy. *Psychological Reports,* 1966, *18,* 767–74.

DIAZ-GUERRERO, R. Interpreting coping styles across nations from sex and social class differences. *International Journal of Psychology,* 1973, *8,* 193–203.

DOOB, L. W. The behavior of attitudes. *Psychological Review,* 1947, *54,* 135–56.

————. An introduction to the psychology of acculturation. *The Journal of Social Psychology,* 1957, *45,* 143–60.

————. Just a few of the presuppositions and perplexities confronting social psychological research in developing countries. *Journal of Social Issues,* 1968, *24,* 71–84.

DURKHEIM, E. *The elementary forms of religious life.* New York: Free Press, 1954.

EDGERTON, R. B. "Cultural" vs. "ecological" factors in the expression of values, attitudes, and personality characteristics. *American Anthropologist,* 1965, *67,* 442–47.

ELAM, E. H. Opinion profiles of seven cities. In J. M. Stycos, *Ideology, faith and family planning in Latin America.* New York: McGraw-Hill, 1971.

ENGLAND, G. W., & LEE, R. The relationship between managerial values and managerial success in the United States, Japan, India and Australia. *Journal of Applied Psychology,* 1974, *59,* 411–19.

FAWCETT, J. T., ARNOLD, F., BULATAO, R. A., BURIPAKDI, C., CHUNG, B. J., IRITANI, T., LEE, S. J., & WU, T. *The value of children in Asia and the United States: comparative perspectives.* Paper of the East-West Population Institute, no. 32, 1974.

FISHBEIN, M. Attitude and the prediction of behavior. In M. Fishbein (Ed.), *Readings in attitude theory and measurement.* New York: Wiley, 1967, pp. 477–92.

FISHBEIN, M., & AJZEN, I. Attitudes toward objects and predictors of single and multiple behavioral criteria. *Psychological Review,* 1974, *81,* 319–42.

————. *Belief, attitude, intention and behavior.* Reading, Mass.: Addison-Wesley, 1975.

FORD, C. S. *Cross-cultural approaches: readings in comparative research.* New Haven, Conn.: HRAF, 1967.

FREEDMAN, R., HERMALIN, A. I., & CHANG, M. C. Do statements about desired family size predict fertility? The case of Taiwan, 1967–1970. *Demography,* 1975, *12,* 407–16.

GODWIN, R. K. *Attitudes and behavior related to modernization.* Population Program and Policy Design Series, No. 6. Carolina Population Center, University of North Carolina at Chapel Hill, 1972.

————. The relationship between scores on individual modernity scales and societal modernization. *Journal of Developing Areas,* 1975. *9,* 415–32.

GOLDBERG, D., SHARP, H., & FREEDMAN, R. The stability and reliability of expected family size data. *The Milbank Memorial Fund Quarterly,* 1959, *37,* 369–85.

GORDON, L. V. Value correlates of student attitudes on social issues: a multination study. *Journal of Applied Psychology*, 1972, *56*, 305–11.

GULLAHORN, J. E., & LOOMIS, C. P. A comparison of social distance attitudes in the United States and Mexico. *Studies in Comparative International Development*, 1966, *2*, 89–103.

HAIRE, M., GHISELLI, E. E., & PORTER, L. *Managerial thinking: an international study.* New York: Wiley, 1966.

HEIDER, F. *The psychology of interpersonal relations.* New York: Wiley, 1958.

HINES, G. H. Cross-cultural differences in two-factor motivation theory. *Journal of Applied Psychology*, 1973, *58*, 375–77.

HOVLAND, C. I., & MANDELL, W. Is there a "law of primacy" in persuasion? In C. I. Hovland, W. Mandell, E. H. Campbell, T. Brock, A. S. Luchines, A. R. Cohen, W. J. McGuire, I. L. Janis, R. L. Feierabend, & N. Anderson (Eds.), *The order of presentation in persuasion.* New Haven: Yale University Press, 1957.

HOVLAND, C. I., & WEISS, W. The influence of source credibility on communication effectiveness. *Public Opinion Quarterly*, 1951, *15*, 635–50.

HOVLAND, C. I., HARVEY, O. J., & SHERIF, M. Assimilation and contrast effects in reactions to communications and attitude change. *Journal of Abnormal and Social Psychology*, 1957, *55*, 244–52.

HOVLAND, C. I., JANIS, I. L., & KELLEY, H. H. *Communication and persuasion.* New Haven: Yale University Press, 1953.

HOVLAND, C., LUMSDAINE, A., & SHEFFIELD, F. *Experiments on mass communication.* Princeton, N.J.: Princeton University Press, 1949.

INKELES, A. Industrial man: the relation of status to experience, perception, and value. *American Journal of Sociology*, 1960, *66*, 1–31.

―――. Making men modern: on the causes and consequences of individual change in six developing countries. *American Journal of Sociology*, 1969a, *75*, 208–25.

―――. Participant citizenship in six developing countries. *American Political Science Review*, 1969b, *63*, 1120–41.

―――. The role of occupational experiences. In C. S. Brembeck & T. J. Thompson (Eds.), *New strategies for educational development.* Lexington, Mass.: D. C. Heath, 1973, pp. 87–99.

―――. The school as a context for modernization. In A. Inkeles & D. B. Holsinger (Eds.), *Education and individual modernity in developing countries.* Leiden: E. J. Brill, 1974.

―――. Understanding and misunderstanding individual modernity. *Journal of Cross-Cultural Psychology*, 1977, *8*, 135–76.

JACCARD, J., DAVIDSON, A. R., TRIANDIS, H. C., MORALES, M. L., & DIAZ-GUERRERO, R. A cross-cultural test of two models for the prediction of behavioral intention. University of Illinois, Champaign-Urbana, Ill., 1975. (Mimeograph.)

JAHODA, G. Psychology and social change in developing countries. In *Proceedings of the XVIth International Congress of Applied Psychology*, Amsterdam: Swets and Zeitlinger, 1969, pp. 140–48.

JAKOBOVITS, L. A. Comparative psycholinguistics in the study of cultures. *International Journal of Psychology*, 1966, *1*, 15–37.

JOHNSON, N. B., MIDDLETON, M. R., & TAJFEL, H. The relationship between children's preferences for and knowledge about other nations. *British Journal of Social and Clinical Psychology*, 1970, *9*, 232–40.

KAHL, J. A. Modern values and fertility ideals in Brazil and Mexico. *Journal of Social Issues*, 1967, *23*, 99–114.

————. *The measurement of modernism: a study of values in Brazil and Mexico.* Austin, Texas: University of Texas Press, 1968.

KALISH, R. A., MALONEY, M., & ARKOFF, A. Cross-cultural comparisons of college student marital-role preferences. *Journal of Social Psychology*, 1966, *68*, 41–47.

KATONA, G., STRUMPEL, B., & ZAHN, E. *Aspirations and affluence: comparative studies in the United States and Western Europe.* New York: McGraw-Hill, 1971.

KELLEY, H. H., SHURE, G. H., DEUTSCH, M., FAUCHEUX, C., LANZETTA, J. T., MOSCOVICI, S., NUTTIN, J. M., RABBIE, J. M., & THIBAUT, J. W. A comparative experimental study of negotiation behavior. *Journal of Personality and Social Psychology*, 1970, *16*, 411–38.

KOHN, M. L. *Class and conformity: a study of values.* Homewood, Ill.: Dorsey, 1969.

LAMBERT, W. E., & KLINEBERG, O. *Children's views of foreign peoples.* New York: Appleton-Century-Crofts, 1967.

LAMBERT, W. E., ANISFELD, M., & YENI-KOMSHIAN, G. Evaluational reactions of Jewish and Arab adolescents to dialect and language variations. *Journal of Personality and Social Psychology*, 1965, *2*, 84–90. (Reprinted in W. W. Lambert & R. Weisbrod (Eds.), *Comparative perspectives on social psychology.* Boston: Little, Brown, 1971, pp. 174–84.)

LAMBERT, W. W., TRIANDIS, L. M., & WOLF, M. Some correlates of beliefs in the malevolence and benevolence of supernatural beings: a cross-cultural study. *Journal of Abnormal and Social Psychology*, 1959, *58*, 162–69.

LINDGREN, H. C., & VU, R. Cross-cultural insight and empathy among Chinese immigrants to the United States. *Journal of Social Psychology*, 1975, *96*, 305–06.

LINDGREN, H. C., SILVA, I., FARACO, I., & DA ROCHA, N. S. Attitudes toward problem solving as a function of success in arithmetic in Brazilian elementary schools. *The Journal of Educational Research*, 1964, *58*, 44–45.

LOOMIS, C. P., LOOMIS, Z. K., & GULLAHORN, J. E. *Linkages of Mexico and the United States.* Research Bulletin 14, Agricultural Experiment Station, Michigan State University, East Lansing, Mich., 1966.

MALPASS, R. Theory and method in cross-cultural psychology. *American Psychologist*, 1977, *32*, 1069–79.

MARTIN, J. G., & WESTIE, F. R. The tolerant personality. *American Sociological Review*, 1959, *24*, 521–28.

McCLELLAND, D. C. *The achieving society.* Princeton, N.J.: Van Nostrand, 1961.

McGINNIES, E. Studies in persuasion: II. Primacy-recency effects with Japanese students. *Journal of Social Psychology*, 1966a, *70*, 77–85.

————. Studies in persuasion: III. Reactions of Japanese Students to one-sided and two-sided communications. *Journal of Social Psychology*, 1966b, *70*, 87–93.

————. Studies in persuasion: IV. Source credibility and involvement as factors in persuasion with students in Taiwan. *Journal of Social Psychology*, 1968, *74*, 171–80.

MELIKIAN, L., & PROTHRO, E. T. Sexual behavior of university students in the Arab Near East. *Journal of Abnormal and Social Psychology*, 1954, *49*, 59–64.

MIDDLETON, M. R., TAJFEL, H., & JOHNSON, N. B. Cognitive and affective aspects of children's national attitudes. *British Journal of Social and Clinical Psychology*, 1970, *9*, 122–34.

MILLER, K. A., & INKELES, A. Modernity and acceptance of family limitation in four developing countries. *Journal of Social Issues*, 1974, *30*, 167–88.

MIRO, C. A. Some misconceptions disproved: a program of comparative fertility surveys in Latin America. In B. Berelson (Ed.), *Family planning and population programs: a review of world developments*, Chicago: University of Chicago Press, 1966, pp. 615–34.

MULLER, E. N. Cross-national dimensions of political competence. *American Political Science Review*, 1970, *64*, 792–809.

MUNROE, R. L., & MUNROE, R. H. Population density and affective relationships in three East African societies. *Journal of Social Psychology*, 1972, *88*, 15–20.

MURDOCK, G. P. World ethnographic sample. *American Anthropologist*, 1957, *59*, 664–87.

OSGOOD, C. E. Speculation on the structure of interpersonal intentions. *Behavioral Science*, 1970, *15*, 237–54.

———. Objective cross-national indicators of subjective culture. In Y. H. Poortinga (Ed.), *Basic problems in cross-cultural psychology*. Amsterdam: Swets and Zeitlinger, 1977, pp. 200–35.

OSGOOD, C. E., MAY, W. H., & MIRON, M. S. *Cross-cultural universals of affective meaning.* Urbana, Ill.: University of Illinois Press, 1975.

OSGOOD, C. E., SUCI, G. J., & TANNENBAUM, P. *The measurement of meaning.* Urbana, Ill.: University of Illinois Press, 1957.

PEABODY, D. Trait inferences: evaluative and descriptive aspects. *Journal of Personality and Social Psychology Monograph*, 1967, *7 (Whole No. 644).*

———. Group judgments in the Philippines: evaluative and descriptive aspects. *Journal of Personality and Social Psychology*, 1968, *10*, 290–300.

PERLIN, L. I., & KOHN, M. L. Social class, occupation, and parental values: a cross-national study. *American Sociology Review*, 1966, *31*, 466–79.

PETTIGREW, T. F. Personality and sociocultural factors in intergroup attitudes: a cross-national comparison. *Journal of Conflict Resolution*, 1958, *2*, 29–42.

PIKE, K. L. *Language in relation to a unified theory of human behavior.* The Hague: Mouton, 1966.

POORTINGA, Y. H. Limitations on intercultural comparison of psychological data. *Nederlands Tijdschrift van de Psychologie*, 1975, *30*, 23–39.

PORTES, A. The factorial structure of modernity: empirical replications and a critique. *American Journal of Sociology*, 1973, *79*, 15–44.

PROTHRO, E. T. Socialization and social class in a transitional society. *Child Development*, 1966, *37*, 219–28.

RAPP, D. W. Childrearing attitudes of mothers in Germany and the United States. *Child Development*, 1961, *32*, 669–78.

ROKEACH, M. *The open and closed mind.* New York: Basic Books, 1960.

ROSENBLATT, P. C. A cross-cultural study of child rearing and romantic love. *Journal of Personality and Social Psychology,* 1966, 4, 336–38.

ROSENZWEIG, M. R. Comparison among word associations with responses in English, French, German and Italian. *American Journal of Psychology,* 1961, 74, 347–60.

SAARBOURG, E. A. Frustration und Autoritarismus.Unpublished doctoral dissertation, University of Koln, 1958.

SCHAFFER, M., SUNDBERG, N., & TYLER, L. Content differences on word listings by American, Dutch and Indian adolescents. *Journal of Social Psychology,* 1969, 79, 139–40.

SCHUMAN, H., INKELES, A., & SMITH, D. H. Some social psychological effects and noneffects of literacy in a new nation. *Economic Development and Cultural Change,* 1967, 16, 1–14.

SEARING, D. D. The comparative study of elite socialization. *Comparative Political Studies,* 1969, 1, 471–500.

SEWARD, G. H., & WILLIAMSON, R. C. A cross-national study of adolescent professional goals. *Human Development,* 1969, 12, 248–54.

SHERIF, M., & HOVLAND, C. I. *Social judgment: assimilation and contrast effects in communication and attitude change.* New Haven: Yale University Press, 1961.

SIMONETTI, S. H., & WEITZ, J. Job satisfaction: some cross-cultural effects. *Personnel Psychology,* 1972, 25, 107–18.

SLOCUM, J. U., JR., & TOPICHAK, P. M. Do cultural differences affect job satisfaction? *Journal of Applied Psychology,* 1972, 56, 177–78.

SLOVIC, P., & LICHTENSTEIN, S. Comparison of Bayesian and regression approaches to the study of information processing in judgment. *Organization Behavior and Human Behavior,* 1971, 6, 649–744.

SMITH, R. J., RAMSEY, C. E., & CASTILLO, G. Parental authority and job choice: sex differences in three cultures. *American Journal of Sociology,* 1963, 69, 143–49.

SOMMER, R. Intimacy ratings in five countries. *International Journal of Psychology,* 1968, 3, 109–14.

SPIRO, M. E., & D'ANDRADE, R. G. A cross-cultural study of some supernatural beliefs. *American Anthropologist,* 1958, 60, 456–66.

STEPHENS, W. N. A cross-cultural study of menstrual taboos. *Genetic Psychology Monographs,* 1961, 64, 385–416.

STRODTBECK, F. L. Considerations of meta-method in cross-cultural studies. *American Anthropologist,* 1964, 66, 223–29.

SWANSON, G. E. *The birth of the gods: the origin of primitive beliefs.* Ann Arbor, Mich.: University of Michigan Press, 1960.

SZALAY, L. B., & BRYSON, J. A. Measurement of psychocultural distance: a comparison of American blacks and whites. *Journal of Personality and Social Psychology,* 1973, 26, 166–77.

SZALAY, L. B., & LYSNE, D. A. Attitude research for intercultural communication and interaction. *The Journal of Communication,* 1970, 20, 180–200.

SZALAY, L. B., WINDLE, C., & LYSNE, D. A. Attitude measurement by free verbal associations. *The Journal of Social Psychology,* 1970,82, 43–55.

TAJFEL, H., JAHODA, G., NEMETH, C., CAMPBELL, J. D., & JOHNSON, N. The development of children's preference for their own country: a cross-national study. *International Journal of Psychology,* 1970, *4,* 245–53.

TAJFEL, H., JAHODA, G., NEMETH, C., RIM, Y., & JOHNSON, N. B. The devaluation by children of their own national and ethnic group: two case studies. *Journal of Social and Clinical Psychology,* 1972, *11,* 235–43.

TANAKA, Y. A study of national stereotypes. In H. C. Triandis (Ed.), *The analysis of subjective culture.* New York: Wiley, 1972, pp. 117–80.

THURSTONE, L. L. Attitudes can be measured. *American Journal of Sociology,* 1928, *33,* 529–54.

TONG, W. F. Teacher attitude and personality as determinants of success in the performance of graduate teacher trainees. Unpublished thesis, University of Malaya, 1967.

TRIANDIS, H. C. Factors affecting employee selection in two cultures. *Journal of Applied Psychology,* 1963, *47,* 89–96.

———. Interpersonal relations in international organizations. *Organizational Behavior and Human Performance,* 1967, *2,* 26–55.

———. Culture training, cognitive complexity, and interpersonal attitudes. In R. Brislin, S. Bochner, & W. Lonner (Eds.), *Cross-cultural perspectives on learning* New York: Wiley/Halsted, 1975, pp. 39–78.

———. *Interpersonal behavior.* Monterey, Calif.: Brooks-Cole, 1977a.

———. Some universals of social behavior. *Personality and Social Psychology Bulletin,* 1977b, *4,* 1–16.

TRIANDIS, H. C., & FISHBEIN, M. Cognitive interaction in person perception. *Journal of Abnormal and Social Psychology,* 1963, *67,* 446–53.

TRIANDIS, H.C., & TRIANDIS, L. Race, social class, religion and nationality as determinants of social distance. *Journal of Abnormal and Social Psychology,* 1960, *61,* 110–118.

———. A cross-cultural study of social distance. *Psychological Monographs,* 1962, *76,* 1–21.

TRIANDIS, H. C., & VASSILIOU, V. Frequency of contact and stereotyping. *Journal of Personality and Social Psychology,* 1967, *7,* 316–28.

———. Interpersonal influence and employee selection in two cultures. *Journal of Applied Psychology,* 1972, *56,* 140–45.

TRIANDIS, H. C., DAVIS, E. E., & TAKEZAWA, S. I. Some determinants of social distance among American, German, and Japanese students. *Journal of Personality and Social Psychology,* 1965, *2,* 540–51.

TRIANDIS, H. C., KILTY, K., SHANMUGAM, A. V., TANAKA, Y., & VASSILIOU, V. A cross-cultural study of role perceptions. In H. C. Triandis (Ed.), *Analysis of subjective culture.* New York: Wiley, 1972a, pp. 263–98.

———. Cognitive structure and the analysis of values. In H. C. Triandis (Ed.), *Analysis of subjective culture.* New York: Wiley, 1972b, pp. 181–262.

TRIANDIS, H. C., MALPASS, R. S., & DAVIDSON, A. R. Psychology and culture. In P. Mussen & M. Rosenzweig (Eds.), *Annual Review of Psychology,* Vol. 24. Palo Alto, Calif.: Annual Reviews, Inc., 1973, pp. 355–78.

TRIANDIS, H. C., TANAKA, Y., & SHANMUGAM, A. V. Interpersonal attitudes among

American, Indian and Japanese students. *International Journal of Psychology*, 1966, *1*, 177–206.

TRIANDIS, H. C., VASSILIOU, V., & NASSIAKOU, M. Three cross-cultural studies of subjective cultures. *Journal of Personality and Social Psychology Monograph Supplement*, 1968, *8*, pp. 1–42.

VASSILIOU, V., TRIANDIS, H. C., VASSILIOU, G., & McGUIRE, H. Interpersonal contact and stereotyping. In H. C. Triandis (Ed.), *The analysis of subjective culture*. New York: Wiley, 1972, pp. 89–115.

WEIGERT, A. J., & THOMAS, D. L. Socialization and religiosity: a cross-national analysis of Catholic adolescents. *Sociometry*, 1970, *33*, 305–25.

WHITTAKER, J. O., & MEADE, R. D. Sex and age as variables in persuasibility. *Journal of Social Psychology*, 1967a, *73*, 47–52.

————. Sex of the communicator as a variable in source credibility. *Journal of Social Psychology*, 1967b, *72*, 27–34.

————. Retention of opinion change as a function of differential source credibility: a cross-cultural study. *International Journal of Psychology*, 1968, *3*, 103–08.

WILLER, D. *Scientific sociology: theory and method*. Englewood Cliffs, N.J.: Prentice-Hall, 1967.

3

Values

Marisa Zavalloni

Contents

Abstract

This chapter reviews literature on values from both a cross-cultural and an interdisciplinary perspective. Originally, the empirical study of values was introduced as the main objective of social psychology, seen as a general science of the subjective side of culture. Social anthropologists and sociologists used the concept of values to express central features of cultures, or of society. Further developments may be noted: for example, the culture and personality school considered values as the result of early socialization practices. In a parallel development, analytical schemes were developed by cultural anthropologists and sociologists for systematic cross-cultural comparisons. The survey approach to the study of values constitutes a further development of empirical research in the last thirty years. The results point to consistent and sometimes striking differences between cultures. The problem left unanswered by this method is how to explain the underlying mechanisms that produce these differences. This leads to the necessity of studying the cognitive and motivational bases of values in a cross-cultural context. An alternative approach to empirical research on values has been developed in the test-oriented field of psychometrics. The results are evaluated in a context of growing scepticism with regard to the validity and meaningfulness of such measures. Values research is then assessed in the light of a renewed interest in the study of cognitive processes. The idiographic versus nomothetic controversy is analysed in line with this new cognitive emphasis in psychology. Moreover, it is argued that values research will be influenced by a current view of society as the expression of conflicting interests, rather than as a reflection of common values. As a result values research is best seen as a part of research on social influence.

Introduction

Values refer to orientations toward what is considered desirable or preferable by social actors. As such, they express some relationship between environmental pressures and human desires.

Since values represent a meeting point between the individual and society, values research is potentially well suited to explore cross-cultural variations within an interdisciplinary framework, by articulating the goals of cultural anthropology, sociology, and psychology: "The concept of values supplies a point of convergence for the various specialized social sciences, and is a key concept for integration with the study in humanities" (Kluckhohn, 1951, p. 389).

However, in spite of some promising starts toward interdisciplinarity, particularly the efforts of C. Kluckhohn (1951, 1956) and F. Kluckhohn and Strodtbeck (1961), this direction has been comparatively neglected; each field pursues values research from one point of view. Smith (1969) is basically right when he states that "the handful of major attempts to study values empirically have started from different preconceptions and have altogether failed to link together and yield a domain of cumulative knowledge" (p. 98).

Since empirical research on values has been conducted by people who "differ widely in disciplinary origin, in substantive theoretical interests and modes of investigation" (Inkeles & Levinson, 1969, p. 435), it is not surprising to find that the term "values" has been used with many different connotations. However, a definition that expresses a common direction that underlies the observed differences may be adopted.

Kluckhohn (1951) provided a definition that captures "the fluid state of value studies . . . and the ambiguity of the term value" (Albert, 1968, p.

288). Its vagueness expresses the common denominator underlying these differences: "A value is a conception explicit or implicit, distinctive of an individual or characteristic of a group, of the *desirable* which influences the selection from available modes, means and ends of action" (Kluckhohn, 1951, p. 395). This definition, a quarter of a century old, hints at some communality between the individual and the sociocultural sphere without specifying its nature. Now, as then, a good understanding of the way an individual functions in his social and cultural context is yet to come.

The notion of values "as distinctive of an individual or characteristic of a group" is ambiguous in that it assumes isomorphism between the individual and the collective aspect of values. In the history of empirical value research of the last twenty-five years, this issue is raised over and over again and dominates the epistemological debate in various social science disciplines.

As Kluckhohn and Murray (1948) stated, a man is

a. like all other men,
b. like some other men,
c. like no other man.

The same is true for his values.

When studying values, social scientists solved the intricacies between what is unique and what is shared in different ways; none of the solutions are acceptable to all.

Cultural anthropologists see the individual as a culture carrier and an informant who can provide information about a group's values, when speaking about his own. Anthropologists who assumed no within-culture variance adopted this view: "Any member of a group, provided that his position with that group is specified, is a perfect sample of the group-wide pattern on which he is acting as an informant" (Mead, 1953, p. 6).

This alleged isomorphism between an informant and the group may appear today as an oversimplification. At the time it was proposed, the use of a group member as a provider of information about values in a society represented an innovation in cultural anthropology. Cultural anthropologists until then had relied on the traditional ethnographic sources, such as religious beliefs, general behavior items, artistic works, etc. to study values. Similarly, sociologists, who are both members and observers of their society, have oftentimes provided descriptions of its values by relying essentially on their own analytical powers.

In a different research tradition, as in the use of the survey approach for the study of values, the communality between the individual and the group is determined by the use of aggregate responses obtained from a sample of individuals and expressed through average frequencies. Similar methods, including complex statistical procedures, are to be found in the extension of the psychometric approach to the cross-cultural study of values.

Social psychologists of the symbolic interactionist school are more likely to conceptualize the relationship between individual and group values by hinting at still poorly known processes through which individual values emerge and eventually modify the sociocultural environment.

In an influential paper on personal values, Smith (1969) also adopts the symbolic interactionist perspective and sees values as central in the organization of personality to the extent that they are constitutive of the self. According to him, it is misleading to assume that general cultural values, as defined by anthropologists, are also the personal values held by an individual. He conceives personal values as the result of complex transactions between the individual and the environment, thus reopening the issue of the relationship between interindividual and intraindividual measures of values. This position is widely influential whenever values are discussed from a theoretical point of view; but it is not able to generate concrete cross-cultural research.

The task of developing research on values that may capture the dialectical relationship between the individual and the environment remains formidable. As a prerequisite, it may require abandoning the epistemological tradition of academic social psychology. In this field, research has been almost entirely conducted by measuring variables on an aggregate of individuals and by determining statistically their covariation (nomothetic approach). This method permits the extraction of configurations and clusters of responses, which provide useful descriptions of attitudes and values in a sample of individuals. However, it is not appropriate for the study of psychological *processes*. In other words, to translate Smith's theoretical position into concrete research would require the development of a structural social psychology paralleling Piaget's structural approach to genetic psychology. It should seek a direct access to the organizational principles and to the processes, conscious or unconscious, that produce a given value system. Developments along this epistemological line are taking place in a new field identified as *cognitive science* (Norman & Rumelhart, 1975; Bobrow & Collins, 1975), an interdisciplinary endeavor concerned with the analysis of underlying structures and processes of cognitive functioning. Several authors in personality research (Mischel, 1973; Bem & Allen, 1974) and social psychology (Harré & Secord, 1973) provide similar arguments. In parallel developments the sociological literature emphasizes the importance of understanding the microprocesses underlying the macrolevel and favors the adoption of the mathematics of general systems theory as an alternative to the use of statistics (Buckley, 1972).

Claiming to represent what Kuhn (1962) has defined as a "paradigmatic shift," a growing number of researchers underline the importance of exploring the relations between elements of a single system (an individual for instance) as opposed to the study of covariation among variables generated by an aggregate of individuals. Since values are part of the cognitive structure and of the personality of an individual, idiographic research on values, aiming to identify some intrapsychic processes that generate them in particular individuals living in different cultures may become relevant, thus creating a bridge between anthropology and psychology. The relevance of a structural-idiographic approach to cross-cultural research on values will be outlined later. This trend toward an increased differentiation and complexity in the study of an individual structure parallels the increased differentiation and complexity in the study of cultures at a macrolevel, where complex models that include ecological, cultural, and social components are developed as particular applications of system dynamics (Berry, 1975).

Thus, if empirical research on values has failed to develop an autonomous body of cumulative knowledge, it reflects to a certain extent a given state of the art in the social sciences; its future development may be linked to the general theoretical orientations that will prevail at that time. In sharp contrast with the neighboring and somewhat overlapping field of attitudes, values research has never developed a body of specific measuring techniques comparable to attitudes scales, which are somewhat independent of the substantive interests of those using them. The different ways of measuring values are inextricably linked to the particular ways a researcher conceptualizes the term, selects an aspect of what may be conceived of as the "desirable," and follows a given theoretical orientation. This precludes the presentation of a section specifically concerned with "measures" of values as distinguished from substantive and theoretical issues. To review cross-cultural research on values requires the presentation of the larger theoretical and disciplinary frames that produced it.

Early Developments in Anthropology and Sociology

Znaniecki (1918) is credited with being the first to introduce to the social sciences the notion that values could be approached empirically, and could form the center of a new discipline, social psychology, which he conceived as a general science of the subjective side of culture. Social psychology "may claim to *be* the science of consciousness as manifested in culture, and its function is to render service as a general auxiliary science, to all the special sciences dealing with various spheres of social values" (p. 78).

A few decades later, cultural anthropologists gave a prominent place to the study of values as part of a comparative science of culture. According to the social anthropologists, it was through values that the cultural determinants of behavior could be studied.

Values were seen as the result of traditional ideas transmitted historically, and were reflected as the essential core of culture (Kroeber & Kluckhohn, 1952). Values were variously defined as the unconscious canons of choice (Benedict, 1934), cultural themes (Opler, 1954), the unconscious system of meanings (Sapir, 1949), a world view (Redfield, 1953), and the central core of meaning (Kluckhohn, 1956). Value configurations were the analytical concepts expressing these central features of cultures, and representing an "abstraction" of the researcher (for instance, in Benedict's classification of culture as "Dionysian and Apollonean"). This distinction was borrowed from Nietzsche's (1901) early work, *The Birth of Tragedy.*

Before the fifties, value configurations were established according to traditional methods of anthropological field work: observation of natural behavior, the questioning of informants, inspection of cultural material (religion, art), etc.

In his early work, for instance, Kluckhohn (1949) attributes to Americans a "good time ideology" on the basis of their high expenditures for alcoholic beverages, theater and movie tickets, tobacco, cosmetics, and jewelry.

To some authors this kind of inference appears redundant (Blake & Davis, 1972). If "good time ideology" summarizes various elements of social behavior it cannot be expected to explain it. However, at the time of these early formulations, analytical abstractions derived from observing patterns of every day life, and expressed as "values," constituted the goal of anthropological analysis and appeared as the antecedents of behavior. Culture was seen as a logical construct, the network of abstracted patterns generalized by the anthropologist, and at the same time these patterns were seen as internalized by the individuals (Kluckhohn, 1954).

In the earliest stage of the development of cultural anthropology, descriptions of values and explanations of behavior appear interchangeable. "Operationally the observer notes certain kinds of patterned behavior. He cannot 'explain' these regularities unless he subsumes certain aspects of the process that determines concrete acts under the rubric 'values'" (Kluckhohn, 1951, p. 396).

At the time of these early formulations, cultural anthropologists were concerned with cross-cultural comparisons of relevant cultural dimensions in mapping the range of cultural relativism. Each culture was studied in its own terms, or emicly, as one would say today (Brislin, 1976). Similar analyses of values appeared concurrently in sociology where the emphasis was placed on within-culture value variations rather than on between-cultures comparisons. A well known example is Parsons's (1949) description of values associated with age and sex roles in American society. Following implicitly the assumption that social values are accessible to society members, Parsons, an American, did not base his analysis on field work, but followed the German tradition—the method of *Verstehen*, that consists of a thorough understanding of the phenomena under study. Parsons distinguished the having-a-good-time value of the youth culture from the dominant American adult values of achievement in the professions and business community.

In this context, values indicate preferences that are close to observed concrete behavior. Values are not seen as expressing the common core of a culture but as keys to differentiating social positions in a functional perspective.

From these early descriptive essays, cross-cultural research on values branched off in four ways: (1) The culture and personality school (Benedict, Mead, Gorer, Kardiner) displaced the search for antecedents of cultural differences in behavior from values to psychological variables derived from psychoanalysis; (2) C. and F. Kluckhohn and Parsons independently developed classification schemes, highly abstract in content, for a systematic comparison of value emphasis in different cultures; (3) An interdisciplinary approach to the study of values was initiated by F. Kluckhohn and F. Strodtbeck, and (4) In sociology with Parsons, values became the analytical basis of functional analysis.

Culture and Personality School

The culture and personality school was based on the assumption that values as behavior are an expression both of cultural institutions and of individual personality and that the influence of culture is always mediated by individuals.

Values were seen as the result of early socialization like other elements of behavior and not as antecedents of behavior. Causal determinants of behavior were expressed in quasi-psychoanalytical terms such as early frustrations (Kardiner, 1939), impulse structure (Mead, 1962), or patterns of child rearing. For instance, severe early cleanliness was supposed to create a repressed rage in Japanese infants, which accounts for some of their adult characteristics, such as brutality in war (Gorer, 1943), or concern for neatness and orderliness (Benedict, 1946). Similarly, La Barre (1945) described the Japanese as the most compulsive people in the world "ethnographic Museum," for similar reasons. A long and severely restricting swaddling, practiced by Great Russians, was allegedly associated with a manic depressive personality exhibited by a group of Soviet defectors (Gorer & Rickman, 1949). Some of these studies, which were conducted during World War II and the cold war period, had enemy nations as a target, and raised the "hope that a diluted version of psychoanalysis could solve the major international problems of our time" (LeVine, 1973, p. viii).

This line of research was largely abandoned since follow-up studies failed to confirm the nature of the antecedent variables, e.g., the severe toilet training of the Japanese (Norbeck & Norbeck, 1956; Lanham, 1956) or the character of the Russian exiles (Inkeles, Haufman, & Beier, 1961).

Comparisons of Value-Emphasis in Different Cultures

C. Kluckhohn (1951, 1956) worked toward the development of an analytical scheme that may be applied to systematic comparisons of value-emphasis in different cultures. It represented an effort to develop etic concepts, in contrast to the main concerns of many anthropologists who rely on emic concepts. It was, of course, congruent with the cultural relativist view that human populations vary widely in their cultural values and moral outlook, and that it is important to represent accurately the indigenous perspective, but comparisons require universal analytic constructs. The development of a typology of values was seen as a way of combining a justified emphasis on the specificity of a culture with the requirement of a systematic study of cultural variations. His goal was to reduce the wide range of regularities in a culture to a few categories or thematic principles, trying to do what factor analysts have done with different methods. At the time it appeared almost self-evident that the substance of the social sciences was to detect central tendencies in all the phenomena studied.

In a first attempt C. Kluckhohn (1951) distinguished between three dimensions of values: (1) Dimension of modality (positive and negative values); (2) Dimension of content (aesthetic, cognitive, and moral values); and (3) Dimension of intent (preferred style of action). He also distinguished between *instrumental* values, and *goal* values: "Instrumental values are those which actors and groups conceive as means to further ends. *Goal* values represent the aims and virtues which societies and individuals make for themselves" (p. 413).

C. Kluckhohn differentiates *values* from *value orientations* that consist of "generalized and organized conceptions influencing behavior, of nature, of man's place in it, of man's relation to man, and of the desirable and nondesirable as they may relate to man-environment and interhuman relations" (p. 411). In his later work, C. Kluckhohn (1956) developed a systematic approach to cross-cultural comparisons of value orientations that consists of a set of binary oppositions representing value emphases.

The actual content of value emphasis represents broad categories of human experience as revealed in history, philosophy, psychology, and the arts, and is, therefore, abstract. Such a high degree of abstraction in a classification of values is justified by the assumption that in a given culture, basic values are dependent upon that culture's conception of the ultimate nature of things. This typology of values is represented by three clusters of dichotomies:

- *Cluster 1—Man and Nature:* This refers to a conception of Man and of Nature:
    1a. Determinate-Indeterminate. This reflects a contrast between a state of affairs based on lawfulness as opposed to chance or caprice.
    1b. Unitary-Pluralistic. The world is seen as a single entity as contrasted to a conception of it as segmented into two or more spheres in which different principles prevail.
    1c. Evil-Good. Nature may be seen as threatening or beneficent.
- *Cluster 2—Man and Man:* This refers to interpersonal relations and to personal goals. It also reflects man's relations to nature:
    2a. Individual-Group. Priority given to the individual or to the collectivity.
    2b. Self-Other. Relative emphasis placed on egoism as opposed to altruism.
    2c. Autonomy-Dependency. Primacy is given to either individual or to group goals.
    2d. Active-Acceptant. Nature seen as being dominating or subjugated.
    2e. Discipline-Fulfillment. Apollonean-Dionysian contrast; Opposition between safety and adventure.
    2f. Physical-Mental. The intellectual as opposed to the sensuous.
    2g. Tense-Relaxed. Intense activity as opposed to easy-goingness.
    2h. Now-Then. A conception of time: the present here and now, as opposed to either past or future.
- *Cluster 3—Both Nature and Man:* This refers to value emphasis linking existential and evaluative assumptions:
    3a. Quality-Quantity. Measurement as opposed to the qualitative.
    3b. Unique-General. Discreteness and particularity as contrasted with abstraction and universality.

Philosophical influences are apparent in the content of this classification that as Kluckhohn states, was arrived at by successive approximations. His acknowledged influences are those of Morris and Northrop, the philosophers, as well as a variety of philosophical and anthropological literature.

Whatever the relevance of C. Kluckhohn's classification in expressing universal value emphases, the empirical problem remained as to how to determine the specific value emphasis of a culture. In a preliminary test of the fitness of his classification scheme for the cross-cultural comparisons of values C. Kluckhohn (1956) relied on the judgment of experts, e.g., anthropologists familiar with different features of the cultures studied. It was widely accepted at the time that: "All or almost all aspects of the social life of a people give expression in varying ways and varying degrees, to be sure, to the basic values which are characteristic of one culture as opposed to another" (F. Kluckhohn & Strodtbeck, 1961, p. 9). However, the development of quantitative methods in the fifties paved the way for an integration of traditional anthropological field work with the survey technique, and thus led toward an interdisciplinary approach to the study of values.

Interdisciplinary approaches

F. Kluckhohn and Strodtbeck: Study of Values (1961)   F. Kluckhohn and Strodtbeck (1961) studied variations of value orientations in five different rural and cultural communities of the American Southwest: Spanish-American, Mormon, Texan, Zuni, and Navaho. The authors' goal was to test the assumption that existential and evaluative beliefs are interrelated and may meaningfully differentiate various cultures. Standardized interview schedules were administered to samples of twenty-five individuals from each community.

The interdisciplinarity of this research resides in the fact that the theoretical predictions are made on the basis of ethnological data; their testing is conducted through statistical analysis of survey data and the interpretation of the results is again provided by anthropologists who are "experts" on the communities studied.

F. Kluckhohn and Strodtbeck (1961) define value orientations as

> complex but definitely patterned (rank-ordered) principles, resulting from the transactional interplay of the analytically distinguishable elements of the evaluative process—the cognitive, the affective and the directive elements— which give order and direction to the ever-flowing stream of human acts and thoughts as these relate to the solution of 'common human problems' (p. 4).

This comprehensive definition is, in practice, restricted to the testing of the few highly abstract categories similar to those developed above, and represents a limited number of common human problems for which all people at all times must find some solution: (1) the relation of man to nature (man-nature orientation); (2) the temporal focus of human life (time orientation); (3) the modality of human activity (activity orientation); (4) the modality of man's relationship to other men (relational orientation); and (5) man's nature (good/bad; mutable/immutable).

These existential notions are assumed to guide concrete behaviors, and are represented in the survey schedule by situations that rural people face everywhere. The range of value orientations is provided by short stories whose outcomes have to be ranked in order of preference by each respondent.

1. The *man-nature orientation* is represented by three alternatives: subjugation to nature, harmony with nature, mastery over nature.

2. The orientation toward *time* is represented by past, present, and future.
3. The *activity* orientation emphasizes being, being-in-becoming, and doing.
4. The *relational* orientation refers to man's relation to other men. The emphasis can be on lineal (ordered positional succession within the group), collateral (primacy given to goals and welfare of lateral extended groups), or individualistic (predominance of individual) goals.
5. The *nature of man* is assumed to be good, bad, or neither, and mutable or immutable. This last value orientation was not included in the interview schedule.

Here is an example of a set of alternatives provided to measure a past, future, or present value orientation:

> Someone says that whatever water comes in should be divided just like water in the past was always divided. Others want to work out a really good plan ahead of time for dividing whatever water comes in. Still others want to just wait until the water comes in before deciding on how it will be divided (Kluckhohn & Strodtbeck, 1961, p. 90).

Each respondent has to indicate the best alternative.

The content of the interview schedule makes it suitable for testing in a peasant community; however its relevance to other groups (e.g., urban dwellers) is doubtful.

In general, the results confirmed the predictions made by the authors: within-culture regularities and between-culture differences emerged.

The outstanding results were that Spanish-Americans preferred a *present* time orientation, the *being* alternative of the activity orientation, and the *subjugated-to-nature* position on the man-nature orientation. Mormons and Texans presented similar value patterns. Both were high on the *doing* orientation, but Mormons were slightly higher. The Mormons gave a somewhat lesser emphasis than the Texans to the *individualistic* orientation. They were also less favorably disposed to the dominance-over-nature as opposed to the with-nature alternative of the *man-nature* orientation. Finally, the Mormons showed a slightly greater tendency than the Texans to choose the *past* alternative of the *time* orientation over the *present* alternative. The Zuni exhibited a strong preference for the *doing* alternative of the *activity* orientation, and for the mastery-over-nature position of the *man-nature* orientation. The Navaho showed a preference for the *present* alternative of the *time* orientation, the with-nature alternative of the *man-nature* orientation, and for the *doing* alternative of the *activity orientation.*

According to the authors, their work demonstrated that it is possible to study the value orientation of a culture through the testing of individuals. The value orientations that were measured through the interview schedule reflected patterns of family organization, economic activities, religious beliefs and rituals, political behavior, attitudes toward education, and intellectual and aesthetic interests as determined independently by anthropologists who were experts on each culture.

This does not mean that the individual consciously holds an abstract notion of his value orientations as defined by the anthropologist. For, if "ideally one would prefer to test directly at the high level of abstraction at which the value orientations themselves are formulated," this is not possible "for not even those few persons who are highly sophisticated in matters of cultural variation are sufficiently well aware of their own implicit value-orientations to give clear distinction on all orientations at this level of analytical abstraction" (F. Kluckhohn & Strodtbeck, 1961, p. 345).

Cultural anthropology is thus seen as providing the means of arriving at scientifically derived abstractions about value orientations and of capturing the essence of a culture. These orientations may escape the phenomenal consciousness of a culture's members. Value orientations are operationalized as concrete choices that must be made in everyday life and then inferred from specific choices of alternatives. This epistemology fits naturally into the logic of survey research. It typifies the view prevalent at the time, of using indicators for abstracting and generalizing from empirical data. The quarrel between the qualitative and the quantitative viewpoints was thus limited to the problem of how to produce indicators. F. Kluckhohn's and Strodtbeck's work combines qualitative observation with quantitative testing and points to a convergence between the results obtained from the two approaches.

Rokeach (1973) criticized the content of the value survey schedule because it is far removed from what is ordinarily meant by a "conception of the desirable": "A person may indeed believe that man is subjugated to nature but circumstance does not necessarily imply that he has a value for 'subjugation to nature,' that he believes such a state of affairs to be desirable, or that man 'ought' to be subjugated to nature" (p. 22).

This criticism, however, does not take into account the complex theoretical relationships between the existential and the evaluation dimensions that constitute the basis of C. Kluckhohn's (1951, 1956) and F. Kluckhohn and Strodtbeck's work. Kluckhohn and Strodtbeck did not ask people whether they "value" subjugation to nature, but what was the best way of planting and taking care of crops; nor did they ask whether or not people could do anything about increasing life expectancy. The existential or general beliefs were seen as influencing concrete choices in everyday life.

Morris's Ways to Live   A comparable effort to measure value as philosophical orientations of peoples through empirical research and statistical analysis was carried out by Charles Morris (1956).

Morris's empirical research on values is directly derived from his own philosophical work; it is based on a series of value scales, defined as ways to live, and represents for the most part conceptions of a desirable life as embodied in the main religious and ethical systems. While Kluckhohn and Strodtbeck's schedule was appropriate mainly for a peasant population, Morris's instrument is suited mainly for highly educated respondents.

The basic values reflected in the different ways of living, according to Morris, are the Dionysian (release and indulgence of existing desires), the Promethean (active tendency to manipulate and to remake the world) and the Buddhistic (self-regulation and holding of the desires in check). The overlap with Kluckhohn's classification is noticeable. These basic values are combined to produce thirteen different ways of living. Each way is described by one paragraph. The essence of each way is shown below.

Way 1: preserve the best that man has attained
Way 2: cultivate independence of people and things
Way 3: show sympathetic concern for others
Way 4: experience festivity and solitude in alternation
Way 5: act and enjoy life through group participation
Way 6: constantly master changing conditions
Way 7: integrate action, enjoyment, and contemplation
Way 8: cultivate capacity for simple enjoyment
Way 9: attain joy and peace through receptivity
Way 10: control unruly impulses
Way 11: cultivate the self through the contemplative life
Way 12: use body energy for daring deeds
Way 13: cultivate humility and closeness to persons and nature.

It may be noted that the first six ways embody values important to the continuing operations of a society (stressing the conservation of what has been achieved, sympathetic concern for others, and reconstruction in the face of new problems), while the last seven are essentially individualistic and contain no stress on social responsibility.

Each way is represented by a lengthy statement that each subject is asked to rank according to a scale (ranging from: "I like it very much" to "I dislike it very much"). This instrument has been applied in a cross-cultural investigation among college students from the United States, India, Japan, China, and Norway. The results indicate that United States students, when compared to the other groups studied, were activist and self-indulgent in their values, and also less subject to social restraint and receptivity. The Indian value pattern was characterized by a strong emphasis upon social restraint and self-control. The value pattern of the Japanese students indicated a general orientation toward people and society; there was also respect for inwardness as well as a receptivity to nature. The Chinese students had the highest score on a factor indicating enjoyment and progress in action as well as withdrawal and self-sufficiency.

Jones and Bock (1960) applied multiple discriminant analysis to the same data. The principal results indicate that the American sample favored a *balanced involvement with all aspects of life* in contrast to the Japanese preference for *independence from others and openness to experience*. Indian students were high on a factor indicating acceptance of values related to dignity, refinement, and self-control suggesting *responsibility for maintaining a high social position*.

Prothro (1958) obtained Arab responses to the Morris ways-of-life questionnaire. The Arabs preferred ways involving activity, group participation, and self-control; they rejected receptivity, contemplation, and carefree enjoyment.

The values research reviewed so far has attempted to prove that there is a link between broad and abstract value orientations as defined by cultural anthropologists or philosophers and the experiences of people in their everyday life. In addition, value orientations are considered to represent crucial variables for the comparison of cultures.

In the last ten years, the field of cultural anthropology has all but abandoned this theoretical orientation. Cultures have since been conceived as cognitive phenomena, and the philosophers' concern with values has been replaced by techniques borrowed from structural linguistics.

The stated goal of this "new ethnography" is to discover how different people organize and use their culture; this is done inductively by relying entirely on the people's definitions rather than on preestablished categories constructed by a researcher. Cultural anthropology, according to this perspective, is concerned only with those events that are expressions of underlying thoughts (Tyler, 1969). Superficially, this statement may appear congruent with Kluckhohn and Morris's goals of discovering the central values of cultures. However, cognitive anthropology emphasizes the necessity of using inductive methods in order to explore cognitive structures and rejects the testing of abstract classification schemes that are derived exclusively from a researcher's analysis. Brislin (in Volume 2 of this *Handbook*) discusses this approach in greater detail.

This conception of ethnography requires that the units by which the data of observation are segmented, ordered, and interrelated be delimited and defined according to contrasts that are inherent in the data themselves (Frake, 1962). In practice, the discovery of objects and events that are significant for defining concepts, formulating propositions, and making decisions in the culture, has been entirely conducted by studying the organization of a particular semantic domain: kinship system, illness, botanical terms, etc. This method, used by the new ethnography, relies on questioning informants through a technique of "controlled elicitation" that produces sentence frames derived from the language of the people under study, and subsequently uses methods of formal analysis. The best known is componential analysis (Goodenough, 1956). Taxonomies, paradigms, and branching are then used to describe different semantic domains (Tyler, 1969).

According to some researchers, the ultimate goal of ethnographic semantics is *the understanding of the evaluations, emotions, and beliefs that lie behind word usage''* (Colby, 1966). However, the gap between the stated goals and the practices of the researcher may appear too wide to some observers. Even if values and beliefs could be analysed through componential analysis, the method seems more appropriate to the study of the denotative rather than of the connotative aspect of a semantic domain. Moreover, the equating of the simple taxonomies of a particular semantic domain with the cognitive map of a group of people appears to be less and less convincing to certain critics (Harris, 1968; Wieder, 1970). However, this new orientation toward a cognitive anthropology is not necessarily restricted to the methods used thus far. According to Tyler (1969) the goals of cognitive anthropology, the psychologist's renewed interest in cognitive processes, and the sociologist's concern with the presentation of the self may possibly converge. Such convergence may result in new perspectives for the cross-cultural comparisons of values.

Values may eventually reappear as a focus for cross-cultural research, but as components of the cognitive map of individuals. Along these lines, there are indications of new developments in cross-cultural research that will be reviewed later (Triandis, Vassiliou, Vassiliou, Tanaka, & Shanmugam, 1972; LeVine, 1973; Zavalloni, 1975).

Values will be seen less tied to philosophical arguments concerning the "essence" of a culture, and more connected to the concept of the organization of the cognitive structure of individuals. They will be seen as an emergent product of past experiences.

Sociology and the Study of Values

With the exception of a few dissenters (Blumer, 1969; Becker, 1964; Dahrendorf, 1958), the basic assumption in the mainstream of academic sociology explained social order by a hypothetical but apparently self-evident consensus of values, e.g., basic normative principles that are shared by all of society's members.

The more elaborate version of the theory of values can be credited to Parsons (1953 and Parsons & Shils, 1951) whose analysis of the social system is based on a classification scheme that is the value orientations pattern; this consists of the following dichotomies:

• Affectivity—affective neutrality
• Self-orientation—collectivity-orientation

- Universalism—particularism
- Ascription—achievement
- Specificity—diffuseness

This classification is somewhat similar to the classification of values developed independently by C. and F. Kluckhohn that determined the essence of a culture. However, Parsons developed a theoretical framework in which values are used as analytical tools for a multiplicity of purposes that range from the description of a general cultural orientation to role differentiations within a culture as well as to basic elements of the personality. Thus, Parsons attempts to integrate the cultural, the social, and the individual level of analysis into a general theory of the social system based on the *value-orientation pattern variables*.

Comparisons between cultures. According to Parsons, the essence of different cultures can be expressed by various combinations of the pattern variables. For example,

Table 3-1. Types of Combination of Value-Orientation Components' Major Social Value-Orientations

	UNIVERSALISM	PARTICULARISM
	A. Universalistic Achievement Pattern	B. Particularistic Achievement Pattern
Achievement	Expectation of active achievements in accord with universalized standards and generalized rules relative to other actors.	Expectation of active achievements relative to and/or on behalf of the particular relational context in which the actor is involved.
	C. Universalistic Ascription Pattern	D. Particularistic Ascription Pattern
Ascription	Expectation of orientation of action to a universalistic norm defined either as an ideal state or as embodied in the status-structure of the existing society.	Expectation of orientation of action to an ascribed status within a given relational context.

(From Parsons & Shils 1951, p. 102)

The Universalistic Achievement Pattern (Cell A) represents the American ethos, and its philosophy of pragmatism. The Universalistic Ascription Pattern (Cell C) represents the idealist philosophic writing as found in the German cultural ideal. The Particularistic Achievement Pattern (Cell B) reflects the classical Chinese cultural pattern, as exemplified by Confucianism. Finally, the Particularistic Ascription Pattern (Cell D) approximates the Spanish-American culture.

Lipset (1963) has applied Parsons's pattern variables to a comparative analysis of United States, Australia, Canada, and Great Britain. The United States emphasizes achievement, egalitarianism, universalism, and specificity. Canada is lower than the United States on all these dimensions. Great Britain in turn ranks lower than Canada. Australia was found more egalitarian but less achievement-oriented, universalistic, and specific.

Within culture comparisons.   According to Parsons, at the social level of analysis, the value-orientation pattern designates the characteristics of an actor which are required by the social system and are also congruent with the expectations of his roles:

> Role-expectations are the definitions by *both* ego and alter of what behavior is proper for each in the relationship and in the situation in question. . . . These expectations are institutionalized when they are integrated with or express value orientations *common* to the members of the community (Parsons & Shils, 1951, p. 154).

During the process of socialization, the value orientation patterns are internalized, and become basic features of the actor's personality.

An extension to social psychology of the value-consensus assumption is provided by Sarbin and Allen (1968). They define social identity as the evaluation from the social system of an individual performance in an ascribed (e.g., male, husband, father) or achieved status which would result in *downgrading* or *upgrading*. A need for conformity to apparently universally shared norms or values is seen as the motor of people's behavior. F. Kluckhohn and Strodtbeck (1961) indicate that this theorizing leads to a polarization of social action in terms of conformity-deviation. The individual either conforms or alienates himself from the role expectations that are highly unitary characteristics of society. They argue that a greater emphasis should be given to possible variations in value orientations to account for differences in behavior. Recently Cicourel (1973), an ethnomethodologist, has pointed to additional weaknesses in using common values embedded in role expectation to explain behavior. This view fails to answer the crucial question of "what passes as 'common' and how our actors decide on their own or some collectivity's 'common' value-orientations" (Cicourel, 1973, p. 21).

Today the trend is toward considering culture as a part of the environment rather than as an internalized feature. Stokes and Hewitt (1976) consider culture as a field of objects that are environmental to action and to which people must relate as they form lines of conduct.

Other ethnomethodologists underline the difficulty of knowing how the observer or the actors perceive what are the proper role expectations, and of deciding the link between Ego and Alter perspectives (Garfinkel, 1967; Douglas, 1970). They propose the search for "interpretative" procedures as the base for understanding emerging values in society. The idea of interpretative procedures replaces the rather static notion that internalized values predispose certain kinds of action. The researcher must specify how the actor negotiates and constructs possible action, and then evaluates the result of the completed action.

The value-consensus assumption—the view of society as a homogeneous system—was never completely accepted in Europe where ideological conflicts have always been predominant. According to Touraine (1973), a French sociologist, society cannot be seen as the expression of common values but rather as an ensemble of cultural tensions and of social conflicts. Society is never fully integrated through values or power. Conflict and protest are endemic and society should be considered as a *champ de création conflictuelle*.

Dahrendorf (1959), a German sociologist, observes that the value-consensus assumption underplays the reality of conflicting groups' interests. Groups or quasi groups have different interests in the maintenance or change of the status quo. As a result, conflicts of values expressing these differences are always likely to exist.

In the United States, the opposition to the value-consensus assumption was voiced by some sociologists or social psychologists identified with the symbolic interactionist point of view. Blumer (1969) argues that

> to seek to encompass, analyze and understand the life of a society on the assumption that the existence of a society necessarily depends on the sharing of values can lead to strained treatment, gross misrepresentation, and faulty lines of interpretation (p. 76).

Values are important only in so far as they enter into the process of interpretation and definition, from which joint actions are formed. Values should not be invoked as causes of social behavior, but should be seen as an *emergent* product of social interaction. As a consequence of this shift from cultural transmission to cultural creation, values, seen as the expression of central tendencies or of dominant ideologies of a society transmitted from generation to generation, appear to be losing most of their relevance as causal constructs used to analyze society. More efforts will be directed to understand the dynamics of innovation and change by focusing on values of creative minorities as "cultural agents" or *"idéologues"* as the French would say. The social scientists are asked to give a closer look to their own values. Thus Gouldner (1969) proposes the creation of a reflexive sociology to keep the sociologist aware of who and what he is, as a member of a specific society at a given time, and of how his social role and his personal life affect his professional life. Social scientists can be said to introduce a political dimension in their work insofar as their observations coincide with their personal values and views of society. Myrdal (1969) has echoed similar concerns when evaluating the role of social scientists' own values in conducting psychological research. A serious tackling of this issue, which would bring research and social reality to an interesting confrontation, may provide a new impetus to cross-cultural research on values and provide a first step toward fulfilling what to Moscovici (1970) appears to be the principal vocation of social psychology: to understand the creation and function of ideology in society. Also relevant to these issues are the numerous studies on alienation reviewed by Seeman (1975). According to his formulation, "the idea of cultural estrangement points to the perceived gap between the going values in a society (or subunit thereof) and the individual's own standards" (p. 93).

The Survey Approach and the Study of Values

The development of quantitative methods during the fifties provided a new impetus to cross-cultural comparisons of values. New methods became available to determine those elusive differences between people and cultures that had been so painstakingly pursued by earlier anthropologists, who were obliged to rely on methods that some considered inexact and subjective.

Responses obtained from representative samples of a group could replace the unreliable questioning of informants. At the same time, quantitative techniques could correct the highly speculative exercises of the classical sociological tradition. C. Kluckhohn's definition of values as the expression of the desirable still fits the content of research on values conducted through the survey method. However if some of his preoccupations with ultimate meanings are reflected in the questions asked, the focus of his research is on the desirable, operationalized as the final goals of individuals. In addition, values related to sociopolitical issues appear frequently in the questions asked.

Buchanan and Cantril

In one of the first applications of survey methods to the study of values, Buchanan and Cantril (1953) assessed mutual stereotypes that were held by representative samples in several countries. Open-ended questions that dealt with general values were also included: "What are your hopes for the future? What would life have to be like to be completely happy?" The authors did not want to impose any standard value scheme on their respondents. However, the responses were coded using a limited number of categories.

In a later study, Cantril (1965) undertook a cross-national comparison of values in fifteen nations as reflected through people's definitions of their basic strivings and personal concerns. The instrument used was a *self-anchoring scale.*

The subject was asked to think of the best and the worst possible world and to place his own world on a point between these two extremes. In addition, questions tapped the respondent's key concerns, wishes and hopes, and worries and fears.

Cantril insists, rightly, on the importance of ascertaining the respondent's own frame of reference. However, since the results are presented as aggregated frequencies, the initial strength of the method becomes a weakness. Specifically, interpretation is difficult because of (a) the difference of meaning obtained on the scale (it is difficult to interpret the meaning of aggregate anchoring points); (b) there are no reasons to assume that the frames of personal references are the same in a sample of individuals, even if it represents a relatively homogenous group; and (c) the use of aggregate responses obviously destroys the specificity of individual patterns. It is regrettable that this issue is not clarified by Cantril.

General results show that there are wide variations in the total volume of concerns expressed by people in different nations. These are interpreted as a function of the political situation of the countries studied. This may be considered a plausible level of analysis, but other more psychological or culturalist explications could have been equally plausible. In Cuba and the Dominican Republic, where radical political changes had occurred, a strong involvement with national problems was frequently expressed. A similar pattern was found in Nigeria, Yugoslavia, and Israel that, at the time, were all gaining independence. By contrast, Indian respondents expressed very little personal involvement with national problems. A similar lack of involvement with national affairs characterized the answers of respondents from Brazil and the United States.

The ambiguity of these results suggests that there is a built-in limitation in cross-cultural survey research in attempting to determine differences in values. If reliable techniques have been developed to get data from representative samples, the interpretation of these results remains plausible at best, and is always vulnerable to what Campbell (1969) has termed "rival hypotheses." An example is the time of data gathering.

Survey data are most useful in obtaining a spectrum that represents cultural differences in values. They obviously do not allow for an explanation of these differences in any unequivocal and compelling way. As a result, if the introduction of rigorous quantitative methods seemed to spell the end of speculative activity in the cross-cultural comparison of values to some observers, it also meant the beginning of a new field for speculations: interpreting the results. Cantril implies that the low involvement of Indians with national affairs has to be interpreted in the context of a "people whose nation achieved independence some years ago and who still have hardly become aware of and begun to solve the problems connected with their development" (p. 253). Finding that there are no appreciable differences between blacks and whites in their degree of self-respect and self-confidence, Cantril comments: "By 1959, the time of our survey, Negro Americans had apparently been able to shed the lack of self-respect that had so long haunted many of them vis-à-vis the white norms they had learned" (p. 272).

A review of the evidence about blacks' lack of self-respect and their alleged internalization of white norms indicates that this survey is not a true reflection of black psyche, but white social scientists' projections of how they would feel if they were suddenly to become black (Zavalloni, 1973a). Cantril's interpretation is not helpful in clarifying this problem. By invoking hypothetical changes and without questioning the views themselves, Cantril adopts contradictory evidence to fit current views. Moreover, many of the findings may compound cultural differences with differences in the time when the data were collected.

Cross-Cultural Studies of Youth Values

A number of researchers have been convinced by Gillespie and Allport's (1955) argument, namely, that if a comparative approach to the study of values were to be developed, an effort should be made to apply similar instruments providing etic measurements to comparable samples in different countries. In their pioneering work, Gillespie and Allport compared values of university students in nine countries. The instrument consisted of an Autobiography of the Future ("Describe your life from now to the year 2000") and a questionnaire that contained multiple choice and open-ended questions that dealt with occupational aspirations and basic values. For example, "What two things would you be most proud to accomplish during your lifetime?"

American students were found high in *privatism;* they were concerned with their own private world and an exciting life. This is a picture of young Americans similar to the one presented by Cantril. In contrast, a nationalistic orientation was typical of Egyptian and Mexican students.

Using the same instrument, Hyman, Payaslioglu, and Frey (1958) found Turkish students high in nationalism. In comparing Bantus, Indians, and whites, Danziger (1963b) found that whites expressed higher *privatism* than the other samples.

Gillespie and Allport (1955) also found that the expressed desire to become an important person was much more common among students from emergent nations than among students of industrially developed countries. Danziger (1963a) reported similar results when he compared aspirations of African and European high school students in South Africa. Stoetzel (1955) reported the same in Japan; his results indicate a widespread desire for fame and high achievement among Japanese university students.

The cleavage between non-Western and Western self-values was confirmed by Rubin and Zavalloni (1969) who used this same instrument to compare values of high school students differing on ethnic and socioeconomic characteristics in Trinidad, W.I., a multiracial society.

A content analysis of the autobiographies of the future[1] of Trinidad youth indicated that East Indian and black students were more likely to express spontaneously the goals of great achievement than did the white or racially mixed respondents. The East Indian students ranked highest in expectations of great achievement[2] closely followed by the black students. The East Indian students valued scientific or political achievements more than wealth, although wealth may be an inherent corollary of these achievements. The black students chose evenly between the attainment of scientific or political fame and the attainment of wealth. On the other hand, white and racially mixed students tended to give priority to the attainment of wealth per se. When socioeconomic differences were examined, intragroup variations were seen only among the East Indian students. Wealth, as a primary goal, was more likely to be emphasized by East Indians of the upper socioeconomic group than by either the middle or lower socioeconomic groups. Compared to 45 percent in the lowest socioeconomic group, only 14 percent of those in the high socioeconomic groups expressed the wish to "become a great person."

Comparing occupational choices of high school students from Ghana with those of British secondary school graduates, Veness (1962) and Jahoda (1966) found the students from Ghana much more ambitious than the British students in their choice of professions. In another study, comparing Maori youth with Pakeha (white) youth in New Zealand, Ausubel (1961) found that, particularly in relation to remote goals, the Maori youth had more unrealistic aspirations.

Glicksman and Wohl (1965) compared values of Burmese and American university students. They asked the respondents to write short essays describing what they wanted from life. The Burmese tended to be far more ambitious than the Americans in their expressed desire for great wealth. Americans expressed more concern with religious values, and with the discovery and realization of personal potential.

These converging results indicate the existence of deep-seated differences in self-values among youth from developed and less developed countries. However, the reasons for these differences are unclear, since the reasons cannot be elucidated by the survey method. One explanation of the difference that has been proposed is "ecological demographic." In the less developed countries there are few educated people. Thus, anyone who is educated is much more likely to occupy the few high level positions that are available. Also, the needs of these countries for high level positions that do not yet exist are far greater than the needs of the developed countries. Even if this explanation is plausible, the importance of determining more precisely the antecedents of such representations of the self in the world, which may remain unrealistic despite some objective opportunities, is evident. (A more idiographic approach, as reported in the section on the idiographic-nomothetic controversy in this chapter, may be relevant.)

Danziger (1963a) developed an "index of self-rationalization" for the analysis of the autobiographies of the future. The index was derived from Weber's (1922) notion that there is an increased rationalization in industrial society that would tend to suppress uncontrolled emotional action and from Mannheim's (1935) corollary notion that people who live in a highly rationalized society show a high degree of self-rationalization as shown in their control of drives and fantasy. In short, self-rationalization induces modest goals.

The index of self-rationalization was applied by Danziger to the analysis of autobiographies of the future of black and white students from South Africa. African girls showed the least degree of self-rationalization by expressing a desire for fame and prestige. On the other hand, both American and Japanese girls expressed a high degree of self-rationalization. Thus, there exists an interrelationship between industrialization and self-rationalization.

Comparable results were obtained by Morsbach and Okaki (1968), who applied the index of self-rationalization to autobiographies of the future that were written by adolescent girls in Africa, Japan, and the United States. The "industrialization hypothesis" may appear to be an unconvincing explanation of complicated cognitive functioning expressed through values and aspirations. Would this reasoning, then, imply that people of preindustrial Europe would have entertained such high aspirations about themselves?

Rokeach Value Survey (RVS)

In the surveys reviewed so far, values were assessed mostly through open-ended questions or essays.

The RVS combines the practical requirements of developing short, easy to administer instruments with the logic of survey research. It consists of two separate check lists in which a respondent is asked to rank order thirty-six value statements. The first list measures "terminal" values represented by eighteen concepts such as salvation, equality, world peace, lasting contributions, comfortable life, exciting life, and social recognition that refer to preferred end states of existence. The second list measures "instrumental" values through eighteen adjectives such as courageous, responsible, honest, polite, and clean that describe some preferred modes of conduct.

Rokeach (1973) compared samples of people from different ethnic and social origins in the United States, as well as samples of students in different countries. Age and sex were also used as independent variables. In the United States, males tended to rank a "comfortable life" higher and "salvation" lower than females, the poor and uneducated ranked a "clean and comfortable life" higher than did the affluent. Sometimes a high ranking value was interpreted as representing a state that has been attained and sometimes as a state that is not attainable. For instance, black Americans compared to white Americans placed a greater value on "comfortable life," and in being "clean" and "obedient." A lower value was placed on "a world of beauty," "family security" and "loving." Rokeach sees as antecedents or determinants of these choices the segregated conditions and the relative deprivation found in black ghettos. The temptation to transform descriptive data, through speculative interpretation into *determinants* of a phenomenon, is an endemic weakness of survey research.

One of the major problems of the Rokeach method is the basic ambiguity between its theoretical and its empirical aspect. Values are defined as "a standard that guides and determines action, attitudes toward objects and situations ideology, presentations of self to others, evaluations, judgments, justifications, comparisons of self with others, and attempts to influence others" (1973, p. 25). Obviously, this is a complex construct that cannot be reduced to the eighteen concepts and eighteen adjectives of the RVS. Moreover, even if Rokeach operationalization is accepted, according to him a value system is an enduring *organization* of beliefs that concern preferable modes of conduct or end-states of existence *along a continuum of relative* importance. This implies that the "value system" of an individual will be derived idiographically from the total configuration of his ranking of values. Yet, on the empirical side, the results are presented as median rankings of each value concept when taken separately and produced by a subsample that is characterized by demographic variables.

Moreover, the rank-order procedure is an ipsative procedure, in the sense that it generates nonindependent data within individuals. Therefore, it is not clear what the psychological meaning of some statistically significant differences among groups may be. For instance, a finding, which Rokeach accords some importance to, asserts that the mean rank of an end state value such as "social recognition" is 13.8 for men and 15.0 for women. One could interpret these results by saying that for both sexes such an end value ranks very low. Rokeach considers this finding a confirmation of the greater value placed on "social recognition" by men than by women in our society. This issue is twofold: (a) a ranking position of 13.8, which is objectively very low, acquires by comparison to another mean an opposite meaning[3]; (b) the difference in the ranking position of a particular value may be due to the importance attributed by the respondents to some other values rather than to the intrinsic meaning of the value.[4]

Given the importance of other variables on values, sex per se may not necessarily be a crucial variable to account for the results. The sex differences on ranking means need to be "controlled" by the level of education, socioeconomic status, occupational status, etc. of the respondent.

Cross-cultural comparisons were conducted with several samples of United States, Australian, Canadian, and Israeli students. United States students were found to be more oriented toward materialistic achievement but less hedonistic and less concerned with equality. Feather and Hutton (1973) applied the RVS to compare Australian and Papua students in New Guinea. The Papua New Guinea students gave much higher priorities to equality, national security, salvation, social recognition and a comfortable life than did the Australian students. These differences are interpreted in terms of broad social influences, the church, local tradition, etc.

At the same time the authors raise some pertinent methodological questions about the cross-cultural utilization of the RVS. People from different cultures may interpret the value concepts in different ways, and some of the values may be outside the range of experience of indigenous students in developing countries. Feather (1975), while restating these points, considered that both lists of RVS cover a wide enough range of values and that "they should provide useful indicators of cross-cultural differences in future comparative research among people who have had a reasonable standard of education" (p. 228). However, the fact remains that in terms of its relevance for cross-cultural comparison, the instrument is western and in no sense appropriate for other cultures. It is an imposed etic, not an emic measure. Because it is easy to administer and to analyze the RVS may appeal to some as a useful instrument for getting quick results. It tells little about values defined as complex intrapsychic constructs. To tackle this problem will require finding means for exploring idiographically the underlying processes and mechanisms that *relate* values, perceptions, judgments, and behavior—in other words, to bring social psychology closer to developments of modern cognitive psychology.

Finally, a note of caution should be raised on the use of student samples as if they constituted a homogenous group for cross-cultural comparisons. Such an assumption underestimates within-culture variations on values. In a survey on student values of thirteen countries (Klineberg,

Louis-Guérin, Zavalloni, & BenBrika, 1978), it was found that large differences in personal and cultural values existed in each of these countries due to the political orientation of the respondents.

Moreover, a factor analysis of the data of this study obtained in France, Great Britain, and the United States (Louis-Guérin, 1973) indicates that the cluster of values associated with a leftist orientation varies in these three countries. French leftists emphasize purely political and ideological values. In contrast, leftist students from the United States and Great Britain are more likely to adopt innovative cultural values, including life styles.

These results indicate the danger inherent in considering a sample of students sufficiently homogenous to provide a satisfactory basis for cross-cultural comparison.

Self, Political, and Moral Values

There are a number of cross-cultural surveys dealing with specific value orientations such as nationalism, modernization, or moral values. Klineberg and Zavalloni (1969) compared the relative strength of tribalism over nationalism in six African countries: Ethiopia, Nigeria, Senegal, Congo, Ghana, and Uganda. One of the instruments used was the "Who am I?" test (Kuhn & McPartland, 1955). It measures self-concept; a respondent is asked to answer the question "Who am I?" twenty times.

The results indicate that Congolese students were the most, while the Ghanian and Nigerian students were the least ideologically oriented. Students in Senegal expressed philosophical-existential values as important aspects of their self-concept. As compared to Nigerian, Ugandan, Ghanian, and Senegalese students, the Congolese and Ethiopian students were more extreme in their nationalistic orientation. The tribal origin of the respondents was inversely associated with a nationalistic orientation. The findings also indicated an inverse relationship between saliency of tribal identification and a nationalistic orientation. McLeod (1959) found nationalism to be dominant in the Middle East. Inkeles and Smith (1974) developed a general scale to measure modernism: the OM scale (overall modernity measure). Interviews with almost 6,000 industrial workers, urban employees, and cultivators of six developing countries confirmed the existence of a general syndrome of modernization. (Details of this research can be found in Davidson & Thomson and Berry in this volume of the *Handbook*.)

Kahl (1968) did research on the general value syndrome of modernism on the basis of seven Likert scales that represented: activism, relative preference for urban life, individualism, low community stratification, mass media participation, low stratification of life chances. The results indicated that people in small towns in the interior of Brazil and Mexico were

traditionalists while people in Rio de Janeiro and Mexico City were mod-
ernists. An important determinant of modernism was social status. Cross-
cultural surveys on moral values are scattered and few. Rettig and Pasamanick (1962) compared American and Korean subjects' notions of fifty
morally prohibited behaviors. The conceptions of morality were similar,
except for an emphasis on "puritanical morality" in the American sample
and on "personal welfare" in the Korean sample.

Pepitone (in preparation) is studying cross-cultural attitudes toward
normative violations, such as crimes, and the kinds and amounts of sanctions recommended for them. Preliminary results indicate that the Japanese samples favor more severe punishment for crimes than do
comparable samples of Americans. (See also Tapp's chapter in Volume 4
of this Handbook; and Kohlberg (1969) on stages of moral development).

To summarize the empirical implications of the survey method as applied to the cross-cultural study of values, the following points are
important:

1. The results point to consistent and sometimes striking differences between cultures without providing explanations of the underlying mechanisms that produce these differences.
2. Thus there is an evident need to study the cognitive and motivational
   basis of self-values in cross-cultural contexts. At the same time, without a clear-cut and consistent mapping of cultural differences obtained
   by questioning large samples from different cultures, as is done
   through the survey method, the study of values (as the results of intrapsychic processes) will lack substance.
3. To conclude, the very success of the survey method makes its principal
   weakness salient: that is its compelling tendency to rely, for interpretation of the results obtained, on inferences that may appear to some as
   too speculative[5] and always vulnerable to what Campbell (1969) calls
   "rival hypotheses."

The progress of the survey approach from an early, purely descriptive
level to an analytical one through cross-tabulations, correlations, and
clustering is still short of providing tools for studying the underlying
processes that generate manifest responses. As Powers (1973) states, "statistical facts entice us to overlook the individual organismic properties that
must underlie all statistical facts" (p. 231). The understanding of the function of human values in different cultures will require a convergence between social psychology and modern cognitive theory. In this domain
there is a trend toward a neoidiographic approach to exploring underlying
processes that may be relevant to the study of values.

Knowledge has advanced so that a mapping of gross differences between cultures in self-values is attainable. The parameters that indicate

the frequencies of given variations in the populations studied can be established. Exploring the underlying dynamics of values, as psychic content, would require a consideration of survey data but such data should not be used for speculations about cultural determinants of psychic processes. Rather, since survey data provide information on variations of value differences, small subsamples, expressing these differences, should be selected for an intensive idiographic study to discover the interconnections between modal values and psychological or cultural antecedents.

The logic of survey research, in the comparison of values, is still an expression of the general search for "central tendencies," which until recently has dominated comparative value research.

While the studies reviewed earlier concern the views of the majority in a given culture, today a greater emphasis is given to minority views and to values as sources of social influence (Moscovici, 1972). The theoretical focus is on intrapsychic processes, of which values are an expression, rather than on determining the frequency of their various expressions. This is not intended to mean that survey research has outgrown its utility. On the contrary, the data obtained through these techniques, which are likely to become more powerful and refined through advanced computer programming, will still provide indispensable and basic information on the fundamental beliefs of a society, at a given moment. What will probably change are the usages and the inferences from the results thus obtained. These may very well become sources for elaborating variables more suitable to the study of *processes* and of *complex structures* in individuals and groups. Such research will eventually permit an integration of the nomothetic and idiographic perspectives in the study of values.

Psychometrics and the Cross-Cultural
Study of Values

Under this rubric is an extension of the methods derived from the test-oriented field of psychometrics (Guilford, 1954) to the cross-cultural study of values. Their *raison d'être* was that of developing easy to administer, standardized tests. Originally, these tests were not intended for cross-cultural comparisons of values, but were part of the field of personality testing, of which the Minnesota Multiphasic Personality Inventory (MMPI) probably constitutes the best known example. Many of these instruments consist of forced-choice schedules, in which a respondent is asked to check a number of items constructed by the researcher. A person's responses are typically assessed against *norms*, or average responses that were obtained from a group possessing similar characteristics. The existence of these *norms* constituted an incentive to obtain equivalent data in different countries: this would be an easy way to generate cross-cultural comparisons. However, most of these instruments measure imposed etic variables and comparison is methodologically indefensible. Moreover, with perhaps the exception of the Allport, Vernon, and Lindzey's (1960) test, the relevance of these instruments for the study of values is somewhat doubtful.

The Allport, Vernon, and Lindzey Study of Values

This paper-and-pencil instrument represented the first, and for a long time the only, procedure available for the study of personal values. It was inspired by Spranger's philosophical view that personalities of men are best known through a study of their values.

It attempts to assess the relative prominence of basic interests or motives in personality, by operationalizing Spranger's types (aesthetic, economic, theoretical, social, religious, athletic). The content of the test may be considered as clearly culture bound (e.g., who do you think is a more important historical character: Socrates or Abraham Lincoln?). There are also references to the U.S. Supreme Court, Leonardo da Vinci, and so on. This makes it unsuited for cross-cultural research. In spite of these limitations it has been used in a few cross-cultural studies of values, which will not be reviewed since they are methodologically indefensible. Even more ambiguous measures of values are supplied by the two following scales that were originally developed for the assessment of individual differences in personality.

The Edwards Personal Preference Schedule

The Edwards Personal Preference Schedule was designed to measure fifteen needs motives from Murray's list of: (1) Achievement; (2) Deference; (3) Order; (4) Exhibition; (5) Autonomy; (6) Affiliation; (7) Intraception; (8) Succorance; (9) Dominance; (10) Abasement; (11) Nurturance; (12) Change; (13) Endurance; (14) Heterosexuality; and (15) Aggression.

Although Edwards's schedule is intended to measure motives (whose relation to value is at best indirect), it has been applied to measure differences between Japanese and American values by Berrien (1966), and Berrien, Arkoff, and Iwahara (1967).

The Gordon Survey of Personal Values

The Gordon Survey of Personal Values (SPV) is intended to measure six ways in which the individual can cope with his environment. These are:

P—Practical Mindedness; A—Achievement; V—Variety; D—Decisiveness; O—Orderliness; and G—Goal Orientation.

The SPV was used for cross-cultural comparisons between Japanese and American students (Kikuchi & Gordon, 1966, 1970). These results suggest that the Japanese are less materialistically oriented than are the American students who have a lower achievement motivation and a lesser need for change and diversity. In contrast, the Japanese place a higher value on a well organized and routinized life, and on systematic approaches to relatively well defined goals.

The usefulness of applying standardized forced-choice schedules for cross-cultural comparison is severely limited for a variety of reasons. The schedules were developed for selection procedures, vocational guidance, and counseling. Along with other information, the obtained scores were supposed to be interpreted for a single individual. Originally the average or group scores constituted norms, or a basis for assessing an individual score. In their cross-cultural extensions these "norms" become a hypothetical "modal personality" characterizing a culture equally as artificial as the "ideal types" that are derived from more impressionistic methods of describing cultures. Moreover the nature of the information obtained is of doubtful significance for the cross-cultural study of values because the content of the items is not a convincing expression of values, and the items do not sample local conceptions of what is desirable.

Furthermore, there is a growing and pervasive scepticism concerning the theoretical import and meaning of personality testing (LeVine, 1973; Mischel, 1973). Doubts about the meaningfulness of regarding personality "as a matter of mere deviations from standard norms in respect to a certain number of common variables" (Allport, 1947, p. 35) have gained momentum in recent years. As a reviewer of psychometric literature underlines it: "The vast literature on personality testing failed to produce a body of knowledge generally acceptable to psychologists. In fact all personality instruments may be described as controversial, each with its own following of devotees" (Buros, 1970, p. 25).

In addition to the doubtful validity of the measures, there is also the artificiality of presenting average scores, or other statistical measures, as representative of meaningful cultural differences in values.

A growing number of psychologists are beginning to implement Brunswick's (1952) admonition to make psychology less artificial and more representative of real life. They do so both by taking into account ecological aspects of behavior and by viewing all behavior within a larger matrix of the subject's life situation (Loevinger, 1966). In this perspective values will be part of a diversified approach to each individual seen as a complex system, representing a cognitive dimension of such a system.

Cognitive Measures of Values

This section will review cross-cultural research on values, as reflected in the cognitive functioning of people. A general focus of this research is to study values through indirect measures, as emerging constructs elicited from cognitive activities.

Triandis's Antecedent-Consequent Method

Triandis's (1972) antecedent-consequent method is based on what may be called a *natural logic*. This refers to the function of *implication*, if X then Y (e.g., if large army, then national security), through which one concept is tied to another.

In this study respondents were asked to select antecedents and consequents of a given concept (e.g. progress, knowledge, power). Thus, values were derived from a cognitive operation, the implicative logic that ties antecedents to consequents of a number of concepts.

The antecedent-consequent method was used to determine the implications of twenty concepts,[6] referring to different domains:

Emotions: anger, courage, fear, and laughter.
Ambiguous political or individual concepts: freedom, peace.
Abstract philosophical: truth.
Social control: punishment.
Social disruption: crime.
Achievement: knowledge, power, progress, success, and wealth.
Nonachievement: death and defeat.
Basic social relation: love, respect, sympathy, and trust.

An elicitation procedure resulted in emic antecedents and consequents of these concepts. Then, each respondent had to choose five antecedent and five consequent concepts out of a pool of sixty.

Example: if there is_____, then there is PROGRESS.

	Research
	Ambition
ANTECEDENT:	Diligence
	Courage
	Endeavor

If there is PROGRESS, then there is_____.

CONSEQUENT:
Success
Achievement
Well-being
Respect
Expansion

The concepts expressing the antecedent (As) and the consequent (Cs) represent controlled associations. Common themes found among As and Cs would reveal underlying values that are defined by Triandis as relationships among abstract categories that have a strong affective component, and also as cultural patterns of preferences for certain outcomes (consequences). Cross-cultural comparisons were obtained with samples of university students in the United States, Greece, India, and Japan.

The results indicated the existence of both universal and culturally specific themes. Morality, proper behavior, and good personal characteristics appeared as antecedents of valued concepts in all of the samples studied.

Cultural differences also appeared in what was considered desirable. Americans stressed achievement, drive, and hard work; Greeks emphasized patience and will power, followed by diligence, honesty, ability, and motivation; Indians stressed discipline, tact, openness to experience, courage, and luck; Japanese stressed achievement, concern with being right, high motivation, enthusiasm, and faith: The *consequents* that follow from "good" concepts emphasized the following themes:

AMERICAN. Individual progress, self-confidence, good adjustment, status, serenity (peace of mind), and satisfaction (achievement, joy).

GREEK. Societal well-being (civilization, glory, victory) and individual success (desire for more love, more appreciation by others).

INDIAN. Increased status of the individuals, glory, and societal well being.

JAPANESE. Serenity, aesthetic satisfaction, general satisfaction, contentment, self-confidence, responsibility, peace, advancement, and good adjustment.

This was the first time that *implication* as a cognitive function was explored in social psychology; it is a promising instrument for cross-cultural comparison since it throws some light on the relationship between values, natural logic, and the associative structure of the mind. In order to facilitate comparisons across samples Triandis et al. consider it more efficient to study *controlled-word* associations instead of *free-word association* (e.g., if there is progress, then there is————). The possibility remains that free-worded antecedents and consequents may produce some unanticipated findings on cross-cultural logical functioning and values production. However, free-word associations as cognitive products are difficult to compare if the unit of analysis is an aggregate (or sample) individual, as in the current nomothetic approach in psychology.

To be useful as tools in values research, free-word associations should appear as elements of a more inclusive cognitive map of each individual studied. The methodological implications of what at first sight may appear as a modest proposition are far reaching since they lead to the development of a structural neoidiographic approach in values research. This issue needs some clarification.

Values and the Idiographic-Nomothetic Controversy

Justifications for studying values were found in their assumed central position in cognitive, behavioral, and affective processes, but very little effort has been spent in determining the nature of intrapsychic processes or the way such processes influence values. Kluckhohn (1951) saw values as influencing selective behavior, but Smith (1969) noted that he never specified the nature of this influence. For Smith, values play an important role in the evaluation processes such as judging, praising, or condemning.

The original view of personal values as part of a complex structure and as the emergent results of intrapsychic and interpersonal processes was overlooked in most of the empirical research that was conducted. Inkeles and Levinson (1969) noted that this represents a limitation of cross-cultural research on values. According to these authors, values and motives as research variables are not assessed within a broader theoretical context, and are not systematically related to other dimensions of personality. Furthermore, the selection of particular values and motives for study might appear arbitrary and fortuitous to some critics. Finally, there is a failure to suggest how different values and motives may interact within the personality. They conclude:

> The individual is seemingly conceived of as a set of slots of varying numbers into which different particular values and motives may be slipped. These are most often considered discretely, or at best as a profile, but little is said of the possible web of relationships among the various motivational, valuational, and other processes—in short, little is said of personality dynamics (Inkeles & Levinson, 1969, p. 439).

While basically agreeing with this statement, the problem of how to approach personality dynamics and its embedded values remains outstanding. Inkeles and Levinson seem to settle for the study of some particular variables: relations to authority, conscious and unconscious self-conceptions, concepts of masculinity, and values in the form of both moral prohibitions and ideals. These values are to be explored through clinical interviews, such as those conducted in the *Authoritarian Personality* (Adorno, Frenkel-Brunswik, Levinson, & Sanford, 1950).[7] The authors fail to acknowledge or to confront the methodological implications of studying values within and between cultures as part of an intrapsychic structure. This structure, used to study the *relations* between the component parts of the cognitive structure or the personality of an individual, may require revision for use in the study of covariations of a few variables measured in an aggregate of individuals.

In fact, the notion that cross-cultural research on values will have to focus on structure, dynamics, and processes will lead inevitably to the reopening of the idiographic versus nomothetic controversy (Allport, 1962) as it has done in the closely related domains of cognitive psychology (Newell & Simon, 1972; Lindsay & Norman, 1972; Underwood, 1975), of social psychology (Harré & Secord, 1973), and of personality research (Mischel, 1973). A brief survey of this issue may be helpful in narrowing the gap between empirical research on values and new theoretical developments in psychology. Values research has been carried out nomothetically, that is, as a search for laws or propositions or variables that hold true for a statistically defined population. This is opposed to an idiographic approach that seeks to understand "the intricacies of internal structure in concrete lives" (Allport, p. 406, 1956). Allport is well aware that the clinical approach per se is not an application of the idiographic perspective. Even though psychiatrists and clinical psychologists use the patient's own story as a starting point, they dismember the complex data obtained into standard dimensions, such as abilities, needs, interests, and values. Until recently, most contemporary social scientists have strongly endorsed the nomothetic perspective, including, with some qualification, Adorno et al., where resulting ambiguity for a psychological study of values is well illustrated. Introducing a detailed analysis of the genesis of authoritarian values in a young man and of democratic values in another, Sanford (1950) states that although their research is concerned with the organization of ideological trends *within* the individual, the bulk of the work is concerned with variables and their relationship: "This is *unavoidable*, for . . . the study of individuals can proceed *only* by analysis into components and the relations of these components can be regarded as significant *only* if they can be, to some extent, generalized" (p. 31). In academic psychology this view was held almost universally and resulted in the absolute primacy given to the aggregate (sample of individuals) over the individual as unit of research, for "to focus upon the individual and the unique" at psychology's present state of development can only lead to sterile speculations (Hall & Lindzey, 1970, p. 293).

At the same time, implicit in this stance is the notion that what is found in an aggregate is pertinent for the understanding of psychological processes characteristic of the individual. Today, the belief that individual responses can be predicted from observed statistical regularity has been questioned in the field of psychometrics (Loevinger, 1966) and of personality research (Mischel, 1973). Yet it remains alive in most empirical research on values. The ambiguous definition of values as characteristic of a group and/or of an individual, which was first introduced by Kluckhohn (1951), reflects this assumed interchangeability and provides the justification for the nomothetic approach in the field. Recent developments in the field of cognitive and personality research conducted within an information processing perspective permit a clearer understanding of the limits of the nomothetic approach for the study of values, seen as the result of intrapsychic processes. These developments will lead to the consideration that a legitimate problem area in psychology is the discovery of how new experiences are processed by a specific conceptual structure that results from a particular life history. This new "cognitive science" (Norman & Rumelhart, 1975; Bobrow & Collins, 1975), which is seen as an interdisciplinary endeavor, is leading toward a neoidiographic approach, thus displacing the focus of psychological inquiry from the aggregate to the individual. In the area of values research, the recurrent question on the nature of cognitive processes, conscious or unconscious, relating cultural values and the representations of self and the social world, may acquire a new meaning through a neoidiographic approach.

Recently, in the field of personality measurement, Mischel (1973), a behaviorist, advocated behavioral assessments that involve the exploration of the unique or idiographic aspects of the single case. This position results from a growing awareness of the magnitude of the cognitive transformations of the stimuli that are specific to each individual. A similar awareness of the role played by a *person parameter* in social psychological experiments is shown by Harré and Secord (1973). The importance of studying psychological processes as idiosyncratic outcomes for discovering general psychological laws has been emphasized by Underwood (1975) who until recently has been a staunch defender of both the nomothetic paradigm and the rule of the single variable in the psychological experiment. He states that "we cannot deal constructively with individual differences when we identify the important variables as age, sex, grade, IQ, social status, and so on. The critical variables are process variables" (1975, p. 134). These examples clearly indicate a major shift in psychology toward structural and process models, which are idiographic and removed from the traditional nomothetic model that attempts to establish correlations between discrete sets of variables. This new orientation may be called neoidiographic insofar as it sets for itself the task of reaching general psychological principles by *directly* studying psychological processes. Such processes were to be inferred as hypothetical constructs in the traditional nomothetic perspective. This position is congruent with those of the symbolic interactionists presented earlier and with those who follow a general systems theory (Buckley, 1972).

Traditionally general systems theory has opposed dealing with an aggregate of independent elements; it prefers observing a coherent whole. In psychology this theory has asserted itself mostly through general statements emphasizing the importance of focusing on the *relations* among psychological dimensions at the individual level (Bertalanffy, 1972), and making holistic statements. It is important, however, to distinguish between the neoidiographic approach and the traditional *holistic* argument in psychology. The neoidiographic approach leads to far-reaching methodological changes that may justify the claims of its supporters of a "paradigmatic shift;" the classic *holistic* argument does not go that far.

Superficially the neoidiographic stance may seem similar to Inkeles and Levinson's (1969) quest for studying values as part of the study of personality dynamics. It may also appear consistent with Sanford's (1970) arguments in favor of a holistic approach to values research in the name of a problem-oriented and humanistic psychology. Sanford goes so far as to deplore the psychologist's emphasis on defining and manipulating variables, while ignoring processes-in-the-person; nevertheless, he does not reach the more radical conclusion since he still supports the study of abstracted part-functions as a means of generalizing and favors the traditional search for hypothetical constructs. Particular individuals can be studied insofar as they express general traits such as authoritarianism in order to illustrate how authoritarianism, a hypothetical construct, works and how it originates from a particular style of socialization. In other words, the study of the individual has meaning only insofar as it represents the general. Yet the proposed link between authoritarian values and style of socialization remains hypothetical, and a number of rival hypotheses have been proposed (Christie & Jahoda, 1954).

To understand the *processes* through which the particular conceptual structure and value system of an individual develops may always have appeared to most psychologists a much more complex task than identifying a hypothetical relation among some variables. What is new today is that the study of individual complexity seems a feasible and worthwhile enterprise. This is because there are computers and a diminished acceptance of inferential leaps used to explain observed relationships among variables. Moreover, individual differences and idiosyncratic systems appear to be the rule rather than the exception (Lindsay & Norman, 1972) and to know how some if not all of them really work, appears an advance over the traditional procedure of abstracting variables in an aggregate. The challenge of the neoidiographic approach lies in its insistence on the importance of studying how an individual's cognitive activities, such as valuing and judging, interact with the conditions of his life and are translated as internal states of experience (Mischel, 1973).

It should be noted that the single major influence in reorienting psychological research toward a structural model is probably due to Piaget.

His emphasis on demonstrating that cognitive operations are "the results of a governing totality, whose laws of composition it is crucial to discover" (Flavell, 1963, p. 34) is echoed in the neoidiographic stance. Piaget's (1929) experimental technique, the *clinical method* in which entire sequences of cognitive responses are obtained to determine the mechanism of reasoning, is obviously idiographic and not suitable for statistical manipulation.

The methodological implications of the neoidiographic approach, for the cross-cultural study of values, may be summarized as follows: there is an emphasis on the necessity of studying directly (1) how values, judgments, and representations of the world are related; (2) psychological processes that are idiosyncratic and individual rather than central tendencies in an aggregate; (3) what makes new experiences possible and how information is integrated in a preexistent cognitive network that is organized as a function of past experience. The psychological laboratory is thus open to the study of psychological processes, as they occur in everyday life, in natural settings; and (4) the emphasis on the study of psychological processes within the individual requires psychological data that are cognitive productions, idiosyncratic in content, such as free categorizations or thinking aloud, rather than stimuli or propositions provided by the researcher, as is usually done when studying an aggregate (see Zavalloni, 1978).

One may predict that as a consequence of the development of a neoidiographic approach in psychology much effort will be spent on redefining the relations between what is unique and what is general in psychology. This may clarify the ways collective and individual values are linked. As a result the cross-cultural study of values will study the articulation of the macrolevel and the microlevel. The new trends in ecological psychology within the framework of general systems theory, as represented by the work of Berry (1975), may be eventually integrated with this neoidiographic approach by distinguishing and then articulating the properties of the various systems: ecological, societal, and personal.

The basis for an idiographic approach to the study of values, as presented here, was grounded in recent trends in cognitive psychology. It is striking to note that similar arguments are provided by LeVine (1973), an anthropologist, attempting to revive culture and personality research.

In his approach, intensive observations of individuals in different cultures reporting on their every day life activities will be required. In the long run this idiographic approach, according to LeVine, will be combined with a nomothetic approach to developing a population psychology analogous to population biology. Individual psychological characteristics will be statistically aggregated and compared across populations differing in characteristics of the social and cultural environment. The author is fully aware of the complexity of this project:

The direct study of the individual involves an enormous amount of data collection. It might well be wondered whether in this direction could lie such an extended detour into clinical investigation . . . that it may never return to the main road of comparative population studies (LeVine, 1973, p. 286).

LeVine does not specify, however, how an intensive clinical exploration can be combined with a statistical analysis of aggregate data.

The Multistages Social Identity Inquirer (MSII)

In line with the preceding discussion, the MSII (Zavalloni, 1971, 1973, 1975) may be seen as an attempt to integrate the nomothetic and the idiographic approaches to the study of values. It permits a quasi-experimental approach to the study of thinking, as it occurs in everyday life. This method attempts to uncover the recoding rules and underlying values an individual applies when perceiving, valuing and judging self, alter, and society. The MSII can be considered as an indirect assessment of values, since these emerge from successive levels of probing, starting from the perception of one's environment (subjective ecology) and then tracing down the underlying links to the self-concept and to the basic values that orient one's actions. The aim of MSII is not simply to identify some important values a person may possess. This can be done more economically through simpler methods. Its purpose is to observe how values are part of the generative mechanisms at work in the construction of one's phenomenal world.

The method begins with a universe of stimuli represented by the social identity cluster shown in Fig. 3–1.

The search procedure consists of questions that probe three distinct but interdependent levels by using (1) free representations of the social identity cluster; (2) a focused introspection technique (FIT); and (3) associative network analysis (ANA).

Representations of Social Identity: The *first level* aims to generate, through the use of free association, the representational units (RU) people use when thinking about the *self* and the *alter*, e.g., "You as a Frenchman, you are . . ."; "They, the French, are . . ." The material that is obtained is defined as *first-order data,* that is, as stimuli to be submitted to the respondent for the generation of *second-order data.* The cognitive substrates of surface data can become manifest, and the structural relations that exist between each representational element may be uncovered when this procedure is used.

The Focused Introspection Technique (FIT) provides the *second level* of MSII: it is devised to search for some aspects of the underlying structure of a person's phenomenal world.

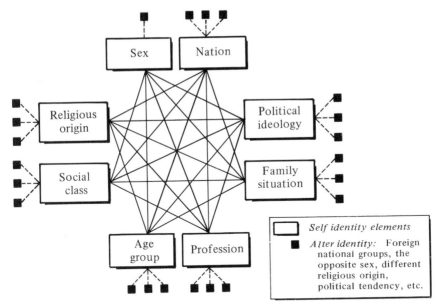

Figure 3–1. Social Identity Cluster: The Interdependence between elements. (From Zavalloni, 1975, p. 202.)

FIT consists of several stages. In *Stage 1,* the respondents are asked to go over their responses and (a) rank each representational unit (RU) on a four-point scale (from completely applicable to nonapplicable to the *self*), and (b) indicate the valence (positive, neutral, or negative) of each RU. In *Stage 2,* the respondents are asked to indicate whether groups' descriptions apply to the groups as a whole or to a subgroup thereof. The results indicate a general tendency to recode the original stimulus (e.g., men) as a subgroup similar to *self* when qualified by *we.* The opposite is true when the stimulus is qualified by *they.* This recoding seems to occur automatically. In *Stage 3* the respondents are asked to indicate the *differential meaning* of each RU when applied to the *self* and when applied to the group. Results indicate a tendency for each RU to acquire positive meaning when applied to the *self.* For example, *individualist* when applied to the French means a "lack of social concern and egocentrism" but when applied to the *self* it means "I value my freedom and independence."

The results obtained through FIT may be used both in a nomothetic and an idiographic way. In the first case, quantifiable variables can be obtained through content analysis and processed through standard statistical procedures, to provide *information on cross-cultural variations.* The meaning attached to being a man, a woman, to belonging to a given social class, or to a religious group are examples of the possible cross-cultural variations.

The values associated with a given social identity can be studied in a comparative perspective on selected samples. Results obtained with FIT by comparing French and American students (Zavalloni, 1971, 1973) and Kenyan students (Smetanka, 1977) indicate the generality of the recoding process and the existence of few recoding rules expressing values and influencing the representations of one's subjective identity (Zavalloni, 1975).

Data provided by FIT can be used in an idiographic perspective through the Associative Network Analysis (ANA) (Zavalloni and Louis-Guérin, 1976) that constitutes the MSII's *third level* of analysis. ANA aims to uncover the basic rules a person applies in his recoding of reality and the links among values, cognition, memories of the past, and actual behavior. This is done by using the responses obtained in FIT stage 1 (valence and self-relevance) and stage 3 (differential meaning of self-applicable RU) as the experimental stimuli for ANA. The respondent will be asked what he means by "valuing freedom." Probing will continue until the following elements are obtained for each RU: (1) *The field of actualization* (private, interpersonal, social, political), (2) *implicit value* (motivation, expectations, needs expressed through a given RU), (3) *Self realization* (doing or being), (4) *modalities of action* (coping style, instrumental behavior, initiate or react), (5) *perceived congruence between personal and environmental values* (integration), and (6) the *biographical source* of the RU.

The results obtained in cross-cultural research conducted in France among immigrants of differing ethnic and national origins (Zavalloni and Louis-Guérin, 1977) indicate that intergroup representations describing social identity elements are rooted in a coherent and organized structure, relating values and perceptions of the world, which has been identified as an *Intrapsychic Operant Synthesis* (IOS). Similar results have been obtained among Kenyan students by Smetanka (1977). IOS may be conceived as a *personal parameter* of a dynamic nature to be used in various ways both in a laboratory setting and in a more clinical one. For instance, memory processes can be studied by tracing how new information on social identity issues (e.g., sex rules, political ideology) is assimilated, as a function of the initial state of IOS. Since IOS represents a state of mind toward the *self* and the world at a given moment in time, it may be used for the study of social influence in a variety of cultural settings, and as a baseline for the observation of how behavior, cognition, and values interact in everyday life. The theoretical insights of symbolic interactionism concerning the relations between values, social representations, and cognitive processes, can thus be operationalized.

Eventually, IOS could also be used in conjunction with LeVine's psychoanalytical approach to culture and personality research, in order to explore the interface between values, social representations, and the deeper levels of personality, conscious or unconscious, in a variety of cultures.

Conclusion

The basic definition of values as a notion of the desirable that influences behavior may fit, by its very vagueness, the new theoretical orientations of the fields that originally promoted research on human values. Value research still remains an eventual focus of interdisciplinary efforts, oriented to the study of the individual and of social action. Both are set against a background of historical and cultural differences.

During the last decade, different features of social action and of individual identity have emerged that are relevant to the study of society and to the content of values research. As a result, the articulation between sociology, anthropology, and psychology is likely to change.

In sociology, the functionalist's emphasis on "values" as the integrative forces in society finds a less widespread acceptance today than was the case earlier. Society appears more as the expression of conflicting interests than as reflecting values that are differentiated in terms of role expectations. Society is seen as a field of creation of conflicting values that is dominated by opposing cultural agents and thus reproducing and creating incompatible choices (Ansart, 1974). Similarly, the cultural anthropologists assumed an isomorphism between group values and individual values[8] that may appear less convincing as the "common" body of values recedes into obscurity.

Consequently cultural outcomes will not be as exclusively located in early socialization processes, which have been the traditional center of values reproduction from generation to generation in social science. Greater emphasis will be given to the motives and activities of cultural agents (les idéologues as the French would say) and on the processes that lead to the creation and development of various social movements. If the social actor is seen as the target of a multiplicity of social influences, rather than as the expression of rules and duties which emanate from a general consensus among groups in a society, the notion of antecedents of values will obviously change. Until now, these antecedents have been identified in some demographic or ecological variables; future emphasis will be on "processes." Parallel developments have occurred in social psychology. According to the perspective of symbolic interactionism, values may be studied as an "emergent" product. Values result from the confrontation between groups mediated by cultural agents as part of the political process of a society.

As stated succinctly by Moscovici (1972) the question shifts from: "Who socializes the individual?" to "Who socializes society?" In the midst of drastic social change, the interest focuses on the development of new values, as a result of both social interaction and intrapsychic processes.

Values research will thus be a part of the research on social influence. Values research may gain more than it loses from this shift of emphasis from cultural reproduction to cultural creation. The change will be in the direction of moving away from static and descriptive data, toward an emphasis on processes that occur within a context of social conflicts and in a climate of struggle for influence. At the same time that values appear to be dethroned as the causal agents of behavior, as links to transmit social reality from generation to generation, and as the roots of social order, values now reappear as a major focus of psychological research. Thus they will become the mediating factors through which social influence operates.

Notes

1. It should be noted that Gillespie and Allport (1955), Hyman et al. (1958), and Stoetzel (1955) did not analyze the autobiographies of the future. Their results are based on the questionnaire.

2. It is striking that Triandis et al. (1972), using a different instrument, the antecedent-consequent method, found a similar result in India: "The Indians hope for a state in which they will have status, glory, and fame. The image of a Maharaja on top of an elephant in a glorious procession suggests itself. Perhaps such images are the distillations of the values of these cultures" (p. 259).

3. To clarify this point: this is comparable to saying that a group with a mean IQ of 80 is intelligent, after comparing this group with a group with a mean IQ of 60. Most of Rokeach's results are of this kind. The correct way to state the findings is that both groups are low and one group is lower than the other.

4. The interpretation of the results might have been less ambiguous if, instead of using a *ranking* procedure, the author had asked the subject to *rate* each value from "very important" to "not at all important."

5. It may also be noted in the recent literature that dissatisfaction is growing with the artificiality of deriving "ideal types" from survey data, as if they had a concrete reality. "The original individuals are now changed into the sociologist's aggregate. *Their* beliefs, *their* values, *their* norms are now attributed to this personage as *social* beliefs, *social* values and *social* norms. It is then perfectly within the bounds of ordinary sociological thinking that social beliefs, norms and values be treated as causing behavior" (Smith, 1974, p. 42).

6. For each concept the semantic differential profiles obtained from indigenously developed semantic differentials were also available and thus permitted the comparison of the results obtained by the two methods.

7. The authoritarian personality, as noted by Rokeach (1973), can be interpreted, in values terms, as referring to people who value obedience, cleanliness, politeness, and place lower value in being a broad-minded intellectual or an imaginative individual.

8. Not complete, but a qualified isomorphism to be sure: "Each people, it is true, has a distinctive set of values. However, no two individuals within the same so-

ciety share identical values. Each individual adds a little here, subtracts a little there, makes this emphasis a bit stronger than most of his neighbors and makes that emphasis a little less strong" (Kluckhohn, 1951, p. 416).

References

ADORNO, T. W., FRENKEL-BRUNSWIK, E., LEVINSON, D. J., & SANFORD, R. N. *The authoritarian personality.* New York: Harper and Brothers, 1950.

ALBERT, E. Value systems. In D. L. Sills (Ed.), *International encyclopedia of the social sciences*, Vol. 7. New York: Macmillan, 1968, pp. 287–91.

ALLPORT, G. W. *The use of personal documents in psychological science.* New York: Social Science Research Council, 1947.

———. The general and the unique in psychological science. *Journal of Personality,* 1962, *30*, 405–22.

ALLPORT, G. W., VERNON, P. E., & LINDZEY, G. *A study of values.* Boston: Houghton Mifflin, 1960.

ANSART, P. *Les idéologies politiques.* Paris: Presses Universitaires de France, 1974.

AUSUBEL, P. *Maori youth.* Wellington, New Zealand: Price Milburn, 1961.

BECKER, H. *The other side.* New York: Free Press, 1964.

BEM, D. J., & ALLEN, A. On predicting some of the people some of the time. *Psychological Review,* 1974, *81*, 506–20.

BENEDICT, R. *Patterns of culture.* Boston: Houghton Mifflin, 1934.

———. *The chrysanthemum and the sword.* Boston: Houghton Mifflin, 1946.

BERRIEN, F. K. Japanese and American values. *International Journal of Psychology,* 1966, *1*, 129–42.

BERRIEN, F. K., ARKOFF, A., & IWAHARA, S. Generation difference in values: Americans, Japanese-Americans and Japanese. *Journal of Social Psychology,* 1967, *71*, 169–76.

BERRY, J. An ecological approach to cross-cultural psychology. *Nederlands Tiidschrift voor de Psychologie,* 1975, *30*, 51–84.

BERTALANFFY, L. The history and status of general systems theory. In G. J. Klir (Ed.), *Trends in general systems theory.* New York: Wiley, 1972, pp. 21–41.

BIESLEUVEL, S. Moral judgments of African and European South Africans. *Journal of Social Sciences,* 1957, *53*, 309–14.

BLAKE, J., & DAVIS, K. Norms, values and sanctions. In L. Faris (Ed.), *Handbook of modern sociology.* Chicago: Rand McNally, 1972, pp. 456–83.

BLUMER, H. *Symbolic interactionism.* Englewood Cliffs, N.J.: Prentice-Hall, 1969.

BOBROW, D. G., & COLLINS, A. *Representation and understanding.* New York: Academic Press, 1975.

BRISLIN, R. W. Comparative research methodology: cross-cultural studies. *International Journal of Psychology,* 1976, *11*, 215–29.

BRUNSWIK, E. The conceptual framework of psychology. *International Encyclopedia of Unified Science,* 1952, *1*, No. 10, pp. IV; 102.

BUCHANAN, W., & CANTRIL, H. *How nations see each other*. Urbana, Ill.: University of Illinois Press, 1953.

BUCKLEY, W. A system approach to epistemology. In G. J. Klir (Ed.), *Trends in general systems theory*. New York: Wiley, 1972, pp. 188–202.

BUROS, O. *Personality: tests and reviews*. Highland Park, N.J.: Gryphon Press, 1970.

CAMPBELL, D. Perspective: artifact and control. In R. Rosenthal & R. Rosnow (Eds.), *Artifact in behavioral research*. New York: Academic Press, 1969, pp. 351–82.

CANTRIL, H. *The pattern of human concerns*. New Brunswick, N.J.: Rutgers University Press, 1965.

CHRISTIE, R., & JAHODA, M. (Eds.), *Studies in the scope and method of "The Authoritarian Personality."* Glencoe, Ill.: Free Press, 1954.

CICOUREL, A. V. *Cognitive sociology*. Baltimore: Penguin Books, 1973.

COLBY, B. N. Ethnographic semantics: a preliminary survey. *Current Anthropology*, 1966, *7*, 3–32.

DAHRENDORF, R. *Class and class conflict in industrial society*. Stanford, Calif.: Stanford University Press, 1959.

DANZIGER, K. Psychological future of an oppressed group. *Social Forces*, 1963a, *42*, 31–40.

———. Validation of *e* measure of self-rationalization. *Journal of Social Psychology*, 1963b, *59*, 17–28.

DOUGLAS, J. D. *Understanding everyday life*. Chicago: Aldine, 1970.

FEATHER, N. T. *Values in education and society*. New York: Free Press, 1975.

FEATHER, N. T., & HUTTON, M. A. Value systems of students in Papua, New Guinea and Australia. *International Journal of Psychology*, 1973, *9*, No. 2, 91–104.

FLAVELL, J. H. *The developmental psychology of Jean Piaget*. Princeton, N.J.: Van Nostrand, 1963.

FRAKE, C. The ethnographic study of cognitive systems. In T. Gladwin & W. G. Sturtevant (Eds.), *Anthropology and human behavior*. Washington: Anthropological Society of Washington, 1962, pp. 72–85.

GILLESPIE, J. N., & ALLPORT, G. W. *Youth's outlook on the future*. New York: Doubleday, 1955.

GARFINKEL, H. *Studies in ethnomethodology*. Englewood Cliffs, N. J.: Prentice-Hall, 1967.

GLICKSMAN, M., & WAHL, J. Expressed values of Burmese and American university students. *Journal of Social Psychology*, 1965, *65*, 17–26.

GOODENOUGH, W. Componential analysis and the study of meaning. *Language*, 1956, *32*, 195–216.

GOULDNER, A. W. *The coming crisis of western sociology*. London: Heinemann, 1969.

GORER, G. Themes in Japanese culture. *Transactions of the New York Academy of Science*, Série II, 1943, *Vol. 5*, pp. 106–24.

GORER, G., & RICKMAN, J. *The people of Great Russia*. London: Cresset, 1949.

GUILFORD, J. P. *Psychometric method*. New York: McGraw-Hill, 1954.

HALL, C. S., & LINDZEY, G. *Theories of personality*. New York: Wiley, 1970.

HARRÉ, H., & SECORD, P. F. *The explanation of social behaviour*. Totowa, N.J.: Littlefield, Adams, 1973.

HARRIS, M. *The rise of anthropological theory.* New York: Columbia University Press, 1968.

HYMAN, H. H., PAYASLIOGLU, A., & FREY, F. W. The values of Turkish college youth. *Public Opinion Quarterly*, 1958, 22, 275–91.

INKELES, A., HAUFMAN, E., & BEIER, H. Modal personality and adjustment to the Soviet socio-political system. In B. Kaplan (Ed.), *Studying personality cross-culturally.* Evanston, Ill.: Row, Peterson, 1961, pp. 201–24.

INKELES, A., & LEVINSON, J. National character: the study of modal personality and sociocultural systems. In G. Lindzey & E. Aronson (Eds.), *Handbook of social psychology,* Vol. 4. Reading, Mass.: Addison-Wesley, 1969, pp. 418–506.

INKELES, A., & SMITH, D. H. *Becoming modern: individual change in six developing countries.* Cambridge, Mass.: Harvard University Press, 1974.

JAHODA, G. Social aspirations, magic and witchcraft in Ghana: a social psychological interpretation. In P. C. Lloyd (Ed.), *New elites of tropical Africa.* London: Oxford University Press, 1966, pp. 199–212.

JONES, L. V., & BOCK, R. D. Multiple discriminant analysis applied to a "way to live": ratings from six cultural groups. *Sociometry*, 1960, 23, 162–76.

KAHL, J. *The measurement of modernism: a study of values in Brazil and Mexico.* Austin, Texas: University of Texas Press, 1968.

KARDINER, A. (Ed.), *The individual and his society.* New York: Columbia University Press, 1939.

KIKUCHI, A., & GORDON, L. V. Evaluation and cross-cultural application of a Japanese form of the survey of interpersonal values. *Journal of Social Psychology*, 1966, 69, 185–95.

————. Japanese and American personal values: some cross-cultural findings. *International Journal of Psychology*, 1970, 5, 183–87.

KLINEBERG, O., LOUIS-GUÉRIN, C., ZAVALLONI, M., & BENBRIKA, J. *Students, values and politics.* New York: Free Press, 1978.

KLINEBERG, O., & ZAVALLONI, M. *Tribalism and nationalism.* The Hague: Mouton, 1969.

KLUCKHOHN, C. *Mirror for man.* New York: McGraw-Hill, 1949.

————. Values and value orientations in the theory of action. In T. Parsons & E. A. Shilds (Eds.), *Toward a general theory of action.* Cambridge, Mass.: Harvard University Press, 1951, pp. 388–433.

————. Culture and behavior. In G. Lindzey (Ed.), *The handbook of social psychology,* Vol. 2. Reading, Mass.: Addison-Wesley, 1954.

————. Toward a comparison of value-emphases in different cultures. In L. D. White (Ed.), *The state of the social sciences.* Chicago: University of Chicago Press, 1956, pp. 116–32.

KLUCKHOHN, C., & MURRAY, H. A. (Eds.), *Personality in nature, culture and society.* New York: Knopf, 1948.

KLUCKHOHN, F. R., & STRODTBECK, F. L. *Variations in value orientations.* Evanston, Ill.: Row, Peterson, 1961.

KOHLBERG, L. Stage and sequence: the cognitive-developmental approach to socialization. In D. A. Goslin (Ed.), *Handbook of socialization theory and research.* Chicago: Rand McNally, 1969, pp. 347–480.

KROEBER, A. L., & KLUCKHOHN, C. *Culture: a critical review of concepts and definitions.* Cambridge, Mass.: Peabody Museum, *Vol. 47*, No. 1, 1952.

KUHN, M. H., & MCPARTLAND, T. S. An empirical investigation of self attitudes. *American Sociological Review, 1955, 19, 68–76.*

KUHN, T. S. *The structure of scientific revolutions.* Chicago: University of Chicago Press, 1962.

LABARRE, W. Some observations on character structure in the Orient: the Japanese. *Psychiatry, 1945, 8, 326–42.*

LANHAM, B. Aspects of child care in Japan: preliminary report. In D. Haring (Ed.), *Personal character and cultural milieu.* Syracuse, N. Y.: Syracuse University Press, 1956, pp. 565–83.

LEVINE, R. A. *Culture, behavior and personality.* Chicago: Aldine, 1973.

LINDSAY, P. H., & NORMAN, D. A. *Human information processing,* New York: Academic Press, 1972.

LIPSET, S. M. The value patterns of democracy: a case study in comparative analysis. *American Sociological Review, 1963, 28, 515–31.*

LOEVINGER, J. Psychological tests in the conceptual framework of psychology. In K. R. Hammond (Ed.), *The psychology of Egon Brunswik.* New York: Holt, Rinehart and Winston, 1966, pp. 107–49.

LOUIS-GUÉRIN, C. *Étude comparative sur la structure des attitudes sociopolitiques d'étudiants dans trois pays: France, Grande Bretagne, États-Unis.* Unpublished Ph.D. Thesis, Université de Paris V, 1973.

MANNHEIM, D. *Mensch und Gesellschaft im Zeitalter des Umbaus.* Leiden: A. W. Sijthoff's Uitgewersmaatschappij N.V., 1935.

MEAD, M. Retrospects and prospects. In T. Gladwin & W. L. Sturtevant (Eds.), *Anthropology and human behavior,* Washington, D. C.: Anthropological Society of Washington, 1962.

———. National character. In A. L. Kroeber (Ed.), *Anthropology today.* Chicago: University of Chicago Press, 1953, pp. 642–67.

MACLEOD, R. B. The Arab Middle East: some social psychological problems. *Journal of Social Issues, 1959, 15, 70–75.*

MISCHEL, W. Toward a cognitive social learning reconceptualization of personality. *Psychological Review, 1973, 80, 252–83.*

MORRIS, C. W. *Varieties of human value.* Chicago: University of Chicago Press, 1956.

MORSBACH, H., & OKAKI, C. A cross-cultural study of future expectations and aspirations among adolescent girls. *Proceedings of VIIIth Congress of Anthropological and Ethnological Sciences,* Tokyo, 1968, pp. 381–85.

MOSCOVICI, S. Preface. In D. Jodelet, J. Viet, & P. Besnard (Eds.), *La psychologie sociale: une discipline en mouvement.* The Hague: Mouton, 1970.

———. Social psychology and society. In H. Tajfel & J. Israel (Eds.), *The context of social psychology.* London: Academic Press, 1972.

MYRDAL, G. *Objectivity in social research.* New York: Pantheon Books, 1969.

NEWELL, A., & SIMON, H. A. *Human problem solving.* Englewood Cliffs, N.J.: Prentice-Hall, 1972.

NIETZSCHE, F. The birth of tragedy. In F. Nietzsche, *The complete works.* Edinburgh and London: Allen & Unwin, 1901–1911.

NORBECK, E., & NORBECK, M. Child training in a Japanese fishing community. In D. Haring (Ed.), *Personal character and cultural milieu.* Syracuse, N. Y.: Syracuse University Press, 1956, pp. 651–73.

NORMAN, D., & RUMELHART, D. E. *Explorations in cognition.* San Francisco: Freeman, 1975.

OPLER, M. E. Themes as dynamic forces in culture. *American Journal of Sociology,* 1945, *51,* 198–206.

PARSONS, T. *Essays in sociological theory: pure and applied.* Glencoe, Ill.: Free Press, 1949.

———. *The social system.* New York: Free Press, 1953.

PARSONS, T., & SHILS, E. A. *Toward a general theory of action.* Cambridge, Mass.: Harvard University Press, 1951.

PEPITONE, A. Personal communication, 1974.

PIAGET, J. *The child's conception of the world.* New York: Harcourt, Brace, 1929.

POWERS, W. T. *Behavior: the control of perception.* Chicago: Aldine, 1973.

PROTHRO, E. T. Arab students' choices of ways to live. *Journal of Social Psychology,* 1958, *47,* 3–7.

REDFIELD, R. *The primitive world and its transformations.* Ithaca, N.Y.: Cornell University Press, 1953.

RETTIG, S., & PASAMANICK, B. Invariance in factor structure of moral value judgments from American and Korean college students. *Sociometry,* 1962, *25,* 73–84.

ROKEACH, M. *The nature of human values.* New York: Free Press, 1973.

RUBIN, V., & ZAVALLONI, M. *We wish to be looked upon.* New York: New York Teachers College Press, Columbia University, 1969.

SANFORD, N. The decline of individualism. *Mental Health Digest,* March 1970, *85,* No. 3, p. 57.

SANFORD, R. N. The contrasting ideologies of two college men: a preliminary view. In T. W. Adorno, E. Frenkel-Brunswik, D. J. Levinson, & R. N. Sanford (Eds.), *The authoritarian personality.* New York: Harper and Brothers, 1950.

SAPIR, E. *Selected writings.* D. Mandelbaum (Ed.). Berkeley, Calif.: University College Press, 1949.

SARBIN, T., & ALLEN, V. Role Theory. In G. Lindzey & E. Aronson (Eds.), *The handbook of social psychology.* Reading, Mass.: Addison-Wesley, 1968.

SEEMAN, M. Alienation studies. *Annual Review of Sociology,* 1975, *1,* 91–123.

SMETANKA, J. National identity through focused introspection. Mimeograph, 1977.

SMITH, D. Theorizing as ideology. In R. Turner (Ed.), *Ethnomethodology.* London: Penguin, 1974, pp. 41–44.

SMITH, M. B. *Social psychology and human values.* Chicago: Aldine, 1969.

SPRANGER, E. *Kultur und Erziehung.* Leipzig: Quelle and Meyer, 1923, p. 199.

STOETZEL, J. *Without the chrysanthemum and the sword.* New York: Columbia University Press, 1955.

STOKES, R., & HEWITT, J. P. Aligning actions. *American Sociological Review,* 1976, *41,* 838–49.

TOURAINE, A. *Production de la société.* Paris: Seuil, 1973.

TRIANDIS, H. C., VASSILIOU, V., VASSILIOU, G., TANAKA, Y., SHANMUGAM, A. V. (Eds.). *The analysis of subjective culture.* New York: Wiley, 1972.

TYLER, S. A. *Cognitive anthropology.* New York: Holt, Rinehart and Winston, 1969.

UNDERWOOD, B. J. Individual differences as a crucible in theory construction. *American Psychologist,* 1975, *30,* 128-35.

VENESS, T. *School leavers: their aspirations and expectations.* London: Methuen, 1962.

WEBER, M. *Wirtschaft und Gesellschaft.* Tuebingen: J. C. B. Mohr (Paul Siebeck), 1956.

WERNER, O., & CAMPBELL, D. Translating, working through interpreters, and the problem of decentering. In R. Naroll & R. Cohen (Eds.), *A handbook of method in cultural anthropology.* New York: Natural History Press, 1970, pp. 398-420.

WIEDER, L. D. On meaning by rule. In D. Douglas (Ed.), *Understanding everyday life.* Chicago: Aldine, 1970, pp. 107-36.

ZAVALLONI, M. Social identity: perspectives and prospects. *Social Sciences Information,* 1972, *12,* 3, 65-91.

———. Social identity and the recoding of reality. *International Journal of Psychology,* 1975, *10,* 197-217.

———. L'approche néo-idiographique en psychologie: convergences interdisciplinaires. *Sciences de l'Homme,* 1978, *9,* 57.

ZAVALLONI, M., & LOUIS-GUÉRIN, C. *Identité sociale et construction de la réalité: images, pensées et action dans la vie quotidienne.* Mimeograph. University of Montreal, 1977.

ZNANIECKI, F. Methodological note. In W. I. Thomas, & F. Znaniecki, *The Polish peasant in Europe and America.* Boston: Bodger, 1918-1920.

4

Behavior Exchange in
Cross-Cultural Perspective

Kenneth J. Gergen,
Stanley J. Morse,
and Mary M. Gergen

Contents

Abstract

This chapter examines the results of a range of cross-cultural studies relevant to processes of social exchange. Sociological and anthropological work is included along with traditional social psychological research. The exchange framework as conceptualized by seminal thinkers such as Homans, Thibaut, Kelley and Blau generally employs a hedonic perspective in which it is assumed that people will select activities which maximize pleasure and minimize pain. Social relations are thus conceptualized in economic terms; each participant furnishes behavioral outcomes having a certain value to others and may receive behavioral outcomes from other participants in return. The general framework may be applied to a wide number of issues including law, morality, leadership, power and social attraction.

The norm of reciprocity, that is returning positively valued outcomes to those from whom they are received, is postulated by theorists such as Gouldner and Blau as central to all exchanges. Sahlins describes three forms of reciprocity: balanced, generalized, and negative. Social psychologists typically prefer a definition of reciprocity which focuses on internal motivational states related to an exchange. Individuals strive to balance the value of inputs and outputs. Research on reciprocity indicates that while reciprocity can be found in highly varied cultural settings, many exchanges do not follow a pure reciprocity model. Of particular interest has been the problem of overpayment. What do people do when they are overcompensated for a task? Research indicates that in order to achieve reciprocity, overpaid people may sometimes do more or better work or alter their perceptions of the situation to justify the overpayment. Cross-cultural variations in preference for equity are also noted.

The question of reciprocity gives way to that of equity in the distribution of rewards. In many situations people do seem to employ an equity model (i.e. distributing rewards to each according to his inputs), while in other situations people distribute rewards according to an equality model (i.e. each receives an equal share). Various characteristics of a situation which might enhance equality distributions include: stress on group interdependence and harmony; reward amounts which are large and publicly made; great discrepancies in performance; emphasis on social approval for sharing; and the anticipation of interchanging roles. It is also suggested that children, women and those high in resources are more likely to make equal divisions of rewards.

The Foa and Foa structural model of resources exchange is elaborated, along with supportive research. Foa and Foa argue for a pattern of resource exchanges which is universal and stable. Studies which support the general framework and elaborate cross-cultural variants are discussed. An instrument designed to cope with cross-cultural differences in exchanges, the cultural assimilator, is described.

Cross-cultural studies on giving and receiving help are reviewed. While cross national differences in giving help are difficult to interpret, social class and donor's level of resources seem to affect helping in many cultures. Reactions to receiving are both positive and negative. Research indicates that the characteristics of the donor, the aid, the recipient and the aid context may all influence reactions to the aid. Similar effects are found in many different cultures.

The chapter concludes with a brief discussion of the hazards of cross-cultural research, particularly problems of testing hypotheses, predicting behaviors, and generalizing from findings. In spite of problems at the empirical level, exchange theory is found to be a rich and comprehensive framework for understanding behavior in widely divergent cultural settings.

Introduction

For the psychologist whose interests span the cultural frontiers, the road to knowledge is a treacherous one. Without substantial resources of time, money, and cultural access the journey can scarcely commence. Once embarked, it is soon discovered that comparisons across cultures are extremely hazardous. Stimulus conditions are virtually impossible to replicate across cultures; interpretations of cultural differences are little more than guesswork; subtle differences in languages and meaning systems hinder generalization; ideological investments create resistance to various theoretical outlooks or cause distortions of interpretation. Of course, it would be inhuman to allow such Herculean difficulties to stand in the way of pursuing psychology cross-culturally; curiosity impels psychologists to continue investigation even if the major outcome is only a better understanding of the immensity and complexity of the quest.

From time to time, developments in the field nurture their hopes that the route is navigable. It is to one of these developments that the present chapter is devoted. One of the major problems in the field is the immense fragmentation of interests and conceptual orientations that prevails. Not only are cross-cultural comparisons of behavior carried out by separate professional guilds within most nations (viz., psychology, anthropology, sociology, political science, economics, geography), but within each of these guilds various subgroups have developed specialized interests. This same type of fragmentation occurs within each separate culture as well, with the major result that communication is inhibited both within and between cultures. Each specialized group within each nation tends to pursue its narrow ends in intellectual solitude. Such fragmentation dampens any hope of reaching an integrated understanding of cultural diversity; the parts remain unassembled and researchers are insulated from considerations of the whole. Further, they fail to see the relationships among diverse areas and the potential parallels between work within separate specialties and nations. The same discoveries must endlessly be rediscovered.

It is within this light that the development of a broad conceptual framework is of special significance. If the framework is sufficiently abstract, conceptually rich, and metaphorically suggestive it may integrate many of the specialized concerns into a compelling unity; parts may be assembled, relationships realized, and parallels established. Within recent years, many have felt that the emerging theory of social exchange may furnish just such a framework. The first major elaborations of exchange theory were provided by the classic works of Homans (1961), Thibaut and Kelley (1959), and Blau (1964). Although the works were independently conceived, their similarity suggested that the authors had captured important elements of the intellectual *zeitgeist*. In one form or another, each of the volumes essentially adopts a hedonistic perspective. The human being is viewed as motivated by a search for pleasure and a reduction of pain. Activities that provide pleasure or minimize pain will be sought, and such activities will be maintained as long as they maximize hedonistic outcomes. In order to obtain such rewards and to reduce punishment from others, it is generally necessary that the individual perform various behaviors. These behaviors may also be intrinsically rewarding or punishing in various degrees. Thus, we may view the individual as constantly involved in a series of social transactions in which rewards and punishments (in the form of behavior) are being exchanged among parties. Using the economic motif that pervades the theoretical terminology, social life is a market in which each individual attempts to maximize his or her gains while reducing costs to a minimum.

Such a view of social behavior has a number of immediately integrative features. For one, the framework indicates that individuals should develop preferred types of exchanges, essentially those that provide them maximal payoffs. These preferred arrangements should then become reflected in the norms of the relationship, or indeed, of the society as a whole. Norm sanctions are often established to reduce deviations from these preferred exchange patterns. Such norm sanctions may often be elaborated in the legal codes of the society and buttressed by armed force. One major task of socialization is to instill an appreciation of commonly preferred exchange patterns and a distaste for exploitation. Morality can thus be translated into socioeconomic laws (see Lempert, 1972). Social institutions are further viewed in terms of normative exchange arrangements governing certain areas of life. Leadership and power are also implicated. Where group leaders are needed, the individual who provides maximal reward at minimal cost to the group should obtain senior status. Differences in social power may be cast in terms of the ability of the individual to obtain costly behaviors from others at little expense to self. Social attraction may also be understood in terms of exchange: attraction is generated when another provides high rewards at low cost.

It is beyond the scope of this chapter to provide a full account of the exchange framework. However, it is important to note that since its inception the framework has been utilized throughout the social sciences. Within social psychology, the framework has been applied to such diverse phenomena as social conformity (Nord, 1969), the development of status in informal groups (Harsanyi, 1966), helping behavior (Greenberg, Block, & Silverman, 1971; Bar-Tal, 1976), the search for uniqueness (Fromkin, 1975), reactions to assistance (Gergen & Gergen, 1971), social attraction (Huesmann & Levinger, 1975), the perception of pay (Weick, 1966), and reward distribution (Leventhal & Michaels, 1971; Leventhal, 1976), to name but a few. Sociologists have found the framework fruitful in examining organizational behavior (Evan, 1962), interorganizational relations (Levine & White, 1960), the attractiveness of work roles in the kibbutz (Yuchtman, 1972), administrative decision making (Gamson, 1961), collective decision making (Coleman, 1966), social obligation (Muir & Weinstein, 1962), as well as a variety of other phenomena (see Emerson, 1962, 1971; Sampson, 1977). Anthropologists have utilized the exchange formulation in understanding such diverse behavior as gift giving (Befu, 1966; Lebra, 1973), Polynesian ceremonials (Hogbin, 1971), and social structure in primitive cultures (Schwimmer, 1970). Within political science, Waldman (1964) has relied upon the exchange framework to integrate understanding of wide-ranging political activities. Economists such as Boulding (1973) and Rapoport and Chammah (1965) have used a form of exchange theory to account for conflict, negotiation and decision making in both the interpersonal and international arenas. Within the field of law, Lempert (1972) has also adopted the exchange approach to account for the development of legal codes. The integrative potential of the framework seems highly apparent.

It will be the aim of the present chapter to examine empirical investigations within the exchange tradition from a cross-cultural perspective. The initial task will be to review several major lines of psychological research conducted on a cross-national basis. One major concern in this review will be the extent to which major propositions remain valid from one culture to another. To put it another way, to what extent do various exchange propositions approximate human universals? Coupled with this concern is an interest in cultural differences. When various propositions are not found reliable across cultures, to what extent can meaningful conclusions be drawn about cultural variations? After reviewing a number of major research domains, a more general inquiry will be made into the problem of cultural universals, and the utility of their exposition both within the framework and without. Finally, a critical look will be taken at the function of exchange theory in cross-cultural research. Specifically, the argument is for a reorientation of the scope and purpose of future explorations in this area.

Reciprocity and Equity in Social
Exchange

Without some form of assurance that one's activities on another's behalf will eventuate in a return of positive outcomes, social organization would cease to function. In the simple case, unless Person (P) is prepared to provide Other (O) with rewards in exchange for the rewards obtained from O—especially if O incurs costs in providing these rewards—there is little reason for O to continue interacting with P. Without reciprocity on P's part, O would simply be experiencing costs and would gain little pleasure from interacting with P. If reciprocity is valued in society, it also seems likely that members who do respond reciprocally will be rewarded and those who do not will be punished. Further, there should be an attempt to socialize people so that adherence to the "reciprocity norm" becomes a moral imperative. In keeping with this line of reasoning, Gouldner (1960) refers to a universal "norm of reciprocity" and argues that without such a norm, societies might disintegrate into warring factions and groups would have difficulty retaining those whose contributions are necessary for effective group functioning. According to Gouldner, for example, tribal chiefs obtain the allegiance of members of the tribe in return for distributing food and other resources to them. Blau (1964) indicates that group members with expertise in a given area, who help others and thereby aid the group as a whole, are accorded status and respect.

In a similar vein, anthropologists have looked at reciprocity as a cohesive force holding societies together. Malinowski (1926) was probably the first anthropologist to analyze societies in this way in his description of the *kula* ring in the Trobriand Islands. A comprehensive treatment of reciprocity in primitive cultures is also provided by Mauss (1954) in his classic essay *The Gift: Forms and Functions of Exchange in Archaic Societies*. Levi-Strauss (1949) further singled out women as a primary "medium of exchange" in preliterate societies. Reciprocity systems have also been delineated within Japanese (Befu, 1966) and Trukese (Goodenough, 1967) cultures. The anthropological literature on the role of reciprocity in social exchange is reviewed and systematized by Sahlins (1965), who described three basic types of reciprocity. In *balanced reciprocity*—which approximates the meaning social psychologists typically give to reciprocity—P is expected to repay O for rewards received from him. The value of the goods or services returned by P or O must more or less equal the value of the goods and services received from O and the reciprocity must occur within a fairly limited period of time. Balanced reciprocity, according to Sahlins, is a rather general phenomenon throughout preliterate societies. The reader interested in the contrast between the social "economies" of preliterate and more complex societies should also see Firth (1967).

Aside from balanced reciprocity, Sahlins also distinguishes between *generalized reciprocity* and *negative reciprocity*. Like balanced reciprocity, generalized reciprocity involves the strict adherence to obligations. In this case, the obligation is to help those in need without expecting immediate repayment. Negative reciprocity, in contrast, is differently motivated. It is behavior designed to obtain "commodities" (goods, services, and so on) from others without providing commodities of equal value in return—if one can successfully avoid doing so through skilled bargaining. While Sahlins himself seems to see negative reciprocity as confined to ingroup/outgroup interactions, others see it as more pervasive. Pryor & Graburn (in press) conclude that Eskimo families exhort generalized reciprocity, but do not in fact practice it. This tendency for exchange theorists to overlook this "rather elementary methodological point in anthropology" of separating the exhortation from the action is emphasized by Befu (1977, p. 256).

Most social psychologists interested in reciprocity in social exchange, however, employ a more complex and somewhat more general model that focuses on internal motivational states. In the terminology typically employed in this area, "outcomes" are equivalent to rewards received from a relationship. "Inputs" are usually viewed as the individual's costs. Generally, inputs are whatever the individual believes entitle him to rewards. In a group situation, for example, each person's contribution to the successful functioning of the group constitutes a set of inputs. In a business firm, inputs might involve P's level of education or length of service with the firm and so on. Outcomes in this case might involve the salary and fringe benefits received from the firm.

Adams (1965) suggests that individuals strive for what they believe is an "equitable" balance between outcomes and inputs. An imbalance between the two creates internal tension. This idea is based on the notion that when outcomes exceed or fall below inputs, dissonance results (Festinger, 1957). To reduce this dissonance, according to Adams, individuals will attempt to bring their outcomes into line with their inputs. When a person feels he is overpaid for performing a task and cannot reduce his level of pay (his outcomes), for example, he may increase his inputs by doing more or higher quality work. This formulation suggests that individuals will repay rewards received from others because by doing so they will raise their inputs, bringing them into line with their outcomes. Of course, it also implies that should P feel he is entitled to the rewards received from O, he will not feel it necessary to repay O for them. The North American literature relevant to this approach is reviewed by Adams and Freedman (1976), Leventhal (1976) and Walster, Walster, and Berscheid (1978). The latter authors seem to minimize the internal tension-reduction of what is called "equity-restoration." They focus, instead, on social factors which may prompt P to maintain an equitable balance between outcomes and inputs—both his own and others'—maintaining that groups reward those who behave in an equitable way and punish those who do not. Similarly, Homans (1961) suggests that adherence to a norm of "distributive justice" guides group life. Those who incur high inputs should be rewarded with high outcomes; those with low inputs should receive low outcomes.

Research on Reciprocity and Equity

In the United States it has been demonstrated that at least under certain conditions people will help those who have previously helped them (Goranson & Berkowitz, 1966) and that the more rewards P receives from O, the more he gives O in return (Pruitt, 1968; Tjosvold, 1977). Schopler (1970) briefly reviews the North American literature on reciprocity and discusses some of the conditions that may affect the amount of reciprocity displayed. As far as cross-cultural research is concerned, Gergen, Ellsworth, Maslach and Seipel (1975) employed a noncompetitive "wagering game" in which undergraduates from the United States, Sweden, and Japan unexpectedly received a gift of money from another player without which they would have had to withdraw from the game. It was found that in each country when subjects were allowed an opportunity to repay the donor, they did so. Morse, Gergen, Peele, and van Rynefeld (1976) found that white South African high school students who received help in a contest willingly offered to help the aid-giver in return. Morse, Gergen, and Gergen (1976) report further that Italian college students who received help from an experimental assistant on a task did more work for the assistant afterwards than those who had not received help. Finally, Morse (1972) found that Italian university students who received help from an assistant conformed more with the assistant's attitudes on an attitude scale than those who had not received help. Attitudinal agreement was the only form of reciprocity possible in this experiment.

As a group such studies show that reciprocity behavior can be experimentally induced in wide-ranging cultural contexts. Some form of reciprocity may be found in all cultures. But what relationship is there between the *amount* of benefits received and the *amount* returned? Apparently, individuals in exchange relationships do not follow a simple one-for-one, tit-for-tat strategy. Thus, Gergen et al. (1975) found that subjects in the three countries studied actually returned fewer resources than they had received. And Morse, Gergen and Gergen (1976), using the

Italian university students as subjects, *did not* find that the amount recip-rocated increased as the amount of help increased. Only studies by Ber-kowitz (Berkowitz, 1972; Berkowitz & Friedman, 1967) show such an effect. Adolescent subjects in both England and the United States worked harder for a stimulus person who had previously provided ample, as op-posed to little, help. It should be noted, however, that these studies by Berkowitz were specifically designed to investigate the operation of what he calls the "norm of social responsibility." As a result, after receiving help from *O*, *P* found himself in a situation in which *O* was very depen-dent upon him and in which *P did not* have the option to disregard *O*.

One major way in which the equity problem has been explored is to provide individuals with unreasonably high outcomes for performing a given task. The major question is whether the person, thus overpaid, will bring his resulting inputs into line with his undeserved outcomes. For ex-ample, will an overpaid worker increase his productivity or the quality of his work? Many North American studies do find such an effect. Overpaid subjects have been found to do more or better work than subjects paid an "equitable" wage. This line of research is summarized by Adams and Freedman (1976) and by Walster, Berscheid, and Walster (1976). Such findings have also been subject to serious question (see Lawler, 1968). A recent study by Morse, Gruzen, and Reis (1976) further suggests that overpaid subjects may, in fact, work harder not because "Positive ineq-uity" is uncomfortable but because restoring equity may be a way of win-ning social approval (in this case, the experimenter's). Whatever interpretation one gives to these American findings, cross-cultural studies *do not* show that overpaid subjects work harder than equitably paid sub-jects. Neither Wilke and Steur (1972), working with Dutch subjects, nor Gergen, Morse, and Bode (1974), using Italian and American subjects, found that level of payment influenced task performance.

The latter authors argue that there are two major ways an overpaid in-dividual may restore equity—by either working harder or by altering his perception of the task and the value of his pay. In the latter case, overpay-ment might cause the individual to reevaluate the work as more difficult or the task more deserving of greater pay. A person can justify to himself that his outcomes, in fact, do not exceed his inputs. Thus, Gergen, Morse, and Bode (1974) found that overpaid subjects rated the task as more diffi-cult and more demanding than equitably paid subjects. This experiment was conducted in both Italy and the United States, with similar results. Overpaid Italian subjects also increased their estimate of a fair wage. As a group, available research studies thus indicate that although a reciprocity norm may often influence whether reward or punishment is returned in kind, strict principles of behavioral equity often fail to operate. In particu-lar, people often find ways of justifying their failure to match the rewards they received with an equal return.

Cross-cultural differences in this domain have received only scant attention to date. An experiment by Feldman (1968) on helping behavior suggests that Americans may be more strongly motivated than many others to prefer situations in which outcomes match inputs. Stimulus persons overpaid cashiers for purchases made in pastry shops in Paris, Athens and Boston. Forty-six percent of the Parisians refunded the overpayment, compared with forty-nine percent in Athens. In contrast, eighty-two percent of the cashiers in Boston did so. Bostonians, that is, were apparently less willing to accept outcomes exceeding inputs. Perhaps economics provides the key to this United States/European difference. The more limited a person's resources, the more willing he may be to accept positive inequity. In this connection, Johnson (1973) reports that American subjects from upper class backgrounds who were overpaid for performing a task, did more work than equitably paid subjects. Those from lower class backgrounds did not. Thus, it seems when a person is not compelled by situational pressures to align inputs with outcomes, wealthier individuals may be more inclined to do so than poorer individuals.

Research on Reward Distribution

Closely related to the problem of equity is the question of how individuals distribute rewards to themselves and to others when working effectively. To what extent are rewards distributed according to principles of equity (each according to his contribution) or equality (each evenly regardless of contribution)? To what degree does favoritism or personal attraction enter the decision-making process? Such questions are extremely important in their relevance to building alternate social structures. On a concrete level, however, we may consider a group of individuals working on a common task. Some people do better on the task than others. When one person is singled out to distribute rewards to the others in any way he or she sees fit, how will the task be accomplished? Will rewards be allocated according to equity considerations, with higher outcomes accruing to people with higher inputs? Or will inputs be disregarded and the rewards distributed equally to everyone? Also, no matter how rewards are distributed to others, will the individual provide himself or herself with outcomes proportional to inputs or with the highest outcomes possible? In more general terms, what comparative weight is placed on equity, equality, and self-gain?

There has been much research on these questions. Again, thorough reviews of the North American literature are provided by Walster et al. (1976), Leventhal (1976), and Adams and Freedman (1976). In general, it appears that North American subjects often distribute rewards to themselves and to others in such a way that outcomes are proportional to inputs. The literature in this area, however, is highly complex. Lerner (1973), for example, found that American college students distribute rewards on the basis of equality, rather than equity (ignoring individual differences in input) when the interdependence between group members was stressed. Reis and Gruzen (1976) report that a person charged with distributing rewards overrewarded himself when information about the way in which he distributed the reward to himself and to others was to remain strictly private. This limited research suggests the conclusion that tendencies to distribute reward equitably may be limited to specific situations (Greenberg, 1978).

In cross-cultural research do individuals distribute rewards to themselves following an equity principle? That they do so is indicated in an experiment by Pepitone, Faucheux, Moscovici, Cesa-Bianchi, Magistretti, Iacono, Asprea, and Villone (1967). These researchers placed United States, French, and Italian undergraduates in a situation in which they could provide themselves with different levels of outcomes by selecting different responses in a variant of a nonzero sum game. Before playing the game, subjects were given false feedback about their abilities. In this way, a high ability (high input) group and a low ability (low input) group were created. As the results showed, high ability subjects generally provided themselves with greater rewards than low ability subjects; that is, they followed an equity principle. The results were similar in the United States, and France. The Italian results were ambiguous.

Another study, however, demonstrates a clear difference between the self-rewarding behavior of Americans and Italians. Pepitone, Maderna, Caporicci, Tiberi, Iacono, Di Majo, Perfetto, Asprea, Villone, Fua, and Tonucci (1970) used an experimental situation similar to that employed by Pepitone et al. (1967). This time, however, subjects who were led to believe they had more ability were given a monetary reward before the game began, while those who were led to believe they had less ability did not receive the reward. In the United States, subjects receiving the reward (the high ability group) provided themselves with higher outcomes than those not receiving the reward. This finding is consistent with equity theory predictions. However, Italian subjects who had not received the reward (the low ability group) rewarded themselves more than those receiving it. Such findings suggest that Americans operate on an equity principle, while Italians may prefer an equality model. The authors, however, prefer not to accept this interpretation and argue that the ability manipulation may have been less successful in Italy than in the United States. This would make the Italian and American results noncomparable since, in effect, the American sample would then consist of a high and a low input group. In another condition, subjects received or did not receive the initial reward on what appeared to be a completely arbitrary basis (in other words, input differences were not invoked to justify the initial reward distribution). In this case, both American and Italian subjects who did not receive the reward subsequently provided themselves with greater rewards for their task performance than those who did receive the initial reward.

The possibility of cross-cultural differences in reward distribution is not limited to the Pepitone et al. (1970) research. Mikula (1972) used pairs of Austrian servicemen as subjects and varied the relative task performance of each. With total performance measured on a 100-point system, some subject pairs found that one of their numbers received a performance or input score of 75 and the other a score of 25. In comparison groups, the performance or input ratio was 62.5 to 37.5 or 55 to 45. After working on the task and achieving these different input levels, each pair of subjects was required to divide a monetary reward. In the 75/25 and 62.5/37.5 conditions, subjects tended to allocate the reward more or less equally, ignoring input differences. Only in the 55/45 condition was the reward divided in such a way that the outcomes received were proportional to inputs. In effect, as long as there were great discrepancies in performance, equality of rewards was maintained. However, where the others' inputs became competitive, reward distribution may have been used to emphasize the differential performance.

In a second experiment by Mikula (1974), subjects were pairs of Austrian and American undergraduates (the latter then studying in Austria). Within each pair, one subject's performance was superior to the other's. Each person was asked independently to distribute the reward. Among both Austrians and Americans, those who performed poorly distributed the reward more in accordance with performance than did those who performed better. However, the American students who did better than their partner took *less* than their Austrian counterparts. (Nationality did not affect reward distribution among those who did worse than their partners.) This would seem to contradict the idea that Americans may be more concerned with equity and Europeans with equality. Mikula however, points out that these American results may reflect the fact that, as foreigners in Austria, his American subjects probably felt an unusually high degree of ingroup solidarity. He, thus, compared his Austrian results with those obtained by Leventhal and Lane (1970) in a similar study in the United States. These authors found that, in distributing rewards, Americans do indeed seem to strive for equity between outcomes and inputs and Austrians for equality between one person's outcomes and another's. The crucial factor, once again, may of course not actually be nationality, but resources.

In this latter regard, it is useful to look at relevant anthropological literature. Sahlins (1965) discussed what he terms "generalized reciprocity," which is more or less equivalent to altruism. To a certain extent, opting for equality rather than equity in the distribution of resources indicates that the individual is prepared to sacrifice his own interests in order to maintain solidarity within the group or in order to help someone with low inputs. It is therefore interesting to note Sahlins argument that generalized reciprocity will occur more frequently when resources are scarce. It is also found more often between individuals connected by kinship and other ties than between relative strangers. If generalized reciprocity is equated with attempts by those with superior inputs to achieve equality in resource distribution, the results of the experiments reviewed so far would appear to fit this pattern. Europeans seem more inclined to equalize resources than Americans (and Americans are generally wealthier than Europeans); ingroup solidarity also appears to generate a preference for equality over equity.

Preference for a particular distribution of rewards may also be produced by an awareness of the impact of one's choice on the social approval or approbation that it may yield. While one might prefer to take all one can get, it may not be socially graceful to do so. Verification of this perspective comes from a study by Kahn, Lamm, and Nelson (1977) who show how American and German observers view allocators in various situations. Kahn et al (1977) studied the reactions of observers to high input and low input allocators who were either equitable or equal in their distribution of rewards. In the United States, subjects, especially females, preferred the low input allocator who chose the equity mode (took less for himself) and the high input allocator who chose an equality solution (also took less for himself). Generosity was preferred over self-interest in all cases.

In Germany, the results were less consistent; male subjects preferred a nongenerous allocator to a generous one. Allocators who kept what they made were seen as more powerful than others.

Increasingly, American theorists and researchers are arguing for the need to keep the rules relevant to preferred allocational strategies flexible. While equity norms are important, other considerations loom important, especially in the "real" world (von Grumbkow, Deen, Steensma, & Wilke, 1976; Leventhal, 1976). When allocators are motivated by social responsibility norms, equality may be the guiding force (Leventhal, 1976); when return help is expected, equality may also be high (Bar-tal, 1976; Tjosvold, 1977), and when harmonious relations are desired, equality is preferred (Austin & McGinn, 1977). Yet, under some conditions, particularly in the private assessments made by males of high input allocators, equity may often be the preferred strategy (Austin & McGinn, 1977; von Grumbkow et al., 1976).

The few existing cross-cultural studies that employ children as subjects, interestingly enough, do not report significant cross-cultural differences. With United States and Austrian children, Mikula (1972) found that rewards were distributed in each country in accordance with performance differences. In a different type of experiment, Stephenson and Barker (1972) had English children play an electric racing car game. A subject found himself in a privileged (high initial income) or deprived (low initial income) condition. This initial reward distribution was presented to the subject as being either justified or not justified. The major dependent variable was how much cheating subjects did. The results of this experiment parallel those obtained by Stephenson and White (1968) in the United States. Cheating was highest in the unjustified/deprived and justified/privileged condition. These results are consistent with equity theory. In the unjustified/deprived condition, subjects apparently believed they deserved higher outcomes than they had received because their initially low outcomes were not based on inputs. Justified/privileged subjects, in contrast, were led to believe that they were entitled to receive high outcomes, and, therefore, provided themselves with them.

These two experiments, then, suggest that cultural differences may affect the behavior of children less than the behavior of adults. If the reasoning concerning the role of economic circumstances is correct, then economic factors rather than cultural ones are involved; this may be because children are both less able than adults to assess their relative economic standing and are less concerned with material resources in general.

In conclusion, both North American and cross-cultural research on reward distribution show that many variables must be taken into account. It cannot be said that individuals will invariably distribute rewards to themselves and to others so that outcomes are proportional to inputs. North Americans may well be more prone than Europeans to distributing rewards in accordance with inputs. Finally, cultural differences in reward allocation may increase with age, and ingroup solidarity and lower resources are often associated with a preference for equality over equity. Cultural differences may thus be attributed to differing economic conditions.

Resource Exchange

Investigations of reciprocity, equity and reward allocation have largely taken place without consideration for the specific resources in question. Implicit is the assumption that one might reciprocate for what is received by returning virtually any resource that could benefit the donor. Such an assumption is clearly misleading. People are often very concerned with the character of the resources to be exchanged, and exchange theory must be importantly concerned with preferred patterns of resource exchange and their underlying rationale. The most extensive research on such patterns was conducted by Foa and Foa (1974). These investigators maintain that certain patterns of exchange are preferred within all cultures. From the Foas' vantage point all resources may be placed into one of six groups: love, status, services, money, goods, and information. These resources are said to be arranged along two dimensions: (1) particularism, or the importance of the giver or receiver's identity to the exchange, and (2) concreteness, or the extent to which the resource has face-value as opposed to symbolic significance. Thus, love is highly particularistic (one normally cares about the identity of the giver), and medium in concreteness (the symbolic significance of loving is often more important than its concrete existence). Money, in contrast, is said to be low in particularism (it has the same value regardless of the donor) and is medium in concreteness. For convenience, the resource array is depicted in Figure 4–1.

The theoretical premise underlying this structural interpretation of

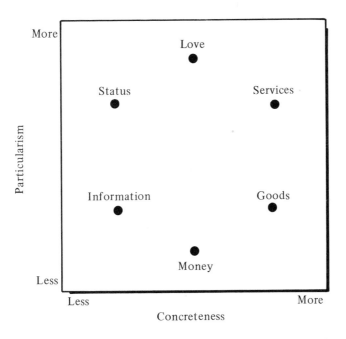

Figure 4–1. The Cognitive Structure of Resource Classes

resources is that those resources that are closest to one another within this two-dimensional array are also closest in terms of meaning or within the cognitive structure of the individual.

Within the United States, Turner, Foa, and Foa (1971) tested the hypothesis that the more proximal the resources in the structure, the more they are perceived as being similar. In general the hypothesized order was displayed. In exchange relationships, the theory posits that greatest satisfaction will accrue when resources that are most similar (e.g., love for love) are exchanged and that least satisfaction will occur when resources that are most dissimilar are exchanged (e.g., love for money).

The universality of such preferences is traced to the common experience of the developing child. A developmental sequence is suggested whereby the infant is said to be completely undifferentiated at a cognitive level. He or she is aware only of the reception of a unitary resource. Through increased experience the child later comes to differentiate self versus other, giving versus taking, and service versus love. Further differentiations occur at later periods, yielding a cognitive structure mapped by the circular formation in Figure 4–1. The cross-cultural applicability of this structure has been demonstrated in Israel, Greece, Hawaii, India, and Senegal (Triandis, Vassiliou, & Nassiakou, 1968; Foa, Triandis, & Katz, 1966; Osgood and Chatterjee as reported in Foa & Foa, 1974). Because the basic exchange structure remains invariant across cultures, a framework exists for exploring differences among cultures. These differences are produced by variations in cultural traditions that produce unique patterns of differentiation among relevant elements within the exchange context. Thus family or institutional roles or patterns of giving or taking may differ across cultures, but an underlying stability can be discerned beneath the deviations. For example, mothers and wives may be treated more alike than mothers and fathers if sex differentiation is stronger than power differentiation. However, in a culture where power differences are more significant than sex differences, mother and father may be treated more alike than mother and wife. Befu (1977) reports data from Japan in which greater expressiveness and affection among people lead to greater social utility in terms of goods and services. In Japan it appears that particularism characterizes all resource exchanges more than in the western world.

From this interlocking view of structural stability and cultural differentiation, a cultural assimilator technique to sensitivity training in cross-cultural settings has been developed. With this technique the individual learns to respond to socially relevant vignettes as a native of the culture might. The vignettes are selected after an analysis of cultural variants in resource structuring is made. Theoretically, the assimilator's function is to illustrate to the learner where differences in cognitive differentiation between the local people and the foreigner are to be found.

Long-term gains in interpersonal skill and job success have been found among samples where this training has been carried out (Stolurow, 1965; Chemers, Lekhyananda, Fiedler, & Stolurow, 1966; Michell & Foa, 1969).

The structural approach as propounded by Foa and Foa (1974) has much to recommend it over the piecemeal, empirically grounded research generally done by social psychologists in cross-cultural settings. Rather than attempting to construct general principles from the ever increasing complexity of accumulated research findings, the Foas have commenced with a broad overview, based primarily on rational considerations. Research data in this case are illustrative rather than attempts at proof. In this sense the Foas elaboration of the exchange framework follows the initial tradition, in which theory is used primarily for catalytic and sensitizing purposes rather than for prediction.

Altruism and the Helping Relation

The view of exchange prevailing thus far within the present chapter is one in which individuals are assumed to maximize their own profits to the greatest possible extent within social arrangements that attempt to insure reciprocity. One might conclude from such an analysis that the reciprocity norm is necessary to prevent a competition of all against all. However, this conclusion is unwarranted, for the attempt to maximize one's own return does not necessarily imply the conclusion that human behavior tends always toward exploitation. Much research has taken place within the exchange tradition on the conditions fostering exploitation as opposed to cooperation among people, and cross-cultural research in this domain has been reviewed by Mann in Chapter 5 of this volume. This literature makes it clear that although exploitation is highly pervasive, conditions can often generate strong motives for cooperation. Research on altruism and helping is additionally enlightening, for such research demonstrates an array of conditions in which people appear to sacrifice their rewards in order to benefit other people. Such behavior does not violate the hedonistic premise of exchange theory; it primarily points to an important source of reward for many people. Rewards in benefitting others often prove greater than the sacrificial costs incurred in doing so. A brief consideration of cross-cultural research within this important area follows.

Within the United States, many studies have been conducted on altruism over the past decade. A useful collection of papers on various facets of altruism is contained in Macaulay and Berkowitz (1970). Krebs (1970) critically examines the concept of altruism and reviews a wealth of literature on this topic. Liktorius and Stang (1975) have also compiled an exhaustive, up-to-date bibliography. In spite of the significance of the area of research, cross-cultural study has only begun to receive attention. Most of this work has been concerned with cross-cultural differences. Which cultural milieus tend to foster a more altruistic orientation to social relations? It does seem clear that general levels of altruistic behavior should differ from one society to another? Almond and Verba (1963) asked respondents in five countries which two qualities they admired most in people. In Great Britain, 65 percent cited "generosity." This compared with 59 percent in the United States, 42 percent in West Germany, 36 percent in Mexico, and 25 percent in Italy.

One of the most thorough experimental studies on altruism in a cross-cultural setting was conducted by L'Armand and Pepitone (1975). They employed an experimental situation in which subjects wager money on a series of events, each having an explicit and objective probability of success. In one condition, subjects place bets on their own behalf. The major dependent variable in this study is the payoff that subjects earn for either themselves or their partner. Indian and United States university students were used as subjects. The results were clear cut. United States subjects wagered more effectively (that is, produced higher outcomes) when they were wagering on their partner's behalf than on their own. Indian subjects did the opposite, wagering more effectively when they were to retain the earnings than when their partner was to do so.

It was also found in this experiment that Indian subjects earned more money for their partner when he was of the same caste as they (Brahmin versus non-Brahmin) than when he was of another caste. This is consistent with the findings of various American studies that show a stronger tendency to help similar than dissimilar others (Sole, Marton, & Hornstein, 1975). Feldman (1968), however, reports that individuals in Paris, Boston, and Athens in most instances helped foreigners and compatriots equally. Where a distinction was made between foreigners and compatriots, on the other hand, the results in Paris and Boston confirm the hypothesis that perceived similarity between P and O increases P's propensity to help O. The results in Athens seem contrary. Greeks gave more help to foreigners than to fellow Greeks. These American and Greek results seem to confirm Triandis's (1973) observation that Americans are more oriented toward helping outgroup members than are Greeks. It is also possible that Greeks include visitors in their concept of the ingroup, but not fellow Greeks that they do not know.

Feldman (1968) also reports that Americans in general are more altruistic—in terms of giving directions and mailing a letter for someone—than Greeks and the French (at least in certain cases). However, Innes (1974) shows that Scottish citizens are more willing to mail a letter for a stranger than Americans are (see Langer & Abelson, 1972). Perhaps the high degree of social solidarity said to characterize the Scots carries over to their relations with foreigners.

Earlier it was found that social class or economic standing appears to influence social exchange. Does this seem true for altruism as well? Sahlins (1965) suggests that "generalized reciprocity" will frequently characterize relations between wealthy and poor individuals. In line with this finding, both the Feldman (1968) and L'Armand and Pepitone (1975) experiments found that socioeconomic status correlated positively with altruistic behavior—among Frenchmen, Greeks, and Americans in the first study and among Indians in the second (no relevant data are provided by L'Armand and Pepitone for their American subjects). Almond and Verba (1963) report, in addition, that the percent of respondents admiring generosity in others increased with socioeconomic status in all countries except Mexico (where it remained stable). These varied findings lend force to Berkowitz and Friedman's (1967) conclusion, as reported in the section on reciprocity, that in England and the United States, individuals from "bureaucratic" middle class backgrounds were more willing than lower class individuals to help someone who is dependent upon them. It should be noted, however, that Ugurel-Semin (1952) found that poor children in Istanbul were more willing to share with others than children from middle class or upper class families. This finding also seems to confirm an observation made by Sahlins (1965), that sharing will be most extensive when economic conditions are harshest.

As far as other variables are concerned, the investigations by both Innes (1974) and Langer and Abelson (1972) found that compliance with a request depends upon both its perceived "legitimacy" and the way O presents it to P. In Scotland and the United States when O made an "illegitimate" request for help, he received more help when he emphasized P's responsibility to help others in general than when he stressed his own plight. When he made a "legitimate" request, however, he received more help when he stressed the specific plight he was in than when he emphasized P's generalized obligation to help others.

Later, some of the general problems inherent in such comparisons will be discussed. For now, it may simply be concluded that far too little evidence exists on which to base broad conclusions. Further research would be much improved by shifting the focus from differences between cultures in absolute amount of generosity or altruism to differences or similarities in function forms. Do variations in various factors have similar or opposing effects from one culture to another?

Reactions to Aid

While altruism across cultures is just beginning to be understood, a substantial body of findings is accumulating on the problem of receiving aid. The problem is an especially interesting one as aid may often create hostility and resentment in the recipient. In both the case of foreign aid and social welfare, for example, aid recipients are often negative to those who help them, dislike the aid, fail to cooperate with the donor, and do not reciprocate for what is received. In terms of social exchange, any transaction may furnish both rewards and punishments. The actual aid received in a transaction is only one factor to be considered. A host of other factors may also enter into the transaction and if the hedonic value of such factors is negative, reactions to the episode may be negative.

Research to date has concentrated on four classes of factors that may influence the outcome of aid transactions: donor characteristics, benefit characteristics, recipient characteristics, and characteristics of the benefit context. Each of these will be discussed in turn.

Gergen and Gergen (1971) assayed the opinions on foreign aid of fifty-six aid officials from twenty-one donor and recipient nations. When asked which factors were most critical in determining the results of aid exchange, the characteristics of the donor were considered the most crucial. Of particular significance was the motivation of the donor, whether selfish and manipulative or based on concern for the recipient. The opinions of these officials are reflected in a number of American studies. For example, Dickoff (1961) found that ulterior motives undercut subjects' appreciation for positive comments from another; Jones, Jones, and Gergen (1963) found that conformity, a form of benefit, was evaluated more negatively when it seemed insincere; Jones (1973) also found a lack of positive regard when donor motives were questionable. Nadler, Fisher, and Streufert (1974), in a simulation of multinational negotiations, found that suspiciousness of motives dampened acceptability of aid offered by an "enemy." Greater liking for helpfulness only accrued to friends. The same assistance received from an enemy appeared less valuable than when received from a friend. Moving to the cross-cultural arena, motives of a donor have been investigated by secondary analyses of public opinion surveys in various nations where aid has been received. Across diverse cultures (e.g. Iran, Brazil, India and Uruguay) evidence indicates that the perception of the donor's good will correlates strongly with acceptability and appreciation for donor and aid (Gergen & Gergen, 1974).

Other characteristics of the donor have been researched. Of particular interest have been the degree of similarity between donor and recipient, the attractiveness of the donor, and the donor's wealth. In the case of similarity, a number of American studies do indicate that increasing similarity of donor and recipient may have beneficial effects. Similarity has been found conducive to a coalition formation (Thibaut & Kelley, 1959), personal attraction (Byrne, 1971), friendship formation (Newcomb, 1961), marriage adjustment (Levinger & Breedlove, 1966), and interpersonal understanding (Triandis, 1960). However, it would be naive to assume that similarity inevitably operates in positive fashion. Two American studies contradict the traditional assumptions about the value of similarity. Fisher and Nadler (1974) found that when aid was received from a similar, as opposed to a dissimilar other, subjects' self-esteem was reduced. In a study by Clark, Gotay, and Mills (1974), the "tension of obligation" appeared greater when the donor was similar to oneself. Recipients were willing to accept more aid without being able to return the aid when the donor was dissimilar. While these two isolated laboratory studies are not robust enough to be generalized extensively, it appears that similarity can be a deterrent to a satisfactory aid exchange.

The effects of donor attractiveness have been examined in the United States by Stokes and Bickman (1974). Again, the obvious, oft-found relationship between attractiveness and liking (e.g., Walster, Aronson, Abrams, & Rottman, 1966) is not supported. Subjects in the Stokes and Bickman study preferred to ask help of an unattractive rather than attractive person. In exchange terms, this can readily be explained as a cost-reduction technique. Less attractive people have fewer resources to expend in doing a favor than attractive ones, unless, as the study found, it is the duty of the attractive person to provide assistance. In this case, attractiveness can be a special bonus to the recipient. In spite of these results, public opinion surveys in diverse cultures suggest that donor attractiveness generally has a positive impact (Gergen & Gergen, 1974). For example, in Iran, if the United States is perceived as peace-loving, its aid is considered effective; results from Nigeria show that, if the USSR is seen to be powerful in military might or in space technology, its aid is seen as imperialistic or domineering; if the USSR is seen as imperialistic in Turkey, its aid programs are not well received; if minority groups suffer in America, this has negative implications for United States aid acceptability in Brazil, Nigeria, and Senegal. In general, nations are seen as "good" or "bad" and this halo effect seems to encompass its aid exchanges as well.

Turning to the effects of the donor's wealth on aid transactions, research results tend to converge across cultural boundaries. Laboratory research in Sweden, Japan, and the United States indicates that recipients of aid are more attracted to a poor donor than to a wealthier one (Gergen, Ellsworth, Maslach and Seipel, 1975). Questionnaire research conducted in Japan, United States, South Africa, Scotland, Korea, and Taiwan corroborate the same conclusion (Morse, Gergen, & Gergen, 1976). Yet, in spite of the increased liking enjoyed by the low resource donor, they may not be selected as partners in coalitions. In the Gergen et al. (1974) study, high resource donors were preferred over low resource donors for future collaboration, even though they were less well liked.

The discussion now turns from the influence of donor characteristics to aspects of the benefit. Thus far research has concentrated on the obligations attached to aid and to its amount. The earlier discussion of reciprocity is most relevant to a discussion of obligation. Reciprocity considerations suggest that people may often prefer to be obligated to return favors they have received. Indeed, Dillon (1968) credits the failure of the United States to allow the French to reciprocate for the massive aid that they received after World War II with the development of French animosity toward the Americans. Laboratory research by Gergen et al. (1974) supports this argument by showing that in Sweden, Japan, and the United States, subjects are more attracted to a donor who asks for an equal return of aid than they are to an offer of "something for nothing." Yet such results are clearly not decisive. As questionnaire research in Japan, United States, South Africa, Scotland, Korea, and Taiwan shows, when people are asked about their preference they seem to prefer aid that is free of any encumbrances (Gergen, Morse & Kristeller, 1973). It is possible that in the abstract people do prefer aid free of obligation; however in the concrete interpersonal setting, shame is avoided when one is obliged to balance the ledger.

In the case of amount of aid, it has been important to consider whether recipients perceive more aid as better. Certainly, receiving aid can have positive effects on recipients' feelings toward a donor. In a survey study (Gergen & Gergen, 1974), Latin Americans answered questions about the success of the United States supported Alliance for Progress in meeting its goals. The more successful the program, the more positive the recipient was toward the United States. In a laboratory study in the United States, Broll, Gross, and Piliavin (1974) found that greater amounts of aid related to more positive feelings toward the donor. Yet, there are certainly limits to such findings. As the amount of aid is increased, the value of the individual unit of aid is likely to be reduced. At the same time, the tension of obligation may steadily increase as aid increases. At a certain point, the tension of obligation should exceed the benefit derived from the aid, and reactions should move from positive to negative.

The personal characteristics of recipients as predictors of reactions to aid has been the focus of research in several cross-cultural settings. Specific attention has been given to the need-state of the recipient, the expectancy of assistance, the autonomy of the recipient, and recipient self-perceptions. Although it seems clear from reinforcement theory that greater deprivation or need should enhance the value of the satisfier and those who provide it, few cross-cultural studies have clearly shown this. A variant of this was found, however, in a simulated cross-national study by Gergen and Morse (1971). In this experiment, six fictitious nations were represented by subjects who competed for aid from a seventh nation. The six nations had either a high or low level of material need and requests for assistance were either approved or denied on a random basis. For none of the nations was donor attraction greatly enhanced by receiving of aid; however, high need-state subjects were significantly more antagonistic toward the donor who denied them aid than were low-need subjects. In effect, high need did not increase the liking of a donor, but it did increase hostility when aid was withheld. Another way of approaching the issue of need-state has been through an assessment of general world view. Specifically, reactions to help may depend on whether one's world view is one of "limited" as opposed to "unlimited" good. Poorer cultures tend to harbor a limited good view, which means that anyone's gain may be their loss (Foster, 1964). Banfield (1961), McClelland and Winters (1969) and L'Armand and Pepitone (1975) have found evidence of this outlook in diverse cultures. In such cultures one might anticipate a positive reaction only when one personally receives the aid. Aid to others in the same culture may be resented.

Whether aid is expected or not may further influence recipient reactions. In an early American study, Spector (1956) found that expectations tend to reduce the value of a reward, in this case, a promotion. It is the unexpected promotion that is most appreciated. Morse (1972) achieved similar results in Italy. Subjects receiving unexpected help on a task proved more willing to reciprocate than those who expected help.

A recipient's needs for autonomy may also be threatened by the offer of assistance. Brehm's reactance theory (1966) illuminates the efforts of those whose freedoms are violated to reestablish their autonomy despite the loss of material gain that may occur. On a cross-national basis, Gergen et al. (1973) asked people in six nations (Japan, United States, South Africa, Scotland, Korea, and Taiwan) about the acceptability of aid and appreciation of the donor, when aid was given with much or with little control over its use. In all countries, positive feelings toward aid and the donor were found when little control was placed over its use, and negative feelings toward the aid and donor were evidenced when autonomy was threatened. Again, there may be limits to the value of freedom. As Broll et al. (1974) found in the United States, recipients would rather be offered help than be allowed the freedom to seek it out.

Self-perception variables, particularly self-esteem, have also been important in cross-cultural research. In Italy, Morse (1972) found strong negative reactions to help when subjects' intelligence was thrown into question by the offer. The same help without such implications was greeted positively. In their six-nation questionnaire, Gergen et al. (1973) found that when one's self-esteem was adversely affected by aid, people indicated that they would dislike a donor as well as their aid. However, Japanese and Chinese respondents were somewhat less negatively affected by the self-deprecating benefit than were respondents from Scotland, South Africa, Korea, and the United States. Buddhist teachings with their strong condemnation of esteem striving may have reduced the effects of esteem-deprecation in the former nations.

Exchange Theory and Cross-Cultural Similarities

Having reviewed several major lines of research bearing on social exchange theory, this chapter is now in a position to inquire into the more general success of the inquiry. Two major questions have dominated the discussion, and both deserve summary attention. The first is the extent to which exchange theory propositions are found valid across cultural boundaries. Is it possible that these are human universals? In empirical terms, this questions the degree of cross-cultural generality to be found in various function forms.

In order to deal with this question adequately, it is first important to note that exchange theory as a whole is comprised of very few testable propositions. In his volume *Social Behavior: Its Elementary Form*, Homans (1961) does succeed in laying out a handful of formal propositions. However, such propositions form the exception within the domain of theoretical writings. It is more fruitful to view exchange theory as an orientation to understanding than as a set of interlocking propositions from which a series of point-predictions about human social behavior can be derived. In this sense, the theory is more akin to behaviorist, Gestalt, or phenomenological frameworks. In each case, the theoretical framework provides a useful terminology allowing the researcher to deal with a highly variegated set of phenomena; it suggests a way of looking at human behavior, bringing certain of its features into clearer focus; it sensitizes one to a variety of processes or factors potentially operating in various situations; and it facilitates a broad integration of many findings. Thus, while the various propositions that have been tested are thoroughly compatible with exchange orientation, they are not strictly derived from its basic tenets.

Turning more directly to the cross-cultural generality of such propositions, it is useful to consider a *continuum of propositional abstraction*. On one hand, there are theoretical propositions of highly abstract character. The reciprocity principle is of this variety; the principle itself makes no specific predictions about concrete cases. A lesser degree of abstraction is embodied in the hypothesis that people generally avoid exchanges of love and money. Greater specificity is embodied in this proposition than in the case of the generalized reciprocity principle. Few exchange propositions exist at a low level of abstraction, that is, where specification is made of the exact, concrete conditions under which the proposition is valid. In the case of highly general or abstract propositions, confirming evidence may be generated with relative ease. One need only consider the rich body of behavior offered by the society as a whole and select those instances which confirm the theory. Because human behavior is complex and variegated, it should be possible to find support for virtually any abstract proposition, along with its opposite. Thus, in cases of reciprocity and equity it is wise to anticipate the generalization of data indicating universality. All cultures will provide sufficiently rich arrays of behavior so that supportive data may be obtained. In this sense, all principles of broad generality are universal. As investigators turn to theories of lesser abstraction, they have fewer degrees of freedom. The propositions increasingly bind them to making specific predictions about very particular forms of behavior. Thus, although behavior in any society is highly complex and varied, it is typically more difficult to obtain confirmation in specific circumstances. As a rule, then, the lower the level of abstraction, the less likely that universally valid propositions will be discovered.

Several additional conclusions stem from this line of reasoning. For one, it may be said that general propositions may be highly useful as sensitizers, but they are of little utility in making concrete predictions in specific cases. In effect, one must be familiar with the concrete case before the general principles can be applied successfully. In contrast, specific hypotheses about concrete cases may be very useful in making predictions. However, both their generality and their contribution to intellectual life may be highly limited. This view additionally suggests that the bulk of the research reviewed here (viz. experiments replicated in various cultural settings) represent a delimited form of scientific activity. The results may lend credence to a particular proposition or viewpoint. However, as support can probably be generated for all reasonable propositions, such research is hardly decisive. To the extent that cross-cultural psychology wishes to concern itself with real-world predictions, cross-cultural experiments of the traditional variety are not likely to prove useful. Experiments may optimally be viewed as systematic illustrations that add credibility, not proof, to one's theoretical speculations.

Exchange Theory and Cultural Differences

These various arguments also prove relevant to the second summary concern: what does existing research on social exchange tell about cross-cultural differences in behavior? Can valid generalizations be made about the French versus the Chinese, or the Japanese versus the Indians? This is not only to ask whether differences in function forms are displaced differentially from one culture to another. It is possible that giving love does not lead to a return of love in all cultures. The exchange function may differ from one culture to another. However, if love is always exchanged for love, some cultures may be more pronounced in this tendency than others.

As a general surmise, it may be said that whether cultural differences are found will largely depend on the particular means used to test the hypotheses or make the comparison. Regardless of its level of abstraction, any proposition must inevitably be tested in a set of concrete circumstances. The selection of circumstances is critical in determining whether cross-cultural differences are found. For example, if researchers wished to know whether Mexicans are more or less aggressive than Americans, and they observed the reactions of randomly selected Mexicans or Americans to a bullfight, they should conclude, by any measure employed, that Mexicans are more aggressive. Yet, the experience of the two groups with the bullfight is entirely different. If they had selected the American football game as the context in which to make the comparison, the opposite results would be found. Nor can it be argued that the bullfight should be used to test Mexicans and an equivalent context like the football game in the United States or the soccer match in Europe. The athletic contests differ in so many ways that no valid conclusions could be reached about cultural differences in aggression. This same argument applies to any experimental procedure employed in cross-cultural research. Each culture has its own particular contexts in which aggression is displayed, its own arenas in which reciprocity occurs; love is exchanged for status, an attractive donor generates good will, and so on. These contexts may further change over time within a given culture (see Gergen, 1973). In this light, it is extremely hazardous, if not wholly misleading, to draw conclusions about cultural differences "in general" from any particular test. When differences in either function form or displacement on a given dimension are encountered, it is wholly gratuitous to draw conclusions regarding cultural tendencies in general. The findings cannot be extricated from the particular context selected for study.

In effect, the many studies reviewed here allowed only minimal coverage of generalized differences in cultural characteristics. Interesting differences do emerge, and such differences sometimes confirm common stereotypes. However, such findings might best be viewed as goads to sharper analysis.

Conclusion

The exchange metaphor has proved immensely powerful in providing a coherent framework for unifying the focus of highly diverse disciplines, and in catalyzing exploration in a variety of domains. However, the primary gains from empirical exploration thus far are not in the validation of theoretical premises. Empirical research has first served to sharpen thinking about the issues at hand; in the execution of the research one must confront the issues in their concrete complexity, so that the result is typically a further elaboration of the theory. Second, research to date has demonstrated the overwhelming problems faced by the behavioral scientist bent on establishing empirically based theories of cross-cultural generality. Given the emerging cognizance of such problems, it seems inefficient to continue replicating such demonstrations. Required at this point are additional inquiries demonstrating the viability of the exchange orientation in multiple arenas. That is, research may usefully challenge one's conception of the ordinary, and demonstrate the advantages of an alternate interpretation. Exchange theory is only one such alternative, but a rich and compelling one with far-reaching implications.

References

ADAMS, J. S. Inequity in social exchange. In L. Berkowitz (Ed.), *Advances in experimental social psychology*, Vol. 2. New York: Academic Press, 1965.

ADAMS, J. S., & FREEDMAN, S. Equity theory revisited: comments and annotated bibliography. In L. Berkowitz (Ed.), *Advances in experimental social psychology*, Vol. 9. New York: Academic Press, 1976.

ALMOND, G. A., & VERBA, S. *The civic culture*. Princeton, N. J.: Princeton University Press, 1963.

AUSTIN, W., & McGINN, N. C. Sex differences in choice of distribution rules. *Journal of Personality*, 1977, 45, 379–94.

BANFIELD, E. C. *Political influence*. Glencoe, Ill.: Free Press, 1961.

BAR-TAL, D. *Prosocial behavior: theory and research*. Washington, D.C.: Hemisphere, 1976.

BEFU, H. Gift giving and social reciprocity in Japan. *France-Asia*, 1966, 188, 161–77.

——. Social exchange. *Annual Review of Anthropology*, 1977, 6, 255–81.

BENEDICT, R. *The chrysanthemum and the sword*. Boston: Houghton Mifflin, 1946.

BERKOWITZ, L. Social norms, feelings, and other factors affecting helping and altruism. In L. Berkowitz (Ed.), *Advances in experimental social psychology*, Vol. 6. New York: Academic Press, 1972, pp. 63–108.

BERKOWITZ, L., & FRIEDMAN, P. Some social class differences in helping behavior. *Journal of Personality and Social Psychology*, 1967, 5, 217–25.

BLAU, P. M. *Exchange and power in social life*. New York: Wiley, 1964.

BOULDING, K. E. *The economy of love and fear*. Belmont, Calif.: Wadsworth, 1973.

BREHM, J. W. *A theory of psychological reactance*. New York: Academic Press, 1966.

BREHMER, B. A note on the cross-national differences in cognitive conflict found by Hammond et al. *International Journal of Psychology*, 1974, 9, 51–56.

BROLL, L., GROSS, A., & PILIAVIN, I. Effects of offered and requested help on help seeking and reactions to being helped. *Journal of Applied Social Psychology*, 1974, 4, 244–58.

BYRNE, D. *The Attraction Paradigm*. New York: Academic Press, 1971.

CHEMERS, M. M., LEKHYANANDA, D., FIEDLER, F. E., & STOLUROW, L. M. Some effects of cultural training on leadership in heterocultural task group. *International Journal of Psychology*, 1966, 1, 301–14.

CLARK, M. S., GOTAY, C. C., & MILLS, J. Acceptance of help as a function of similarity of the potential helper and opportunity to repay. *Journal of Applied Social Psychology*, 1974, 4, 224–29.

COLEMAN, J. S. Foundations for a theory of collective decisions. *American Journal of Sociology*, 1966, 71, 615–27.

DICKOFF, H. Reactions to evaluations by another person as a function of self-evaluation and interaction context. Unpublished doctoral dissertation, Duke University, 1961.

DILLON, W. S. *Gifts and Nations*. The Hague: Mouton, 1968.

EMERSON, R. Power-dependent relations. *American Sociological Review*, 1962, 27, 31–41.

————. Exchange theory: the problem of appropriate data. Paper presented at American Sociological Association, Denver, Colo. August, 1971.

EVAN, W. M. Role strain and the norm of reciprocity in research organizations. *American Journal of Sociology*, 1962, 68, 346–54.

FELDMAN, R. E. Response to compatriot and foreigner who seek assistance. *Journal of Personality and Social Psychology*, 1968, 10, 203–14.

FESTINGER, L. A. *A theory of cognitive dissonance*. Evanston, Ill.: Row, Peterson, 1957.

FIRTH, R. (Ed.), *Themes in economic anthropology*. London: Tavistock, 1967.

FISHER, J. D., & NADLER, A. The effect of similarity between donor and recipient on recipient's reaction to aid. *Journal of Applied Social Psychology*, 1974, 4, 230–43.

FOA, E. B., & FOA, U. G. *Societal structures of the mind*. Springfield, Ill.: Charles C Thomas, 1974.

FOA, U. G., TRIANDIS, H. C., & KATZ, E. W. Cross-cultural invariance in the differentiation and organization of family roles. *Journal of Personality and Social Psychology*, 1966, 4, 316–27.

FOSTER, G. R. Authoritarianism in early adolescence. *Dissertation Abstracts*, 1964, 25, 612–13.

FROMKIN, H. L. The search for uniqueness and valuation of scarcity: neglected dimensions of value in exchange theory. In K. J. Gergen, M. J. Greenberg & R. H. Willis (Eds.), *Social exchange: advances in theory and research*. New York: Wiley, 1975.

GAMSON, W. A. A theory of coalition formation. *American Sociological Review*, 1961, 26, 373–82.

GERGEN, K. J. Social psychology as history. *Journal of Personality and Social Psychology*, 1973, 26, 309–20.

GERGEN, K. J., ELLSWORTH, P., MASLACH, C., & SEIPEL, M. Obligation, donor resources and reactions to aid in a three nation study. *Journal of Personality and Social Psychology*, 1975, 31, 390–400.

GERGEN, K. J., & GERGEN, M. M. International assistance from a psychological perspective. *Yearbook of World Affairs*, Vol. 25. London: Institute of World Affairs, 1971, pp. 87–103.

――――. Understanding foreign assistance through public opinion. *Yearbook of World Affairs*, Vol. 28. London: Stevens and Sons, 1974, pp. 125–40.

GERGEN, K. J., & MORSE, S. J. Material aid and social attraction. *Journal of Applied Social Psychology*, 1971, *1*, 150–62.

GERGEN, K. J., MORSE, S. J., & BODE, K. A. Overpaid or overworked? Cognitive and behavioral reactions to inequitable rewards. *Journal of Applied Social Psychology*, 1974, *4*, 259–74.

GERGEN, K. J., MORSE, S. J., & KRISTELLER, J. L. The manner of giving: cross-national continuities in reactions to aid. *Psychologia*, 1973, *16*, 121–31.

GOODENOUGH, W. H. *Property, kin, and community on Truk*. Hamden, Conn.: Archon, 1967.

GORANSON, R., & BERKOWITZ, L. Reciprocity and responsibility reactions to prior help. *Journal of Personality and Social Psychology*, 1966, *3*, 227–32.

GOULDNER, A. W. The norm of reciprocity, a preliminary statement. *American Sociological Review*, 1960, *25*, 161–78.

GREENBERG, J. Effects of reward value and retaliative power on allocation decisions: justice, generosity or greed? *Journal of Personality and Social Psychology*, 1978, *36*, 367–79.

GREENBERG, M. S., BLOCK, M. W., & SILVERMAN, M. A. Determinants of helping behavior: person's rewards versus other's costs. *Journal of Personality*, 1971, *39*, 79–93.

HARSANYI, JOHN C. A bargaining model for social status in informal groups and formal organizations. *Behavioral Science*, 1966, *11*, 357–69.

HOGBIN, H. J. Polynesian ceremonial gift exchange. In A. Howard (Ed.), *Polynesia: readings on a culture area*. San Francisco: Chandler, 1971, pp. 27–45.

HOMANS, G. C. *Social behavior: it's elementary forms*. New York: Harcourt, Brace, 1961.

HUESMANN, L. R., & LEVINGER, G. Incremental exchange theory: a formal model for progression in dyadic social interaction. In L. Berkowitz & E. Walster (Eds.), *Advances in experimental social psychology*, Vol. 9. New York: Academic Press, 1976.

INNES, J. M. The semantics of asking a favour: an attempt to replicate cross-culturally. *International Journal of Psychology*, 1974, *9*, 57–61.

JOHNSON, D. A. Equity theory and overpayment: the behavior of children of differing socio-economic backgrounds. Unpublished manuscript, University of California, 1973.

JONES, E. E. *Ingratiation: an attributional approach*. New York: General Learning Press, 1973.

JONES, E. E., JONES, R. G., & GERGEN, K. J. Tactics of ingratiation among leaders and subordinates in a status hierarchy. *Psychological Monographs*, 1963, *77*, whole no. 566, no. 3.

KAHN, A., LAMM, H., & NELSON, R. E. Preferences for an equal or equitable allocator. *Journal of Personality and Social Psychology*, 1977, *35*, 837–46.

KELLEY, H. H., & THIBAUT, J. W. Group problem solving. In G. Lindsay and E.

Aronson (Eds.), *Handbook of social psychology*, 2nd Ed., Vol. IV. Reading, Mass: Addison-Wesley, 1969, pp. 1-101.

KREBS, D. Altruism: an examination of the concept and a review of the literature. *Psychological Bulletin*, 1970, *73*, 258-302.

LANGER, E. J., & ABELSON, R. P. The semantics of asking a favor: how to succeed in getting help without really trying. *Journal of Personality and Social Psychology*, 1972, *24*, 26-32.

L'ARMAND, K., & PEPITONE, A. Helping to reward another person: a cross-cultural analysis. *Journal of Personality and Social Psychology*, 1975, *31*, 189-98.

LAWLER, E. E. Effects of hourly overpayment on productivity and work quality. *Journal of Personality and Social Psychology*, 1968, *10*, 306-14.

LEBRA, T. S. Compensative justice and moral investment among Japanese, Chinese, and Koreans. *The Journal of Nervous and Mental Disease*, 1973, *157*, 277-91.

LEMPERT, R. Norm-making in social exchange: a contract law model. *Law and Society Review*, 1972, *6*, 278-91.

LERNER, M. J. Social psychology of justice and interpersonal attraction. In T. Huston (Ed.), *Perspectives on interpersonal attraction*. New York: Academic Press, 1973.

LEVENTHAL, G. S. The distribution of rewards and resources in groups and organizations. In L. Berkowitz and E. Walster (Eds.), *Advances in experimental social psychology*, Vol. 9. New York: Academic Press, 1976.

LEVENTHAL, G. S., & LANE, D. W. Sex, age, and equity behavior. *Journal of Personality and Social Psychology*, 1970, *15*, 312-16.

LEVENTHAL, G. S., & MICHAELS, J. W. Extending the equity model: perception of inputs and allocation of reward as a function of duration and quantity of performance. *Journal of Personality and Social Psychology*, 1969, *12*, 303-09.

LEVINE, S., & WHITE, P. E. Exchange as a conceptual framework for the study of interorganizational relationships. *Administrative Science Quarterly*, 1960-1961, *5*, 583-601.

LEVINGER, G., & BREEDLOVE, J. Interpersonal attraction and agreement: a study of marriage partners. *Journal of Personality and Social Psychology*, 1966, *3*, 367-72.

LEVI-STRAUSS, C. The principle of reciprocity. In C. Levi-Strauss (Ed.), *Le principle de reciprocité* (Chapter 5). 1949.

LIKTORIUS, A., & STANG, D. Altruism, bystander intervention and helping behavior: a bibliography. *Journal Supplement Abstract Service*, 1975, Manuscript #1096.

MACAULAY, J., & BERKOWITZ, L. *Altruism and helping behavior*. New York: Academic Press, 1970.

MALINOWSKI, B. *Crime and custom in savage society*. London: Routledge-Kegon Paul, 1926.

MARWELL, F., & SCHMITT, D. R. Cooperation and interpersonal risk: cross-cultural and cross-procedural generalizations. *Journal of Experimental Social Psychology*, 1972, *8*, 594-99.

MAUSS, M. *The gift*. Glencoe, Ill.: Free Press, 1954.

McCLELLAND, D. C., & WINTERS, D. G. *Motivating economic achievement.* New York: Free Press, 1969.

MIKULA, G. Nationality, performance and sex as determinants of reward allocation. *Journal of Personality and Social Psychology,* 1974, *29,* 435–40.

MILLER, M. J., BREHMER, B., & HAMMOND, K. R. Communication and conflict reduction: a cross-cultural study. *International Journal of Psychology,* 1970, *5,* 75–87.

MITCHELL, T. R., & FOA, U. G. Diffusion of the effect of cultural training of the leader in the structure of heterocultural task groups. *Australian Journal of Psychology,* 1969, *21,* 31–43.

MORSE, S. J. Help, likeability and social influences. *Journal of Applied Social Psychology,* 1972, *2,* 34–46.

MORSE, S. J., GERGEN, K. J., & GERGEN, M. M. Reciprocity and receiving help. Unpublished manuscript, 1976.

MORSE, S. J., GERGEN, K. J., PEELE, S., & VAN RYNEFELD, J. Reactions to receiving expected and unexpected help from a person who violates or does not violate a norm. Manuscript submitted for publication, 1976.

MORSE, S. J., GRUZEN, J., & REIS, H. T. The nature of equity-restoration: some approval-seeking considerations. *Journal of Experimental Social Psychology,* 1976, *12,* 1–8.

MUIR, D. E., & WEINSTEIN, E. A. The social debt: an investigation of lower-class and middle-class norms of social obligation. *American Sociological Review,* 1962, *27,* 532–39.

NADLER, A., FISHER, J. D., & STREUFERT, S. The donor's dilemma: recipient's reactions to aid from friend or foe. *Journal of Applied Social Psychology,* 1974, *4,* 275–85.

NEWCOMB, T. *The acquaintance process.* New York: Holt, Rinehart and Winston, 1961.

NORD, W. R. Social exchange theory: an integrative approach to social conformity. *Psychological Bulletin,* 1969, *71,* 173–208.

PEPITONE, A., FAUCHEUX, C., MOSCOVICI, S., CESA-BIANCHI, M., MAGISTRETTI, G., IACONO, G., ASPREA, A., & VILLONE, G. The role of self-esteem in competitive choice behavior. *International Journal of Psychology,* 1967, *2,* 147–59.

PEPITONE, A., MADERNA, A., CAPORICCI, E., TIBERI, E., IACONO, G., DiMAJO, G., PERFETTO, M., ASPREA, A., VILLONE, G., FUA, G., & TONNUCCI, F. Justice in choice behavior: a cross-cultural analysis. *International Journal of Psychology,* 1970, *5,* 1–10.

PRUITT, D. G. Reciprocity and credit building in a laboratory dyad. *Journal of Personality and Social Psychology,* 1968, *8,* 143–47.

PRYOR, F. L., & GRABURN, N. H. The myth of reciprocity. In K. Gergen, M. Greenberg, & R. Wills (Eds.), *Behavior exchange: advances in theory and research.* New York: Wiley, in press.

RAPOPORT, A., & CHAMMAH, A. M. *Prisoner's dilemma.* Ann Arbor, Mich.: University of Michigan Press, 1965.

REIS, H. T., & GRUZEN, J. On mediating equity, equality and self-interest: the role of self-presentation in social exchange. *Journal of Experimental and Social Psychology,* 1976, *12,* 487–503.

SAHLINS, M. D. On the sociology of primitive exchange. In Association of Social Anthropologists of the Commonwealth, Monograph 1. *The Relevance of Models for Social Anthropology*. New York: Praeger, 1965, pp. 139–238.

SAMPSON, E. E. Psychology and the American ideal. *Journal of Personality and Social Psychology*, 1977, *35*, 767–82.

SCHOPLER, J. An attribution analysis of some determinants of reciprocating a benefit. In J. Macaulay & L. Berkowitz (Eds.), *Altruism and helping behavior*. New York: Academic Press, 1970, pp. 231–38.

SCHWIMMER, E. G. Exchange in the social structure of the Orokaiva. Ph.D. Dissertation, University of British Columbia, 1970.

SOLE, K., MARTON, J., & HORNSTEIN, H. A. Opinion similarity and helping: three field experiments investigating the bases of promotive tension. *Journal of Experimental Social Psychology*, 1975, *11*, 1–13.

SPECTOR, A. J. Expectations, fulfillment, and morale. *Journal of Abnormal and Social Psychology*, 1956, *52*, 51–56.

STEPHENSON, G. M., & BARKER, J. Personality and the pursuit of distributive justice: an experimental study of children's moral behavior. *British Journal of Social and Clinical Psychology*, 1972, *2*, 207–19.

STEPHENSON, G. M., & WHITE, J. H. An experimental study of some effects of injustice on children's moral behavior. *Journal of Experimental and Social Psychology*, 1968, *4*, 460–69.

STOKES, S. J., & BICKMAN, L. The effect of the physical attractiveness and role of the helper on help seeking. *Journal of Applied Social Psychology*, 1974, *4*, 286–94.

STOLUROW, L. Idiographic programming. *National Society Programmed Instruction Journal*, 1965, *3*, 10–12.

THIBAUT, J. W., & KELLEY, H. H. *The social psychology of groups*. New York: Wiley, 1959.

TJOSVOLD, D. Commitment to justice in conflict between unequal status persons. *Journal of Applied Social Psychology*, 1977, *7*, 149–62.

TRIANDIS, H. C. Subjective culture and economic development. *International Journal of Psychology*, 1973, *8*, 163–80.

————. Some determinants of interpersonal communication. *Human Relations*, 1960, *13*, 279–87.

TRIANDIS, H. C., VASSILIOU, V., & NASSIAKOU, M. The cross-cultural studies of subjective culture. *Journal of Personality and Social Psychology, Monograph Supplement*, 1968, *8*, No. 4, 1–42.

TURNER, J. L., FOA, E. B., & FOA, U. G. Interpersonal reinforcers: classification, interrelationship, and some differential properties. *Journal of Personality and Social Psychology*, 1971, *19*, 168–80.

UGUREL-SEMIN, R. Moral behavior and moral judgment of children. *Journal of Abnormal and Social Psychology*, 1952, *47*, 463–76.

VON GRUMBKOW, J., DEEN, E., STEENSMA, H., & WILKE, H. The effect of future interactions on the distribution of rewards. *European Journal of Social Psychology*, 1976, *6*, 119–23.

WALDMAN, S. R. Exchange theory and political analysis. *Sociological Inquiry*, 1964, *34*, 76–82

WALSTER, E., ARONSON, V., ABRAMS, D., & ROTTMAN, L. Importance of physical attractiveness in dating behavior. *Journal of Personality and Social Psychology,* 1966, 4, 508–16.

WALSTER, E., BERSCHEID, E., & WALSTER, G. New directions in equity research. In L. Berkowitz & E. Walster (Eds.), *Equity theory: toward a general theory of social interaction.* New York: Academic Press, 1976.

WALSTER, E., WALSTER, G. W., & BERSCHEID, E. *Equity, theory and research.* Boston: Allyn and Bacon, 1978.

WEICK, K. E. The concept of equity in the perception of pay. *Administrative Science Quarterly,* 1966, *11,* 414–39.

WILKE, H., & STEUR, T. Overpayment: perceived qualifications and financial compensation. *European Journal of Social Psychology,* 1972, *2,* 273–84.

YUCHTMAN, E. Reward distribution and work-role attractiveness in the kibbutz—reflections on equity theory. *American Sociological Review,* 1972, *37,* 581–95.

5

Cross-Cultural Studies of Small Groups[1]

Leon Mann

Contents

Abstract

In all societies people belong to small primary groups that enforce conformity to norms and require cooperation to achieve group goals. Most work on cross-cultural aspects of small group behavior has sought to test differences between cultures in the scope and intensity of conformity and cooperative behavior. In the main, this research has been conducted by western investigators within a limited range of cultures, with the aid of instruments and procedures developed for laboratory experimentation, e.g., the Asch conformity procedure, the nonzero sum game, the risky shift procedure. Because of these limitations, generalizations about similarities and differences in group behavior across cultures must be made with due caution.

Conformity in the face of group pressure has been found in all countries studied with the aid of the Asch (1956) procedure. The percentage of subjects yielding to group pressure in replications of the Asch study in various countries is approximately 33 percent, the figure obtained in the United States by Asch (1952); thus in Lebanon the rate of yielding was 31 percent, in Hong Kong 32 percent, in Brazil 34 percent (Whittaker & Meade, 1967), and among Fijians 36 percent (Chandra, 1973). A lower frequency has been found in Germany (22 percent) and a higher frequency among Rhodesian Bantu (51 percent) (Timaeus, 1968; Whittaker & Meade, 1967). Anticonformity, the tendency to go against the group, even when it is correct, is rare, but has been found among Japanese subjects who apparently resent the social pressures imposed by an ad hoc group of strangers (Frager, 1970). Two antecedents of conformity have been identified: (a) in subsistence societies, an economic system based on sedentary agricultural or herding arrangements is associated with a high incidence of conformity (Berry, 1967, 1974; Munroe, Munroe, & Daniels, 1973); (b) in tribal societies, cultures with stringent sanctions against deviance are associated with more conformity (Whittaker & Meade, 1967). The existence of a strong peer culture does not necessarily lead to a high level of conformity, as revealed by kibbutz data (Shapira, 1970).

Experimental research on cooperation-competition across cultures has been confined almost entirely to the study of response patterns of pairs or groups of subjects in highly structured game situations, nonzero sum games for adults, and cooperative games for children. So far, unlike the anthropologists who have observed marked differences in intensity of cooperation-competition across cultures (Mead, 1961), experimental psychologists have failed to find systematic differences. Inadequacies of the nonzero sum game as a method for studying cooperation, as well as variations in the exact nature of the game used, may be responsible for the lack of solid research findings on adult cooperation. Research on cooperation among children across cultures has been systematic and cumulative. The data reveal a strong subculture effect, with rural samples in Mexico, Israel, United States, Canada, and New Zealand more cooperative than urban samples (Madsen & Shapira, 1970; Thomas, 1975). No marked differences have emerged between urban samples across cultures in the level of cooperative responses. However, field studies have shown that greater cooperation may be found among children in cultures with no specialized caste or class structure, and where they are assigned meaningful chores (Whiting & Whiting, 1975).

Cultures also vary in other aspects of group functioning: the nature of pressures imposed by groups on deviate members to elicit adherence to group norms; the power of the group of produce attitude and value change by means of group discussion and decision; and the effects of variations in leadership and communication structure on group productivity and morale. Cross-cultural researchers have found a widespread tendency for groups to reject their deviate members (Schachter, Nuttin, De Monchaux, Maucorps, Osmer, Duijker, Rommetveit, & Israel, 1954) and for group decisions to function as a powerful source of commitment on members (Lewin, 1947; Misumi & Shinohara, 1967). The tendency for group decisions made after discussion to be more risky than individual decisions is a widespread western phenomenon that has not been found in African cultures that value caution (Carlson & Davis, 1971). Studies of work groups have shown that in some cultures democratic forms of leadership and participatory types of communication structure are the most preferred and effective, while in others, autocratic and centralized styles of leadership and communication are preferred (Meade, 1967; Misumi, 1972). In all societies the group exerts pressures toward conformity and cooperation. The exact nature and strength of the relationship between the two processes is a problem that awaits investigation.

The Universality of Natural Groupings

Throughout their lives people belong to small primary groups such as the family, play, interest, and association groups, in which interaction between members is face-to-face, intimate, and personal. Such natural groups are found in all kinds of societies at all levels of complexity. The anthropologist Coon (1946) maintained that natural groups are characteristic of all kinds of human beings everywhere, and that the only difference between traditional and modern societies in respect to natural groupings is quantitative. The simpler the society, the greater the role of the primary group; the more complex the society, the more numerous and complex its groups, and the greater the possibility for the individual to join and leave these groups.

In order to make a meaningful analysis of the differences between group behavior across societies, the nature and function of groups must first be recognized. Most of our knowledge regarding small group behavior is derived almost entirely from the study of ad hoc, artificially formed groups of strangers in the laboratory. The laboratory group does have some affinity with the many temporary groupings prevalent in modern society, such as ad hoc committees, study groups, assemblages of ship passengers, and bands of resort vacationers. However, it has little correspondence to any of the groupings that exist in small primitive societies, in which members know one another intimately and interact more or less continuously.

In the most primitive human societies known, such as those of the Andaman Islanders, Tasmanians, Yaghans of Terra del Fuego, Indians of Lower California in the Jesuit days, the family is the only group of any permanency, and beyond it is a slightly larger group of several families that move about together hunting, gathering wild vegetable foodstuffs, fishing and so on. All of the people in such a group know each other intimately. All have found some way of adjusting their several personalities into a working institution (Coon, 1946, p. 164).

Murdock (1949), in a worldwide survey of 241 communities, noted that approximately 16 percent were organized into bands, rather small, mobile and unstable groupings of around fifty people, the members of which regularly fell out and joined or formed other bands. Some groups met only intermittently; among the Plains Indians, for example, the tribe constituted an actual group only during a relatively brief period in the summer when they gathered to kill bison (Honigmann, 1959).

In sum, while groups are a naturally occurring, universal human phenomenon, their continued significance for the individual may vary considerably across societies, so that in small traditional societies the individual may belong to one major group that controls virtually all that affects him, while in larger modern societies he may have membership in many groups, some small and intimate, others large and amorphous, but with the freedom to quit groups, join groups, or form others at different periods of his life. Any attempt to compare small group behavior cross-culturally must take this fundamental difference into account as it sets the limits to any generalization from studies of groups in western societies.

Why is group membership important? In the first place, individuals depend on others for the satisfaction of most needs, and, in turn, the group mediates a variety of goals to its members. Only within the group is food, shelter, sexual satisfaction, and protection against external threats normally provided. In times of stress and danger, people who stay together in a group are better able to sustain themselves than isolated individuals, and the group becomes a source of comfort and reassurance to its members. The group is the avenue for the achievement of goals that require such cooperative efforts as a buffalo hunt (e.g., the Dakota Indians), the building and manning of canoes (e.g., the Maori), and the use of large fish traps (e.g., the Samoans). Groups also allow most members the satisfaction of social needs such as approval, recognition, and friendship, and for some members the fulfillment of power and leadership needs. In larger and more complex societies, individuals may form groups in order to express beliefs and have them confirmed by others. When *objective* reality is not readily accessible, group membership enables the individual to have his opinions and judgments validated by social reality. Festinger (1954) spoke of a drive for social comparison, a need "to know that one's opinions are correct, and to know precisely what one is and is not capable of doing" (p. 217).

All people derive a sense of belonging and support from membership in groups. According to Sherif & Sherif (1964), groups are formed to provide their members with mutual support and to give them a feeling of personal worth. This is the source of the group's power to influence the attitudes and habits of its members.

A number of important social processes arise as a consequence of the interdependence and close ties that occur in primary groups. Conformity to norms is enforced in order to maintain the group's cohesion and stability. Cooperation between members is encouraged in order to ensure that the group moves towards its goals. In order to shape the manner and efficiency with which these goals are realized, the group becomes differentiated along the dimensions of friendship, leadership, communication, and responsibility for tasks.

Because such forms of interaction as conformity and cooperation are crucial to social existence, every society tends to elaborate on them as cultural values, and through the process of socialization, give them tangible expression by producing an individual who, within his group, is at least to some degree conformist and cooperative. There are, of course, differences in emphasis across societies, and to some extent this is a function of the size, complexity, structure, social, and economic resources of the society. But, as Mead (1961) concluded in her review of thirteen "primitive" societies,

> . . . no society is exclusively competitive or exclusively cooperative. The very existence of highly competitive groups implies cooperation within the groups. Both competitive and cooperative habits must coexist within the society. There is furious competition among the Kwakiutl at one stratum of the society—among the ranking chiefs—but within the household of each chief cooperation is mandatory for the amassing of the wealth that is distributed or destroyed. Similarly among the Manus the competitive exchanges between the wealthy entrepreneurs are dependent upon a degree of cooperation within the constellation of related persons who support the leader (p. 460).

Similarly, all societies require some compliance or conformity to the basic values, even when the approved pattern of conduct is basically individualistic (the Ojibwa), competitive (the Kwakiutl), or cooperative (the Zuni). Again, there may be quantitative differences, with strict compliance emphasized more among the predominantly cooperative cultures, and with correspondingly stronger social disapproval for nonconformity. Thus the highly cooperative Dakota Indians and the Zuni of New Mexico use strong public disapproval and gossip (shaming) to punish deviant conduct (see Mead, 1961; Adair & Vogt, 1949).

This chapter on cross-cultural aspects of group behavior begins with a consideration of the group as an agent of socialization, focusing on the role of the peer group. Next is an analysis of conformity responses elicited when the individual is subjected to social pressure by a group of strangers.

This analysis discusses the developmental aspects of conformity across cultures, the significance of ecocultural variables as an antecedent of conformity behavior, and the relationship between conformity and obedience. Groups elicit conformity not only by direct social pressure but also through discussion and exchange of information; accordingly, another section considers the effects of group discussion on member's attitudes and values. The effect of group structure on the productivity and morale of its members and whether the group is led and organized on democratic or authoritarian lines is a related problem to be considered from a cross-cultural perspective. Cultures vary in the nature of their societal arrangements for allocating resources and therefore it might be expected that such variations are reflected in the degree of cooperation or competition maintained between group members as they seek to obtain material rewards. Studies conducted on the level of cooperation in children's groups and adult's groups are dealt with in this chapter. Finally, the analysis of group dynamics is extended to encompass the problem of crowd behavior in different cultures. The chapter concludes with an examination of some needs and shortcomings in the literature on cross-cultural aspects of group behavior.

The validity of cross-cultural comparisons depends on the extent to which the entities arrayed for comparison can be accurately conceptualized and defined as cultures and not blurred with other entities (e.g., nations, socioeconomic classes, rural-urban groups). If the aim is to relate phenomena on a cultural level to those on a social psychological (group) level, then the investigator must be alert to the definition of culture and the precise features of culture that are supposed to influence social behavior—language, economic factors, ecology, urbanization, level of education, child rearing practices, belief systems, and so on. Unfortunately, a good deal of the cross-cultural work involving small groups either ignores this conceptual problem or confounds the operation of culture with some other factor, often social class or urban-rural difference. The tendency to blur culture and subnational entities is pervasive. Recognition of this problem does not, however, ensure that it can be dealt with, for usually there is insufficient empirical data to enable the reviewer to disentangle the specific effects of culture from other factors. This chapter includes a number of studies that could be labeled national and subnational comparisons rather than cultural comparisons.

The reliability of any generalization concerning cross-cultural differences and similarities depends on the validity of the methods employed to make observations relating to the behavior under investigation. (For a full discussion of the methodology employed in cross-cultural psychology see Volume 2 of this *Handbook*.) In the cross-cultural study of group behavior, a variety of methods have been used: these include laboratory experiments in which subjects in artificially formed (ad hoc) groups of strangers interact, are exposed to social pressure, work together on tasks, engage in discussion, and make decisions; gaming studies in which pairs of subjects interact in highly structured situations; questionnaire techniques in which individuals respond alone, while the salience of the group is manipulated; and field observations on social conduct in naturally occurring groups. The validity of cross-cultural comparisons becomes an urgent problem whenever methods are applied directly from one culture to another without due consideration and allowance for their culture-specific associations and limitations. For this reason, throughout the chapter, evaluation of the research methods used by the cross-cultural investigator accompanies the discussion with an assessment of the findings generated by the work.

Crucial for the development of a cumulative field of cross-cultural psychology is the introduction of research designs that generate reliable knowledge about the role and function of groups in different societies. Several major meta-methods have been identified in cross-cultural research (see Strodtbeck, 1964). Within the area of group behavior three meta-methods dictate the research strategy: (a) the search for cross-cultural differences, (b) replication and the search for cultural universals, and (c) serendipitous or hypothesis-generative research. An appendix at the end of the chapter outlines the logic of cross-cultural inquiry into small groups, with examples of the three methods derived from studies discussed in the chapter.

The Group as an Agent of
Socialization

In socializing the individual, culture does not work in the abstract, but rather through its agents—parents and siblings (the family group), teachers, age-mates (the peer group), and so on. This fact provides several linkages between culture and social behavior. Since each of these groups is a culture "carrier" or "transmitter" of values it is important to learn first, when each group achieves prominence as a socializing agent, and second, to what extent each group complements, rivals, or outweighs the influence of other agents of socialization. This chapter focuses on studies of groups consisting of age peers who are relative strangers to one another—accordingly, the peer group is most relevant to the discussion. In many societies the peer group emerges as most influential during the period of adolescence. But this is far from universal. For example, in kibbutz society the peer group, a highly cohesive entity, asserts a significant role from an early age, and steadily increases in importance during middle childhood and adolescence. The second question, which relates to the degree of harmony versus conflict between agents of socialization, takes on greater meaning in societies that are undergoing rapid social and historical change as traditional adult values become challenged by emerging values of youth. There has been some work on this problem as it affected the American youth culture, especially during the 1960s (see Coleman, 1961; Feuer, 1969), but little systematic work on the role of peer group influences has been conducted cross-culturally.

An important experimental program that demonstrates the influence of the peer group is that of Bronfenbrenner and his colleagues (Bronfenbrenner, 1967, 1970a; Shouval, Venaki, Bronfenbrenner, Devereux, & Kiely, 1975; Garbarino & Bronfenbrenner, 1976) who compared the reactions of twelve-year-old children to the rival pressures of peer group norms and adult norms. Bronfenbrenner's procedure was to administer sets of "moral dilemmas" to samples of twelve-year-olds in thirteen countries and then to manipulate the salience of either the school class or parents as a reference group by informing subjects that either their classmates or their parents would get to see their responses. The responses were then scored as either peer oriented or adult oriented.

The Bronfenbrenner dilemmas experiment has been conducted in thirteen countries with widely differing sociopolitical systems and systems of child rearing (Garbarino & Bronfenbrenner, 1976). A considerable amount of interesting data have emerged from this energetic research program (see Table 5-1). For the present discussion, the main interest is in the way children in various cultures responded in the peer pressure condition. Most cultural samples (Czechoslovakia, Poland, Japan, Canada, United States, Israel, Holland, Scotland, and Switzerland) when in the peer condition gave responses indicating a greater readiness to engage in mischievous or antisocial activity as urged by the peers. However the Soviet children, and to a lesser extent the Hungarian and West German children, become more conventionally moral in the peer condition. Although the clusters are not perfect, the major variables that appear to differentiate one group of countries from the other are the qualities of ideological strictness and political centralism. The Communist bloc countries, in particular the Soviet Union and Hungary, are committed to political orthodoxy, and thus conventional moral standards are reinforced by adult and peer pressures. Whereas in western countries, which are pluralistic in orientation, peer pressures strengthen any tendencies toward rejection of the conventional moral response.

These data are suggestive then, of somewhat different socializing roles (at least reference group function) performed by the peer group in different cultures. It has often been asserted that in western Europe and in the United States the peer group frequently acts in opposition to adult values. The Bronfenbrenner data showing the significant effect of peer pressures in shifting responses in a peer direction are consistent with this assumption. However, it would be incorrect to conclude that in the USSR the peer

Table 5-1. Bronfenbrenner's Dilemmas Experiment: Mean Conformity Scores to Conventional, Adult-approved Moral Standards as a Function of Social Pressure under Three Experimental Conditions*

Country	Base Condition	Peer Condition	Adult Condition
USSR			
Boarding School (Collective)	13.82	15.04	15.62
Day School (family)	11.81	12.32	12.49
Hungary	13.28	13.74	15.17
Czechoslovakia	10.36	7.64	10.38
Poland	6.94	3.90	7.60
Japan	3.77	2.90	4.62
Canada	3.58	.91	4.27
West Germany	1.79	2.26	4.43
United States	2.43	1.27	2.96
Israel			
Kibbutz (Collective)	2.26	.62	1.80
City (family)	2.77	.52	1.22
Holland	1.27	.16	2.10
Scotland	1.31	−1.89	1.77
Switzerland	−1.59	−3.91	− .76

* Based on Table 6, Shouval et al., 1975, p. 485. A high score signifies readiness to conform to conventional adult-approved moral standards.

group is weak. In the USSR the peer group endorses the adult value system. From the time children enter school the peer group reinforces desirable societal behaviors through Communist organizations for younger children (the Pioneers) and for adolescents (the Komsomol) (see Mead & Calas, 1955). Social pressure from peers is tantamount to social pressure from adults, and it has a marked effect on producing a more adult response. This research program on social pressures highlights the close relationship between the dominant value system of a culture (in terms of its emphasis on conventional morality) and the role played by the peer group, either as a supporter or opponent of that value system.

In tribal societies there are also considerable variations in the role of the peer group. For example, in some cultures the adolescent male experiences intense peer group contacts and isolation from the parental home as part of tribal initiation rites (Whiting, Kluckhohn, & Anthony, 1958). The point is that cultures vary in the role played by the peer group—both in the intensity of peer group experience and the peer group's position vis-a-vis adult authority. Therefore the meaning and significance of the group as an agent of social control and reinforcement must be taken into account in comparing the results of studies of group behavior derived from different countries.

Culture and Conformity

The aim of socialization in all societies is to induce individuals to conform willingly to the major ways of society and to the groups to which they belong. Although in most societies independence training is introduced in childhood so that the individual is not wholly dependent upon his parents and other adults for the satisfaction of his needs, there is nonetheless substantial pressure on the individual to be conventional in behavior and attitudes. In adulthood, after the person learns what is expected, greater variation in conduct may not only be permitted but encouraged. Rigid conformity is not regarded as ideal behavior in most societies, especially changing societies, because the person may be unable to adjust to changing circumstances. This section examines the tendency of individuals in different countries to yield when put under social pressure by a group of strangers. (Note that very few studies have investigated pressures to conformity in naturally occurring groups in which the individual has ongoing membership).

The problem of maladaptive conformity and independence has been of central interest to cross-cultural researchers since the classic work of Asch (1952, 1956) on individual reactions to majority group pressures. The unexpected finding that 32 percent of a sample of American male students yielded to the majority against their own judgment on at least half of the pressure trials, led some commentators to speculate that Asch had tapped a peculiarly American phenomenon confined to the McCarthyist era of the 1950s. Replications and variations of the Asch experiment both within the United States and in other countries reveal, however, that the disconcerting level of conformity found by Asch is quite widespread. A discussion of cross-national studies that followed the Asch procedure will be presented first and then studies that use other techniques to investigate conformity will follow.

Using the Asch conformity test, Whittaker & Meade (1967) studied conformity in four cultures—Brazil, Lebanon, Hong Kong, and Rhodesia (Bantu). In three of the four countries, the frequency of yielding was remarkably similar to that found by Asch more than a decade earlier in the United States (33 percent): viz. Brazil (34 percent); Lebanon (31 percent); and Hong Kong (32 percent). Only in Bantu subjects from Rhodesia, a tribe with extremely stringent sanctions for nonconformity, was yielding significantly greater (51 percent). Interestingly, among Chinese subjects, for whom yielding and compliance is recognized as a virtue, conformity was not greater than elsewhere. A replication of the Asch procedure in Fiji (Chandra, 1973) obtained a conformity rate of 36 percent among indigenous Fijians. The remarkable similarity of the findings across cultures might indicate that regardless of cultural influences, there is some powerful experimental force that produces the effect. Whittaker & Meade mention possible biases due to the fact that their samples consisted of volunteers. Another possibility is that since the subjects were all college students, they belonged to a relatively homogeneous subculture whose values transcend factors of national background.

Replications conducted in Germany (Timaeus, 1968) and in Japan (Frager, 1970) obtained significantly less conformity than was exhibited by Asch's American students in the early 1950s. Timaeus (1968) predicted on the basis of Lewin's (1948) and Hofstatter's (1963) analysis of the German personality in social situations a lower level of conformity than for Americans. His sample of University of Cologne subjects indeed produced a lower conformity response (22 percent). However, it is possible that age was a factor, as the German students were considerably older (and therefore probably more independent) than the typical American subject (Luck, 1975, personal communication). Frager's study of Japanese conformity is surprising for two reasons. An analysis of the literature led him to expect that in Japan social pressures would be strong and therefore conformity responses prevalent; however, the frequency of conformity responses (25 per cent) was somewhat lower than that found by researchers in other countries. Further, a strong anticonformity response was shown by 34 percent of the subjects; this is the tendency for the subject on neutral trials to call the wrong answer deliberately when the majority give the correct answer—a phenomenon rarely observed in conformity research. This unexpected finding raises some important questions regarding the differing forms that conformity and anticonformity responses might take in various societies, e.g., whether such strong anticonformity is unique to Japanese populations.

An important consideration is the significance to a Japanese subject of an ad hoc group of strangers gathered together in the laboratory. Nakane (1970) and others have commented on the strong loyalty Japanese have to one group and to that group alone. It would be incorrect therefore to conclude on the basis of Frager's findings that the Japanese are in general nonconformist. This striking display of contrary behavior in response to a group of strangers leads us to conclude that in Japan conformity can be elicited only by the natural group to which the individual already owes strong allegiance.

Frager also found that anticonformity was closely related to subjects' scores on an alienation measure. The alienation of Japanese college students was clearly evident in the epidemic of riots and strikes that plagued Japanese campuses in the 1960s. So it is possible that Frager tapped a particularly strong anticonformity theme of that period. If indeed the prevailing climate of alienation and protest has a marked effect on conformity and anticonformity responses, it clearly is no longer acceptable to use

Asch's 1950 findings, obtained in a quieter era, as a standard for comparison. Replication within the culture as well as across cultures is obviously called for, and on a variety of samples, not just students (see Gergen, 1973).

Milgram (1961), using a modified version of the Crutchfield (1955) technique for studying conformity, compared the level of yielding among French and Norwegian students. In one of the experiments students sat in booths and listened to tones through earphones. They then heard what they thought were other subjects expressing judgments about the tones, after which they had to give their own judgment. In reality, what they heard were pretaped judgments made by experimental confederates who had been coached to give incorrect responses on approximately half of the trials. Milgram predicted that the Norwegian students would be more conformist than the French because of the greater cohesion or consensus of Norwegian society as contrasted to the tradition of dissent and argument in French political life. In this study the general climate and institutional values of the two societies were reflected in the level of conformity shown. Across tasks Milgram found between 50–75 percent of Norwegian subjects yielded to the fake majority, while between 34–59 percent of French subjects yielded. Note, however, that the level of conformity displayed by the French students, who enjoy a reputation for independence, was remarkably high, especially considering that the Crutchfield technique ordinarily elicits only modest levels of conformity at least among American subjects. This is a study, then, where the cultural difference is not the sole interest. The level of the response shown provides a goad that at least questions the accuracy of the ethnographic account of French society.

Developmental Aspects of Conformity across Cultures

The manner in which conformity responses develop and function in different countries is another area that has received attention. If conformity is a product of socialization, especially peer group socialization, then conformity may be described and understood developmentally. Shapira (1970) used a variation of the Asch paradigm, which might be called the "misleading peers" procedure, to compare conformity of nine- to eleven-year-old city and kibbutz children in Israel. It might be predicted that if kibbutz children are, by virture of their socialization, more peer group oriented (Spiro, 1958) then they would be more conformist when pressured by their peers. The procedure used by Shapira is highly practical. Each subject is seated with three other children his age. The children are each given books with four lines on a page and are told to say which of the three lines (numbered 1, 2, and 3) is similar in length to the fourth, comparison line. The naive subject always answers last and unknown to all the children, his book differs systematically from theirs. As in the Asch procedure, the subject is forced to choose between responding correctly or "yielding" to the group. On twelve pages there are eight critical trials. Shapira (1970) found no differences in conformity between the kibbutz and city children in this situation, which suggests that the peer group is equally important in both Israeli subcultures.[2]

A study conducted by Kagan (1974) which also used the "misleading peers" procedure compared seven- to nine-year-old rural Mexican children with urban Anglo-American children. The mean number of conformity responses given by the Mexican children (10.4 out of a possible 15) was significantly greater than the number given by American children (5.9 out of 15). However, it is important to note that while 31 percent of the Mexican children completely resisted yielding, not one of the American children remained entirely independent. In brief, if rural Mexican children conformed at all, they were more likely to conform frequently, as against American children who were sporadic in their conformity. It should be recalled that the group in this procedure is naive as to why the subject is making errors, and, as might be expected, the group tends to voice its disapproval. Kagan observed that in the United States there was a greater number and intensity of disapproving comments to the subject. This may have been responsible for the universal tendency among the American children to yield at least once. This finding hints at the intriguing possibility that tolerance for deviation is lower among American children, but the pressures brought to bear are less effective in moulding conformity. Kagan recognized that urban-rural differences and several factors other than "culture" could explain the difference he found. It would therefore be important to replicate this study with such extraneous variables controlled. The "misleading peers" procedure, apart from its ease of administration and psychological impact, is a most promising procedure in that it can be used to study conformity and group pressures simultaneously in one paradigm, thereby bringing together two experimental traditions—group pressure studies (see below) and research on conformity.

A study by Sistrunk, Clement, and Guenther (1971) is one of the few attempts to examine developmental aspects of conformity across cultures. They studied American and Brazilian subjects from nine to twenty-one years old. (Recall that Whittaker & Meade, 1967, found no difference between Brazilian students and Asch's subjects in their conformity study.) Conformity behavior was measured in an Asch-type task in which group "pressure" was conveyed by the experimenter, who informed the subject on critical trials that "the majority of others" chose a certain line as the longest, and that this information could be used "to help in making your choice, or not used, as you wish." Magnitude of conformity produced by this procedure was understandably slight, especially among American subjects, for whom the manipulation virtually failed at every age level. Brazilian subjects, however, showed a modest tendency to conform. It would be worthwhile to replicate this study with a stronger conformity procedure.

Ecocultural variables and conformity

Probably the most important work for the development of a theory of culture and conformity is Berry's (1967, 1974) research into conformity responses in subsistence societies. Berry took as his point of departure Murdock's categorization of subsistence societies into low and high food accumulators (hunters and fishermen *versus* farmers and shepherds). He predicted that high food accumulators would exhibit greater conformity because, in accord with their interdependent economic systems, such societies adopt socialization practices to enforce compliance (see Barry, Child, & Bacon, 1959). For example, the Temne of Sierra Leone are high food accumulators. They raise one crop of rice each year, and the yield is collected by the village to be shared out to each family during the year, according to its requirements and the amount available. Such a system makes for a high degree of interdependence. Consistent with this, the Temne expect strict conformity to norms (e.g., corn must be planted on time, a hungry Temne must follow the rules about the use of the storage bins), punish deviation severely (e.g., accusations of witchcraft are used as a social sanction), and emphasize group reliance. In an Asch-type situation a high incidence of conformity would be expected.

Berry thus looked for the antecedents of conformity behavior in two interrelated variables—the nature of the economy and the severity of socialization practices to elicit compliance. His investigation of conformity among the high food accumulating Temne, the low food accumulating Eskimos of Baffin Island (a society in which hunting is carried out independently in small family groups), and the intermediate Scots, represents a good example of a test of a true culture-related hypothesis. Berry's procedure involves a "false-norm" pressure situation. Each subject takes a test in which a reference line is followed by eight lines of varying length. The subject is asked to say which of the comparison lines is the same length as the reference line. The experimenter offers to "help" the subject by suggesting that most people say it is, for example, the sixth line. The maximum conformity score obtainable is 15. In support of the hypothesis, the high food accumulating Temne had a mean score of 9.04, the Scots 4, and the low food accumulating Eskimos a score of 2.5.[3] It should be noted that Berry's procedure departs markedly from the Asch group pressure procedure, and is indeed not a true group pressure situation. In essence it contains a package of social pressures—a suggestion by the experimenter that certain information is helpful, as well as reference to an alleged majority viewpoint. Thus, cultural differences in (a) response to the demand implied by the experimenter's endorsement, and (b) reaction to the normative implication that "most people" hold a certain position, both enter the situation, and perhaps in unpredictable ways.

Berry (1974) extended research on the effect of ecocultural setting on conformity to encompass high and low food accumulating samples from traditional and transitional cultures including Sierra Leone, Australia, New Guinea, and Canada. The hypothesis that high food accumulating cultures would be associated with high conformity scores on the normative pressure task was again supported, and this occurred for both traditional and transitional cultures. However, a third study (Berry & Annis, 1974), which compared high and low food accumulating cultures among the North Western American Indians, failed to obtain systematic differences in conformity scores. In this region the ecocultural variable had no apparent effect on conformity, possibly because of the very narrow range of cultures investigated, or perhaps because the normative pressure task was unsuitable for the sample.

Other researchers have tested the ecocultural model of conformity behavior. Munroe et al. (1973) investigated the relationship of subsistence economy to conformity in three Kenyan societies; the Kipsigis (a herding society), and the Gusii and the Logoli (two societies with limited herding activities). Consistent with the hypothesis, the Kipsigis conformed more than either the Gusii or Logoli on two "false norm" pressure tasks involving estimates of dots and lines.

Berry & Annis (1974), in summarizing work on psychological differentiation and conformity in subsistence societies, warn of the danger of trying to impose a concept universally. In this important program of research the focus has been confined to cross-cultural comparisons of subsistence societies. But even within this select category, it appears that the relationship between ecosystem and conformity to normative pressure is complex and no doubt complicated by other variables, such as population size and crowding, role differentiation and stratification, and contact with other cultures.

Several comments might be made about the cross-cultural study of conformity. Most of the work, with the exception of Berry (1967, 1974) has focused primarily on Western societies. These studies (e.g., Milgram, 1961; Whittaker & Meade, 1967) have tended to rely on quasi-ethnographic descriptions of national character (e.g., the "independent" French, the "conformist" Japanese) as a basis for the choice of cultural samples and the prediction of how they will differ in response to group pressure. In essence, what these studies seek to do is test and confirm national stereotypes and reputations in a controlled situation by the use of a standardized measure. The ecosystem model, however, begins with the postulate that basic ecological-economic factors govern patterns of socialization that in turn determine levels of conformity. In effect, it offers a true cross-cultural theory from which, given information about the ecology and food gathering habits of a community, it is possible to predict how its members will respond to conformity pressures. The model could be refined, perhaps at the level of (a) distinguishing between cooperative, competitive, and individualistic structured societies (see Mead, 1961), and (b) distinguishing between societies in which the peer group is an active socialization agent (here the Asch procedure might produce high levels of conformity) and those that are almost exclusively adult dominated. Research could also be extended to include the insular Pacific region, in which substantial numbers of high and low food accumulating societies are to be found (see Whiting, 1968). Moreover, the range of procedures for eliciting conformity might be extended to tap various facets of conformity, such as normative conformity (in which yielding is based on the prospect of acceptance or rejection by the group), informational conformity (in which exchange of information indicates a new social reality), and even ingratiation conformity (calculated "yielding" in order to curry favor) (see Deutsch & Gerard, 1955; Jones, 1964). This is important because in some cultures conformity may be based on informational factors (e.g., rapidly changing societies in which the group defines social reality for its members) rather than normative pressures (e.g., traditional societies in which adherence to group norms is rigidly enforced). The Asch procedure and its variants tap predominantly the normative basis of conformity (Allen, 1965). A final point relates to the size of the majority arrayed against the naive subject in the Asch procedure. Asch found in the United States that a majority of three was sufficient to produce the maximum conformity effect; increases in the opposition, even up to a majority of fifteen, produced no increase in the percentage of yielding responses. This intriguing finding, which suggests that a majority of three becomes defined as a social reality for purposes of eliciting conformity, should be tested in other cultures. It is possible that the point at which individuals are coerced into conformity varies from culture to culture: as a function of the number of groups to which individuals belong, previous experience of deviance, and so on. But, it is possible that the "optimal-three" principle may generalize beyond the one or two cultures in which it has been found to constitute a remarkable "law" of social behavior.

Obedience

While the essence of conformity is yielding to group pressure, the process of obedience relates specifically to compliance to authority. Like conformity, obedience may be either productive and adaptive, or mindless and destructive. Milgram (1965) devised a procedure for the study of destructive obedience. His intention was to investigate the predisposition toward obedience among Germans, a problem posed by the inhumane behavior of many German soldiers and citizens during the period of the Third Reich. Milgram's pilot studies at Yale University yielded such startling findings that he never proceeded to the German study but carried out his entire program of research in the United States.

Subsequently, other investigators conducted replications of the Milgram procedure with subject samples in Germany (Mantell, 1971), Italy (Ancona & Pareyson, 1968) and Australia (Kilham & Mann, 1974), but differences in methods of recruitment, subject populations and even procedure make cross-cultural comparisons rather hazardous. Milgram found that 65 percent of his adult male American subjects were fully obedient, i.e., followed the experimenter's orders to administer an extremely painful electric shock to a victim. A similar percentage of Yale undergraduates were fully obedient. In a close replication of the Milgram "base-line" condition in Germany, Mantell (1971) found that 85 percent of a sample of adult Munich males were fully obedient. A replication in Rome by Ancona and Pareyson (1968) also yielded a higher level of obedience than that reported by Milgram. In Australia, Kilham and Mann (1974) studied Sydney University students in a variation of the Milgram procedure. While the level of obedience among males was high (40 percent) it fell below the 65 percent reported by Milgram for his executant condition. It is likely that the *Zeitgeist* in Australia in 1971, a period of widespread public protest against the war in Vietnam, was different from the climate in the United States in 1961 when Milgram conducted his studies. However, there may also be national differences in the ideology of obedience, as suggested by surveys comparing Australian and American responses to the question of obedience to military orders (Mann, 1973) which reveal a significantly higher obedience orientation in the United States than in Australia.

Research on the problem of destructive obedience has an uncertain future, given the understandable concern about the ethical problems raised by the Milgram procedure (see Kelman, 1967; Baumrind, 1964). It is likely then that unless a more acceptable experimental procedure is devised, it will not be possible to investigate experimentally the moral and social factors that bind obedience in different countries. One possibility, however, is the development of procedures in which the subject is ordered by adults to perform nondestructive prescriptive and proscriptive tasks such as "pick up the mess" or "don't touch the box." Such procedures have been used to study obedience in children in the United States (Landauer, Carlsmith, & Lepper, 1970; Minton, Kagan & Levine, 1971) and in the Kikuyu of East Africa (Munroe & Munroe, 1972; 1975). The Munroes' research reveals that the Kikuyu children in comparison with the United

States children were more obedient, which is consistent with ethnographic evidence of strong compliance training in many East African societies (Doob, 1965).

Obedience refers to the action of the person who complies with authority; conformity describes the response of an individual who submits to his peers, people of his own status, who have no special right to direct his behavior (see Milgram, 1974, p. 113). The interest in this chapter is on conformity rather than obedience. However, a relationship between conformity and obedience can be postulated, with the most conformist also tending to be the most obedient people. Indeed, a common assumption in the cross-cultural literature is that some societies, because of their harsh socialization practices, produce a generally dependent type who is compliant to both authority figures (obedience) and to group pressures (conformity), whereas other societies produce an independent type who is capable of withstanding both authority and group pressure. Such an assumption may be valid for integrated societies in which *all* agents of socialization operate in harmony to reinforce each other's goals and values. But in societies in which one agent is dominant, or where agents are divergent in their values (e.g., some Western societies), or where there are sharp discontinuities in practices, the notion of a generally compliant citizen who submits readily to any kind of pressure—from legitimate authority, the natural primary group, ad hoc collections of strangers, etc., may be quite erroneous. Thus it might be possible to find cultures in which high conformity is coupled with low obedience, and *vice versa*. It is tempting to speculate that this might be the case in Germany, where relatively low conformity to a group of strangers (Timaeus, 1968) coincided with high obedience to an experimenter (Mantell, 1971), and perhaps also in Japan where low conformity to a group of strangers (Frager, 1970) may go together with a strong tendency to obey the authority of a single primary group and its leader (see Nakane, 1970). The implication is that in order to understand and predict conformity in different cultures it may be necessary first to analyze the function of both organized and relatively informal group life, especially as it relates to the peer group, in the regulation and control of behavior. Traditional societies in which conduct is strictly regulated by adults and teachers may produce high levels of obedience but still be associated with quite low levels of conformity if the peer group is a relatively unstructured and unimportant social unit.

Adherence to Group Norms

As a condition of retaining group membership the individual is required to change his way of acting or thinking to correspond, at least in some measure, to the group norms. Such adherence is mediated through direct social pressure (the process of normative conformity) and through ex-change of information in the course of interaction (the process of infor-mational conformity). Group norms are enforced by a variety of formal and informal pressures conveyed through discussion and communication between members. This section deals with the effects of group discussion on members' attitudes as studied cross-culturally. Unfortunately, there is little systematic evidence on this question.

Group Pressures on the Deviate Member

In all societies pressure is brought to bear upon deviate group members. Coon (1946) observed that in small traditional societies based on bands of hunter-gatherers, "discordant members are either ejected or they leave voluntarily to form the nuclei of new groups" (p. 164). Again, in more complex agrarian societies, such as the valley-dwelling Riffians of North-ern Morocco where resources are scarce, if a person could not get along easily with other members of the clan he was forced to leave home. He either headed for the city or joined another clan in some distant valley where there was a shortage of manpower. Among the Zuni of New Mex-ico, an agrarian society with a scarcity of land, aggression and pride were regarded as deviant behavior. Shaming and gossip were used to pressure the deviate, and often the most "progressive" members were made to feel so uncomfortable that they left the pueblo (Adair & Vogt, 1949). In most small agrarian societies, public opinion and gossip function as mecha-nisms by which the group maintains adherence to accepted standards of behavior (e.g., the kibbutz).

In western societies also, a variety of social pressures, including argu-ment, criticism, the threat of rejection, and ultimate explusion are used to enforce conformity to group norms. Research on this aspect of group functioning was initiated by Schachter (1951), who found that communi-cation to a member increases in direct relation to the extent of his devia-tion from the group norm. If the group cannot bring the deviant back into line it is likely to reject him. A most ambitious cross-cultural project on the problem of how groups react to their deviate members was carried out by Schachter et al. (1954) in seven western countries—Holland, Sweden, France, Norway, Belgium, Germany, and England in 1952–53. The experi-menters created numerous aviation clubs for boys in each of the countries studied. At the first meeting an interclub competition was announced with a prize offered to the club that built the best model airplane. The experi-menters explained the different models the club members could build to-gether. While almost all of the boys favored working on an attractive model, one member of each group (a stooge-deviator) deliberately insisted that the group work on a rather unattractive glider. Schachter et al. had no specific cross-cultural hypothesis in mind. Rather their intention was to test the generality of the predicted group reaction, a tendency to reject the deviate. This was indeed found in all countries, but the failure of the manipulation to "take" in several countries appears to have caused the investigators some discomfort. Actually, the awkward and less featured aspects of the findings turn out to be perhaps the most interesting. Table 5–2 presents the basic findings of the Schachter et al. study—

1. There were distinct cultural differences in the tendency for groups not to reach uniformity of opinion after discussion, with lack of unanimity most prevalent in England (43 percent), Belgium (34 percent) and Germany (32 percent). The failure of group members to agree among themselves in opposition to the deviate meant, of course, that conditions necessary to pressure and threaten the deviate were missing.
2. A quite unexpected tendency was found for the deviate to win over the majority to his viewpoint, and this varied cross culturally, e.g., 20 percent of British groups ended up coming across to the stooge's preference. The problem of minority influence (Doise, 1969; Moscovici & Faucheux, 1972; Zavalloni, Chapter 3 in this Volume), which has been virtually ignored in the literature, may be of great interest cross-culturally.
3. Cross-national differences occurred in the magnitude of rejection of the deviate, with rejection greatest in France, Norway, and Sweden, and lowest in England and Germany.
4. There was a high degree of correspondence between the tendency to reach uniformity in opposition to the deviate and strong rejection of the deviate. The French and Norwegian data provide an illustration of this; almost all of these groups achieved uniformity and in addition rejected the deviate most intensely.

While alternate conclusions and explanations are possible, including that of methodological nonequivalence, what emerges from the data is that conformity pressures differ across cultures, with pressures highest in France and Norway, lowest in Britain and Germany. These data, when juxtaposed with Milgram's (1961) finding of high levels of conformity among both Norwegian and French students, and Timaeus' (1968) finding of low conformity among his German subjects, add up to a consistent set of data. However, cross-national differences in pressures toward and reactions to conformity may be fragile and ephemeral; this is because the effects obtained are sensitive to cultural changes over time, the kind of tasks and procedures used in the research, and the nature of the samples studied, usually homogeneous groups of students.

Communication and Conflict Reduction

The problem of intragroup differences of opinion is another area to be investigated by cross-cultural researchers (e.g. Hammond, Bonauito, Fau-

Table 5-2. Some Results from the Schachter et al. (1954) Cross-Cultural Experiment on Threats to and Rejection of a Deviate.

	Number and % of groups in which agreement is reached against the deviate (1)	Mean rejection of deviate (2)	% of groups in which members did not reach agreement (3)	% of groups in which members come to agree with deviate
Holland (n=53 groups)	40 (75%)	3.47	13%	12%
Sweden (n=44 groups)	29 (66%)	4.50	25%	9%
France (n=37 groups)	35 (95%)	6.00	6%	0%
Norway (n=40 groups)	32 (80%)	5.09	17%	3%
Belgium (n=38 groups)	24 (63%)	3.88	34%	3%
Germany (n=48 groups)	24 (50%)	2.01	32%	18%
England (n=30 groups)	11 (37%)	3.04	43%	20%

(1) From Schachter et al., p. 408, Table 1.
(2) Only for those groups who reached agreement against the deviate, calculated across all experimental conditions from Schachter et al., p. 423, Table ix.
(3) From Schachter et al., p. 421.

cheux, Moscovici, Frohlich, Joyce, & DiMajo, 1968). The interest in this work is the examination of the role of communication in conflict reduction in various countries. The standard procedure involves the bringing together of subjects with different policies to solve a set of problems. Hammond et al. (1968) found that under conditions of total communication American subjects showed more conflict reduction than did European subjects. However, Brehmer (1970) failed to replicate these findings, and it is probable that procedural differences in the running of American and Western European subjects rather than true national differences were responsible for the pattern of findings in the earlier study (Brehmer, 1974). It would be premature, however, to foreclose on this problem area, as it is likely that people in various countries adopt different strategies, such as appeasement, bluff, aggression, compromise, etc., in the face of interpersonal disagreements, and it is important to investigate this matter.

Group Discussion and Attitude Change

Only a few studies examine *informational* social influence (see Deutsch & Gerard, 1955) cross-culturally. The interest in these studies is whether the social group exerts a greater influence on members' attitudes in certain countries. These studies take as a point of departure anthropological accounts of the significance of group membership in traditional societies (e.g., Hsu, 1953). Meade and Barnard (1973) compared the reactions of United States and Hong Kong Chinese when opposed in their stated opinions by the rest of the group. The experiment was introduced as an "opinion poll," in which the naive subject and five experimental confederates gave their opinions on several social and political issues. The subject was asked to give his opinions first, then each of the stooges indicated why they opposed those of the subject. The experimenter then informed the group that members would have the opportunity to amend their original opinions. It was found that fewer American than Chinese subjects shifted in the direction of the group, but when they did they showed significantly greater amounts of change than the Chinese (note: this is not consistent with Whittaker and Meade's, 1967, finding of no difference in conformity levels between American and Hong Kong Chinese). An incidental finding is that some American subjects showed negative or boomerang shifts reminiscent of the anticonformity exhibited by Frager's (1970) Japanese subjects in a conformity situation. This is indicative of the diversity and heterogeneity of the American sample.

Klauss and Bass (1974) investigated the effects of group discussion on individual opinions cross-culturally. The subjects were an accidental sample of adult male managers participating in training programs in eleven European and two Asian countries (Japan and India). As part of the program, the managers from each country were formed into groups of six to seven members. First, individually, they filled in an "exercise attitudes" questionnaire, after which they took part in a group discussion on their attitudes, the purpose of which was to reach a group rating on each item. Finally, each manager reanswered the questionnaire anonymously. The measure of group influence was the number of subjects who shifted toward the group rating. The investigators found that shifts toward the group position were most prevalent among German and Swiss managers and least prevalent among British and Austrian managers. On a measure of anticonformity (shifts away from the group rating) Japanese managers were especially prominent (see Frager, 1970). Again for the Japanese subjects, it is highly likely that rejection of the group was a function of rejection of any artificial or ad hoc group to which the individual owed no strong allegiance. Apart from sampling difficulties, this study suffers from inadequate reporting of data (only the relative national rankings, not the precise numbers who changed, or magnitude of change was presented).

Group Decisions

One of the pioneering studies on group influence was carried out during World War II by Lewin (1947) who studied the effect of group decision on the attitudes and habits of members of a group toward strongly held, traditional food preferences. A series of experiments was conducted in the United States to induce housewives to prepare intestinal meats, and to feed cod liver oil and orange juice to their babies. In one experimental treatment the housewives heard a lecture on the desirability of these foods given by a nutritional expert; housewives in the other condition participated in group meetings at which they discussed the merits of the foods and were then asked to indicate by a show of hands whether they intended to serve or use these foods. On follow-up checks Lewin found that housewives who had participated in the group discussion and decision session were more likely to serve the recommended foods than housewives who attended the lecture session.

There are many factors that contribute to the effectiveness of group decision—the value of the discussion, the act of making a decision, public commitment, and the degree of group consensus perceived by members (Bennett, 1958), but they are not pertinent here. What is of interest are the numerous replications of Lewin's work in Japan, by Makita (1952) and his collaborators, Misumi (1956) and his coworkers, Misumi and Haraoka (1958, 1960), Misumi and Shinohara (1967), and Haraoka (1970), and the finding that group decision is a powerful technique for producing attitude and habit change in a variety of work settings (see also Tannenbaum, Chapter 7 of this Volume). The study by Misumi and Shinohara (1967) is typical of this research. They used the group decision method to modify the driving habits of Japanese bus drivers and found a substantial reduction in their accident rates. They also compared bus drivers who participated in the program as a group from the same bus depot and those who participated in ad hoc groups. The group decision technique was more successful in reducing the accident rate among the groups whose members knew each other, indicating the significance of the natural group in Japan as well as the importance of continued social supports after the decision is made. An interesting possibility is that the group decision technique would be more powerful among natural Japanese groups because of their intense loyalties than, for example, natural American groups, but less effective among ad hoc Japanese groups than similar American groups.

Unfortunately lacking in this area are cross-cultural studies of traditional and preferred modes of group decision making. In Japan the traditional form of decision making is the *ringi-sei* (Kerlinger, 1951; Nakane, 1970), a kind of consensus system in which all decisions are made "unanimously." The members never vote on an issue but acquiesce to the "will of the group;" subordinates and leaders are bound together in obligations of loyalty, even if they privately disagree. Studies of Japanese managers and foremen (e.g., Cole, 1971) reveal that the *ringi* system is strongly endorsed in Japanese firms and factories (see Tannenbaum's Chapter 7 in this volume). The measures taken to arrive at and implement group decisions and in particular to enforce commitment may indicate something about the significance of group loyalty and the relationship between leaders and followers in different cultures. This is a neglected area that deserves more attention.

Risky Decisions in Groups

Group decision making not only affects attitudes and habits but also functions to alter the kind and quality of choices made by members. The traditional assumption—that groups tend to be more cautious than individuals acting as decision makers—was rejected in the 1960s following the discovery of the risky shift phenomenon, the tendency for members after participation in group discussions about hazardous alternatives to become riskier in their own preferences (see Kogan & Wallach, 1967, for a review of the earlier studies). The risky shift phenomenon has been obtained in numerous laboratories throughout the United States. Indeed, it is a robust and widespread phenomenon, as group shifts of comparable direction and size have been found in many countries with western European cultures, viz., Canada (Vidmar, 1970), England (Bateson, 1966; Fraser, Gouge, & Billig, 1970), France (Kogan & Doise, 1969), Germany (Lamm & Kogan, 1970), Israel (Rim, 1963), and New Zealand (Bell & Jamieson, 1970).

Many explanations for the risky shift phenomenon have been advanced. Brown's (1965) cultural value hypothesis is probably the one of most interest to cross-cultural research. According to this hypothesis, there is a cultural value for riskiness or for taking a chance in contemporary western society. When group members discuss the hazardous alternatives, the information exchanged supports and reinforces this cultural value. This is because individuals want to be at least as risky as their peers. If in the course of discussion they learn that they were not as risky as they thought, they are moved to adhere to the value and shift to a riskier option. A derivation from the hypothesis is that in societies where the dominant culture value is caution the group discussion should lead to a *cautious shift*, especially on the items for which there is a strong cultural "demand" toward wariness and conservatism.

A direct way to test the cultural value hypothesis is to replicate the group discussion procedure in two societies, one with a strong cultural value of riskiness, the other with a strong value of caution. Such a study was conducted by Carlson and Davis (1971) who compared the effect of group discussions on riskiness in the United States (a high risk culture), and Uganda (a low risk culture). The individual decisions of the Ugandan subjects were initially more conservative than those of the Americans, supporting the premise that Ugandans are less favourably disposed to risk taking than Americans. Consistent with the culture-value hypothesis, the group discussion produced evidence of a shift to caution in the Ugandan sample (conservative shifts occured on two of the eleven problems), but in the American sample there was evidence of a risky shift (significant risky shifts were found on three of the eleven problems). This, incidentally, was not as strong an effect as usually obtained for American samples. Gologor (1977) conducted a test of the risky shift hypothesis in Liberia, a conservative African culture, using culturally appropriate items. As predicted by the culture value hypothesis, the majority of shifts were in a cautious direction.

The rather reliable risky shift phenomenon is associated then with the value system of western cultures but not with African cultures. The Carlson and Davis study is a good example of how cross-cultural research can be used to test directly a social psychological hypothesis. It raises several problems, however, including the question of whether the decision tasks, in particular the Choice Dilemmas questionnaire, have the same meanings for subjects in the two cultures, an instance of the emic-etic problem in cross-cultural research (see Brislin, 1976). Since culture determines the situation for which caution in opposition to riskiness is normative, the continued use of the same set of American-devised items to test the risky shift in the United States and in other cultures raises the additional problem of a culture-fair test of the phenomenon (see Cartwright, 1973). This problem is overcome, however, in Gologor's (1977) study.

Group Structure

This section examines the question of the optimal and preferred structures for work, learning, communication, and so on in social groups. The kind of structure preferred by the group's members depends to some extent upon the activity in which the group is engaged, but it is likely that preferred ways of leading and organizing groups varies across cultures. Two dimensions of group structure will be examined in this section—leadership or power, and communication.

Leadership

The classic study on the effect of various types of leadership on group behavior was that of Lewin, Lippitt, and White (1939) in the United States. Clubs of eleven-year-old children were run by leaders who adopted either autocratic, democratic, or laissez-faire methods. Under the autocratic regime, one group became rebellious, the others were cowed into apathy. The democratic leadership produced an involved, well-knit and industrious group of boys. Under laissez-faire conditions the boys became frustrated and bewildered, uncertain of what to do, and morale and group output was low. The investigators found that on questioning the boys all except one preferred the democratic leadership.

Groups operate in a cultural context; the Lewin et al. findings show how the climate of a group has a marked effect on the behavior of members. Replications of the Lewin et al. study have been carried out in East

Germany, India, Hong Kong, and Japan. In East Germany, Birth & Prill-witz (1959) found, as did Lewin et al. in the United States, that boys in the autocratically led groups were most submissive, most dependent upon the leader, and most lacking in group spirit. Meade (1967) argued that the Lewin et al. findings may be limited to countries that emphasize the value of democratic leadership. In cultures with a high degree of authoritari-anism, groups may function better under authoritarian leadership. This assumption was tested in a replication of the "group atmospheres" study in India (a country with a high degree of authoritarianism, see Meade & Whittaker, 1967) with ten- to eleven-year-old Hindu boys as subjects (Meade, 1967). It was found that in the Indian groups authoritarian leader-ship was associated with better morale and higher productivity than dem-ocratic leadership. Boys in the authoritarian led groups had fewer absences, completed their tasks faster, worked better, and were more ap-preciative of their leader than boys in the democratically run group. Meade (1970) extended the study of leadership "climates" to a compari-son of groups of Hong Kong Chinese and Chinese-Americans in Hawaii under conditions of authoritarian, democratic, and laissez-faire leader-ship. It was assumed that Chinese living in an authoritarian culture setting, Hong Kong, would adapt better to an authoritarian group atmosphere. Unlike the Lewin et al. study, Meade's study dealt with attitude change rather than with group morale and productivity. Subjects were required to rank a set of critical issues before and after meeting in discussion groups led by either authoritarian, democratic, or laissez-faire leaders. Among the Hong Kong Chinese, authoritarian leadership produced greater group agreement or cohesion on the issue than did the democratic leadership. The Chinese-Americans, however, showed no difference between the two leadership styles in level of agreement. Unfortunately this study fails to demonstrate, as claimed, that cultural definitions of leadership are re-sponsible for the effectiveness of different leadership styles, as there may be considerable experimental "demand" associated with the procedure employed, a paper and pencil measure of attitudes administered before and after the experimental manipulation.

In Japan, Misumi and his collaborators (Misumi, Nakano, & Ueno, 1958; Misumi and Nakano, 1960a, 1960b; Misumi & Okamura, 1961) have carried out replications of the leadership "climate" studies. The Japanese groups consisted of ten- to eleven-year-old boys who met under the su-pervision of either authoritarian, democratic, or laissez-faire leaders. Mis-umi and Nakano (1960a) found that the authoritarian-led groups were most highly motivated and produced the best products (a finding contrary to that obtained by Lewin et al. for American subjects). Misumi reasoned that the superiority of authoritarian leadership may have been due to the extreme difficulty of the group task, rather than a cultural tendency for the

Japanese to excel under an authoritarian regimen. In a follow-up study (Misumi & Nakano, 1960b) task difficulty was varied across each of the three leadership climates. An interaction effect was found between leadership style and task difficulty, such that the authoritarian-led group produced more and better work on the difficult task, but the democratically led group excelled on the easy task. It appears then that the effect of "social climates" in children's groups is a function of both cultural and task factors. An intriguing possibility suggested by the Japanese data is that in emerging democratic societies, democratic leadership styles will be effective only as long as the problem confronting the group poses no real difficulties.

Communication

Some limited cross-cultural work has also been carried out on the problem of how different communication networks affect performance and satisfaction in groups. This research takes as its point of departure an early study by Leavitt (1951) on American subjects. Leavitt studied four different communication networks that varied in degree of centrality, i.e., the extent to which they forced communication to be routed to one central person. The two patterns of relevance here are the *wheel*, a centralized network, in which one person, the "hub man," is central to the flow of information, and the *circle*, a completely decentralized network in which all members are equally central. Leavitt found that for simple tasks, the wheel produced faster and more accurate problem solving than the circle, but those who worked in the wheel network were far less satisfied than members of the circle net. Shaw (1964) concluded that for complex problems the circle is not only more satisfying but also faster and more accurate.

As for the "social climates" phenomenon, it can be postulated that certain kinds of group structure would be more effective in different societies; specifically, that the rather "democratic" circle method would be more efficient and satisfactory in democratic societies, while the more "autocratic" wheel network would be more efficient in traditional authoritarian cultures.

Hare (1969) initiated cross-cultural research on this question after observing that groups of Ugandan subjects were more efficient in the *circle* than in the wheel network. He examined the problem-solving performance of groups of college students from the United States, South Africa, the Philippines, and Nigeria (Yoruba and Ibo) placed in the circle and wheel networks. Based on anthropological accounts of the authoritarian ethos of the Yoruba (see LeVine 1966), Hare predicted that they would be more efficient in the wheel than in the circle net. However, in each of the five cultural samples problem solving was faster in the "democratic" circle network than in the wheel, consistent with the pattern to be expected for complex problems (see Shaw, 1964).

Kano (1971) conducted a study of communication structure with Japanese subjects, varying the complexity of the problem to be solved by the group. Consistent with Shaw's (1964) analysis, the wheel net produced quicker solutions to simple problems, but the circle was quicker for complex problems. Also consistent with earlier studies, member satisfaction was greater in the circle net than in the wheel net for both kinds of problems. Unlike the group "climate" studies, there is no evidence to suggest that in reputedly more authoritarian cultures (e.g., Uganda, Nigerian Yoruba) the "autocratic" wheel structure will be more efficient or satisfying to participants. We conclude, as for the research on group climates, that the constraints imposed by the difficulty of the task may outweigh cultural factors to determine the kind of communication structure that will enhance group efficiency and satisfaction; alternatively, that the task may be so artificial in some cultures that it precludes obtaining cultural differences.

Cooperation and Competition

Cultures, both traditional and modern, vary in the arrangements made for the distribution of available resources. In some subsistence societies members tend to be selfish and unconcerned with others (e.g., the Siriono Indians of Eastern Bolivia). In other subsistence societies, highly cooperative arrangements are made for the management of scarce food resources (e.g., the Bushmen of the Kalahari desert). In complex modern societies the dominant political-ideological system (e.g., socialism, capitalism, people's democracy) defines the scope of competition and channels its direction between groups.

While some cultures place stronger emphasis on cooperation than others, the question of cooperation and competition within society is complicated by the fact that even competition presupposes some cooperation, and that intragroup harmony may coincide with intergroup rivalry. Moreover, under the pressure of harsh environmental conditions, a traditionally individualistic culture may change temporarily to a cooperative arrangement (e.g., the Eskimo when threatened with starvation; Mead, 1961). Therefore, while cultures vary in the cooperative-competitive nature of their societal arrangements, these differences may not necessarily pervade the activity of all groups within the society. In brief, although a correspondence exists between the overall cooperative-competitive nature of a culture and the kind of social interaction that characterizes its groups, the relationship will not be perfect.

For the most part, cross-cultural studies of cooperation between group members have been confined to the highly structured interactions of pairs of subjects working to achieve gains or avoid losses in a variety of laboratory games. The literature on cooperative behavior in children's groups, which is considered first, is in general more cumulative than the research on cooperation in adults, which relies entirely on gaming techniques.

Cooperation and Competition in Children's Groups

There has been systematic work on cooperative and competitive aspects of children's groups carried out in several countries, including Mexico, Kenya, United States, Israel, Canada, Australia, and New Zealand.

Madsen (1967) devised a set of game procedures for the study of cooperation in two-person and four-person groups. The essential feature of these games is that on a trial by trial basis cooperative turn-taking yields greatest rewards for each child, whereas competition is maladaptive. On the Madsen cooperation board four subjects must coordinate their strings in order to draw a line through a set of designated circles. On the *circle matrix board*, the two players must take turns if they are to maximize the number of prizes won across trials. The *cooperation box* requires two children to work cooperatively if they are to open a hinged box fastened by four spring latches. In the *marble pull apparatus*, each player has a string connected to a marble holder with magnetic inserts. If a tug of war occurs the marble holder comes apart and neither player gets the marble. But across trials, by taking turns in pulling, rewards can be maximized for both players. These procedures overcome most of the problems of artificiality that plague the typical nonzero sum game utilized in the study of adult cooperative behavior. Although they have the same structure, viz., members of the group can earn larger prizes by working together than they can when they compete against each other, they have a quality of realism which makes their face validity readily apparent.

Madsen and his coworkers, Kagan and Shapira, have used these games in a program of experiments on the cooperative behavior of children in Mexico, the United States, Israel, and South Korea (Madsen, 1967, 1971; Kagan & Madsen, 1971, 1972; Madsen & Shapira, 1970; Madsen & Yi, 1975; Shapira, 1970; Shapira & Madsen, 1969, 1974; Shapira & Lomranz, 1972). In this program they systematically investigated cultural differences, urban-rural differences, and age factors as well as differences attributable to the conditions and nature of the experimental game. It was consistently found that four- to eleven-year-old Anglo-American children compete more in these simple games than both Mexican children and Mexican-American children.[4] Indeed, the Anglo-American children showed such pervasive competitiveness that they tended to be irrational and self-defeating. Most American children adopted competitive strategies even when they were nonadaptive, a reflection perhaps of the strong emphasis on competition in the American milieu. Mexican children, on the other hand, exhibited a high level of cooperative, unselfish behavior in these games, consistent with the emphasis on cooperation and control of competition that is a prominent characteristic of Mexican culture (see Romney & Romney, 1963; Madsen, 1964).

The scope of the Madsen project is impressive, but there are methodological flaws. The Anglo-American samples were drawn almost exclusively from Los Angeles, California—rural samples were not taken. In Mexico, rural and urban samples were investigated, but most of the cross-national comparisons were between the rural Mexican sample and urban American sample, a confounding of cultural and subcultural variables. Further, the Mexican rural sample was drawn from the small village of Nuevo San Vicente, Ensanada (population 800), which makes it possible that the Mexican children were well acquainted with each other and therefore accustomed to cooperative interaction. Perhaps the major weakness of the project is the dependence on a single method to generate the data. It is hazardous to seek cultural differences on the basis of a single method, particularly if it involves only one setting, the laboratory. Cultures vary on a myriad of attributes, any of which can interact with the method to generate a difference that reflects the attribute rather than the culture. The Madsen program would be strengthened considerably by the introduction of other methods in other situations, such as observation of free play in field situations (see Sutton-Smith, in Volume 4 of this *Handbook*) and tests of sharing versus hoarding in the classroom to establish the construct validity of the key measure. Methodological weaknesses aside, the irrational competition of the American children, especially the older ones as they interacted under conditions of individual reward, was quite striking, and sets a standard for assessing competitive behavior in groups of children from other cultures.

The work carried out on cooperation and competition in Israel by Shapira and others utilizes the procedure devised by Madsen, but generally avoids the sampling weaknesses of the American-Mexican research. Shapira (1970) drew her Israeli urban sample from ten different schools and drew the kibbutz sample from seventeen different *kibbutzim*. As predicted, kibbutz children (who had grown up together) were more cooperative than a sample of urban Israeli children (who were acquaintances), who were in turn about as cooperative as the urban American children mentioned above (Shapira & Madsen, 1969, 1974). Shapira (1976) found that this difference between kibbutz and city children in level of cooperativeness held up across different ages from five to eleven years. Arab village children in Israel were more cooperative than Israeli urban children, but not as cooperative as kibbutz children (Shapira & Lomranz, 1972).

Put together, these studies in United States, Mexico, Israel, and Korea reveal that cooperation is elicited quite readily under conditions of *group* reward, but under the incentive of *individual* reward, when turn-taking and coordination are required to gain prizes, children from the rural subcultures—Israeli kibbutz, and Arab, Mexican, and Korean villages—continued to cooperate, while children from urban subcultures—American, Israeli, Mexican and Korean cities—began to compete in a nonadaptive manner. The urban Mexican sample was somewhat more cooperative than the American, Israeli, and Korean urban samples, but the major difference to emerge was subcultural rather than cultural—a useful reminder that in making cross-cultural comparisons it is hazardous to draw conclusions from only urban samples.

In Canada, Miller (Miller & Thomas, 1972; Miller, 1973) tested Caucasian and Blackfoot Indian children from nonintegrated schools on the Madsen cooperation board. In the first study, Indian children cooperated effectively while the urban Canadian children competed disruptively. The second study investigated samples of Caucasian and Blackfoot children from an integrated school. The amount of cooperative behavior, similar for both samples of children, fell between the strong cooperation of the Indian children and the weak cooperation of the Caucasian children in the first study. It appears, then, that acculturation and integrated schooling virtually eliminates differences between Indians and Caucasians, at least in cooperative behavior.

Research on children's cooperative behavior has also encompassed Australia and Papua-New Guinea. Sommerlad and Bellingham (1972) compared the performance of samples of Australian aboriginal and white children on the Madsen cooperation board. The value of cooperation, which is stressed in the aboriginal culture, was evident in the significantly greater cooperative responses of the aboriginal children than of the white children. Thomas (1975) investigated samples of New Zealand children using the Madsen cooperation board. In traditional Polynesian and Maori society the value of cooperation is emphasized. Thomas found that Cook Islands children (Polynesian) and rural Maori children were more cooperative than European and urban Maori children. Munroe and Munroe (1977) compared Kikuyu children from a semitraditional community in Kenya with suburban United States children using the circle matrix board. In subsaharan Africa there is a cultural emphasis on children's assistance in cooperative household tasks. This was reflected in a significantly higher level of cooperativeness of Kikuyu children compared to American children.

These studies of cooperation among children in the United States,

Mexico, Kenya, Israel, Canada, Australia, and New Zealand represent a useful contribution to the field of cross-cultural social psychology. The Madsen apparatus offers a standardized and transportable procedure for the study of social interaction in children from a wide age range in many different cultures. The possibility of making comparisons across groups studied by different investigators makes for cumulative research. To this stage, the research reveals that cooperation under conditions of *group* reward appears to be universal; but under the condition of *individual* reward, cooperation is maintained only in those subcultures that emphasize the value of cooperation, viz., the Mexican village, the Israeli kibbutz, the Arab village, the Korean village, tribalized Blackfoot Indians and Australian aborigines, village Polynesians, and Maoris. In urban subcultures of the United States, Mexico, Israel, Korea, Canada, and New Zealand, the prospect of individual reward signalled the onset of competitive and non-adaptive behavior. And, as found in several studies, the older the children, the more competitive and disruptive the interaction. There is a danger that the ease and availability of the Madsen method will generate a host of co-operation-competition studies that achieve little more than the addition of another point of comparison. Apart from the need to establish the construct validity of the method, there is an urgent need to choose cultures for study in terms of their cultural significance on the cooperation-competition dimension. Thus, replication studies in cultures that have undergone rapid and dramatic change from a totalitarian political system to a socialistic one (e.g., Portugal) would be of considerable interest. Also of value would be studies in which the games, work customs, and folklore pertaining to cooperative themes are directly related to responses on standard and validated measures of the cooperation-competition dimension.

Cooperation and Competition in Adult Groups

Virtually all of the cross-cultural work on cooperative behavior among adults is based on mixed-motive games, so called because of the conflict each player experiences regarding the appropriate strategy for choice. Mixed-motive games hold promise because they supposedly capture in miniature some of the dilemmas of cooperation and competition in real life. Critics of the gaming approach to the study of cooperation maintain that findings are specific to the experimental situation, and that the game paradigm is unrealistic. Criticism has also been made by some European social psychologists that the emphasis upon the two-person mixed-motive game in American research has distorted the study of social interaction (Moscovici, 1972; Faucheux, 1976). On the other hand, mixed-motive games may be useful for investigating and comparing cooperative behavior across cultures. McClintock and McNeel (1966) assert that

the advantage in utilizing games to study the motivational basis of cooperation and competition across societies is that the subjects are involved in an
interpersonal task at the time of measurement. The task seems to be a salient
one in most societies since games represent a relatively universal form of social behavior. Furthermore, the technique has the advantage of being relatively language-free, highly reliable, and readily subject to statistical
treatment (1966, p. 412).

Triandis, Malpass, and Davidson (1972) speculate that gaming studies
could provide useful leads concerning the structure of motives in various
cultures, in particular those in which a delicate state of ecological balance
exists and the population must carefully choose whether to interact cooperatively or competitively.

Two games that have been used extensively in cross-cultural research
of cooperative behavior in adults are the Prisoners Dilemma Game (PDG)
and the Maximizing Difference Game (MDG). In the PDG a competitive
choice may be motivated either by a desire to maximize one's own gain or
to maximize the difference in gain vis-à-vis the other person. The MDG
differs from the PDG in that a competitive response must be based solely
on the desire to maximize the difference in gain. Table 5–3, which compares typical payoff matrices for the PDG and the MDG, illustrates the
different pattern of outcomes for competitive choices in the two games.

One of the first cross-cultural studies of cooperative game behavior
was that of McClintock and McNeel (1966) who investigated cooperative
and competitive responses of Flemish-Belgian and American university
students. They found that the Belgian students were more competitive
than the Americans on the MDG—the Belgian students seemed more
concerned with beating the other person than with obtaining the maximum outcomes for themselves.[5] A study by McNeel, McClintock, and
Nuttin (1972) again found a highly competitive orientation among Belgian

Table 5–3. Payoff Matrices for Mixed-Motive Games

	Maximizing Difference Game					*Prisoner's Dilemma Game*	
		Player 2					Player 2
		C_2	D_2				C_2	D_2
Player 1	C_1	6,6	0,5		Player 1	C_1	3,3	0,5
	D_1	5,0	0,0			D_1	5,0	1,1

Note: Payoffs to player 1 appear on the left in each cell. C= cooperative choice; D=competi-
tive choice (from Carment, D., 1974b, 9, p. 214).

students. A third study, by McClintock and Nuttin (1969), compared the behavior of Flemish-Belgian and American school children on the MDG at three different age levels. While American children in grades two and four were more competitive than the Flemish, by grade six children from the two cultures were equally competitive. Taken together with the results from the first study, these findings suggest that at some stage in adolescence the Flemish children begin to overtake American children in competitiveness. No explicit cross-cultural hypothesis guided this research, but it is of significance, first, because it shows the importance of age sampling before broad cross-cultural comparisons can be drawn; second, because it reveals that in some cultures a social process may emerge most strongly late in development; third, that the stereotype of extreme American competitiveness should be placed in perspective by reference to competitiveness in other cultures. However, Faucheux's (1976) critique of research in this area must be taken seriously, especially as it relates to the interpretation of the motives underlying apparently "competitive" responses made by subjects in various cultures.

Research conducted in cultures other than the United States, such as Canada, provides some useful comparisons. Carment (1974a) investigated the behavior of Canadian university students on the MDG. The proportion of competitive responses made by the Canadians (35 percent) was approximately half that found for the Flemish-Belgians (65 percent) in the McNeel et al. (1972) study. In a second study, Carment (1974b) compared Canadian and Indian students from the University of Delhi on the MDG, and found that the Indians gave a significantly higher percentage of competitive responses (55 percent) than the Canadian subjects (35 percent). Another study by Carment (in press) again showed the greater competitiveness of Indian university students than Canadian students; indeed the competitiveness of the Indians was highly similar to that of the Belgians studied by McClintock and McNeel (1966). Druckman, Benton, Ali, and Bager (1976) examined differences in bargaining behavior in India, the United States and Argentina. Indian subjects were highly competitive, more so than either American or Argentinian subjects. The competitive motivation of Indian subjects may suggest a view of the world as containing limited resources, a perception that corresponds to the economic reality of India, an overpopulated country where prospects for adequate employment are low. Again, the underlying motives for subjects' responses in these games must be carefully examined if valid cross-cultural comparisons are to be drawn.

It should be noted, however, that the exact nature of the game and the conditions under which it is played have marked effects on cross-cultural findings. Alcock (1974) for example, investigated sequential bargaining behavior under conditions of time pressure and found that Canadians were more *competitive* than Indians. In another study Alcock (1975) used a "threat game" in which one player believed he was either the "underdog" or the "top dog"; it was found that Indians were more competitive than Canadians in the "top dog" condition, but the reverse held in the "underdog" condition. These findings indicate that it is extremely hazardous to depend entirely on one type of game or measure for drawing conclusions about the competitive tendencies of subjects from different cultures.

The need to use a variety of games before drawing conclusions is further indicated by Meeker's (1970) study of game behavior among adults of the Kpelle tribe of Liberia. Meeker predicted that the traditional Kpelle would be more cooperative than westernized (Kwii) Kpelle. This was indeed the case on the PDG, but not so for the MDG, on which there was no difference between the two samples, both of which were extremely competitive. A noteworthy aspect of this study is that it was possible to adapt the two forms of mixed-motive game for use in a nonwestern, nonliterate culture, suggestive of the interesting cross-cultural possibilities of experimental game research. Bethlehem (1975) has provided further evidence of the tendency for westernization to produce an increase in competitiveness. In a PDG study conducted in Zambia, traditional Tonga subjects were more cooperative than westernized Tonga and Asian subjects.

The opposite of trying to beat the other person is probably "rewarding the other" in which a person can maximize reward for another without cost to himself. L'Armand and Pepitone (1975) examined "other rewarding" behavior in India and the United States, predicting that in India, a society divided on caste and religious lines, the tendency to reward another person would be weaker than in the United States. Indeed, even when Indian subjects had nothing to lose by being generous to a stranger they failed to help. It is possible that the low level of helping in India reflects a strong competitive tendency engendered by a world view of limited resources (see Foster, 1965). (This finding of Indian "competitiveness" when in a benefactor position is consistent with Alcock's (1975) observation that Indians in the "top dog" position in the threat game were highly competitive.) Americans in the benefactor position were quite generous, but once the game was changed to the typical competitive structure, their generosity vanished.

An interesting series of cross-cultural studies on the effects of interpersonal risk and trust in a game situation has been carried out by Marwell, Schmitt, and Shotola (1971), Marwell and Schmitt (1972), and Marwell, Schmitt, and Boyesen (1973). In the first study, Marwell et al. (1971) observed that when the act of cooperation entailed the risk of exploitation very few players chose to cooperate. A replication conducted in the United States and Norway (Marwell & Schmitt, 1972) revealed that while 15 percent of the American subjects cooperated most of the time, not one of the Norwegian students worked cooperatively while under interpersonal risk. However, when subjects played the game with a stooge who followed a totally pacifist-cooperative strategy (Marwell et al., 1973) 92 percent of Norwegian subjects ended up cooperating, as against 55 percent of American subjects. In sum, the Norwegian subjects showed a dramatic reversal from total noncooperation when under risk of exploitation, to almost complete cooperation when confronted by a pacifist-trusting partner. The American subjects, too, showed this change, but it was less dramatic than that of the Norwegians. This interesting series of studies again indicates that conclusions about cross-national differences in cooperative-competitive behavior must be predicated closely upon the exact nature of the game. Beyond that it is clear that even within the same interpersonal situation subjects from different cultures may respond differently to various threats and risks, overtures and strategies.

Interpersonal negotiation and bargaining was investigated in an ambitious gaming study conducted by Kelley, Shure, Deutsch, Faucheux, Lanzetta, Moscovici, Nuttin, and Rabbie (1970) in five laboratories in the United States and laboratories in Belgium, France, and the Netherlands. No clear-cut differences emerged between countries in the effectiveness of negotiation and production of agreement. Instead, the investigators found that the negotiation situation was defined somewhat differently across laboratories, and it was this factor that affected bargaining behavior rather than any cultural differences. Flament (1967), too, found that comparisons between American subjects and French and Belgian subjects on reciprocal giving produced few clear cut differences. Again it was found that the diverse interpretation of the situation by subjects in the various laboratories produced the major effects. Both of these studies are disappointing in that no strong cross-cultural findings emerged. However, they serve as a reminder of the need for representative sampling of laboratories in different countries in order to avoid the pitfalls of making erroneous conclusions about broad cultural differences when subcultural differences may tell a large part of the story.

To summarize: The work on cross-cultural aspects of cooperative behavior in two person mixed-motive games is not a particularly impressive package. To some extent this may be a consequence of the inherent limitations of the gaming model of social behavior. But a review of the work reveals that few, if any, studies were conducted to test specific cross-cultural hypotheses; rather, the countries appear to have been selected for convenience. Moreover, it is clear that the differences observed between cultural samples may be limited to specific games, played by subjects of a certain age and background (college students) in a highly selected sample of laboratories.

Much of the work is further flawed by a failure to specify in detail the nature of the samples in order to determine the comparability of the student subjects across cultures, as well as a failure to examine in close detail the motives and reasons underlying apparently competitive and cooperative responses. One finding to stem from this work is that American subjects, highly competitive in the children's studies, sometimes emerged as more cooperative than Belgians (McClintock's experiments), Norwegians (Marwell & Schmitt's experiments) and Indians (L'Armand & Pepitone). This raises the question of developmental changes in the balance of cooperation and competitiveness in different cultures, a problem hardly touched on in the literature. Beyond that there is the thorny question of how to assess differences in magnitude or level of a response in different cultures. Strictly speaking, reference to differences of magnitude is useful only if the context and meaning of the particular variable is identical in the two cultures. Otherwise, the investigator must be satisfied with statements about the relative order rather than the magnitude of differences. To do more would require a theoretical analysis in which the construct is validated in the two cultures and it is established that in both it has virtually identical meanings.

There is a tendency in the literature in this area for investigators to focus on the common effect, to mask cultural differences behind general trends observed for the majority of subjects (e.g., McClintock & Nuttin, 1969; Kelley et al., 1970). While this may reflect a cautious policy, given the difficulties of achieving exact replication and comparability at research sites in different countries, it can easily produce a false notion of social psychological "universals" in which real cultural differences become blurred or get explained away (see the Appendix to this chapter).

In the study of cooperation it is clear that there is a wide gap between the anthropologist's level of societal analysis (e.g., Mead, 1961) and tightly controlled, highly abstract situations created by the social psychologist to examine social interaction in dyads. If advances are to be made, this area, more than most, is sorely in need of a proper cross-cultural framework and a valid methodology.

A promising approach to the study of cooperative conduct is to be found in the work of Whiting and Whiting (1975) who made field observations of social interaction in free settings. The Whitings have reported data on altruism (i.e. offering help and support, responsible suggestions) among groups of children aged three- to eleven-years-old in six cultures. The observations consist of numerous five minute segments taken over a period of six to nine months. Each altruistic act initiated by the child is tallied, yielding a percentage of altruistic "interacts" for each culture sample. Among three nonliterate cultures (Gusii of Kenya, Juxtlahuaca of Mexico, and Tarong of the Philippines) cooperative and altruistic interaction was very common. The Whitings maintain that in these cultures in which there is no occupational specialization, no federal authority beyond the village, and no caste, class, or priesthood, children must cooperate in order to perform the many chores and responsibilities assigned to them. In the three more complex cultures (Taira of Okinawa, Japan; Rajput of northern India; and "Orchard Town" of Massachusetts, U.S.A.) in which children compete in school and are not assigned responsible farming and household chores, the incidence of altruistic behavior was significantly lower. An important aspect of this research is that it goes beyond the mere reporting of cultural differences to attempt an explanation in terms of the child's role and responsibilities in the society (Whiting & Whiting, 1975).

Intergroup Cooperation and Competition

The matter of cooperation between groups goes somewhat beyond the scope of this chapter, as it deals with the problem of intergroup rivalry and conflict resolution. One research approach that is worth mentioning before concluding this discussion of cooperation and competition in groups is that of the field experiment used in the study of competition and cooperation between specially created groups. The work of Sherif, Harvey, White, Hood, and Sherif (1961) is interesting because it points the way to an alternate experimental approach to the study of social interaction in groups. In the Sherif et al. (1961) Robber's Cave field experiment, twenty-two American boys, all of them strangers, were brought together at a summer camp. The boys were divided into two groups, the "Rattlers" and the "Eagles." After a sense of group solidarity had developed, the investigators (in their role of camp counselors) introduced tugs of war and other contests to build up intergroup rivalry. Within a few days hostility between the two groups was intense and raids, physical and verbal abuse had broken out between members of the two groups. It was only after the investigators introduced a series of emergency situations that required cooperation between the groups for their resolution that hostility subsided and good intergroup relationships were restored. Diab (1970) attempted a replication of the Robber's Cave experiment at a summer camp in Lebanon. On this occasion the "Blue Ghosts" and the "Red Genies" were the two groups formed by the investigator. While the sequence of group behaviors closely paralleled those found in the American study, there was an unforeseen difference, the inability of the investigators to reduce the acute frustration and hostility felt by one of the groups toward the other. Indeed the camp had to be abandoned before intergroup harmony could be restored. Field experiments of this kind, although fraught with obvious hazards, offer an alternate, promising approach to cross-cultural studies of cooperation in groups.

Groups and Collective Behavior

The cross-cultural analysis of group processes can also be extended into the area of crowd behavior, to encompass the forms and meanings of collective episodes in various countries. This area has been ignored by cross-cultural researchers because of the problems associated with studying collective phenomena per se, complicated by the problem of ensuring equivalence of cross-cultural observations. There are, however, some interesting possibilities for research on crowd conduct in different countries.

One possibility is the study of how groups from different countries react in extreme situations, including natural disasters, panics, and prison camps. Probably the major determinant of individual reactions to stressful situations is the availability of the group as a source of support. For example, it might be hypothesized that members of strong peer group cultures will be especially resistant to coercive persuasion when confined together in groups. Consistent with this hypothesis, the lower incidence of collaboration among Turkish prisoners than American prisoners held captive in the Korean POW camps 1951–52 has been attributed, among other things, to the maintenance of a hierarchical group structure among the Turks and to a breakdown of group supports among the Americans (Schein, 1958). Another area of interest is the study of how groups in different cultures cope with natural disaster. Religious beliefs about reincarnation and myths regarding the role of deities in natural events determine reactions of resignation and of panic in the face of impending and actual disasters (see Lachman, Tatsuoka, & Bonk, 1960).

Another aspect of collective behavior that is amenable to cross-cultural analysis is the investigation of common crowd forms, including queues, commuter groups, bystanders, and audiences. The dimensions of conformity and cooperation-competition, which provide a conceptual link between culture and social behavior in the small group, also operate in the larger, anonymous crowd. For example, conformity pressures on commuters to join a bus queue are much more effective in Australia than in the United States and Israel (see Mann, 1970, 1977). Again, the principle of waiting one's turn, which is the essence of cooperation in the queue situation, varies across cultures, so that "queue etiquette," which is highly developed in England is practically nonexistent in some countries (Mann, 1970).

While the more routine and orderly forms of collective behavior are readily investigated by means of surveys, field observation, and field experiments, the less scheduled and ordered forms, such as riots, panics, and rumors can only be approached by means of case study and archival analysis. Cross-national studies of riot behavior in Japan, France, and India (Mann, 1974; Mann & Newton, in press) were based upon the archival analysis of material from newsfilm and newspaper reports. These analyses revealed that in India, a nation with a high level of structural violence in contrast to the other two countries, riot activity was remarkably constant, general and pervasive, involving many groups in society and encompassing many issues.

Across cultures the structural conditions that are conducive to various forms of collective behavior vary considerably. Such factors include population density and norms governing interpersonal distance (conducive to the spread of rumor and panic), climate (which attracts people to public places) as well as the obvious political and social factors that govern the expression or suppression of group protest and demonstration. These factors must be taken into account in any attempt to compare the frequency, forms, and meanings of crowd behavior across countries.

Summary

Here is a brief summary of what is known and not known about group behavior from a cross cultural perspective. Consideration is given to three aspects: group dynamics, conformity and cooperation-competition.

1. The study of group dynamics, initiated in the United States by Lewin and his associates, prompted a spate of replications in other countries, but a systematic transcultural view of group processes has still not developed. Either autocratic or democratic group leadership may be more effective depending upon whether the country is authoritarian (see Meade, 1967) and the task easy or difficult (Misumi & Nakano, 1960b). Across a number of cultures, the most efficient and preferred group structure is the decentralized "democratic" circle rather than the centralized wheel (Hare, 1969; Kano, 1971). Group decision, an effective social influence technique, generalizes beyond the United States to at least Japan (Misumi & Shinohara, 1967; Haraoka, 1970). And the shift to risk after group discussion is a widespread western phenomenon, but is not found in cultures that value caution (Carlson & Davis, 1971; Gologor, 1977). In all cultures studied so far there is a tendency to reject the person who deviates from the group's norm (Schachter et al., 1954). Lacking in the field at present is an understanding of how people come together in groups, how norms emerge, and the factors that underlie group change and transformation.

2. Conformity to group pressures has been found in all countries investigated by means of the Asch procedure or its variants; the incidence of the phenomenon falls within the range of 22 percent to 51 percent (Germany and Rhodesian Bantu respectively). The usual frequency is about 33 percent (the proportion obtained in the United States by Asch): thus,

Lebanon 31 percent, Hong Kong 32 percent, Brazil 34 percent (Whittaker & Meade, 1967), and Fiji 36 percent (Chandra, 1973). Anticonformity, the phenomenon of deliberately going against the group even when it is correct, is uncommon, but emerges quite strongly in Japanese students (Frager, 1970), and to some extent among Japanese managers (Klaus & Bass, 1974), both samples apparently reacting against the ad hoc group of strangers who were trying to pressure them. Among the antecedents of conformity are (a) sedentary agricultural or herding cultures (high food accumulators) as shown in Berry (1967, 1974) for the Temne and others, and by Munroe et al. (1973) for the Kipsigis of Kenya, and (b) tribal societies with stringent sanctions against deviance, e.g., the Bantu of Rhodesia (Whittaker & Meade, 1967). The existence of a strong peer culture does not necessarily produce a high level of conformity (see the kibbutz; Shapira, 1970). While a body of knowledge has emerged on the problem of conformity, largely ignored in the literature is (a) the significance of conformity in natural groups (as distinct from ad hoc or artificially put together groups), (b) the role of conformity in the overall system of compliance, especially in relation to obedience, (c) the distinction between normative and information-based conformity as it relates to different cultures, and (d) sanctions and pressures that arise to elicit conformity.

3. Cross-cultural research on cooperation-competition has been confined, with notable exceptions, such as Whiting and Whiting's (1975) field observations of social interaction, to the study of nonzero sum games (for adult subjects) and cooperative games (for children). Among adult samples, no evidence of systematic or meaningful cross-cultural differences in cooperative behavior has emerged, the exact nature of the game producing apparently contradictory trends. Research on children, which has been more cumulative, reveals (a) a strong subculture effect, with rural samples more cooperative than urban samples, conceivably because of the variable of prior acquaintance in the rural samples, and (b) no marked difference between urban samples across cultures (this may be consistent with findings for adults). Spurts and discontinuities in competitiveness across age groupings occur, as was found for Belgian subjects (McClintock & McNeel, 1966; McClintock & Nuttin, 1969). In general, with age, children of many cultures become less cooperative (Kagan & Madsen, 1971; Madsen, 1971). There has been no real search for the antecedents of cooperative behavior, although it appears that in cultures that stress the value of cooperation (e.g., rural or traditional communities such as the Israeli kibbutz, tribal Australian aboriginals, and Mexican, Kikuyu, Polynesian, and Maori villages) such behavior predominates. Observations indicate that greater cooperation occurs in cultures with no specialized caste or class structure and where children are assigned important chores, e.g., Gusii, Juxtlahuaca, and Tarong (Whiting & Whiting, 1975). In general, the study of intragroup cooperation is at a relatively undeveloped stage and urgently requires a systematic framework to enable specification of the nature of cooperative

interaction across cultures and a methodology for precise, valid investigation.

4. Despite obvious gaps, work on conformity and cooperation processes has received considerable attention, and attempts should be made to tie the processes together conceptually. The key question is the nature of the relationship between conformity and cooperation in various cultures. A close link might be expected in that highly interdependent groups require both conformity and cooperation to realize their goals. It is expected then that in cultures where there are strong pressures toward compliance there would also be pressures toward cooperation. There is evidence of an association between cooperation and conformity, as observed by anthropologists (Zuni, and Dakota Indians; Mead 1961), and found by psychologists (rural Mexican children; Kagan, 1974; periurban Kikuyu children in Kenya; Munroe & Munroe, 1973, 1975, 1977). But this is not universal, as shown for kibbutz children where there is a high level of cooperation (Madsen & Shapira, 1969) but modest conformity (Shapira, 1970). In all societies a certain amount of conformity and cooperation is inevitable, but the exact locus and its magnitude are the questions that remain unanswered. Psychologists and anthropologists might most profitably combine to locate and measure across cultures the interrelationships between social processes, a task that remains to be done.

Conclusion

The literature on cross-cultural group behavior reveals a remarkable ethnocentric imbalance. The field has been dominated by western researchers, studying American samples (at least 75 percent of empirical studies cited in this chapter involved an American comparison), with procedures devised in an American context (e.g., nonzero sum games, the Asch procedure). Even Asian and European researchers have tended to adopt *in toto* these procedures (see Diab, 1970; Misumi et al., 1958, 1960a; Timaeus, 1968). No doubt the impression of American domination of the field is compounded by the limited availability of foreign language journals reporting work in other regions, and a selection process whereby only those researchers who replicate or extend classic American studies come to the attention of the western audience. However, the strong "American connection" in cross-cultural research on social groups is indisputable, and while there are advantages to a firm vantage point, the view of social behavior it affords is inevitably filtered and incomplete.

The argument for broadening and diversifying the problems, procedures, and samples that constitute the cross-cultural investigation of groups can be made on several grounds, namely, as a corrective to the overreliance on American models and approaches (the attack on American social psychology by European social psychologists, e.g., Moscovici, 1972; Tajfel, 1972; and Faucheux, 1976, is interesting in this regard). But more important, it is crucial that knowledge about the diverse processes that underlie group behavior is advanced before unique forms of social organization disappear, and cultures become homogenized under the impact of western influence.

A valid cross-cultural social psychology depends ultimately on the validity of its methods and procedures. In this respect almost total dependence on the laboratory method may retard the field. It is probable that across cultures, individuals view science, experimentation, and the subject role itself, in a variety of ways ranging from curiosity, through fear and suspicion, to resentment. Many of the standard social psychological procedures, such as the use of experimental accomplices or stooges (as in the Asch conformity procedure), the assembly of ad hoc groups of strangers (as in the risky shift experiments), and the requirement to respond in precise and controlled ways, become distorted, even ludicrous, in many non-western culture settings. Frijda and Jahoda (1966) also make this point:

> Much of the work on group behavior would be difficult, if not impossible to replicate in a tribal non-literate culture. This is because such studies usually entail the bringing together of persons unknown to each other, followed by suitable treatments designed to produce particular types of interaction relevant to the hypothesis being tested. The difficulty, rather briefly and crudely, would be that pre-existing social relationship would determine the nature of the interaction; if the people involved did not know each other, they would either seek to find some such basis in terms of remote kinship, or they would have insufficient common ground for effective interaction. It therefore cannot be taken for granted that all experiments do lend themselves to direct cross-cultural replication (p. 112).

The implication is clear: the typical artificially created laboratory group may have little relevance to the study of group behavior in less developed societies. For the meaningful investigation of social behavior in these, and perhaps in all cultures, field studies and field experimentation must become the major research instruments. While the favored social psychology method, laboratory experimentation, still retains an important role, its inherent limitation needs to be recognized.

Appendix

The Logic of Cross-Cultural Inquiry into Small Groups

In a seminal paper, Strodtbeck (1964) analysed the logic underlying various cross-cultural research designs. What follows is an elaboration of Strodtbeck's classification to identify the major types of metamethod in cross-cultural research on small group behavior.

1. *The Search for Cross-Cultural Differences*   On the basis of scope and ratio-nale, three kinds of method can be identified relating to the search for culture differences in group behavior.

a. Studies that predict the *direction* and *magnitude* of the difference between cultures usually stem from a general theory. Each culture selected for investigation varies on the independent variable (such as type of family organization, resource availability, dominant ideology, climate, etc.) to enable a test of a general, culture-related hypothesis. An example is Berry's (1967) test of the relationship between societal food accumula-tion and conformity behavior, with the Temne, Scots, and Eskimos rep-resenting three values on the independent variable. Another example is Carlson and Davis's (1971) test of Brown's culture-value explanation for the risky shift phenomenon which predicted that groups of Americans (risk takers) and Ugandans (cautious) would exhibit a risky shift and a shift to caution respectively. This is the most ambitious and impressive type of cross-cultural research, in that it uses each culture as the equiva-lent of a different experimental treatment, but it is still, unfortunately, a rare occurrence.

b. Differential incidence studies predict the *direction* (but not extent) of the difference between cultures. Frequently the aim of such research is to check and substantiate ethnographic observations about cultural differ-ences on a specific dimension. Put crudely, the social psychologist sets out to check and refine the impressions of nation-watchers (e.g., Gorer, 1955) and the observations of anthropologists. Thus, there is an attempt to establish whether indeed subjects from culture *A* show "more of" standardized behavior *X* than subjects from culture *B*. One example is Milgram's (1961) conformity experiment which predicted, on the basis of national reputations, that Norwegian subjects would conform more than French subjects in Asch-type situations. Another example is Kagan and Madsen (1972), who predicted on the basis of anthropological re-ports that Mexican children would be more cooperative than American children in two-person games. The virtue of this quite common type of research is that it provides a check on the accuracy of observations and impressions about cultures.

c. In a third type, some difference might be expected between cultures (since differences do frequently arise) but no direction or extent is spec-ified. Such studies test for the effect of culture as a variable in much the same way social surveys routinely test the effect of social class, sex, and age variables. Cultures under investigation may be selected quite arbi-trarily, or the choice might be dictated by considerations of conven-ience, availability of research sites, collaborative arrangements, and so on. For all their shortcomings, such studies are useful at an early stage in the development of a field in that they provide the rudiments of a data base. Studies in this category include comparisons of college students from various countries on the Prisoner's Dilemma Game and the Maxi-mizing Difference Game.

2. *Replication and the Search for Cultural Universals*   The fundamental aim of cross-cultural research is ultimately to check the generality of psychological laws and principles of human behavior. The strongest form of transcultural comparison leads to a statement that a behavioral process is universal. A more modest but more realistic statement is that a given behavior is not culture-specific, but generalizes to at least several cultures. An example is Schachter et al.'s (1954) test of how boys' groups in various countries reject deviate members. Investigation of the seven national groups provided an opportunity to conclude that despite unexplained differences, the tendency for deviates to be rejected by their peers is a widespread phenomenon.

Other research of this type is the "other-culture" replication study, a follow-up by an investigator of an earlier finding reported by another investigator in another culture-setting. The aim, implicitly, is to attempt generalization beyond the original culture. A good deal of the risky shift research, as well as replications of Lewin's group decision experiments in Japan by Misumi and others, belongs in this category, raising questions about the applicability of emic concepts and measures closely associated with one culture in the investigation of another; see Brislin (1976).

Frequently investigators who focus on psychological universals are inclined to disregard statistical differences between groups in preference of a conclusion along the line of "we're all remarkably alike." The difficulty, a real one, is that statistical differences may sometimes be more apparent than cultural differences, especially when the cultures sampled fall within a narrow range on the continuum. The basic problem can often be traced to a failure of investigators to specify in advance what constitutes a meaningful cross-cultural difference for the behavior under investigation (and occasionally a confusion between surface differences—a concern with merely ordering cultures on some criterion measure—and common underlying processes—a concern with the psychological relationships basic to human conduct). The matter of establishing criteria for cultural (as distinct from statistical) differences, e.g., rules regarding nonoverlapping distribution, difference ratios, and so on is clearly an important but neglected problem.

3. *Serendipitous or Hypothesis-Generative Research*   The development of new hypotheses is the aim of the researcher who views culture as a locus for the discovery of new categories of experience. Hypothesis-generation is a desirable aspect of any research; as such this type of study is identified post facto when compelling, totally unexpected findings have been unearthed, rather than in advance by its aims. Such research may involve the comparison of several cultures or the systematic examination of a single culture, the investigator implicitly retaining his own culture as a standard for comparison. Single culture studies occasionally produce surprising or

serendipitous findings that stimulate fresh thinking about a social process. Frager's (1970) experiment on conformity in Japan is an example of serendipitous research: surprisingly, one-third of his subjects made anticonformity responses, a finding that contradicts assumptions about Japanese compliance and represents the first observation of anticonformity in the laboratory.

Theory Testing in Group Research

The first method, which conceptualizes culture as an experimental treatment, represents an ideal, in that it presupposes a theory approach to cross-cultural psychology. Its neglect is unfortunate, as prospects for advancement of the field depend largely on this model. Examples of culture-equivalent variables that may prove to be fruitful foci for theory building and testing in the area of group behavior include the following:

1. "guilt" versus "shame" cultures (Benedict, 1946) and their relationship to the kind of group pressures put upon deviate members (e.g., appeals to normative standards versus embarrassment techniques).
2. the relationship between cultures of plenty and want to the tendency to display a shift to risk or caution in group decision making.
3. beleaguered versus secure cultures (Cuba, Israel, Rhodesia versus Sweden, Switzerland, New Zealand) and the degree of ingroup solidarity and belief in the inherent morality of their actions.
4. cultures continually threatened by natural disasters such as floods, disease, and famine versus immune cultures, and the differences placed on individual versus group survival in an emergency.
5. recently victorious versus defeated nations and their preferences for autocratic versus democratic leadership styles (post-World War I Germany, post-World War II Britain).
6. the incidence of rumors, panics and entry stampedes, as a function of cultures that prescribe close versus loose interpersonal distance.

These are examples, some more obvious than others, of potential linkages between culture-equivalent variables and social group processes. The point of the exercise is to indicate that the social psychologist must go beyond the social process itself—conformity, group decision making, leadership preferences—by asking questions about how they vary across cultures, and proceeding to a careful analysis of the characteristics and attributes of cultures. He must remain alert to the key variations that create the conditions for a crucial test of a culture-related hypothesis.

Notes

1. Acknowledgments: Richard Brislin and Harry Triandis for their valuable comments on the manuscript, and to Harumi Befu, John Berry, Helmut Luck, and Ariella Shapira for their useful suggestions.

2. This conclusion is supported by the Shouval et al. (1975) finding that kibbutz and city children responded almost identically on the Bronfenbrenner dilemmas, especially in the peer pressure condition. It is possible, of course, that the incidence of conformity would be greater among kibbutz children than among urban children on tasks that have implications for group goals. The Asch procedure, in as much as it involves a task with no implication for the maintenance of the group's goal, provides an inadequate picture of the kind of conformity pressures that arise when an individual's independence threatens to undermine the group's capacity to achieve its goals. I am grateful to Ariella Shapira for this suggestion.

3. Dawson (1974), in an important paper on cultural pressures toward conformity, has presented some interesting data on the incidence of left-handedness in the three cultures investigated by Berry (1967). Left-handedness might be considered a rather esoteric measure of nonconformity. However, an impressive relationship was found between incidence of left-handedness and Asch-type conformity scores in various samples from the three cultures. The incidence of left-handedness: Eskimo (11.3 percent); Scot (7 percent); Temne (3.4 percent). We surmise that the Eskimos do not attempt to change handedness, whereas Temne parents, who are concerned with strict adherence to norms, punish children who use the wrong hand.

4. McClintock (1974) compared Anglo-American and Mexican-American children on a maximizing differences game, and consistent with the Madsen group, found that Anglo-American children were more competitive than Mexican Americans.

5. Faucheux (1976) has been highly critical of this program of research comparing Belgian and American subjects, arguing that the investigators' American perspective led them to erroneous conclusions. Faucheux reinterpreted McClintock and McNeel's (1966) data, making a crucial distinction between a so-called competitive response, the purpose of which is to enable a player who is behind to catch up and gain equity, as against a truly competitive response in which the player wants to forge ahead of the other. Consistent with Faucheux's distinction, among the Belgians competitive responses were more frequent when subjects were in a losing position than when they were in a winning position; the reverse was true for the Americans. Accordingly Faucheux concluded that the apparent competitiveness of the Belgians reflects more a concern with the nature of the relationship between themselves and the other player, with equity the dominant value, whereas among the Americans the main concern appears to have been a single-minded quest for points.

References

ADAIR, J., & VOGT, E. Z. Navaho and Zuni veterans: a study of contrasting modes of culture change. *American Anthropologist,* 1949, *51,* 547–61.

ALCOCK, J. E. Co-operation, competition and the effects of time pressure in Canada and India. *Journal of Conflict Resolution,* 1974, *18,* 171–97.

———. Motivation in an asymetric bargaining situation: a cross-cultural study. *International Journal of Psychology,* 1975, *10,* 69–81.

ALLEN, V. L. Situational factors in conformity. In L. Berkowitz (Ed.), *Advances in experimental social psychology,* Vol. 2. New York: Academic Press, 1965, pp. 133–73.

ANCONA, L., & PAREYSON, R. Contributo allo studie della agressione: la dinamica della obbedienza distruttiva. *Archiva di psicologia neurologia e psichiatria,* 1968, *29,* 340–72.

ASCH, S. E. *Social psychology.* Englewood Cliffs, N.J.: Prentice-Hall, 1952.

———. Studies of independence and conformity. A minority of one against a unanimous majority. *Psychological Monograph,* 1956, *70,* No. 9 (Whole No. 416).

BAUMRIND, D. Some thoughts on ethics of research: after reading Milgram's "Behavioral study of obedience." *American Psychologist,* 1964, *19,* 421–23.

BARRY, H., CHILD, I. L., & BACON, M. K. Relations of child training to subsistence economy. *American Anthropologist,* 1959, *61,* 51–63.

BATESON, N. Familiarization, group discussion, and risk taking. *Journal of Experimental Social Psychology,* 1966, *2,* 119–29.

BELL, P. R., & JAMIESON, B. D. Publicity of initial decisions and the risky shift phenomenon. *Journal of Experimental Social Psychology,* 1970, *6,* 329–45.

BENEDICT, R. *The chrysanthemum and the sword.* Boston: Houghton Mifflin, 1946.

BENNETT, E. B. Discussion, decision commitment, and consensus in "group decision." *Human Relations,* 1955, *8,* 251–74.

BERRY, J. W. Independence and conformity in subsistence level societies. *Journal of Personality and Social Psychology,* 1967, *7,* 415–18.

———. Differentiation across cultures: cognitive style and affective style. In J. Dawson & W. Lonner (Eds.), *Readings in cross cultural psychology.* Hong Kong: University of Hong Kong Press, 1974, pp. 167–75.

BERRY, J. W., & ANNIS, R. C. Ecology, culture and psychological differentiation. *International Journal of Psychology,* 1974, *9,* 173–93.

BETHLEHEM, D. W. The effect of westernization on cooperative behavior in central Africa. *International Journal of Psychology,* 1975, *10,* 219–24.

BIRTH, K., & PRILLWITZ, G. Fuhrungsstile und Gruppen Verhalten von Schultkindern. *Zietschrift fur Psychologie,* 1959, *163,* 230–301.

BREHMER, B. A note on the cross-national differences in cognitive conflict found by Hammond et al. *International Journal of Psychology,* 1974, *9,* 51–56.

BREHMER, B., AZUMA, H., HAMMOND, K. R., KOSTRON, L., & VARONOS, D. D. A cross-national comparison of cognitive conflict. *Journal of Cross-Cultural Psychology,* 1970, *1,* 5–20.

BRISLIN, R. W. Comparative research methodology: cross-cultural studies. *International Journal of Psychology*, 1976, *11*, 215–29.

BRONFENBRENNER, U. Response to pressure from peers versus adults among Soviet and American school children. *International Journal of Psychology*, 1967, *2*, 199–207.

————. *Two worlds of childhood: U. S. and U. S. S. R.* New York: Russell Sage Foundation, 1970a.

————. Reaction to social pressure from adults versus peers among Soviet day school and boarding school pupils in the perspective of an American sample. *Journal of Personality and Social Psychology*, 1970b, *15*, 179–89.

BROWN, R. *Social psychology.* New York: Free Press, 1965.

CARLSON, J., & DAVIS, D. M. Cultural values and the risky shift: a cross-cultural test in Uganda and the United States. *Journal of Personality and Social Psychology*, 1971, *20*, 392–99.

CARMENT, D. W. Effects of sex role in a maximizing difference game. *Journal of Conflict Resolution*, 1974a, *18*, 461–72.

————. Indian and Canadian choice behavior in a maximizing difference game and in a game of chicken. *International Journal of Psychology*, 1974b, *9*, 213–21.

————. Indian and Canadian choice behavior in a mixed-motive game as related to score feedback and sex of subjects. *International Journal of Psychology* (in press).

CARTWRIGHT, D. Determinants of scientific progress: the case of research on the risky shift. *American Psychologist*, 1973, *28*, 222–31.

CHANDRA, S. The effects of group pressure in perception: a cross-cultural conformity study. *International Journal of Psychology*, 1973, *8*, 37–39.

COLE, R. E. *Japanese blue collar: the changing tradition.* Berkeley, Calif.: University of California Press, 1971.

COLEMAN, J. S. *The adolescent society.* New York: Free Press, 1961.

COON, C. S. The universality of natural groupings in human societies. *Journal of Educational Sociology*, 1946, *20*, 163–68.

CRUTCHFIELD, R. S. Conformity and character. *American Psychologist*, 1955, *10*, 191–98.

DAWSON, J. Ecology, cultural pressures toward conformity and left-handedness: a bio-social psychological approach. In J. Dawson & W. Lonner (Eds.), *Readings in cross cultural psychology.* Hong Kong: University of Hong Kong Press, 1974, pp. 124–29.

DEUTSCH, M., & GERARD, H. A study of normative and informational social influences upon individual judgment. *Journal of Abnormal Social Psychology*, 1955, *51*, 629–36.

DIAB, L. N. A study of intra-group and intergroup relations among experimentally produced small groups. *Genetic Psychology Monographs*, 1970, *82*, 49–82.

DOISE, W. Intergroup relations and polarization of individual and collective judgments. *Journal of Personality and Social Psychology*, 1969, *12*, 136–43.

DRUCKMAN, D., BENTON, A. A., ALI, F., & BAGER, J. S. Cultural differences in bargaining behavior: India, Argentina, and the United States. *Journal of Conflict Resolution*, 1976, *20*, 413–52.

FAUCHEUX, C. A critique of cross-cultural social psychology. *European Journal of Social Psychology*, 1976, *6*, 269–322.

FESTINGER, L. A theory of social comparison processes. *Human Relations*, 1954, *7*, 114–40.

FEUER, L. *The conflict of generations: the character and significance of student movements.* New York: Basic Books, 1969.

FLAMENT, C. Representations dans une situation conflictuelle: Étude inter-culturelle. *Psychologie Française*, 1967, *12*, 297–304.

FOSTER, C. Peasant society and the image of the limited good. *American Anthropologist*, 1965, *67*, 293–315.

FRAGER, R. Conformity and anti-conformity in Japan. *Journal of Personality and Social Psychology*, 1970, *15*, 203–10.

FRASER, C., GOUGE, C., & BILLIG, M. Risky shifts, cautious shifts and group polarization. *European Journal of Social Psychology*, 1970, *1*, 7–30.

FRIJDA, N., & JAHODA, G. On the scope and methods of cross-cultural research. *International Journal of Psychology*, 1966, *1*, 110–27.

GARBARINO, J., & BRONFENBRENNER, U. The socialization of moral judgment and behavior in cross-cultural perspective. In T. Lickona (Ed.), *Morality: a handbook of moral development and behavior.* New York: Holt, Rinehart and Winston, 1976.

GERGEN, K. J. Social psychology as history. *Journal of Personality and Social Psychology*, 1973, *26*, 309–20.

GOLOGOR, E. Group polarization in a non-risk taking culture. *Journal of Cross-Cultural Psychology*, 1977, *8*, 331–46.

GORER, G. *Exploring English character.* London: Cresset Press, 1955.

HAMMOND, K. R., BONAUITO, G. B., FAUCHEUX, C., MOSCOVICI, S., FROHLICH, W. D., JOYCE, C. R. B., & DIMAJO, G. A comparison of cognitive conflict between persons in western Europe and the United States. *International Journal of Psychology*, 1968, *3*, 1–12.

HARAOKA, K. Group decision and behavioral change, II. In K. Haraoka, *Social psychology of attitude change.* Tokyo: Kaneko Shobo, 1970, pp. 166–74.

HARE, A. P. Cultural differences in performance in communication networks in Africa, the United States, and the Philippines. *Sociology and Social Research*, 1969, *54*, 25–41.

HOFSTATTER, P. R. *Einfuhrung in die Sozialpsychologie.* Stuttgart: Alfred Kroner, 1963.

HONIGMANN, J. S. *The world of man.* New York: Harper & Row, 1959.

HSU, F. L. K. *Americans and Chinese: two ways of life.* New York: Abelard-Schuman, 1953.

JONES, E. E. *Ingratiation.* New York: Appleton-Century-Crofts, 1964.

KAGAN, S. Field dependence and conformity of rural Mexican and urban Anglo-American children. *Child Development*, 1974, *45*, 765–71.

KAGAN, S., & MADSEN, M. C. Experimental analyses of cooperation and competition of Anglo-American and Mexican children. *Developmental Psychology*, 1972, *6*, 49–59.

———. Cooperation and competition of Mexican, Mexican-American and Anglo-American children of two ages under four instructional sets. *Developmental Psychology*, 1971, *5*, 32–39.

KANO, S. An experiment on the interaction of communication structure variables with task variables upon group problem solving efficiency and morals. *Japanese Journal of Educational Social Psychology*, 1971, *10*, 55–66.

KELLEY, H., SHURE, G. H., DEUTSCH, M., FAUCHEUX, C., LANZETTA, J. T., MOSCOVICI, S., NUTTIN, J. M., & RABBIE, J. M. A comparative experimental study of negotiation behavior. *Journal of Personality and Social Psychology*, 1970, *16*, 411–38.

KELMAN, H. C. Human use of human subjects: the problem of deception in social psychological experiments. *Psychological Bulletin*, 1967, *67*, 1–11.

KERLINGER, G. Decision making in Japan. *Social Forces*, 1951, *30*, 36–41.

KILHAM, W., & MANN, L. Level of destructive obedience as a function of transmitter and executant roles in the Milgram obedience paradigm. *Journal of Personality & Social Psychology*, 1974, *29*, 696–702.

KLAUSS, R., & BASS, B. M. Group influence on individual behavior across cultures. *Journal of Cross-Cultural Psychology*, 1974, *5*, 236–46.

KOGAN, N., & DOISE, W. Effects of anticipated delegate status on level of risk taking in small decision making groups. *Acta Psychologica*, 1969, *29*, 228–43.

KOGAN, N., & WALLACH, M. Risk taking as a function of the situation, the person, and the group. In G. Mandler (Ed.), *New directions in psychology*, Vol. 3. New York: Holt, Rinehart and Winston, 1967.

LACHMAN, R., TATSUOKA, M., & BONK, W. Human behavior during the tsunami of May 23, 1960. *Science*, 1960, *133*, 1405–09.

LAMM, H., & KOGAN, N. Risk taking in the context of intergroup negotiation. *Journal of Experimental Social Psychology*, 1970, *6*, 351–63.

LANDAUER, T. K., CARLSMITH, J. M., & LEPPER, M. Experimental analysis of the factors determining obedience of four-year-old children to adult females. *Child Development*, 1970, *41*, 601–11.

L'ARMAND, K., & PEPITONE, A. Helping to reward another person: a cross-cultural analysis. *Journal of Personality and Social Psychology*, 1975, *31*, 189–98.

LEAVITT, H. J. Some effects of certain communication patterns on group performance. *Journal of Abnormal Social Psychology*, 1951, *46*, 38–50.

LEVINE, R. *Dreams and deeds: achievement motivation in Nigeria.* Chicago: University of Chicago Press, 1966.

LEWIN, K. Group decision and social change. In T. Newcomb & E. Hartley (Eds.), *Readings in social psychology.* New York: Holt, Rinehart and Winston, 1947.

———. Some social psychological differences between the U. S. and Germany. In K. Lewin, *Resolving social conflicts.* New York: Harper & Row, 1948, pp. 3–33.

LEWIN, K., LIPPITT, R., & WHITE, R. Patterns of aggressive behavior in experimentally created "social climates." *Journal of Social Psychology*, 1939, *10*, 271–99.

MADSEN, W. *The Mexican-Americans of south Texas.* New York: Holt, Rinehart and Winston, 1964.

MADSEN, M. C. Cooperative and competitive motivation of children in three Mexican sub-cultures. *Psychological Reports*, 1967, *20*, 1307–20.

———. Developmental and cross-cultural differences in the cooperative and competitive behavior of young children. *Journal of Cross-Cultural Psychology*, 1971, *2*, 365–71.

MADSEN, M. C., & SHAPIRA, A. Cooperative and competitive behavior of urban

Afro-American, Anglo-American, Mexican-American and Mexican village children. *Developmental Psychology*, 1970, *3*, 16–20.

MADSEN, M. C., & YI, S. Cooperation and competition of urban and rural children in The Republic of South Korea. *International Journal of Psychology*, 1975, *10*, 269–74.

MAKITA, M. Comparative study on lecture and group decision in motivating a desired behavior. *Japanese Journal of Educational Psychology*, 1952, *1*, 84–91.

MANN, L. Social psychology of waiting lines. *American Scientist*, 1970, *58*, 390–98.

———. Attitudes towards My Lai and obedience to orders: an Australian survey. *Australian Journal of Psychology*, 1973, *25*, 11–21.

———. Cross-national aspects of riot behavior. In J. Dawson & W. Lonner (Eds.), *Readings in cross cultural psychology.* Hong Kong: University of Hong Kong Press, 1974, pp. 327–37.

———. The effect of stimulus queues on queue-joining behavior. *Journal of Personality and Social Psychology*, 1977, *35*, 437–442.

MANN, L., & NEWTON, J. Rioting in India, France, and Japan: an analysis in terms of structural violence and force-type. *International Journal of Group Tensions*, in press.

MANTELL, D. M. The potential for violence in Germany. *Journal of Social Issues*, 1971, *27*, 101–12.

MARWELL, G., & SCHMITT, D. R. Cooperation and interpersonal risk: cross-cultural and cross-procedural generalizations. *Journal of Experimental Social Psychology*, 1972, *8*, 594–99.

MARWELL, G., SCHMITT, D. R., & SHOTOLA, R. Cooperation and interpersonal risk. *Journal of Personality and Social Psychology*, 1971, *18*, 9–32.

MARWELL, G., SCHMITT, D. R., & BOYESEN, B. Pacifist strategy and cooperation under interpersonal risk. *Journal of Personality and Social Psychology*, 1973, *28*, 12–20.

McCLINTOCK, C. G. Development of social motives in Anglo-American and Mexican-American children. *Journal of Personality and Social Psychology*, 1974, *29*, 348–54.

McCLINTOCK, C. G., & McNEEL, C. P. Cross-cultural comparisons of interpersonal motives. *Sociometry*, 1966, *29*, 406–27.

McCLINTOCK, C. G., & NUTTIN, J. M., Jr. Development of competitive game behavior in children across two cultures. *Journal of Experimental Social Psychology*, 1969, *5*, 203–18.

McNEEL, C. P., McCLINTOCK, C. G., & NUTTIN, J. M., Jr. Effects of sex-role in a two-person mixed-motive game. *Journal of Personality and Social Psychology*, 1972, *24*, 372–78.

MEAD, M. (Ed). *Cooperation and competition among primitive peoples.* Boston: Beacon Press, 1961.

MEAD, M., & CALAS, E. Child-training ideals in a post-revolutionary context: Soviet Russia. In M. Mead & M. Wolfenstein (Eds.), *Childhood in contemporary cultures.* Chicago: University of Chicago Press, 1955, pp. 179–203.

MEADE, R. D. An experimental study of leadership in India. *Journal of Social Psychology*, 1967, *72*, 35–43.

———. Leadership studies of Chinese and Chinese-Americans. *Journal of Cross-Cultural Psychology*, 1970, *1*, 325–32.

MEADE, R. D., & BARNARD, W. A. Conformity and anticonformity among Americans and Chinese. *Journal of Social Psychology*, 1973, *89*, 15–24.

MEADE, R. D., & WHITTAKER, J. O. A cross-cultural study of authoritarianism. *Journal of Social Psychology*, 1967, *72*, 3–7.

MEEKER, B. F. An experimental study of cooperation and competition in West Africa. *International Journal of Psychology*, 1970, *5*, 11–19.

MILGRAM, S. Nationality and conformity. *Scientific American*, 1961, *205*, 45–52.

————. Some conditions of obedience and disobedience to authority. *Human Relations*, 1965, *18*, 57–76.

————. *Obedience to authority.* New York: Harper & Row, 1974.

MILLER, A. G. Integration and acculturation of cooperative behavior among Blackfoot Indians and non-Indian Canadian children. *Journal of Cross-Cultural Psychology*, 1973, *4*, 374–80.

MILLER, A. G., & THOMAS, R. Cooperation and competition among Blackfoot Indians and Urban Canadian children. *Child Development*, 1972, *43*, 104–10.

MINTON, C., KAGAN, J., & LEVINE, J. F. Maternal control and obedience in the two-year-old. *Child Development*, 1971, *42*, 1873–94.

MISUMI, J. *Group dynamics in Japan.* The Japanese Group Dynamics Association. Faculty of Education, Kyushu University, Fukuoka, Japan, 1972.

MISUMI, J., & HARAOKA, K. An experimental study of group decision (II). *Research Bulletin of Faculty of Education*, Kyushu University, 1958, *5*, 61–81.

————. An experimental study of group decision (III). *Japanese Journal of Educational Social Psychology*, 1960, *1*, 136–53.

MISUMI, J., NAKANO, S., & UENO, Y. An experimental study of group decision (I). *Research Bulletin of Faculty of Education*, Kyushu University, 1956, *4*, 17–26.

————. A cross-cultural study of the effects of democratic, authoritarian, and laissez-faire atmosphere in children's groups (I). *Research Bulletin of Faculty of Education*, Kyushu University, 1958, *5*, 41–59.

MISUMI, J., & NAKANO, S. A cross-cultural study of the effect of democratic, authoritarian, and laissez-faire atmosphere in children's groups (II) and (III). *Japanese Journal of Educational Social Psychology*, 1960a, *1*, 10–22; and 1960b, *1*, 119–35.

MISUMI, J., & OKAMURA, N. A cross-cultural study of the effect of democratic, authoritarian, and laissez-faire atmosphere in children's groups (IV). *Japanese Journal of Educational Social Psychology*, 1961, *2*, 65–70.

MISUMI, J., & SHINOHARA, H. A study of effects of group decision on accident prevention. *Japanese Journal of Educational Social Psychology*, 1967, *6*, 123–34.

MOSCOVICI, S. Society and theory in social psychology. In J. Israel & H. Tajfel (Eds.), *The context of social psychology: a critical assessment.* New York: Academic Press, 1972, pp. 17–68.

MOSCOVICI, S., & FAUCHEUX, C. Social influence, conformity bias, and the study of active minorities. In L. Berkowitz (Ed.), *Advances in experimental social psychology*, Vol. 6. New York: Academic Press, 1972, pp. 150–202.

MUNROE, R. L., & MUNROE, R. H. Obedience among children in an African society. *Journal of Cross-Cultural Psychology*, 1972, *3*, 395–99.

————. Cooperation and competition among East African and American children. *Journal of Social Psychology*, 1977, *101*, 145–46.

————. Levels of obedience among United States and East African children on an experimental task. *Journal of Cross-Cultural Psychology,* in press.

MUNROE, R. L., MUNROE, R. H., & DANIELS, R. E. Relation of subsistence economy to conformity in three East African societies. *Journal of Social Psychology,* 1973, *89,* 149–50.

MURDOCK, G. P. *Social Structure.* New York: MacMillan, 1949.

NAKANO, C. *Japanese society.* Berkeley, Calif.: University of California Press, 1970.

RIM, Y. Risk-taking and need for achievement. *Acta Psychologica,* 1963, *21,* 108–15.

ROMNEY, K., & ROMNEY, R. The Mixtecans of Juxlahuaca, Mexico. In B. Whiting (Ed.), *Six cultures.* New York: Wiley, 1963.

SCHACHTER, S. Deviation, rejection, and communication. *Journal of Abnormal and Social Psychology,* 1951, *46,* 190–207.

SCHACHTER, S., NUTTIN, J., DEMONCHAUX, C., MAUCORPS, P. A., OSMER, D., DUIJKER, H., ROMMATVEIT, R., & ISRAEL, J. Cross-cultural experiments on threats and rejection. *Human Relations,* 1954, *7,* 403–39.

SCHEIN, E. H. The Chinese indoctrination program for prisoners of war. A study of attempted "brainwashing." In E. E. Maccoby, T. M. Newcomb, & E. L. Hartley (Eds.), *Readings in social psychology* (3rd ed). New York: Holt, Rinehart and Winston, 1958, 311–34.

SHAPIRA, A. Competition, cooperation and conformity among city and kibbutz children in Israel. Unpublished doctoral dissertation. University of California, Los Angeles, 1970.

————. Developmental differences in competitive behavior of kibbutz and city children in Israel. *Journal of Social Psychology,* 1976, *98,* 19–26.

SHAPIRA, A., & LOMRANZ, J. Cooperative and competitive behavior of rural Arab children in Israel. *Journal of Cross-Cultural Psychology,* 1972, *3,* 353–59.

SHAPIRA, A. & MADSEN, M. Cooperative and competitive behavior of kibbutz and urban children in Israel. *Child Development,* 1969, *40,* 609–17.

————. Between and within group cooperation and competition among kibbutz and non-kibbutz children. *Developmental Psychology,* 1974, *10,* 140–45.

SHAW, M. E. Communication networks. In L. Berkowitz (Ed.), *Advances in experimental social psychology,* Vol. I. New York: Academic Press, 1964.

SHERIF, M., HARVEY, O. J., WHITE, B. J., HOOD, W. R., & SHERIF, C. W. *Intergroup conflict and cooperation: the robbers' cave experiment.* Norman, Okla: University of Oklahoma Press, 1961.

SHERIF, M., & SHERIF, C. W. *Reference groups: exploration into the conformity and deviation of adolescents.* New York: Harper & Row, 1964.

SHOUVAL, R., VENAKI, S., BRONFENBRENNER, U., DEVEREUX, E. C., & KIELY, E. Anomalous reactions to social pressure of Israeli and Soviet children raised in family versus collective settings. *Journal of Personality and Social Psychology,* 1975, *32,* 477–89.

SISTRUNK, F., CLEMENT, D. E., & GUENTHER, Z. C. Developmental comparisons of conformity across two cultures. *Child Development,* 1971, *42,* 1175–85.

SOMMERLAD, E., & BELLINGHAM, W. P. Cooperation-competition: A comparison of Australian, European, and Aboriginal school children. *Journal of Cross-Cultural Psychology,* 1972, *3,* 149–57.

SPIRO, M. E. *Children of the kibbutz.* Cambridge, Mass.: Harvard University Press, 1958.

STRODTBECK, F. Considerations of meta-method on cross-cultural studies. *American Anthropologist,* 1964, *66,* 223–29.

TAJFEL, H. Experiments in a vacuum. In J. Israel & H. Tajfel (Eds.), *The context of social psychology: a critical assessment.* New York: Academic Press, 1972, pp. 69–119.

THOMAS, D. Cooperation and competition among Polynesian and European children. *Child Development,* 1975, *46,* 948–53.

TIMAEUS, E. Untersuchungen zum sogenannten konformen Verhatten. *Zeitschrift fur Experimentelle und Angewandte Psychologie,* 1968, *15,* 176–94.

TRIANDIS, H., MALPASS, R. S., & DAVIDSON, A. R. Cross-cultural psychology. *The Biennial Review of Anthropology,* 1972, *24,* 1–84.

VIDMAR, N. Group composition and the risky shift. *Journal of Experimental Social Psychology,* 1970, *6,* 153–66.

WHITING, B. M., & WHITING, J. W. *Children of six cultures: a psychocultural analysis.* Cambridge, Mass.: Harvard University Press, 1975.

WHITING, J. W. Methods and problems in cross-cultural research. In G. Lindzey & E. Aronson (Eds.), *Handbook of social psychology,* 2nd ed., Vol. 2. Reading, Mass.: Addison-Wesley, 1968, 693–728.

WHITING, J. W., KLUCKHOHN, R., & ANTHONY, A. The function of male initiation ceremonies at puberty. In E. Maccoby, T. Newcomb, & E. Hartley (Eds.), *Readings in social psychology.* New York: Holt, Rinehart and Winston, 1958.

WHITTAKER, J. O., & MEADE, R. D. Social pressure in the modification and distortion of judgment: A cross-cultural study. *International Journal of Psychology,* 1967, *2,* 109–13.

6

Social and Cultural Change[1]

J. W. Berry

Contents

Abstract

Although social and cultural change is studied predominantly in other social science disciplines, a developing role for psychology has been recognized by both those other disciplines and psychology. A schematic model is proposed that makes a number of distinctions, among which are differences between the sociocultural and individual locus of change and differences between psychological antecedents and psychological consequents of change. Some conceptual problems are reviewed in order to disentangle such value-laden notions as "development" and "modernization"; in addition, the universality and linearity of change are questioned. The chapter then considers some representative studies of psychological antecedents to change (including modern attitudes, achievement motivation, and some personality and learning approaches) and some psycholog-

211

ical consequents of change (including "shifts" in cognitive, personality, and attitudinal variables, and the rise of "acculturative stress"). The review concludes with suggestions for reorienting the field of enquiry, and for pursuing some urgent research questions.

Why a Psychology of Social and Cultural Change?

One of the largest research traditions in the social sciences is the study of social and cultural change. Economics, political science, sociology, demography, and anthropology all have been concerned with both the origins and impact of changes in their respective variables, be they cultural, institutional, or behavioral. With such a large-scale onslaught, it would be reasonable to expect to find comprehensive and perhaps integrative treatments of the topic in the literature. However, such is not the case; if any notice is taken of variables from another discipline, it is usually only to indicate that the author is aware of other levels of analysis.

Increasingly, these nods of recognition are in the direction of psychological variables. There appears to be a growing awareness among many social scientists that economic or institutional analysis is insufficient to deal with the phenomena of social and cultural change. Increasingly, theoretical and empirical attention is being paid to individual and behavioral variables, both by other social scientists and psychologists.

This chapter brings together this growing literature, viewed conceptually and critically from the perspective of cross-cultural psychology. As such, it shares the same defect noted in the writings from other disciplinary points of view; it makes no claim to be comprehensive in scope, nor integrative of material from more than one discipline. Indeed, it does not consider all the available topics that have been studied within cross-cultural psychology. For example, the phenomenon of the adjustment of returning students (e.g., Eckensberger, 1972; Brislin & Van Buren, 1974) is not touched, and studies of immigrant adaptation (e.g., Gordon, 1964; Taft, 1977) are covered only in selected topical areas. Even the massive changes that have occurred in Japan (e.g., Caudill, 1976; Wagatsuma, 1975) and China (e.g., Fried, 1976; Inkeles, 1976; Rin, 1975) are largely ignored, as are studies that focus on sociological and political change (e.g., Feieraband, 1969).

From this list of exclusions, the reader may legitimately ask: what is there left to include? The answer constitutes a statement of focus and of bias: the chapter is largely devoted to the psychological study of social and cultural change among Third World people, most of whom are (or until recently have been) operating at subsistence-level, and who have been (or who still are) subjected to Western influences over the past three to four hundred years. This particular focus potentially covers all of the Western Hemisphere, Africa, Oceania, and much of Southeast Asia; it is largely to these areas that first anthropologists and now cross-cultural psychologists have directed their attention.

While acknowledging a bias toward people that usually have been studied by anthropology, the chapter will attempt to deal with conceptualizations that are commonly employed in the other social sciences; a later section will outline the approaches to change that these other disciplines have taken. For the present, it is necessary to indicate only the approach taken here: change is an alteration in culture (including language and custom), and in behavior (including beliefs, attitudes and values) which takes place in a group. Although it is possible to propose a distinction between social change and cultural change (de Vos, 1976, p. 8), because this chapter deals primarily with the individual and his behavior, no such general division will be maintained. Rather social and cultural change will be considered as a single cluster, distinct from behavioral or psychological change.

A Preliminary Analysis

Given the need to attend to some basic sociocultural features of change, it may be asked: which aspects of these broader questions have a priori implications for psychological variables? The answer to this question may provide a guide through the massive literature, but it may also blind researchers to unexpected relationships. Despite this hazard, the area of social and cultural change, and its literature, is so voluminous that some preliminary analysis is essential; this section analyses and structures the field so that it is more amenable both to psychological analysis and to the review of the psychologically related materials.

A reading of most of the basic treatises in the area of social and cultural change suggests five major distinctions of psychological import: locus, source, direction, dynamics, and sequence.

Locus

The first issue pertains to the location of change and its level of analysis. Broadly, there are three different loci: *sociocultural, institutional,* and *individual*. At the sociocultural locus, social change involves large systems (such as nations, regions, or cultural groups) and the level of analysis tends to be anthropological, political, economic, or macrosociological. At the institutional locus, social change involves economic or governmental institutions, and the level of analysis tends to be in economic or sociological terms. At the individual locus, social change involves attitudinal, motivational, or cognitive variables, and the level of analysis tends to be socio-psychological or psychological (see Kelman & Warwick, 1973). The focus in this chapter, of course, will be on the individual locus but for reasons that were stated previously, the two broader ranges are necessarily implicated in any analysis of change at the individual locus or at the psychological level of analysis.

Source

A second question is essentially concerned with the source of change. Although no change event may be attributed to a single *external* or *internal* source, it is useful to keep them distinct for conceptual purposes. In general, external sources of change lie in cultural diffusion or development programmes, while internal sources reside in the internal social or psychological dynamics of the cultural or social group. This distinction is an important one, for there tends to be an overwhelming emphasis on external sources in the literature; by drawing this distinction at the outset, more attention may be directed towards internal sources.

Direction

In the discussion of conceptual problems the cultural biases inherent in such terms as *traditional* and *modern* will be examined and an attempt to comprehend some basic dimensions of change will be made. However, here it is sufficient to consider three general directions of change: (1) the direction of becoming "modern" in the usual sense of urbanization and homogenization of world cultures; (2) the direction of a "traditional" life style, when there is a reaffirmation of characteristic values; and (3) some "novel" life style on a dimension that is independent of the usual "traditional-modern" axis. This distinction will have important implications in the consideration of measurement problems.

Dynamics

Numerous writers have distinguished between the *processes* of change and the *states* that exist at some point during the process. Nevertheless, many others appear confused, confusing such terms as "modernization" (a process over time) and "modernity" (a state that results from the process of modernization). This distinction is very important, for it raises serious methodological and research difficulties: the study of the process requires a dynamic conceptualization and a longitudinal design, while the study of the state may only require cross-sectional research.

Sequence

Finally, the distinction made between cause and effect is perhaps most important when working at the individual level. It is useful to separate the psychological *antecedents* from the psychological *consequents* to change, even when the same kind of behaviour is being considered. For example, achievement motivation may be both an antecedent and a consequent of a successful development programme, but some other phenomenon (for example, psychological stress) may also be a consequent. For practical reasons such a distinction is also worth making, for much of the psychological research has been carried out from one or another of these perspectives, but rarely from both.

These five distinctions have been employed in this chapter to assist in the structuring of the voluminous material available. During a first attempt at integrating the material, a schematic overview was developed that provided a fairly simple structure; this is illustrated in Figure 6-1.

Three separate features of this schematic overview should be kept in mind: the first is the *structure*, the second is the set of *relationships*, and the third is the *content*. With respect to the structure, the overview is arranged into two levels (the *sociocultural* and the *individual*, with the *institutional* subsumed under the former); it is arranged horizontally by *sequence* (with *antecedents* on the left and *consequents* on the right). Both *external* and *internal* sources are indicated at the left. All blocks indicate *states*, while lines indicate *processes*. Thus all five features that were considered in the preliminary analysis appear in the scheme.

With respect to relationships, the lines all indicate two-way flows. For example, for diffusion to occur there must be interaction between two cultural systems. The scheme also considers both cultural-behavioral interactions and the mutual behavioral influence of outsiders and indigenous residents. These four sources that are considered to be *antecedent* then enter into an interaction with the *consequents;* however the major direction of influence is stronger from antecedent to consequent than the return influence. Finally a mutual interaction is envisaged between the changed sociocultural system and the changed behaviors.

Third, with respect to content, since the primary interest is the individual, most of this review will focus on that level. Nevertheless, at the sociocultural level a number of variables are implicated: ecological setting and economic resources, political development (among internal sources), and technology and formal education (among external sources). Other implicated features are the relationships between the two cultures, particularly the demographic factors of migration and population dominance, and the nature of intergroup relations (whether plural or monistic and whether positive or hostile).

At the level of individual behavior, a number of psychological vari-

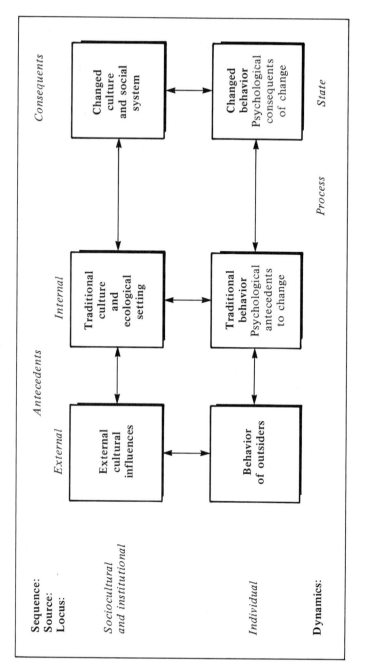

Figure 6–1: Schematic Model of Relationships among the Locus, Source, Direction, Dynamics and Sequence of Change.

ables are important. Among the external antecedents are the behaviors and beliefs brought by educators, missionaries, traders, and colonial officials. Among the internal antecedents are such psychological features as attitudes toward change, achievement orientation, and other personality characteristics. Finally, among the consequents, two classes of behaviors are apparent: (1) *behavioral shifts* are the changes in behavior toward new norms; and (2) *acculturative stress* refers to the disorganization or even disintegration of behavior that often (but not inevitably) accompanies social and cultural change.

Approaches from Other Disciplines

Anthropology

Given the strong theoretical and research ties between cross-cultural psychology and anthropology, it is appropriate to begin this brief overview of other approaches with that discipline. In broad terms, there are two paradigms for research: the first, *acculturation,* has had the longest history and the greatest theoretical impact, while the second, *development,* is a more recent and a more applied orientation.

Perhaps the two best sources for the acculturation paradigm are the classic treatise by Herskovits (1938) and the early attempt to formulate the concept made by the Social Science Research Council (USA) in 1954. The process of acculturation involves the mutual influence of two autonomous cultural systems. Changes are induced in both systems as a result of the diffusion of cultural elements in both directions. However, usually the flow of culture is not balanced, but is stronger in one direction than the other. This imbalance often leads to the view that acculturation is really the process of one culture dominating another; despite this observed imbalance, the concept itself still refers to a two-way flow.

Discussing acculturation in these terms suggests that it is merely an additive or subtractive process, that cultural elements are added or taken away in units that predate the cultural exchange process. However, this relatively static interpretation is not appropriate to the phenomena: "Acculturation is . . . neither a passive nor a colorless absorption. It is a culture-producing as well as a culture-receiving process. Acculturation . . . is essentially creative" (Social Science Research Council, 1954, p. 985). Acculturation is not just an *external* process, but one that triggers dynamics *internal* to the cultural groups involved; the impetus may derive from external sources, but the continuing process is carried on with dynamic resources.

This fairly positive view, however, must be balanced with a statement about the frequent negative consequences of acculturation. In addition to adding new cultural elements, and stimulating new cultural developments, acculturation can also bring about serious cultural disintegration and loss. Sociocultural systems may become stressed to a point where adaptive changes become difficult or impossible (SSRC, 1954, p. 986; Spradley & Phillips, 1972). Thus, the frequent occurrence of cultural breakdown with acculturation has led to the view that the process is inevitably destructive to one of the cultural systems involved.

In summary, the acculturation paradigm within anthropology has been employed to refer to mutual cultural exchange and influence, sometimes imbalanced and destructive, but also containing the possibility that creative and novel cultural forms will develop. Its importance lies not only in its frequent use in anthropological studies of social change, but also as one of the most common conceptualizations in psychological studies of social change.

More recently, as part of a more general movement toward the application of social sciences, the *development* paradigm has come to the fore. These programmes have involved the deliberate changing of a culture in one particular direction, induced by forces *external* to that culture. In a sense, it is "acculturation by design," in which the nature of the eventual cultural adaptation is specified in advance. The direction of change (development) "represents an increase in the capacities of a society to organize for its own objectives, and to carry out its programmes more effectively" (Belshaw, 1972, p. 83). As Belshaw points out, the key to the change is *organization;* "one society is developed and another undeveloped (when) the former is, by comparison with the latter, able to make much more complicated decisions and to do more complicated things" (Belshaw, 1972, p. 83). Although often confused with notions of being "primitive" or "civilized" or with ideas of "cultural evolution," development essentially refers to the process of increasing the complexity and integration of a set of cultural elements; being developed is the state or condition of having a high level of complexity and integration. Defined and approached in such a way, the use of the term *development* in anthropology becomes relatively value-free, and avoids the great ethnocentric problems inherent in such terms as "underdeveloped" or "modernization."

In summary, the development paradigm is a more limited, controlled, and applied approach to change than that of acculturation. Its importance lies not only in its increasing use within anthropology, but also in its relationship to many psychological studies of the process. However, psychologists have not been as wary of value judgments in its use as anthropologists; but this relatively neutral conceptualization within anthropology will serve as a guide to the analysis of psychological studies of "psychological modernity."

Sociology

There are two general paradigms in sociological studies of change: *structural* and *developmental*. The former is largely concerned with an analysis of internal relationships within the structure of a society, while the latter is related to a concern for development, often within the subdiscipline of "rural sociology."

Although structural changes in society are the most general and basic phenomena, this paradigm apparently has had less interest for psychologists than the more applied issues. Nevertheless, it is important to note the fundamental work carried out by Eisenstadt (1973, Chapter 6) and Rogers (1973) among many others. This approach tends to define change as "the process by which alteration occurs in the structure and function of social systems" (Rogers, 1973, p. 76). This process proceeds through communication and diffusion of innovations within the society. Innovations are defined as ideas, practices, or objects which are new (Rogers, 1973). The spread of these innovations is in part determined by the structural and functional features of the society, and they in turn stimulate structural and functional societal change. Although somewhat abstract, this kind of analysis has demonstrated the interdependence of social change and social structure, and has been useful in applied work in the area of agricultural and family planning programmes.

Of greater importance for the psychological study of change has been the sociological approach to development. At the core of the approach are four basic requirements (Balandier, 1972, p. 71): (1) investigation of the structural characteristics of the society (the structural approach); (2) identification of the dynamics that operate within those structures and are potentially capable of bringing about changes in them; (3) detection of the processes at work; and (4) determination of the external relations of the society. When each of these has been examined, applications of specific programmes that are directed toward change may be attempted. Not so clear in the sociological literature, however, is the *goal* of development; is it societal complexity, economic growth, or political stability? Although the conditions of its study have been clearly outlined (and serve its psychological study well), the direction of change is left unspecified. Perhaps this is in the interest of a value-free social science, or (more likely) perhaps it is due to the unarticulated assumption that development inevitably means "modernization." This major issue will be confronted in the following discussions and again in the section on conceptual problems.

Political Science

As this brief overview proceeds from anthropology through sociology to political science, the notion grows that change or development implies some unitary end state, most often termed "modernization" (Apter and Mushi, 1972). This tendency is illustrated by Eisenstadt (1973, Chapter 4) who argues that political modernization involves "the development of a highly differentiated political structure . . ." (p. 74) the "extension of the scope of the central legal, administrative and political activities . . ." (p. 74) "the continuous spread of potential political power to wider groups in the society—ultimately to all adult citizens" (p. 74), and ". . . . the weakening of traditional elites. . ." (p. 74). Supplementing this view is that of Deutsch (1969) who considers that modernization tends to lead to national integration. These dual trends of differentiation and integration are conventional constituents of the process of development at many levels of analysis (including the biological). However, the second element may not always accompany the first; as Lijphart (1975) noted, the rise of ethnic nationalism and regional loyalties in many "modern" states raises important questions about the linearity of change. It may be that initial tendencies toward homogenization will give way to later particularistic reactions. This point is important for the psychological study of social change, for it raises the important question of the linearity of the process of social change, and it serves as the basis for a discussion of psychological studies of attitudes toward assimilation and integration.

Economics

Finally in this overview, we have the discipline with the clearest position on the questions confronting us: economic development involves the growth of production and wealth. Such

> narrow economism made people think that the rapid growth of productive forces would, once firmly established, set in motion the whole development process which would expand more or less spontaneously to take in all branches of human activity (Sachs, 1972, p. 51).

Often this single approach is considered as a necessary condition, and occasionally it is designated as a sufficient condition for development in other sociocultural levels. This narrow identity is important here primarily because it has laid the foundation for numerous psychological studies of change that focus on economic behavior, its basis in personality, and its intentional modification.

Over the course of this set of brief summaries of approaches in other social science disciplines, it was noted that social change tends to be viewed as development, and development tends to be viewed either as "modernization" or as economic development. Although it is important to note these trends and their potential contribution to the psychological study of social change, it is even more important to consider how limited these approaches have become. If the "preliminary analysis" is taken as a general statement of the complexities of social change phenomena (and even that analysis was necessarily limited), the empirical *focus* is found largely at the sociocultural or institutional level (ignoring the individual or behavioral) and the *direction* has primarily been in terms of modernization (ignoring traditional reactions and novel forms). A more balanced view of *sources* was evident, with external origins of change being only slightly emphasized over internal resources. A balanced view of the *sequence* was also evident, with both antecedents and consequents being considered. Finally, the *dynamics* of change were well considered, particularly in the sociological approach. However, there remains a major conceptual problem (one which is accompanied by a measurement problem) that will be discussed next: how is it that the literature of social change has become so identified with the concept of "modernization"?

Some Conceptual Problems

There are essentially three conceptual problems at the sociocultural level of analysis that have not been adequately resolved in the literature. Of course it is not possible to resolve them here, for a large-scale reexamination of the basic concepts is currently underway (e.g. Desai, 1971; Eisenstadt, 1973, Chapter 5; Poggie & Lynch, 1974). However it is possible to make their conventional current use explicit so that the study of social and cultural change at the individual level may be viewed in the context of these three problems: (1) the *value-laden* nature of the concepts of development and modernization, (2) the *universality* of the process and states which mark the various stages of the process, and (3) the *linearity* of the change.

At the sociocultural level of analysis, the identification of social change with development has not been a recent phenomenon. As Nisbet (1971, pp. 98–99) pointed out, "social change was conceived after the pattern of organic growth" as early as classical times. This approach ". . . formed the essential character of a way of envisaging social and cultural change . . . that was to become one of the master ideas of Western thought." However the narrower identification of development with modernization appeared during and following the period of Western colonial expansion (Omvedt, 1971, p. 122). The valuing of development and modernization as "progress" is inherent in both approaches (Srinivas, 1971, p.

149). The historical and intellectual basis of this identification has been located by Mazrui (1968, p. 69) in the tradition of "social Darwinism," complete with its overtones of "racism and ethnocentrism" (p. 70). The forms of social and cultural change most often studied are not value-free; indeed the study may be seen as a normal outgrowth of the values of the Western society in which the social science traditions have been developed. None of this is to say that the study is wrong, naughty, or even neo-colonial; however the value bias is clearly present, and it is important to recognize it at this point, before the psychological literature is examined.

A second problem is in the *universality* of the phenomena of social change. Are the paths and end states similar everywhere all the time? Are "traditional" and "modern" end states the poles between which all societies and individuals pass? Is the path or process similar in all cases? At least three varieties of answers may be discerned in the literature. The first asserts that both process and end states are everywhere similar, that certain features of traditional life are the same, that the modern goals are shared, and that common steps are (or need be) taken to move between the two poles. A second position states that there are only local and unique phenomena, that traditional cultures vary widely, that goals that are sought vary as well (and may indeed not be "modern") and that the steps taken en route must necessarily vary. And finally a third general position maintains that the process and endpoint are similar everywhere, but care must be taken in considering the probable existence of traditional cultural variation at the beginning point. All three positions are maintained by those studying individual behavior in relation to social change, and the question of the "universality" of the process is perhaps the most important of present questions.

Third, is the process of change essentially *linear*, or is there a "reaffirmation" of tradition following exposure to acculturative influences. As early as 1961, Jahoda was reporting such reaffirmation phenomena in West Africa, and much earlier Park (1928) considered one resolution to marginality to be "to swing about and reaffirm" one's traditional culture. More recently, Gusfield (1967) has drawn up "seven fallacies" in the "linear theory of social change," including assumptions about traditional homogeneity, and conflict between "traditional" and "modern" forms of behavior. Even more recently, Kavolis (1970) suggested:

> . . . either that the process of modernization of the personality is in some respect being reversed after modernization has been accomplished or that the conceptualization of psychological modernization is too narrow and has never encompassed all of the essential transformations of the personality during modernization (p. 435).

In a provocative (but impressionistic) analysis, Kavolis argued that many of the "modern" behaviors that are being discussed in the social and cultural change literature are being repudiated by many young people in "modernized societies": an interest in mysticism, and a loss of faith in science and technology (among many indicators) point to the emergence of a "postmodern man."

In both "modern" and "modernizing" societies, then, there is some evidence that suggests that the drift of behavioral change is not linear, that traditional or nonmodern values and behaviors are increasing in frequency. For those studying individual behavior during social change, it would appear unwise to ignore the possible nonlinearity of the phenomena.

The three basic problems suggest that the psychological study of social and cultural change should remain open to many alternative approaches and to a large variety of phenomena. Although this has not been the case, the least that can be done now is to keep these issues open during the review of the psychological literature.

Psychological Factors Associated with Change

As noted earlier, there is a basic division in the social change literature between those who view change primarily in terms of things (technology, institutions, etc.) or in terms of individuals (their attitudes, values, etc.). In the classic volume edited by Weiner (1966) this division was apparent, and in the more recent literature (Desai, 1971; Kunkel, 1966; Campbell & Converse, 1972) it remains as a basic issue. Thus far this chapter has discussed both points of view, but now it will focus primarily on the human factors that appear at the individual level of analysis. In doing so, however, these other issues should remain available for assistance in interpreting the behavioral materials.

A few highly influential names and a few dominant themes stand out in this psychological literature. Since most of these names and themes coincide, it would be tempting simply to proceed with the review, perhaps chronologically, by way of these ready-made divisions. However, a deeper patterning appears in the literature, one that has a strong methodological base: almost all of the theoretical statements and empirical studies have a clear emphasis on either the psychological antecedents to change, or the psychological correlates or consequents of change. Given this more fundamental division and its relevance for the eventual application of psychological knowledge about social and cultural change, it seems advantageous to proceed in this second way.

Within the materials on antecedents to change there are two large research traditions, and a third set of smaller but significant programmes.

These first two are the general area of *attitudes and beliefs* (with workers such as Inkeles, Dawson, and Jahoda), and the area of *achievement orientation* (with McClelland, LeVine, and De Vos); the third set includes many other psychological variables such as *authoritarian socialization* (Hagen), *operant conditioning* (Guthrie), and *modal personality* (Wallace). Any review of these materials must necessarily be highly selective, but this threefold organization appears to sample equitably from the available literature.

In studies of the psychological correlates and consequents of social and cultural change, there appear no large-scale research traditions nor any great single research programmes. The fragmented nature of the literature makes it difficult to review, and the problem is compounded by the large number of studies in the area. More for convenience than ease of fit, the materials are divided into those that are concerned with *behavioral shifts* during and after acculturation (test score changes and shifts in personality patterns with social change) and those that examine the *acculturative stress* associated with social and cultural change (mild mental and behavioral pathology often, but not always, accompanying change).

Despite this fairly clear division in the literature between antecedents and consequents, there is one outstanding worker in the area whose integrated work cannot be divided in this way, and whose ideas may serve as a general introduction. In his classic study, Doob (1960) addressed the two problems jointly,[2] and in a later theoretical statement he again considered the double problem (Doob, 1968). For Doob (1960, p. 3) there are two basic questions "being raised concerning people in less civilized[3] societies: 1. Why do they become more civilized in certain respects? 2. What happens to them as they become more civilized?" His approach to these questions is to present a set of hypotheses that makes predictions about the psychological differences between people who "remain unchanged," those who "have changed," and those who are "changing" (1960, p. 324–26). Empirical evidence is generally presented as a contrast between two groups, one low and the other high on acculturation (p. 66); this acculturation decision is based primarily upon the number of years of formal education of the respondent (p. 49).

The psychological scope of the volume is wide indeed, and Doob admits that his twenty-seven hypotheses are far too broad to be adequately assessed by the evidence he accumulates in his own studies (p. 39). Nevertheless, his broad conceptualization of the psychological components of social and cultural change deserve to be considered at the hypothetical level, for they are an extremely stimulating introduction to the field and most of its basic issues.

Although space does not permit a consideration of all the hypotheses, there are two sets that have centrally addressed the issues of utmost concern. The first set of four hypotheses is devoted to the psychological dynamics of change, and contrasts those individuals in transition with those who have already changed or who remain unchanged:

1. In comparison with those who remain unchanged or who have changed, people changing from old to new ways are likely to be more discontent (p. 74).
2. In comparison with those who remain unchanged or who have changed, people changing from old to new ways are likely to feel more aggressive (p. 80).
8. In comparison with those who remain unchanged or who have changed, people changing from old to new ways are likely to feel more ambivalent toward outsiders associated with those new ways (p. 121).
10. In comparison with those who remain unchanged or who have changed, people changing from old to new ways are likely to be generally sensitive to other people (p. 135).

These four hypotheses suggest that an emotional cluster defined by discontent, aggressiveness, ambivalence, and sensitivity is psychologically characteristic of people undergoing change. Whether these precede the change, or arise as a function of it, may only be determined by a longitudinal study that has yet to be attempted.

A second set of hypotheses is concerned with the psychological characteristics of those who have experienced change:

11. After people change centrally from old to new ways, they are likely to value in others and in themselves traits which indicate independence and self-confidence (p. 141).
16. In comparison with those who remain unchanged, people who are changing or have changed centrally are likely to be more proficient in novel situations; the degree of their proficiency will vary with the perceived similarity between those situations and ones in their past experience (p. 175).
17. After people change centrally from old to new ways, they are likely to develop facility in abstracting (p. 187).
18. After people change centrally from old to new ways, they are likely to be more proficient in making subjective judgments of objective time intervals (p. 191).
19. After changing people learn a new language, they are likely to perceive differently significant stimulus patterns (p. 195).
20. After people change centrally from old to new ways, they are likely to be more proficient in using language to describe and express their feelings and reactions to the external world (p. 200).

All of these behavioral changes are in the direction of greater detachment of self from one's sociocultural context; this theme will be discussed in the last section of this chapter.

Although phrased as hypotheses, Doob's statements are essentially qualitative assessments of the material that was available to him at that time (late 1950s). Some of these materials he gathered himself (in three areas in Africa, and one in Jamaica), and the rest was available in the literature on Amerindian and Middle Eastern peoples. Subsequently Doob (1968) condensed these twenty-seven hypotheses into fifteen principles. These fifteen principles were essentially updated evaluations of his original hypotheses.

In the balance of the chapter, such an integrated approach is no longer feasible since most research is concerned with only a single element. Thus antecedents will be separated from consequents and concomitants, while the latter two will be combined. Although consequents and concomitants should be separable, in fact they are not, given the present lack of longitudinal studies. Indeed, it is only possible to separate antecedents to change from consequents and concomitants because of the relatively strong *theoretical* arguments made by those working in the area of modern attitudes and achievement orientation. If the distinction had to be made on empirical grounds alone, the lack of longitudinal studies would once again hinder the validity of the distinction.

Psychological Antecedents to Change

Attitudes and Beliefs

Perhaps the most researched topic in the psychological study of social and cultural change has been the question of individual attitudes toward change. As already noted, the designation of this research as "antecedent" cannot be made with confidence, for there is undoubtedly a process of attitudinal change that continues during and after social and cultural change. Nevertheless, the theoretical position of most workers in this area allows for a prior attitudinal orientation toward change, and in the absence of disconfirming longitudinal evidence, it is reasonable to assume that such an initial predisposition does exist.

Also noted was that the bulk of the sociocultural literature has been devoted to that segment of social change that has become known as "development" or "modernization"; similarly, the attitudinal literature has become narrowly focused on modernization, or more accurately, on psychological modernity. Because of this, the psychological study of modern attitudes has become bogged down in the controversy surrounding the value, the universality, and the linearity of the notion. But, more than in the case of the sociocultural study of modernization, the psychological approach has forced an examination of the issues because all three parts of the controversy are necessarily implicated in the technique of attitude measurement: the question of value must be attended to before scoring can be done; the question of universality must be considered before item content can be decided; and the question of linearity must be studied before the scales may be put together and techniques of statistical analyses decided.

It is fair to say that these three problems have not been *solved* in the psychological literature, but that in the psychological study of modernity, the assumptions have to be made *explicit*; it is no longer possible to hide the issues when measurement must be made. With respect to value, all the known scales assign high or positive numbers to the "modern" alternative; that does not indicate ultimate value, for the numerical assignment is merely an arbitrary decision. However the fact that all scales are in this direction suggests a general value orientation among workers in this field. For the question of universality, many scales have provided for only one kind of "tradition" and one kind of "modern," betraying an assumption that it is an *etic* that has universal applicability; however others have assumed only the universal applicability of the dimension and provided culturally specific *emic* content for the various traditional and modern items. (For a discussion of *etic* and *emic* approaches to cross-cultural research, see the Introduction to Volume 2 [Methodology] of this *Handbook*.) As for the question of linearity, no systematic measurement work has been carried out, except that some studies have involved the concept of "reaffirmation" attitudes.

Since only universality shows great variation in the literature, this review will follow distinctions in that area. First, there is a large set of studies, mainly within a sociological framework, that assumes the universality of the modernization process. Second, there is an approach that has sought local exemplars of the universal approach. And third, there are a few studies that argue only for a local, culturally relevant study of change.

A universal approach.   Although most of the workers included in this section would probably object to such a characterization, they have developed scales to measure modern attitudes across cultures, but have not altered the scales to take cultural variations (in either the traditional or modern content) into account. The major research workers in this area (Inkeles & Smith, 1974) have constructed their scales as if what they seek to measure is culturally invariant. And such an assumption characterized their earlier statements (e.g. Smith & Inkeles, 1966); nor did Doob (1967) or Kahl (1968) seek to vary their own scales when they were employed in various cultural settings. Despite the criticism, Inkeles and Smith (1974) employed scales of psychological modernity in many countries, and have produced a classic in the field of the psychological study of social change.

Over the past decades, Inkeles and Smith have produced a series of research reports and essays on the Six Country project; these materials are drawn together in a concise monograph (Inkeles & Smith, 1974). The purpose of their study was to "explain the process whereby people move from being traditional to becoming modern personalities" (p. 5); the motive for conducting the study was the realization "that nation building and institution building are only empty exercises unless the attitudes and capacities of the people keep pace with other forms of development" (p. 1).

A conception of "modern," derived in part from "the forms of conduct we saw as likely to be inculcated by work in the factory" (p. 5), initially included twenty-four themes that were considered part of the syndrome (e.g., active public participation, family size restrictions, identification with the nation, kinship obligations, mass media, time and work commitment: Inkeles & Smith, 1974, Table 7–1, p. 101). These themes were "conceived of as manifestations of a more general, unified underlying dimension of modernity . . ." (p. 35) that they termed Overall Modernity (OM).

To pursue this question empirically, Inkeles and Smith developed a sampling strategy that encompassed four kinds of people in six developing nations. Since their concern was with modernization it was important to select countries that were experiencing this kind of change, and that had sufficient internal variation to sample from a variety of groups. Those selected were Argentina, Chile, East Pakistan (now Bangladesh), India, Israel, and Nigeria. In each country a sample of about nine hundred participants was sought that was to be all male, aged eighteen to thirty-two, and working in four occupational categories: (a) experienced urban industrial workers (about 400); (b) inexperienced urban industrial workers (about 200); (c) urban nonindustrial workers (about 100); and (d) rural farm workers (about 100).

An element essential to the design of the study was the multiple comparisons made possible by such a sampling strategy. For example, comparison of samples (a) and (d) (their basic contrast) allows them to check whether men who migrated to the city and acquired industrial experience are now more modern than their "country cousins," while the comparison of samples (b) and (d) allows them to check whether workers migrating to urban industry are "preselected as already modern" (p. 38). A comparison of samples (a) and (b) allows them to examine the "modernizing effect of urban factory experience," while a comparison of samples (a) and (c) permits an "assessment of factory experience alone" since sample (c) is urban as well, but not working in a factory setting.

In five of their six countries (all except India) more refined sampling permitted Inkeles and Smith to divide factories into "traditional" and "modern" types, and in some countries an extra sample of "high education experienced factory workers" was obtained. However, the basic four-group sample was central to their experimental design.

The components of modernity were operationalized by constructing a scale that they refer to as OM (Overall Modernity). A pool of attitude items was generated from the original themes, and each item was tested in at least four of the six countries for relevance and clarity: the seventy-nine items in this pool were designated OM-1. Then more items were developed (seventeen dealt with political modernity, twenty-three were "secondary" questions of the same type as the original seventy-nine, and forty-seven dealt with "objective" test materials) so that a total of 166 items were available for field use (p. 86). In addition to OM-1, four other forms were developed for a variety of special uses. These various scales appear (Table 6-3, p. 96) to be working in almost identical ways; intercorrelations range from +.73 to +.99, with over half being above +.90.

Inkeles and Smith argue that they have been able "reliably to characterize each individual more or less globally as relatively more modern or traditional by using the general or summary measure" of OM (p. 116), and that the "chief theoretical implication of the combined index is that it establishes the existence of a general quality of the personality which may reasonably be called individual modernity" (p. 117). And, more generally, they conclude, "The modern man is a cross-national, transcultural type who can be identified by our scales whatever the distinctive attitudes with which his culture may otherwise have endowed him" (p. 118).

Employing all their independent variables (such as education, mass media exposure, and occupational experience), Inkeles and Smith were able to account (via multiple correlations) for 47 percent of OM scale score variance (a median r of +.69, ranging from +.56 to +.79 from sample to sample). The most useful predictor, in general, was the experience of education (ranging from +.41 to +.71) followed by mass media (median r = +.45), factory experience (median r = +.29), and years of urban residence (median r = +.30).

They conclude that these essentially adult experiences can alter fairly basic attitudes; they base this conclusion both on analysis of OM scores by years of factory experience and by contrasts between matched urban factory workers and rural agricultural workers. This basic shift they term "modernization," and claim that it has four constituents: the modern man is an informed participant citizen; he has a marked sense of personal efficacy; he is highly independent and autonomous in his relations to traditional sources of influence especially when he is making basic decisions about how to conduct his personal experiences and ideas; and he is relatively open-minded and cognitively flexible (p. 290).

In their last chapter, Inkeles and Smith deal effectively with the "values" question and the "universality" problem. On the former, they argue that what is subsumed under their term "modern" is not uniquely European, American, or Western; these characteristics are found in all their samples. And on the latter, they argue that they are not simply assuming some universal character syndrome, but that they have empirically demonstrated it (pp. 290, 295): "we believe it to be of a higher order, indicating a more general human characteristic which is pancultural in meaning and transnational in relevance" (p. 298).

Although they have been confronted with criticisms of their project during the past decade (Inkeles, 1977), and do a neat job of inoculating against some common alternative explanations (Inkeles & Smith, 1974, pp. 292–98), they do not satisfactorily deal with the basic problem of what might be called "input predisposing output." That is, a particular conception of unidirectional change has been operationalized through a series of scales (which assume a traditional to modern dimension); with this input, could they have obtained any other set of results? Admittedly, they had good research cooperation with social scientists in the six countries, and they even developed a "distinctively Indian scale of modernity" (p. 298) that proved to be highly correlated to OM; but these moves away from a universalistic framework are relatively small in relation to the total cast of the theory, the empirical work, the data analyses, and the interpretation.

There is an alternative to this universal approach, one that assumes that there may be a universal *process* and perhaps a universal *dimension*, but that its *measurement* should be culturally specific and indigenous in content.

Local exemplars of a universal process.   Early criticism of both the Kahl and Inkeles approaches was soon evident in both the sociological and psychological literature. For example, Gusfield (1967) criticized the assumed linearity and polarity of the "tradition and modernity" conception. Shortly afterwards, Stephenson (1968) presented a theoretical argument and empirical demonstration of the "local exemplar" approach. He argued that "traditional" and "modern" were appropriate conceptions of a dimension of change, but that the cultural group must be allowed to define the content of these two poles:

> Modernization is the movement of persons or groups along a cultural dimension from what is defined by the cultural norms as traditional toward what is defined by the same culture as modern. Those values defined in the local culture as traditional comprise what may be called traditionalism; those defined as modern constitute modernism (Stephenson, 1968, p. 268).

Prior to these skirmishes in the sociological literature, Dawson (1963) had developed and reported on a technique for conceiving of and measuring the traditional-modern (originally termed traditional-western) dimension using item content from *within* the cultures themselves. In a series of later reports (Dawson, 1967a, 1969a, 1969b, 1969c, 1973a, 1973b; Dawson, Law, Leung, & Whitney, 1971; and Dawson, Whitney, & Law, 1972) he elaborated and applied these ideas in a variety of cultures. In addition to developing this scaling technique for measuring traditional-modern attitudes, Dawson has also developed a theoretical position that attempts to deal with attitudinal conflict and the dynamics of attitudinal change. Basic descriptions of these two aspects of this work appear in Dawson (1967) and Dawson (1969a); this discussion is based mainly on these sources. The more recent extensions and elaborations will be considered following the outline of his basic arguments.

In his scale development, Dawson argued that traditional concepts must be drawn from the cultural life of the group involved, and that these concepts should sample widely from the culture of the people (1967, p. 83). This not only meets the "local exemplar" requirement, but introduces a new concern—that of the representativeness of these exemplars. In addition, he argues that traditional and western content should not simply be stated as alternatives, but intermediate attitudinal positions should be phrased to allow compromise attitudes to be exhibited; this innovation permits some novel positions to be taken (see the introduction to this chapter). Finally, Dawson argued that given Jahoda's (1961) finding of some traditional cultural reaffirmation among western-exposed peoples, the scale should not assume linearity, but allow for the exhibition of attitudinal reaffirmation, if it is in fact present in the samples.

To meet these requirements, Dawson selected eighteen concepts from the culture of his Sierra Leone (West Africa) samples (e.g., on witchcraft, polygamy, gift exchange), and developed four statements about each concept, one each to express a "traditional," "semi-traditional," "semi-western," and "western" attitude. The concepts were selected with the assistance of anthropologists and local informants, and the creation and designation of an item as "semi-traditional," for example, "involved using African and European residents of Sierra Leone acting as judges" (1967, p. 86).

Dawson then used his scales to test a theory of attitudinal change based upon a generalized theory of consistency or congruence (or, conversely, dissonance). In the second of his two basic papers (1969a), Dawson considered the problem of "unresolved attitudinal conflict occurring with individuals exposed to a rapidly changing social environment" (p. 39). He noted that "it is a basic premise of this theory that attitudinal inconsistency will be maladaptive to the individual and that this will result in pressures to reduce or eliminate inconsistency" (p. 41). Many attitudes, he considered, would be easily adjusted by moving to a compromise position (i.e., a "semi" item) but others would constitute a real conflict situation, and this is most likely to occur in "traditional high affect attitudes" such as witchcraft (p. 42).

A technique was developed to estimate the degree of "unresolved attitudinal conflict in T-W scale" (p. 47); this technique employed the discrepancy between "traditional" and "Western" responses, and between "semi-traditional" and "semi-Western" responses. A score could then be calculated for each individual and each concept. As expected, unresolved attitudinal conflict was highest for those more basic value areas (such as witchcraft, parental authority, wife obedience to husband), and lowest for other cultural elements (such as ethical obligations at work). His overall findings were generally (p. 52) that most concepts had the modal response in the "semi" compromises, but that in about a quarter of the concepts (those of great traditional importance) unresolved attitudinal conflict was present.

Finally in Dawson's study of modern attitudes, he outlined a theory that attempts to account for cross-cultural differences in "susceptibility to traditional-modern attitude change" (Dawson et al., 1971; Dawson et al., 1972; Dawson, 1973a, 1973b). Basically, there are two elements to the theory (Dawson et al., 1971, pp. 3–4): "nature of indigenous socialization systems"; and "the degree of culturally determined tolerance for cognitive inconsistency in belief systems." To this he added (1973a) a more basic ecological variable that contrasts sociocultural groups on the basis of their subsistence pattern (Barry, Child, & Bacon, 1959). Not only are group and individual differences expected in attitude change as a function of these variables, but so are differences in achievement motivation and the "potential for economic development" (Dawson, 1973a, p. 216); however, these latter two variables will be treated in the discussion of achievement orientation. The basic theoretical expectations are (p. 219) that agricultural societies (which tend to have formal authority systems and harsh socialization) will exhibit high susceptibility to modern attitude change, high achievement motivation, and high potential for economic development. In contrast, hunting societies (which tend to have no formal authority systems and permissive socialization) will exhibit low susceptibility to modern attitude changes, low achievement motivation, and low potential for economic development. Although some evidence was provided in support of such an expectation (e.g., Dawson, 1973a) the samples were extremely small (e.g., Eskimo samples of fifteen and fourteen persons, and Japanese samples of twenty and eleven), and the theoretical expectations must remain at the hypothetical level for the present time. Nevertheless, the general point of view that the psychological features of change will depend not only on the degree of external influence, but also on the psychocultural characteristics of the group being influenced, is eminently plausible.

Indigenous beliefs.   In contrast to the universalistic approach, some workers have argued that very careful, locally based studies must be conducted if the cultural meaning of social and cultural change is to be discovered. However, given that psychologists are usually searching (via cross-cultural comparison) for generalizations, this approach has not been as popular as it has been in anthropology. Perhaps the most suitable illustration of this more cautious approach is the work of Jahoda (1961, 1962, 1968, 1970) on supernatural beliefs and their relation to social change in West Africa.

A basic two-fold question is to what extent are supernatural (i.e., traditional) beliefs inconsistent with the process of social change (i.e., modernization), and to what extent are these beliefs altered by the experience of such change? Related to this is the extent to which these changes are linear (moving from a "traditional" to a "modern" pole) or alternatively nonlinear (moving to a level of "traditional reaffirmation," after high exposure to external change).

Jahoda (1970) questioned both the universality and linearity of the psychological correlates of social change, and considered even the local exemplars approach to be based on unsupportable assumptions:

> ... it commonly appears to be taken for granted not only that there exists a continuum whose two polar extremes are "traditional" and "Western," but that the various constituent elements of such an orientation will cluster together; for instance, this seems to be the assumption underlying Dawson's (1967b) T-W Scale. However, this view is in conflict with the present writer's observations, and it is therefore desirable to examine systematically the relationship between supernatural beliefs on the one hand and social, economic, and political ideas and attitudes on the other (p. 117).

In part his arguments are based upon the prevalence of traditional beliefs in his original studies of various acculturated African samples (1961, 1962); "the broad picture that emerged was one of a high rate of survival of traditional beliefs among these university students" (1970, p. 120). And in part Jahoda has evidence from his "Index of Supernatural Beliefs" to indicate that even after a further decade of acculturation, traditional beliefs remained at a high level.

This index was developed using ten beliefs (e.g., "twins are different from ordinary children," or "fortune tellers really know the future"); items were formulated in relatively concrete terms. Each item was responded to on a four-choice scale (total belief, probable belief, probable disbelief, and total disbelief) and a score was derived by summing across the ten items. In his recent use of the index, Jahoda found that over two-thirds of a university student sample (n=280) expressed total or qualified belief in the fortune telling item, and a little under two-thirds in witchcraft (Jahoda, 1970, Table 1). When he split his sample in two by age (over and under age twenty-five), he found that the index did not correlate with the Smith and Inkeles (1966) OM scale in the younger sample, but was significantly related (+.24) in the older sample. His analyses led him to the conclusion that traditional beliefs were not only remaining at a high level despite continuing social change, but that they were actually on the increase: "supernatural beliefs are coming to be more widely held by educated Ghanaians" (1970, p. 128), and there appears to be a "revolt against western values" that might be "described as a partial return to traditional West African cosmological notions."

The first meaning of such a finding is that not only the "universal" approach, but also the "local exemplars" approach may be insensitive to the realities of psychological change during social change. If similar locally sensitive work is conducted elsewhere, there may be additional evidence for this view; but if all studies are conducted with some universal assumptions, it may never be known whether such psychological ("antiwestern") change is a common phenomenon.

A second meaning of Jahoda's findings is that there may be no necessary conflict between "traditional" and "modern" points of view, as Dawson and other congruence theorists postulate. The high level of traditional belief present in a highly acculturated population suggests no strong movement toward resolving what westerners might view as a logical inconsistency. Rather as both Jahoda (1968) and Barbichon (1968) suggest, there may very well be a "state of cognitive coexistence" during social and cultural change that is neither maladaptive nor conflict ridden. If such is the case, then the dynamics of attitudinal change may, in the end, be different from the present suggestions based upon dissonance theory.

Necessarily, discussions of these three approaches to the study of traditional attitudes and beliefs have focussed on a key researcher in each to the exclusion of many others. In so doing, others have been ignored, and the key workers may have been "overlabelled." Nevertheless, this dimension of universality (and to a lesser extent that of linearity) has proved to be a real basis for contrasting these various approaches.

An important examination of the universality issue has been conducted by Jones (1977). In that study, items from the Inkeles and Smith and Dawson instruments were supplemented by items from the scales of Kahl (1968) and Guthrie (1970). These were administered to 998 school students in isolated communities in northeastern Canada. Results indicated that each scale is itself factorially complex, and that there is "little significant overlap" among the scales. If modernity is indeed universal, and if these scales all assess it, then surely some degree of factorial similarity should emerge. This study suggests that there are now problems not only of universality, but also of the concurrent validity of these various scales of individual modernity.

Achievement Orientation

Without doubt, the research tradition of "achievement orientation" has been one of the most substantial (both theoretically and empirically) in the recent history of cross-cultural psychology. Because of the scope of the work (and the considerable attention paid to it), it is not possible (nor necessary) to attempt more than a selective review of the field. As in the case of studies of "modern attitudes," attention will be devoted to a few representative workers: McClelland (1961) and McClelland & Winter (1969), as the originator and developer of the tradition; and LeVine (1966) and De Vos (1968) and others, as extenders and critics of the theory.

As in the case of the study of "modern attitudes," the research surrounding the topic of achievement orientation has been plagued by the fundamental questions of value and universality, and to a lesser extent of linearity. These difficulties will be apparent as the theory, the practice, and the critics are reviewed. Finally, and again as in the case of "modern attitudes," the antecedent role of achievement orientation cannot be demonstrated with any confidence. It is most usually conceived of as a personal value that exists in a society prior to economic development (and perhaps necessary to that development) but some critics have placed it chronologically as a correlate or even a consequent or such development (e.g., Inkeles, 1971, p. 273).

McClelland's theory: need for achievement.   A basic argument of McClelland (e.g., 1961, Chapter 1) is that economic development cannot be explained without reference to social and psychological variables. In this early search for such variables, he was struck by the apparent role which a motivation to get ahead played in the process of development; and he hypothesized that "achievement motivation⁴ is in part responsible for economic development" (1961, p. 36). Previous work by McClelland and his associates (1953) on the achievement motive had established reliable and valid techniques for assessing achievement motives, primarily through the content analysis of written or spoken material produced in response to a variety of experimental conditions (see Brislin's chapter in Volume 2 of this *Handbook*).

The interest in studying achievement motivation (or more broadly, achievement orientation) cross-culturally stems from McClelland's demonstration that there is a pattern of sociocultural antecedents (mainly in socialization) to its development in individuals. Since these socialization antecedents are known to vary cross-culturally, there is a ready-made theoretical scheme for its further analysis. Briefly, those individuals who develop high achievement motivation had mothers who expected early self-reliant mastery, placed fewer restrictions on the child, and generally encouraged early achievement (McClelland, 1961, pp. 342–43). In a series of cross-cultural extensions (e.g., Child, Storm, & Veroff, 1958; Rosen, 1959), both with cultural archival and individual sampling material, these socialization antecedents of nAch have been largely confirmed.

The discovery of the patterning of group differences in achievement orientation (in relation to objective indices of development) was the primary purpose of the McClelland (1961) studies; the experimental manipulation of achievement among entrepreneurs for the purposes of economic development was the goal of the McClelland and Winter (1969) study. In the 1961 report, historical, modern, and traditional societies were considered at two levels of analysis: the analysis of cultural products (mainly stories) for indicators of achievement motivation, and the analysis of economic development of the society. To an impressive degree McClelland was able to demonstrate, usually with some temporal lag, the covariation of the frequency of achievement themes in the products of a society and economic development. Two examples of this relationship (one contemporary across nations, and one historical) will serve as illustrations. In the first, McClelland (1961; Table 3-4) relates achievement motivation scores for thirty countries (derived from content analysis of the stories in children's readers in 1925 and 1950) and two estimates of recent economic growth (per capita income, electrical production per capita). The correlations between achievement motivation scores for the 1925 stories and economic growth are significant, but are insignificant for the 1950 stories. McClelland interprets this pattern as supporting not only the relationship between achievement motivation and economic development, but the *prior necessity* of such motivation. In the second example, average achievement levels in English literature (from years 1500 to 1800) are compared with rates of grain and coal imports at London fifty years later (as an indicator of economic activity); the parallel course of these two variables over this 300-year period is striking, and is taken by McClelland (1961, p. 139) again as support for a relationship, with priority attributed to the psychological variable. Recent work by Finison (1976), however, has raised doubt about the generality of these correlations. Over the period 1950 to 1971, Finison found no correlation between nAch and electrical production, and a *negative* correlation between 1950 nAch level and growth in national income (1950 to 1971). He has concluded that the McClelland model may be inappropriate for the present historical period. Given this transhistorical instability within a culture area, it is possible that cross-cultural instability may also exist.

Many other sociocultural factors were considered by McClelland, including the role of religion (the well-known Protestant Ethic thesis of Weber, 1930) and the role of entrepreneurs (McClelland, 1961, Chapters 6 and 7) as individuals most responsible for economic activity. It is this latter factor, and the possibility that achievement motivation might be increased in adults, that led McClelland and Winter (1969) to the second major study.

Starting with the demonstration that achievement motivation systematically varies with and precedes economic growth, and the demonstration that its level in adults (mainly entrepreneurs) could be experimentally increased (McClelland, 1965), these authors set out to "increase achievement motivation in entrepreneurs" (p. 37) in India, Italy, and Tunisia.

The courses to train participants sought "to increase entrepreneurial spirit and improve interpersonal competence ... by emphasizing motivation, planning and cooperative effort." A basic theme was that "participants can initiate and control change by setting reasonable goals for change in themselves, in their firms and in their area, and that this can lead to rapid economic growth for the individual and the area" (McClelland & Winter, 1969, p. 150). The content of the courses varied from a creative thinking session to a discussion on family values and practice in scoring achievement content.

An evaluation of the effects of the course was undertaken, primarily through follow-up interviews with the participants. Those interview materials were scored for "business activity level" (p. 211) and were compared both with precourse activity level and with a group of untrained controls. Their general conclusion was that "the course did change people" (p. 212) in a way consistent with earlier attempts to develop achievement motivation. When scored for "hours worked" and "starting new business," similar significant changes were observed.

Although group comparisons demonstrated significant effects for the training course, it was true that not all individuals changed; some (the 45 percent called "changers") increased dramatically, while others (called "inactives") remained uninfluenced in economic behavior by the course.[5] These two groups did not differ in mean age or education (p. 259), nor on a variety of values and beliefs (such as fatalism or traditionalism; pp. 261–62). In the face of these results, McClelland and Winter concluded (p. 266) that

> . . . . we must be prepared to admit that the connections between traditional values and modernization are neither so obviously true nor so simple as they might be thought to be. We must consider again what many anthropologists have long claimed: that change usually is consolidated not by the disruption and destruction of so-called traditional values, but rather by their reinterpretation or resynthesis together with new actions (Singer, 1966). A man can begin to act differently and yet hold traditional beliefs. Whatever dissonance one would expect from this combination is handled by reinterpreting the old beliefs so that they do not conflict with the new actions. Usually it is not handled by directly abandoning the old beliefs.

What is being asserted is, in one very fundamental sense, a challenge to the research tradition of "modern attitudes": achievement motivation may be increased without any clear effect on the more general set of "modern attitudes" held by individuals; since the former is a demonstrable antecedent to economic development, there may be a minimal relationship between these general modern attitudes and subsequent development.

At a more general level, McClelland and Winter (Chapter 12) address the larger question of the role of psychological education in development. First, they conclude that despite the child socialization-achievement motivation relationship (established in McClelland, 1961), "adult behavior can be changed" (p. 337). Further, those who did change in the direction advocated by the training became "change agents," creating changes in the social and economic life around them. Finally, the retention of traditional values and practices need not interfere with this way of economic change (McClelland & Winter, 1969, p. 349; McClelland, 1971, p. 290); that is, all psychological characteristics need not change in order for one of them to be altered and have significant effects on the process of development. It may be that OM (overall modernity) can be detected in some individuals, and be shown to be related to experience of modern life, but it may not be a necessary precondition of significant social change.

Extensions and criticisms of achievement motivation theory.   The extensive theoretical and empirical work of McClelland has not gone unchallenged. In particular, the questions of the sociocultural origins of achievement motivation (in terms of child socialization and a host of other factors) and of the characteristic expression of it (individualistic entrepreneurial activity or other cultural patterns) have been considered by many workers. This section will look at the work of de Vos (1965, 1968), LeVine (1966), Pareek (1968), Himmelstrand and Okediji (1968), Gallimore, Sloggett, Gallimore, and Kubany, (1970) and Dawson (1973a); this selection is representative of the numerous extensions and criticisms of the theory, but is by no means complete.

Perhaps the most telling critical examination of the generality of McClelland's work has been conducted by de Vos. Basically he questioned the universality of the socialization antecedents of achievement and of the mode of expression of an achievement orientation. In a series of observations and formal studies with the Japanese (1965, 1968), de Vos found a "pervasive preoccupation with achievement and accomplishment no matter where or what group of Japanese was tested" (1968, p. 359). Despite this high level, the Japanese socialization values are not based upon independence and self-reliance, but upon affiliation and a sense of family and group obligation; this, of course, is in sharp contrast to the McClelland position. While "McClelland somewhat singlemindedly emphasizes the role of individualistically oriented entrepreneurial behavior" (de Vos, 1968, p. 360), the Japanese "achieve in the context of social dedication." This is due to the fact that "the western ideal of personal self-realization apart from family or social group has been foreign to the Japanese system of thought . . . the ultimate goals of Japanese life centered on non-instrumental, quasi-religious concepts of family continuity" (de Vos, 1968, p. 362). This is a test case where high levels of achievement motivation can be persistently demonstrated, but where both its cultural *origins* and cultural *expression* are virtually opposite to those reported by McClelland.

These arguments pertain directly to one of the basic problems—that of universality. Depending on one's point of view, one could conclude that this evidence shatters the universality of McClelland's system, or illustrates it. From the first point of view, it is clear that its source and expression are not culturally invariant—the causal and expressive system is relative to the cultural context, and therefore is not *culturally* universal. On the other hand, one could argue that it may be psychologically universal, since it appears in many cultural systems, even in those whose child socialization practices and permissible expressions of economic activity are so different. Of course the resolution to this paradox lies in the meaning of "it"; if we mean a standard *behavior*, then "it" is not universal, but if we mean a standard *motive* whose behavioral manifestations vary, then "it" may be universal. Clearly a good deal more critical thought and empirical work are required before this question of universality may be evaluated.

Another major field worker in studies of achievement orientation has been LeVine (1966). In a study of Nigerian schoolboys from three different ethnic groups (Ibo, Yoruba, and Hausa), he raised the question of the cultural roots of apparent "uneven distribution of achievement motivation" among ethnic groups within a single nation (LeVine, 1966, p. 2). To many observers of African life, there have been obvious and relatively persistent differences in achievement orientation among groups; for example, the Ibo and Kikuyu exhibit remarkable enterprise. Without numerical majority in their countries, they have achieved a strong economic, cultural, and political position; such a situation is ready made for a natural experiment on the cultural roots of achievement orientation.

The African cultural setting, though, is clearly different from those that nurtured the development of the achievement motivation theory of McClelland. First, in most African societies "the pecuniary motive was well developed, and competition for wealth, prestige and political power was frequent and intense" (p. 3); for LeVine this distinguishes most African societies from "folk and peasant peoples in other parts of the world." Second, although most aspire to wealth and status, "they do not generally regard hard work as highly commendable in itself" but seek a "social pattern in which freedom from work is a prerogative of high status" (pp. 3–4). Thus, although different from the cultural expression in Japan noted by de Vos, it is just as clearly different from the entrepreneurial pattern of expression studied by McClelland. This requires an understanding of the problem from within the African cultural system, prior to any study of achievement motivation.

The more general purpose of LeVine's study was to pose (and answer) three questions relevant to all cross-cultural behavioral study: "Are there objectively measurable differences in personality between culturally differing populations? If so, what are the sociocultural causes of such differences? And what are the social consequences of these differences?" (p. 10). To guide the enquiry, LeVine proposed a cultural dimension on which the groups could be shown to differ, and which was theoretically linked to the development of achievement motivation. His concept of "status mobility" emphasized that each society has a "system of ranked statuses in which mobility is possible from one status to another" (p. 17). At the top will be the "ideal man" for that society, and a variety of behaviors could be socially encouraged in order to reach it. LeVine presents a contrast between two hypothetical types: one in which "a person from the lower orders can rise only by first becoming the lackey of the high status person" (p. 17) would tend to encourage obedience, servility, compliance, and deference; and another in which "status mobility is managed largely through outstanding performance in an occupational role" (p. 17) would tend to encourage independence, industriousness, foresight, and daring. In the latter social mobility system, LeVine argues that there is likely to be "a larger proportion of individuals high in achievement than in the first society" (p. 18).

A test of this theory was made by analyzing the mobility systems of the three groups, by sampling and analyzing dream reports and essays for achievement themes, and relating both to evidence for differential achievement attitudes and behavior among the three groups. His findings (1966, Chapter 8) were that there were clear group differences in achievement imagery in dream content, in references to obedience and social compliance values in essays, and to self-development and improvement in living standards in national opinion surveys. These results constitute a clear answer to his first general question; since the ordering is consistent (but not exclusively so) with observed cultural differences in status mobility, the second question may also have received an answer. Finally, the social consequences of these differences appear to have been the creation of a wide variation in economic development, and in general social and cultural change.

LeVine's study, along with the work of de Vos, demonstrates the need to consider local cultural features before an understanding of achievement motivation may be claimed for a particular group; to that extent, the universality of McClelland's system is limited. But to the extent that the motive could be validly assessed, and be shown to relate to some socialization factors consistent with those in McClelland's scheme, LeVine's study suggests some degree of cross-cultural applicability of the concept of achievement orientation.

Finally this section considers briefly a number of smaller, but relatively important extensions and criticisms of the original theory. To Pareek (1968), who was a professional colleague of McClelland's in the Indian programmes, motivation is important for social change, generally, and development in particular; but achievement motivation alone cannot promote development. Two other motives that Pareek calls "extension motivation" and "dependence motivation" must also be considered. The first implies a "concern for other people or the society" and is defined as "a need to extend the self or the ego and to relate to a larger group and its goals" (Pareek, 1968, pp. 118–19); in these terms, it is not dissimilar to the "affiliation" arguments made by de Vos (1968) for achievement in Japanese society. This extension motive is considered to be "super-ordinate," making it useful both for improving intergroup harmony, and (perhaps most importantly) for "sustaining continued motivation of people in development" (Pareek, 1968, p. 119). Although there is no research or empirical evidence available to either establish the existence of this motive or to evaluate its role in social change, Pareek argues (p. 119) that there is considerable historical and political evidence suggesting such a motive, and that there should be serious research into it.

The second motive ("dependence motivation") is also thought to be important in the process of development because it is a negative factor. Pareek (1968, p. 119) defines it as "looking for direction from other sources" and may be manifested in either "excessive dependence—seeking support and guidance, or in excessive counter-dependency—the aggressive rejection of authority." It is characterized by a lack of initiative, avoidance of responsibility, direction seeking, seeking favor of a superior, and overconformity.

In a statement of a general paradigm of development, Pareek (1968, p. 121) suggests that development (D) is a positive function of achievement motivation (AM) and extension motivation (EM), reduced by the degree of dependence motivation (DM) $[D \rightarrow (AM \times EM) - DM]$. To a certain extent, this formulation is only a marginal extension of the views of McClelland. Both recognized that achievement motivation is not all there is to development, and both are concerned with the obvious need for entrepreneurial activity not to be limited to self-gratification (McClelland refers to it as a "concern for the common welfare of all," while Pareek calls it the "extension motive"). Finally, "dependency motivation" once operationalized may turn out to be little more than the polar opposite of achievement motivation, and hence its presence in the paradigm is mathematically redundant. Nevertheless, the elaboration of the complex sets of motives that may be involved in social change is an important task, and Pareek (along with de Vos) must be commended and encouraged to further this line of enquiry.

This pursuit of more complex motives, and their relationships with other psychological (and economic) factors, has been conducted by Himmelstrand and Okediji (1968). As they point out, social and economic development cannot be considered simply as a function of *levels* of resources (including both psychological and nonpsychological resources); the "structure and patterns of resources" must be examined. Basic to their argument is the notion of *resources congruence*; "underdevelopment, we presume, is indicated not only or even mainly by low levels of resources, but rather by incongruous or imbalanced resource structures" (p. 26). At three levels of analysis (individual, group, and societal) they examine some possible kinds of incongruence:

> The Personality Level: Does an individual in his personality combine a need for achievement, skills relevant to achievements, fairly accurate perceptions of alternative lines of action and their possible consequences, receptivity to new information, a capability of negotiating differences with other individuals? Or has he developed some of these traits at the expense of other traits? What type of personality dynamics brings about balanced or incongruous types of personality structures and of human resources respectively?

> The Group Level: Does an individual in his group easily find individuals with complementary resources so that, for instance, his own need for achievement can be complemented by advice from those who have knowledge and skills relevant to achievement, or vice versa, so as to bring about a concurrence of resources and facilities within the group? Or is such complementarity difficult to attain in the given group?

> The Social Level: Is the structure of society, particularly its stratification system and its institutional set-up so constituted that a high degree of concurrence of material and human resources is created by the process of socialization of individuals and by the distributional processes in groups? Or does the social structure hamper such concurrence of resources? (pp. 26–27)

Within the "human resources" factor, Himmelstrand and Okediji (p. 27) argue that psychologists concerned with social change must be prepared to work on at least six topics: general knowledge and skills, more specific skills, receptivity to novel concepts and information, creativity, achievement values, and inclination to empathize or negotiate. Note that only one of these factors involves a concern with motivation; such a view places the role of motivational variables in proper perspective, both from their relative importance to development and from their interactive position with other psychological variables.

Another critic of the role of achievement orientation has been Gallimore who with his associates (Sloggett, Gallimore, & Kubany, 1970) found no clear relationship between achievement motivation and actual school achievement in a sample of Hawaiian school children. Thus the generality of the power to explain actual achievement differences may be limited to one activity area (for example, academic behavior); if this kind of finding persists, then the explanatory role for achievement motivation may be much smaller than many had thought. In a second study (Kubany, Gallimore, and Buell, 1970), the researchers were concerned with the general problem of individualistic achievement (see de Vos, 1968); in a study of Filipino high school students in Hawaii, they found that achievement behavior (in a game) was higher when the students were being observed than when they were performing privately. That is, behavioral expressions of achievement may require culturally appropriate settings; and the measurement of either achievement motivation or of actual achievement outside of these settings will be virtually meaningless as an indicator of achievement in that group.

Finally, this section on achievement motivation returns briefly to the arguments of Dawson, who has proposed a theory to account for the cross-cultural variation in achievement motivation (in addition to variation in "modern attitudes"). For Dawson (1973a) not only attitudes, but also achievement motivation and "potential for economic development" will vary according to the exploitive pattern or subsistence base of a society; this relation is mediated by the variation in authority systems and socialization emphases typically developed by (for example) hunting as opposed to agricultural societies. In a test of his proposal, he found that "achievement independence" but not "achievement conformity" (as measured by the California Personality Inventory, Gough, 1969) differed significantly between a group of Alaskan Eskimo and Japanese high school and university students (with the Japanese scoring higher). However this finding is *opposite* to that which might be expected on the basis of McClelland's (1961) review of the contribution of socialization to group and individual differences; in his view the more achievement-oriented and self-reliant socialization emphases of some societies (the Eskimo are clearly in this group) should lead to higher, not lower, achievement motivation. This one reversal presented by Dawson would not seem to jeopardize the large generalization, and the conclusion might be drawn that a good deal of field work is necessary before any generalizations can be made about group differences in achievement motivation and "potential for economic development."

Other Psychological Approaches

Many other approaches to the study of psychological factors in social and cultural change have been taken. In general there have been three classes of approach, one based upon "personality" psychology, another on studies in "perception and cognition," and the third upon "learning" psychology. Among the many varieties of the "personality" approach, two further subclasses may be discerned. One is the *global* approach, which has developed largely within the school of psychological anthropology, and the other is an attempt to isolate some *specific traits and values* that might account for differential social and cultural change; of course this examination of modern attitudes and achievement orientation, had they not been so complex and distinctive, might have exemplified this subclass, but they have really established themselves as independent research traditions. With respect to the role of perceptual and cognitive variables, a number of factors have been postulated as psychological antecedents to social change, including skills or resources and cognitive structure (complexity, flexibility, and style). Finally among the varieties of the "learning" approach, two subclasses may also be discerned, one based upon classical learning theory, and the other based upon operant theory. This discussion will devote attention to one example of research in each of the five (global personality, specific trait, perceptual-cognitive, classical learning, and operant learning) approaches.

A global personality approach.   This approach is concerned with the congruity between the global personality of the group being influenced and that of the group that is bearing the acculturative pressures. Its history is firmly set in the research traditions of "culture and personality" and of "value orientations"; in particular, the studies by Mead (1956a, 1956b) in Melanesia, Beaglehole (1957) in Polynesia, and Hallowell (1955) and Wallace (1951) among various Amerindian peoples. Although their works were more specifically directed toward constructing the "modal personality" of the peoples they were working with, all considered the question of social and cultural change, and the likely role of the personalities they were describing. A common theme was that if the personalities were oriented toward change, particularly if they were congruent with the life style with which they were increasingly aware, then social change would be relatively smooth and rapid. A number of field studies have now been conducted which, in general, bear out these assumptions.

A specific trait approach.   A good deal of attention has been paid to the theory of social change advanced by Hagen (1962). Although trained as an economist, he turned to psychology for an understanding of why "people of some societies entered upon technological progress sooner or more effectively than others" (p. ix). He considered that "the differences were due only in very minor degree to economic obstacles, lack of information or lack of training" and so he turned his attention "to other possible causes of differences in human behavior—to differences in personality, and hence personality formation and the social conditions affecting it" (p. ix). His overall scheme is represented by a model of society "which stresses the chain of causation from social structure through parental behavior to childhood environment and then that from childhood environment through personality to social change" (pp. 8-9).

With respect to individual development, Hagen concentrated his psychological study on "the first half dozen years of life" (p. xii). This decision led him to rely heavily upon the psychoanalytic literature, and upon the personality formulations that have been derived from it (particularly upon the conception of the authoritarian personality). Two implications of this decision are that Hagen assumes some predictability from early experience to adult behavior, and that early experience has better predictability than other (later) experiences. In part, both Inkeles and Smith (1974) and McClelland and Winter (1969) have challenged this view, and have demonstrated the effects of adult factory and training experience upon attitudes and motives toward social change well into adult life.

The basic argument of Hagen is that in agricultural societies[6] economic and technological growth occurs only gradually. "Contact with technologically advanced societies is a necessary condition" (pp. 34–35), but it is not sufficient. Other elements, such as material resources and social and psychological factors must also be present, and they must be structured in certain ways. Thus the key to growth "seems to be largely internal rather than external" (p. 55), and the central feature lies in the concept of "traditionalism." For Hagen, in a traditional society "behavior is governed by custom, not law. The social structure is hierarchical. The individual's position in the society is normally inherited rather than achieved. And, at least in the traditional state so far in the world's history, economic productivity is low" (pp. 55–56). Such a social system is "stable because the simple folk as well as the elite accepted it" (p. 71).

> Satisfaction in yielding to the judgment and wishes of superiors, and satisfaction in dominating inferiors are interwoven in the personality of the simple folk in traditional societies the world over.... Personalities in which these traits are prominent may be termed authoritarian personalities. We may conclude that the structure of traditional society has lasted as long as it has because the personalities of the simple folk are authoritarian (pp. 73–74).

In contrast to this pervasive authoritarian personality, Hagen defines the "innovational personality" in terms of creativity, positive attitudes toward working in novel fields, and openness to new experience. For Hagen (p. 86) "social change will not occur without change in personality," and it is a change from the authoritarian to the innovational that is required.

A perceptual-cognitive approach.   Many cognitive aspects have been proposed as relevant to social change and development in the history of psychology and anthropology. Perhaps the most widely accepted view was that some peoples simply were not "intelligent" enough to "progress." It is assumed here that this view is not considered seriously any longer, and that the fallacies and ethnocentrism inherent in such a view have been sufficiently aired (e.g., Berry & Dasen, 1974; Cole & Scribner, 1974). However, to dismiss this first approach is not to dismiss the question of group differences (in contrast to deficits) in cognitive abilities and structures, or their possible roles in the process of social and cultural change.

With respect to the question of *skills,* it is clear from the last decade of cross-cultural research in perception and cognition that there are indeed group differences in the perceptual and cognitive skills developed by people to meet their particular ecological and cultural problems (e.g. Berry, 1966, 1976; Dawson, 1967b; MacArthur, 1973, 1975; Vernon, 1969). It is also clear that the perceptual and cognitive skills required by an industrialized and technological life style are of a particular kind; the requirement is for relatively well-developed perceptual (disembedding and spatial) skills, and high development of analytic (cognitive) skills (Deregowski, 1973; Bowd, 1974). One problem of social and cultural change from this point of view, then, is to achieve a match or congruence between the pattern of skills developed and valued in traditional life and those required in a technological life (Berry, 1971b, p. 153; MacArthur, 1975, p. 240). Alternatively, social and cultural change, rather than moving toward a technological life, could move toward a life style that capitalizes on extant skill patterns. In the former, change would involve the deliberate alteration of a skill pattern to prepare for a standard technological life style, while in the latter, change would involve the development of a new life style that better matches the present pattern of perceptual and cognitive skills.

Over and above these relatively basic skills, Himmelstrand and Oke-diji (1968, p. 27) have proposed others of importance (which often come only with some degree of prior culture contact) such as literacy and arithmetic skills; the role of these in promoting social change is self-evident (Jahoda, 1968). In summary, then, a reasonable case can be made for the necessity (but probably not for the sufficiency) of a pattern of perceptual and cognitive skills that are congruent with the social, economic, and cultural goals that are being sought. There is no suggestion that "general ability" or "intelligence" is implicated, since its cross-cultural variation is theoretically and empirically indeterminate (Berry, 1972). Rather, there is the suggestion that groups embarking on a programme of change should possess a set of skills consistent with its goals, or be in a position to acquire them; otherwise problems of adaptation may arise (see section on consequents of change).

From the point of view of the *structure* of perceptual and cognitive life, there have also been numerous proposals. In particular, Triandis (1973) proposed that a requirement for economic development is "cognitive complexity" that involves at least three dimensions: discrimination, differentiation, and integration. For Triandis (1973, pp. 172–73),

> . . . if a culture does not have a sufficiently developed differentiation in an exchange that is important for effective behavior in economically developed settings, this culture has characteristics which *inhibit* economic development. Conversely, some traditional cultures may have developed much differentiation in these exchanges and these cultures will find it easier to develop.

Two other cognitive factors have been proposed in the area of structure. One, by Cohen (1968, p. 11), is the degree of cognitive "flexibility"; this proposal is based upon the observation that "modernization often involves new solutions to older problems." And the second, by Diaz-Guerrero (1973), is "coping style," or the characteristic approach to problem solving employed by an individual. Diaz-Guerrero distinguishes between two coping styles: an "active" style involves changing the physical and social environment, while a "passive" style involves adjusting oneself to the environment. It is argued that the former is more conducive to social change and economic development than the latter.

A classical learning approach. One of the significant workers in the area of psychological anthropology has been Hallowell, whose collected papers (1955) are still a stimulating introduction to a range of topics. His analysis of the effects of acculturation on personality (which will be considered in the next section) provided a great methodological advance, but his analyses of the sociopsychological aspects of acculturation provided an even greater theoretical contribution. As may be judged from these introductory remarks, Hallowell was interested in both the antecedents of change, the "goals and motivations of individuals which *lead* to the acceptance of new cultural items, and the conditions under which social learning takes place" (p. 307), and also the consequents, "the psychological depth of the readjustment, with the cumulative psychological effects which acceptance may bring about in a given population over a period of time" (pp. 307–08).

In his analyses of sociopsychological aspects of acculturation (1955, pp. 310–32) Hallowell argues (p. 315) that "the problem of cultural change hinges on the conditions and processes that bring about socially significant adjustments of the individual behavior." Since culture contact is a necessary but not a sufficient cause of acculturation (p. 316), a wide variety of adaptations should be found whose nature will depend on other (perhaps sociopsychological) factors. Hallowell contrasts two such adaptations, one that leads to fairly radical changes in behavior and culture, and one that is "limited to securing the benefits of specialized goods or services that members of either group can offer" (p. 316). Since both kinds of adaptation may be observed (and indeed many intermediate ones) for similar conditions of contact, then internal sociopsychological variables must provide the clue to the observed variation.

One way to approach these psychological variations is from the perspective of learning theory, "for learning is the psychological crux of acculturation":

> When peoples with different cultural systems come into contact with one another, an examination of the barriers to learning, on the one hand, and the incentives to learning on the other, afford us direct insight into the dynamics of acculturation, although this angle of approach has not yet been systematically explored. The essential questions are the specific conditions under which individuals of either group gain an opportunity to learn about the ways of the other group, how far such learning is promoted or discouraged, what is learned and the various incentives to learning, the kind of people who have taken the initiative in learning, and the results of the process with respect to the subsequent relations of both groups and their cultural systems (p. 318).

The analysis of culture learning is made by Hallowell in terms of motivations (both primary and secondary), imitation, and positive and negative reinforcements (in terms of forced change and forced exclusion, or barriers). With respect to motivation, Hallowell points out that in mankind, secondary drives (such as prestige and appetites for particular kinds of food) are the major concern; since these are learned, they are probably culturally patterned, and hence implicated in the demands made during acculturation. In dealing with the phenomenon of imitation during contact, Hallowell states his assumption that a group "will imitate only those food habits, skills, attitudes or other items that, for one reason or another, satisfy their own culturally acquired drives" (p. 320), and further that there will be " no demand for exactness of imitation if approximate imitation is rewarding" (p. 320). Summarizing to this point, "the study of acculturation processes, then, involves not only an examination of drive and reward, but the details of the process of imitative learning in the transfer of habit patterns" (p. 320).

His analysis then switches to the conditions of positive and negative reinforcement that often prevail during acculturation. Noting that where

> there is freedom for imitative learning to take place in the social interaction between two peoples, it is hardly conceivable that acculturation can be in any sense a disruptive process, since the cultural features of one society that are imitated by members of another become functionally connected with established drives or with new ones that are in harmony with the cultural system of the borrowers (p. 321).

However, acculturation is rarely so simple and easy-going as this; on the contrary there is often a system of coercion and exclusion that forces selective access to features of both the traditional and the introduced culture. Some important traditional features are removed and replaced by introduced ones (for example language and religion) by authorities and institutions such as missionaries and teachers. Conversely, some valued aspects of the introduced culture are kept out of reach (for example physical comforts and economic status) while less valued aspects of the traditional culture are forcefully retained. The result of this system of positive and negative reinforcement has often been a high level of cultural transformation with negative side effects, such as anxiety:

> . . . the fact that European encroachment upon the domain of the nonliterate peoples everywhere created such a large variety of anxiety arousing situations suggests that an examination of the role that anxiety drives of all kinds play as motivation factors in readaptation may be especially valuable (p. 326).

This is a common focus in the literature on psychological correlates and consequents of social change, but its importance here lies in its conceptual role rather than as a final stress reaction (see section on consequents of change).

An operant learning approach.   On the cover of a monograph by Guthrie (1970) is a profile of a peasant superimposed on a pigeon; the intention is not to reduce the peasant to the status of an experimental animal, but to suggest that the behavior of people involved in the complex situations of social and cultural change might be considered anew from the perspective of Skinnerian psychology. Despite this orientation, Guthrie's study uses an eclectic approach to "the role of psychological factors in social change" and the identification of "some of the social factors which impede development" (p. 4). Indeed, a good portion of his empirical work is devoted to the study of modern attitudes, and what he terms the "subsistence attitudes" of peasants, and other psychological variables associated with a cognitive rather than an operant approach.

In his eclectic mood, Guthrie (1970) applied a scale of modern attitudes (drawn from Smith & Inkeles, 1966) and other interview questions to samples in four communities in the Philippines that varied in distance from a major city. In general there were no systematic differences in outlook among the samples (which were intended to represent differential exposure to modern influence) nor between the sexes on topics such as the value of education, traditional beliefs, family obligations, and planning for the future. Some differential reaction was apparent, however, between wealthy and better educated respondents and those who were not. On the whole, though, all groups tended to express attitudes and values that were identifiable as "modern."

On the other hand, the behavior of people in the communities where the samples were drawn was in contrast to these attitudes: many had "the subsistence outlook" (p. 99) of being contented with meeting each day's needs as they arose, of "getting by" and of "leveling" (where sharing and egalitarian values tend to keep everyone at the same level). One resolution to this paradox (suggested by the socioeconomic status differences) lies in "the systems of rewards and reinforcements which are offered" (p. 105); more specifically, "the reinforcement contingencies for modern behavior are very low, even though many have a capacity for modern behavior in their repertoire" (p. 107). This possibility led Guthrie to consider the Skinnerian analysis presented in detail in Chapter 7 of his monograph.

This approach, of course, does away with postulated motives and attitudes, and in its place provides a reinforcement "strategy of social change based on operant-conditioning principles" (p. 115). For example, the "leveling" behavior may be understood in terms of negative reinforcement for productive behavior, while the value placed on education may be understood when one conceives of education as an attainment that cannot be taken away, even by stronger people. In summary, Guthrie outlines the essential advantages of such an approach:

> We have offered this brief and simplified outline of operant conditioning, a body of theory and experiments developed by Skinner and many others, in order to suggest a systematic orientation for observation and experiment in the study of modernization and the understanding of behavior in traditional societies. The theory has proven to be very productive in educational and

clinical psychology; this is an attempt to extend it to research and action programs in other cultures. The orientation is strongly behavioristic in the
sense that it deals with the individual's observable activities. It does not make
use of covert processes such as character traits and other inherent qualities as
explanatory devices (p.117).

*Summary of Psychological Antecedents to Social
and Cultural Change*

The literature on psychological factors in social change tends to be divided
into those features that are viewed as antecedent and those that are
viewed as correlates or consequents of social change. This division (which
was followed in this review) has only marginal empirical support, for the
status of most of the variables results primarily from their positions in a
theoretical analysis, and only occasionally from empirical demonstration.
A more likely relationship between these factors and change is one of
mutual interaction, with some priority given in some situations to psychological variables.

In general, social and cultural change does not proceed without psychological change, and group contact is a necessary but insufficient cause
of change. If this is the case, then psychological variables must constitute
some of the "missing" prior conditions. Also, these initial psychological
predispositions to change probably continue to alter during the larger
process of social change.

In the literature there are two massive research paradigms and a host
of smaller ones. The literature on "modern attitudes" and "achievement
motivation" constitutes the bulk of the theoretical and empirical work,
and both, along with a set of perceptual and cognitive skills, qualify as
psychological variables pertaining to the *characteristics of individuals* in the
change process. Of the other approaches, two ("global" and "authoritarian" personality) belong to this same class, while the other two ("classical"
and "operant" learning) are essentially statements not about individual
characteristics, but about *psychological conditions* during the change process.
Thus, out of this vast array of literature, two basic psychological variables
of interest to the student of social and cultural change may be discerned:
psychological *characteristics* of individuals, and psychological *conditions* of
the situation.

Psychological Consequents of Change

Before plunging into the voluminous literature on psychological phenomena that are often considered to be the result of social and cultural change,
it is worthwhile to recall the following information. First, with respect to

locus of change, the concern remains primarily with the *individual*, but the other two loci (*sociocultural* and *institutional*) are important both for the provision of information about the immediate causes of individual change, and for their role as "interaction variables" whose own variation goes hand in hand with the psychological phenomena. Second, the *source* of these individual changes will be seen to exist at the sociocultural level, and perhaps primarily in *external* cultural sources; however, once again evidence for an interactive process will be discovered where both *external* and *internal* sociocultural features must be taken into account if we are to comprehend the nature of the individual response to change. Third, the *direction* of the individual response to change will be considered in terms of the three alternatives that have been proposed: there will be a discussion of "behavioral shifts" toward the behavioral norms that are prevalent in the more dominant sociocultural system; there will be a consideration of "reaffirmation phenomena" that returns the individual to a quasi-traditional set of behavioral norms; and there will be an examination of some novel behaviors, primarily the phenomena of "acculturative stress." Fourth, the *dynamics* of the individual response will be examined, with an emphasis upon the *states* rather than the *processes*; in the absence of research data, especially of longitudinal research, discussions of the latter are rather difficult. And finally, as the division of these two large sections (on antecedents and consequents) indicates, the psychological phenomena considered here are viewed as correlates or consequences of social and cultural change rather than as antecedents. However, as in the case of the discussion of antecedent variables, the allocation of phenomena to one category or another cannot be made with confidence.

A preliminary analysis of the consequents of social and cultural change suggests the greatest variation in the phenomena lies within the notion of *direction*. The discussion of the literature, then, will be presented with three general features in mind: "behavioral shifts," "reaffirmation phenomena," and "acculturative stress." This categorization necessarily simplifies the complex and interwoven nature of the behaviors being considered, but without such an analytical framework, no sensible display of the material would be possible. The final section will attempt to integrate these three features, not only among themselves, but with the earlier materials on psychological and sociocultural antecedents to change.

Behavioral Shifts

This section is concerned with the changes in those behaviors which existed prior to acculturation, to levels or states that more closely approximate those found in the society that is providing the acculturative influences. In simple terms, the concern is with the "taught" becoming more like the "teacher." Although these changes potentially occur in all or most behavioral domains, there have been four obvious research areas that provide the bulk of the literature: (1) the changing patterns of language use ("language shifts"); (2) the study of perceptual and cognitive behavior, primarily in relation to antecedent educational variables; (3) the study of general personality changes; and (4) the monitoring of changes in attitudes that come about as a result of social and cultural change.

Language shifts.   One of the more obvious shifts that occurs with acculturation is the changing pattern of language use. For some (e.g., Lieberson, 1970), language is the key to acculturation, while for others (e.g., Fishman, 1966) culture may be retained even when a traditional language is unused or even lost; in the latter case, however, the term "ethnicity" may be more appropriate than "culture" to label the group context (Glazer & Moynihan, 1975).

Despite the obviousness of language use, there is real difficulty in determining the degree to which individuals actually shift to the new language during acculturation. For example, language is involved not only in speech, but in writing, reading, and thinking; the ease with which one can monitor language shifts in each area varies tremendously (Fishman, 1972, Section VII). Moreover the choice of language will depend on the nature of the relationship (e.g., boss-worker, or friend-friend) in which language is being used.

These difficulties have led to complex analyses of the dual phenomena of language maintenance and language shift. However a few generalizations have emerged from the literature (e.g., Fishman, 1966, 1972; O'Bryan, Reitz, & Kuplowska, 1975; Taft, 1966, 1977) on North America and Australia, although work in other parts of the world requires more attention (Fishman, Ferguson, & Das Gupta, 1968). These generalizations indicate that during social and cultural change, language use does shift, slowly at first, but very rapidly from the second generation on. Second, the shift tends to be mainly away from languages of minority groups with little prestige toward languages of dominant groups with greater prestige. Third, reverse shifts do occur in which a traditional language is deliberately retained or even relearned in order to provide both a symbol and a vehicle for reaffirming a traditional identity; this latter phenomenon will be apparent in most of the behavioral domains encountered in this section.

Perceptual and cognitive shifts.   It has often been noted that apart from missionary activity, the spread of western education has been the most deliberate attempt to alter the behavior of peoples in the history of contact. Economic and political interests may have been the primary goal of contact in most cases, but behavioral changes flowing from those institutions were largely incidental to the goals. In contrast, when educational institutions were introduced into a society (or more accurately, superimposed on existing educational practices) there were deliberate attempts to change the intellectual and other characteristics of the people. Given this explicit goal, along with the convenience of school classes for psychological research, it is no wonder that the greatest bulk of material is in this area.

Although demonstrations of the influence of education are fairly abundant, there are few clear indications of the precise variables involved in the change. At the simplest level, education can be seen as providing more information than was available previously; perceptual and cognitive shifts may come about because of shifts in *content*. Shifts may occur because new ways of coding and retaining information are provided by the arrival of literacy. Furthermore there has been the assumption that education somehow makes people cognitively more *powerful* by extending their capacities. Before reviewing the material available on the psychological shifts that are induced by education, it is important to note that all societies engage in a process of education; so it is not the process itself that is new, but the *formality* and *content* of the process that is introduced by a dominant society. What had traditionally been a process of informal instruction and observational learning in concrete settings is now supplemented or replaced by formal and institutionalized instruction requiring verbal and other novel forms of learning of more abstract material (Scribner & Cole, 1973). Most important, perhaps, is the introduction of literacy to groups of peoples whose symbolic life had heretofore been unwritten. Do these three facets of education lead to any changes in perceptual and cognitive behavior? The answer usually given is a resounding, if not a unanimous, "Yes." The evidence derives from a large and diffuse body of experimental and observational material, based upon many anthropological and psychological approaches. With so much material available, once again there is a need for selection with an eye to representativeness.

Within the study of cognition and perception there are many points of view concerning the "depth" of the changes that result from education. At one extreme, there is the view that real intellectual and perceptual changes take place, resulting in more developed cognitive functioning (the "deep" or "strong" view); at the other extreme, there is the view that only a few test-taking tricks have been acquired that account for the altered score patterns (the "weak" view). And in between, at least two other views may be discerned: one asserts that the changes are comprised of a little of each of the two above extreme changes, while the other argues that the altered cultural setting nurtures a new set of performance skills deeper than the "tricks" point of view, but which is neither more or less "developed" in terms of the first point of view.

Looking first at research into intellectual functioning, there is strong evidence to support the statement that on many, or even most cognitive tests, scores of acculturated and educated samples shift to a position between the scores of unacculturated groups and those norms for the culture providing the influence. The strongest interpretation of these observed shifts has been in the traditional "intelligence testing" movement, where an instrument is assumed to be "culture-free," and hence higher or lower positions on the scale are considered as more or less intelligent; if an educated sample scores higher, then its "intelligence" has been raised. The ethnocentrism inherent in this kind of argument has been noted often in the recent literature (e.g., Berry, 1972) and need not be repeated here.

An equally strong but different position has been taken by Bruner and his colleagues, based upon performance on cognitive tasks derived from the Piagetian school. For Bruner, education serves as "an agency for empowering human minds" (1971, p. 523); as cultures and their educational systems vary, so too will the power of the intellect (p. 526). If education is not available, the intellectual development is reduced or even ceases (Greenfield, 1966, p. 235). And in his strongest interpretation, in the absence of education, " . . . one finds forms of intellectual functioning that are adequate for concrete tasks but not so for matters involving abstract conception. . . . In short, some environments 'push' cognitive growth better, earlier and longer than others" (Greenfield & Bruner, 1969, p. 654).

At the weakest extreme, changes in cognitive task or intelligence test scores with education specifically, and acculturation generally, may be interpreted in terms of mere test sophistication, including familiarity with a test situation (sitting, responding to questions), motivational and interest factors, and perhaps some perceptual-cognitive consequences of literacy (deciphering and interpreting test materials). It would be difficult to argue for effects only at this level, for as Witkin and Berry have pointed out (1975, p. 71), this interpretation would be possible only if education led to fairly rapid and large-scale alterations in test scores. But this has not occurred; educational and acculturational influences can be easily detected, but differences between cultural groups definitely remain.

In between these two extremes, a position has been outlined by Cole and his colleagues (e.g., Scribner and Cole, 1973) that argues that the culture of a group provides appropriate performance settings, and by implication, a change in culture would provide settings for new performances. Such an interpretation has been made by many workers, in both cognitive and perception studies. For example, ecological and cultural settings for the emergence of a variety of skills have been mapped by Berry (1966, 1971, 1976) and Dasen (1972, 1975). And all have been able to demonstrate consistent changes in these skills as new cultural settings emerge through urbanization, industrialization, and education.

The only possible decision is to admit that the evidence available does not permit selection of either a strong, weak, or intermediate interpretation of the observed intellectual changes. At best, the lack of wholesale changes makes it unlikely that the weak ("tricks") interpretation accounts for them, and the unjustified universalism and ethnocentrism in the strong interpretation makes it unlikely to be the most reasonable interpretation. Clearly a good deal of research work is required before any valid view may be presented.

Turning to the study of perception, a similar set of views may be discerned; however, it is difficult to find an example of the hard interpretation in its strongest form. There have been two large research traditions in the cross-cultural study of perception that have fairly consistently revealed changes in scores with increased education and acculturation. The first (the study of susceptibility to a variety of visual illusions: Segall, Campbell, & Herskovits, 1966) has shown that illusion responses vary according to the nature of the visual ecology that varies according to acculturation (specifically the introduction of neatly carpentered right-angled buildings). In a number of supplementary studies and analyses (e.g., Gregor & McPherson, 1965) however, no clear pattern emerged in relation to degree of acculturation. A further analysis (Berry, 1968) led to the demonstration that if one takes two contradictory effects of acculturation into account (more "carpenteredness," leading to an expectation of higher illusion susceptibility; and greater perceptual development, leading to an expectation of lower susceptibility) both effects can be shown to be operating.

A second research tradition (the study of pictorial depth perception: Hudson, 1962) has shown that there are likely to be "two-dimensional" interpretations of "three-dimensional" pictorial representations by unacculturated samples, while those with higher levels of education tended to make the appropriate "three-dimensional" interpretation. Supplementary studies (e.g., Dawson, 1967b; Kilbride, Robbins, & Freeman, 1968; Deregowski, 1974) were able to demonstrate changes in test scores with education. The meaning of these changes, however, remains a matter of debate (Miller, 1973; McGurk & Jahoda, 1975).

Once again, there is the task of estimating the "depth" of these changes. As in the case of cognitive functioning, it is safe to conclude that a "tricks" interpretation is not the whole answer, and since no one has proposed that profound changes in perceptual processes or development occur, the strong position need not receive undue attention. The strongest argument appears to be that of Dawson (1967b) who refers to changes in "habits of perceptual inference" with training and acculturation. However, a qualitative assessment of the patterning of changes suggests that perceptual change may be relatively superficial; education and urban experience appear to "wipe out" scores of traditional samples more readily than in the case of cognitive test performance. This phenomenon is reasonable, since perceptual activity may be considered as less central, and more in interaction with the changing world than is the case for cognitive activity. However, as in the previous case, no valid assessment of the "depth" of perceptual change may be made at the present time.

Personality shifts.   Many personality variables (e.g., achievement orientation, authoritarianism) considered in the section on antecedents to social and cultural change could be reconsidered in this section on consequents; however since they were conceived of as prior to change, even though they undoubtedly undergo change themselves, they were classified as antecedent. In addition to the predicted rise of achievement orientation and falling of authoritarian values, there have been many studies that have been explicitly devoted to monitoring the changes in general personality as a function of the degree of acculturation (e.g., Hallowell, 1955; Beaglehole, 1957; Spindler & Spindler, 1958; Caudill, 1949; Hoffman, 1961) and in many specific traits (e.g. gratification, Gold, 1967; dependency-fatalism, Graves, 1967; and conformity to group norms, Berry, 1967, 1974a). In this section, representative studies will be used to illustrate the research problems and findings of the area.

Two classical studies of general personality changes have been conducted by Hallowell (1955) and Spindler and Spindler (1958, 1968), both with Amerindian populations in the same culture area (Northeastern Algonkian). In Hallowell's study, he was concerned with two questions: what are the "typical psychological characteristics" of a group; and "do we find continuity or discontinuity in the modal personality . . . at different levels of acculturation?" (1955, p. 345). A further question, of social and personal adjustment, will be considered in the section on stress reactions. Hallowell's basic design was to select three communities of Ojibway Amerindians at differing levels of acculturation, and to administer a projective test (the Rorschach⁷) to samples from these communities. To the extent that there was similarity across groups, Hallowell was able to extract a modal aboriginal personality, and to the extent that there were systematic differences across acculturation levels, he was able to infer changes in general personality due to acculturation. In fact a remarkably stable pattern emerged that was identifiable as "a persistent core of generic traits which can be identified as Ojibway" (p. 351) which "seems generic for the Algonkian peoples of the Eastern Woodlands of the earliest contact period" (p. 351). Even the acculturated sample "are still Ojibway in a psychological sense", there being "no evidence at all of a fundamental psychological transformation" (p. 351). On the other hand, he continues, "the fact of psychological continuity must not be taken to imply that no modifications in the psychological structure of the Ojibway have taken place" (p. 351); indeed, a weakening of the rigid self-control so characteristic of many Algonkian peoples, and the appearance of apathy and frustration, all indicate an effect of acculturation. However, these changes serve to emphasize the remarkable continuity of traditional personality through the process of acculturation found in Hallowell's studies.

In the work of Spindler and Spindler at least five acculturation levels are distinguished among the Menomini Amerindian samples: one they term "nation-oriented," another "ungrouped transitionals," and two others as "acculturated," divided into an "elite" and a lower-status group. A fifth category, which they place between the native-oriented and transitional groups, is a Peyote religious cult that they refer to as a "stabilized form of reactive movement"[8] (Spindler & Spindler, 1968, p. 328–29). Like Hallowell, the Spindlers employed a projective technique (again the Rorschach) and a variety of participant observation techniques to assess relationships between general personality and level of acculturation. At the traditional ("native-oriented") pole, they found a psychological configuration that centered on personal restraint, self-control in interpersonal relations, and dependence on supernatural power. In the "Peyote group" there was a significant relaxing of controls over emotions, while in the "transitionals" there were signs of withdrawal and deviancy (drinking, homicide) and a lack of goal-oriented behavior either toward traditional or new cultural goals. In the two acculturated groups, emotional openness and the pursuit of new goals (e.g., personal success, material acquisition) were apparent; the loss of the old emotional restraints was clear.

This picture of varying personality patterns across an acculturational dimension contrasts with the degree of continuity noted by Hallowell. In a sense, these two studies illustrate the range of material available on general personality continuity and change. It may be the case that the difference is due to the relative degree of acculturation experienced by the groups in the two studies; that is, the most acculturated of Hallowell's samples appear to have been experiencing a degree of acculturation represented in the Spindlers' transitional group. If this is the case, then the contrasting findings may be resolved by hypothesizing a fairly stable shift in general personality from traditional through to transitional stages; in this range the phenomenon of continuity may be the predominant one. Thereafter during transition, however, difficulties of adjustment may break down any observable continuity and lead to the obvious levels of social and psychological stress so often described in the literature. Resolutions of this turbulence may be made either by engaging in "reaffirmation behavior," by seeking novel integrations of the two cultures, or by completing the acculturation process and shifting completely to the life style of the dominant culture. Such a pattern would make sense of the Hallowell and Spindler observations. The material will be examined in the rest of this section on psychological consequents to discover whether further evidence is available to test it.

A topic that is often studied in relation to general personality change is that of ethnic identity. This research tradition also often involves the phenomenon of reaffirmation, and so provides a further opportunity to check the hypothesis. A basic argument (e.g., Glaser, 1958) is that the ethnic category that is self-assigned provides "a frame of reference for ordering social relationships" (p. 31), and as such is an important element in the daily life of people experiencing intergroup contact and social change. In some studies, only linear changes are observed; for example, across generations of migrants to a new country, there is a gradual shift in identity from the ancestral to the host group (e.g. Taft, 1966, 1977). In other studies (mainly with indigenous groups) increased contact also induces a return to identification with the ancestral group (e.g. Jahoda, 1961; Berry, 1970; Wober, 1973). Often there is considered to be an "identity struggle" (e.g., Robbins, 1973a, 1973b) that is resolved either by reaffirming one's ancestral identity or by completing the shift to the new identity (De Vos & Romanucci-Ross, 1975).

The gradual shift in identity appears to be related to an increasing degree of acculturation. For example across nine Amerindian samples (Berry, 1975), the identity choice of respondents was correlated highly with the education of the individual and with the general level of education in the community. Nevertheless, in addition to this general trend, some highly acculturated individuals did reaffirm their ancestral identity. The dynamics of the reaffirmation, however, remains unexplored.

Another question of interest is whether the process of nation building requires a large-scale shift away from a number of local ethnic identities to a new monolithic national identity (Berry, 1974b; Segall, Doornbos, & Davis, 1976). Some nations deliberately seek the assimilation of ethnic groups to a common norm, while others permit or encourage a variety of identities in a "plural" sociocultural system. Whether the shift to a single national identity is necessary or not, the evidence presented in this section suggests that the shift generally does occur, but that there are phenomena of resistance and occasionally of reaffirmation.

Attitude Shifts.   The evidence presented in the section on psychological antecedents showed that modern attitudes not only were implicated in the process of social and cultural change, but also became more "modern" as experience of schools, urbanization, and industrialization became higher. This section is concerned with a programme of attitude research that did not conceive of the attitudes as antecedent to change, but as a correlate and consequent of level of acculturation and differential policies of acculturation.[9] In a series of studies, Berry (Sommerlad & Berry, 1970; Berry, 1970, 1974b, 1975) set out to study how various populations who occupied a minority ethnic status desired to relate to the larger society to which they were being acculturated. A conceptual scheme was advanced that considered two questions: is it valuable to retain one's traditional culture, and is it valuable to have positive relations with the larger society? If one values both, then an attitude of *integration* is defined; if the first is not valued, but the second is, then an *assimilation* attitude is defined; and if the first is valued, but the second is not, then a *rejection* or self-segregation attitude is defined. A series of questions was developed that phrased these two values in a variety of ways. In both studies with Australian Aboriginal respondents (Sommerlad & Berry, 1970; Berry, 1970) there was evidence that acculturation level in general was associated with more positive attitudes towards *assimilation;* however there was also some evidence that not only were less acculturated individuals more in favor of *rejection,* but so too were some highly educated individuals suggesting some degree of attitudinal reaffirmation. In the Amerindian studies (involving nine samples of varying cultural background and acculturation level), the mean sample response in favor of *assimilation* was positively correlated with level of education, while the opposite was the case for attitudes toward *rejection.* Within samples, there was also evidence for individual experience of education to be associated (in the same direction) with the two attitudes; however, once again some highly educated respondents in most samples reversed the general trend and provided reaffirmation responses (Berry, 1975).

These patterns of attitudes toward the larger society suggest both some degree of "shift" as a function of continuing acculturation, but also some "reaffirmation" consistent with the study of supernatural beliefs conducted by Jahoda (1970). Obviously some other factors, at present unspecified, lead to splitting the process into three avenues of further adaptation, one directed toward further assimilation, one toward integration, and one toward a reaffirmation of traditional life. The psychological study of this splitting point is recognized as an urgent and important research question, for it will clarify the apparent nonlinearity in personality, identity, and attitudinal changes with acculturation.

At this point, it will be useful to pause and present a schematic overview of the psychological consequents discussed so far. Such an overview will clarify the trends noted, and will permit an introduction to the next section. Some psychological variables have been displayed as a function of some general dimension of social change, primarily defined in terms of acculturation (mainly education) from external sources.

In Figure 6-2 the four psychological areas reviewed so far are indicated as a function of this general acculturation dimension. At the top is a fifth psychological area, which is perhaps the largest of the research traditions in the literature: acculturative stress.

On measures of perception and cognition, the trend is a fairly straightforward shift from functioning in a traditional manner to obtaining test scores that are more like the norms of the new culture. In the study of personality and identity, there is also some evidence for a similar straightforward shift, but during a midpoint of transition there is some evidence

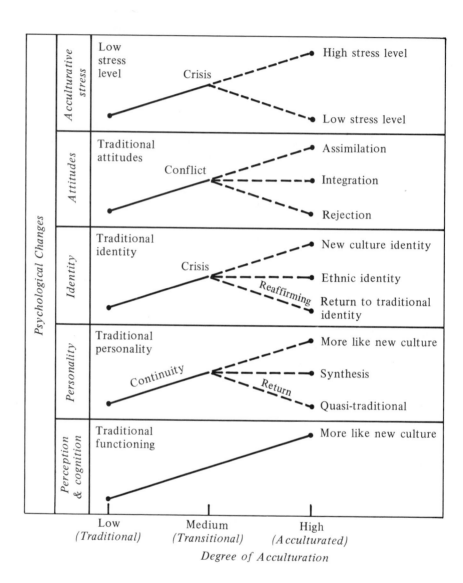

Figure 6-2: The Course of Psychological Change in Five Domains as a Function of the Degree of Acculturation.

of crisis and fragmentation that tends to resolve itself by splitting; one avenue continues the movement toward the new or host culture, one moves toward a quasi-traditional pattern of "reaffirmation," and one seeks an intermediate synthesis or "ethnic" identity. A similar pattern appears in the area of attitude research; there is a fairly straightforward shift toward assimilation attitudes with increasing acculturation, but again there is evidence of attitudinal integration and attitudinal reaffirmation (rejection). This points toward a nearly parallel course for these four separate phenomena associated with acculturation. The hypothetical course of the fifth phenomenon, "acculturative stress," is illustrated at the top of the figure; an examination of the evidence for such stress during acculturation follows.

Acculturative Stress

The discussions of "shifts" in a variety of behaviors with acculturation might have given the impression of a fairly easy psychological transfer between cultures. However, the presence of the reaffirmation phenomena suggests that some turbulence might be present during acculturation. Indeed the belief that social and cultural change always bring with it some emotional difficulties has been widespread in the anthropological and psychiatric literature, but it has been questioned from time to time (e.g., Fried, 1964; Hippler, 1974).

In general, the arguments have been that social disorganization, cultural stress, or communal crises (Leighton, 1959; Spradley & Phillips, 1972; Vallee, 1968) act as a mediating variable between the variables of social change and "acculturative stress." This latter term has been employed by Berry (1971a, p. 326) as a general term to refer to those individual states and behaviors that are mildly pathological and disruptive, including those problems of mental health and psychosomatic symptoms so often observed during social change.

At least three areas of research may be used as sources of evidence. The first, involving change and industrialization within a single nation or cultural group, has exhibited very little evidence of stress reaction. As Fried (1964) has noted, over the periods of industrialization in Western countries (for example the last 150 years), there has been little change in rates of hospitalization for psychoses. And Inkeles and Smith (1970) have found no evidence of maladjustment or strain during industrialization in their Six Country study. However, it should be noted that the samples in the Inkeles and Smith study were "successful" in their move to the city and in their search for employment (Berry & Annis, 1974, p. 384). Those who were not included in the sample, either by nonmigration in the first place, or by return migration following an unsuccessful urban adaptation, might have exhibited higher stress levels. But, of course, these individuals could not be represented in their samples. Furthermore, it is reasonable to assume that urban migrants have better health services available; this would likely have some effect on reported psychosomatic symptoms of stress.

A second area of research, involving migrants to new countries, has usually provided evidence for more acculturative stress and breakdown (Fried, 1964; Sanua, 1970) among immigrants, but this is far from universal (Murphy, 1961, 1965). In some host countries (for example, in the United States) migrant groups have "higher rates of admission to mental hospitals than the local-born population" (Murphy, 1974), whereas in other countries (for example in Canada and southeast Asia) the reverse appears to be the case. One interpretation (Murphy, 1969, 1974) is that in culturally plural societies (those pursuing *integration* policies) it may be possible for ethnic groups to maintain a supportive cultural tradition, especially if their numbers are high; on the other hand, in nonplural societies (those pursuing *assimilation* policies) there is a dominant culture with a "clear set of national attitudes and values which all immigrants had either to adjust to or oppose" (p. 10) leading to pressure, conflict and eventually higher rates of breakdown.

The third research tradition, and the one with which we are most concerned, is that of the acculturation of native peoples by dominating societies, for example in North and South America. In this area there is greater evidence of acculturative stress, but even here, it is not inevitable (Chance, 1965) and may have been overestimated in the past decades of research (Hippler, 1974).

In reviewing this large body of literature, we will once again select a few examples of representative research. Because the cultural conditions for this form largely exist for Amerindian and Aboriginal peoples (in North America and Australia), these cultural areas will be used to provide the appropriate studies. Among researchers of sociocultural and psychological stress in North America, Chance stands out as a key figure: his two large projects, one with Alaskan Eskimos, and the other with the Cree of Quebec, provide a fairly coherent statement about psychological adjustment problems during acculturation. In his Eskimo research, Chance (1960, 1965, 1973) was primarily concerned with the cultural disruption and disorganization generated by the Euroamerican intrusion into the area (the construction of radar bases). In his first study (1960) Chance reported that in general, no community disintegration or loss of morale could be detected despite very dramatic technological change; he interpreted this as being due, primarily, to a built-in predisposition to change, where "a greater value was placed on adaptability than on conformity" (1965, p. 373). Noting that this was in sharp contrast to most other studies of rapid acculturation, Chance turned his attention to an analysis of why this may have been the case. Chance employed three variables: contact, identification, and an estimate of psychosomatic stress based upon the Cornell Medical Index (Brodman, Erdman, Lorge, Gershenson & Wolff, 1952). His hypothesis, that those Eskimos who had low contact with Western life, but strongly identified with it, would have a high level of psychosomatic stress was supported; consistent with this argument, those who had more congruent levels of both variables had lower levels of stress. The generality of this incongruity argument needs to be checked with culturally dissimilar samples (Vallee, 1968, p. 566); however, the value of this finding was in questioning the necessary relation between dramatic social change and psychological stresses that had held until that time.

In his second study, Chance (1968) led an interdisciplinary team to the consideration of the problems of developmental change among a group of Cree Amerindians of northern Quebec. Its purpose was to more fully comprehend the nature of social and cultural change and to apply this knowledge to the economic growth and social well-being of the Cree people (p. 3). Specifically, the Chance team wanted to test further the psychological effects of incongruence amid economic, social, and political change:

> We plan to test the hypothesis that the degree of congruence in the three spheres of development will be directly correlated with the degree of social stability of the population undergoing change; and conversely, that uneven or incongruent rates of development between these three sections will promote conflict (p. 7).

Of greatest interest is the psychological focus of the study conducted by the psychiatrist Wintrob (1968) and the anthropologist Sindell (Wintrob & Sindell, 1972). Working primarily with Cree youth, they were interested in the prevalence of identity problems and of psychopathology that could be related to acculturation. In particular, most of the youth in the study changed their residence each year between a traditional hunting life and a residential school life; this process of "enculturative discontinuity," enhanced by intergenerational conflicts during the return to camp life, brought about identity conflict in almost half the student population, and psychopathological symptoms in an additional 14 percent of cases.

The new dimension of discontinuity has now been added to that of the incongruity dimension of Chance's earlier work, and both should be employed in further analyses. One further study that enabled a partial check on these findings was conducted by Berry and Annis (1974). In that study, they sampled from three different Amerindian cultures (Cree, Carrier, and Tsimshian) varying in degree of cultural disparity with the larger Eurocanadian society. Measures of psychosomatic stress symptoms and feelings of marginality varied across the groups as predicted. This finding provides support for the incongruity hypothesis, but the cultural conditions did not permit a test of the discontinuity hypothesis. However another hypothesis was advanced and confirmed: in most Amerindian samples, levels of psychosomatic stress and feelings of marginality were negatively related to the degree of individual psychological differentiation (Witkin & Berry, 1975). Those individuals who were psychologically differentiated (i.e., field-independent), no matter how disparate their culture from the Eurocanadian norm, experienced fewer stressful effects of acculturation. This factor of differentiation, it will be remembered, was implicated in the process of development as a purely cognitive variable; its more general role will be considered in the next section.

The other cultural area where acculturative stress has been studied is in Australia. A leader in this work has been Cawte. In a series of publications (Cawte, Bianchi, & Kiloh, 1968; Bianchi, Cawte, & Kiloh, 1970; Cawte, 1973) the patterning of psychosomatic stress symptoms among selected groups of Aborigines has been analyzed in relation to acculturation pressures and other external changes. In a first study (1968), responses to a twenty-item modification of the Cornell Medical Index (Brodman et al., 1952) indicated a relatively high level of stress among Aborigines; it was especially high among those who were more economically deprived and those who had immigrated from other areas. It appears as if Cawte and his colleagues were observing an additive effect that combined the stresses of poverty and dislocation with the effects of general acculturation. In a second study (Bianchi et al., 1970), a Guttman scale was constructed to yield an index of "cultural identity" (based upon four aspects of acculturation), but overall correlations between the scales and psychosomatic stress were low. Only one of the four elements (retention of traditional beliefs) proved to be significantly (positively) related to stress levels, leading the authors to conclude that "culture contact of the kind existing on Mornington Island is not a significant causal factor in mental illness" (1970, p. 385). However Bianchi et al. (1970) and Cawte (1973) point out that for the one group whose acculturation has been rapid and conflict ridden, stress levels were indeed higher than for the other groups.

Other studies of acculturative stress with Australian Aborigines (e.g., Berry, 1970) tend to indicate a high level of stress, in relation to other peoples studied previously. Of particular interest is the indication that stress levels may be reduced by assuming an "Australian" identity and more positive attitudes towards assimilation. Further indications that stress increases with acculturation were provided indirectly by Dawson (1969c), who demonstrated a decline in satisfaction with a number of life situations (e.g., education, general treatment) across three levels of acculturation.

Overall, it is clear that earlier assumptions that social change and acculturation tended to be psychologically devastating are no longer maintained. In the research tradition involving native peoples in relation to a dominant society, however, there is fairly persistent evidence for somewhat higher levels of psychosomatic stress among these populations than among nonnative samples. Differences between native groups indicate that the degree of cultural incongruity or disparity may be a factor in inducing stress, and analyses within groups suggest that stress may decline after a decision to further assimilate. However, evidence also suggests that during transition (especially if it is characterized by some discontinuity in cultural expectations) and for those who have reaffirmed, stress levels may be very high. Finally, there is some indication that for those groups who are able to maintain themselves and not experience dominant group pressures to assimilate (as in plural societies), stress levels may be lower. All these, however, should remain at the level of hypotheses, and be the subject of considerable further research. That the question remains a serious one is evidenced by the theme of the 1975 World Congress on Mental Health: "Economic Growth and Mental Health."

Integrative Overview and Future Research

It should be apparent that the state of knowledge about psychology and social change is full of gaps and that no comprehensive summary position is possible. In contrast, over twenty years ago anthropologists were able to draw together an impressive set of materials (Mead, 1953) to assess the state of their knowledge; and more recently (Goodenough, 1963) that discipline was able to prepare a "manual for people engaged in developing 'underdeveloped' countries" (p. 11).

Despite this large difference in the state of the art, there are some bases on which to attempt to construct an integrated model of psychological factors in social and cultural change. First, the psychological study of change is not and should not be independent of the approaches made by those other disciplines; they provide some leads and indications. Second, some extant integrative models and schemas are available in the literature (e.g., Doob, 1960, 1968; McClelland, 1961; Cohen, 1968; Himmelstrand and Okediji, 1968; Dawson, 1973a; Tanaka, 1973), some of which have guided this review of the available materials. And third are some emerging findings and generalizations from the mass of studies reviewed that bear either directly or tangentially upon this topic.

This section will proceed by first referring to the schematic overview presented at the outset (Figure 6-1). Then a number of other schemas and models will be examined to search for points of congruence and incongruence. This second step should lead to observations that have both relatively firm bases for generating hypotheses for future research, and gaps that require further exploration. Finally the field of enquiry will be oriented and suggestions for some topics for future research will be provided.

At the level of individual behavior, a number of psychological variables have emerged in the review. Essentially two clusters appeared, one that may be termed "psychological characteristics" and the other "psychological conditions." Among the former were some personality traits of achievement orientation, authoritarianism, variables of personality, and value congruence with the goals of social and cultural change. Also, there was some evidence for cognitive and perceptual congruence being implicated. Among the latter was the structure of behavioral reinforcements provided by the external culture for the primary and secondary needs of indigenous peoples.

Moving to the consequents, there was frequent mention of the disorganization or even disintegration which occurs at the sociocultural level. Some recent arguments, however, indicate that this is neither inevitable nor universal: the presence or absence of this feature is probably a function of the congruence between the external and traditional cultural variables. In any case the sociocultural system does become changed, and may become disorganized; the new features that were implicated were a more stratified social and political system, greater emphasis on technology and education, and, to emphasize a major feedback loop, an increased emphasis on social and cultural change itself.

Finally at the individual level, there was consistent evidence that many (or most) behaviors shift away from traditional norms to those that are exhibited by norms conveying the change. In such areas as perception, cognition, attitudes, and personality traits, the general drift is unmistakable. However, the process appeared not to be linear, at least not for all individuals; some demonstrated reaffirmation behaviors and some novel integration behaviors in all except perceptual and cognitive functioning. And, consistent with the observed phenomena of cultural disorganization, there are often (but not always) symptoms of acculturative stress behaviors, which appear to be resolved either by further assimilation, or in some cases by reaffirmation behavior.

These are the structure, relations, and content of the reviewed material, set in the context of the schematic overview and analysis based upon other social science disciplines. How does this general overview relate to the other schemes and models referred to previously? It should be noted that in most cases, the other schemes are *research* schemes, and as such tend to overemphasize the variables of particular interest during a particular research project. Nevertheless, most of the other schemes have sought some generality by looking at variables beyond their immediate research problem. To this extent, then, comparisons may be made, and perhaps some insights may be gained to guide future research.

In the introductory section of this chapter considerable attention was devoted to the comprehensive account of Doob (1960). It will be remembered that Doob's hypotheses were very broad, and were proposed in part to stimulate work that might lead to their acceptance or rejection. To what extent has subsequent work supported these hypotheses? In his first set concerned with the emotional tone of those experiencing change, despite a shift away from the point of view that generated the predictions of discontent, aggression, ambivalence, and sensitivity, there is a good deal of evidence to indicate that these emotional states do attend the process of transition (see also Guthrie's chapter in Volume 6 of this *Handbook*). In his second set concerned with the psychological characteristics of those who have changed, there has been some support for his predictions of increased initiative, independence, and abstracting facility. It is possible to argue that such a pattern involves an increase of psychological differentiation (Witkin & Berry, 1975).

Turning now to the set of models already available in the literature (McClelland, 1961; Cohen, 1968; Himmelstrand and Okediji, 1968; Tanaka, 1973; Dawson, 1973a; Inkeles and Smith, 1974), there are a number of similarities in overall conceptualization. First, all of them propose a set of "input" variables that are basically sociocultural and institutional. Second, all of the models move to a set of psychological variables whose core is a motivational-attitudinal-values cluster. And third, most of the models move to a third set of variables that is basically one of economic and political development. It is quite clear from this brief description that consistent with colleagues in economics, there has been a heavy emphasis on "development thinking" and "modernization" among even psychologically oriented researchers. These models also switch their "locus" back and forth between the "sociocultural" and "individual" levels. With their typical concern with sociocultural input and output, and their interest in individual psychological variables mediating them, other phenomena of interest tend to be obscured. In the present model, both the "sociocultural" and the "individual" locus of change are carried through the three stages.

Although the schematic model proposed in this chapter grew out of a consideration of representative work in many areas, it is clear that the relative emphasis on some aspects (as evidenced in the extant models and the large-scale research traditions of achievement orientation and modern attitudes) has overshadowed the work in other areas. This discrepancy in research investment among the various areas is in need of some balancing. To conclude this chapter, suggestions of a reorientation of the field are given below. These, of course, are suggestions based only upon scientific considerations; practical (primarily economic) considerations may continue to influence research trends, but this should not deter the attempt to specify where scientific weaknesses lie.

1. Psychological research on social and cultural change should give at least initial consideration to all six variables in Figure 6–1. The "development" (and "modernity") research traditions have carved a rut through the phenomena available for study, leading to an imbalanced state of knowledge.

2. Research problems should be considered from each of the five perspectives outlined in the preliminary analyses, (and structured in Figure 6–1). The relative emphasis on group or individual level measures, on external or internal sources of change, on antecedents or consequents, on processes or states, and on the linearity of change, should not be prejudged. Many interesting and important dimensions will go unobserved if their nonexistence is assumed.

3. In particular, there has appeared a large overemphasis on states, and a relative neglect of the psychological processes involved in social and cultural change. There is some evidence concerning what the phenomena are, but very little knowledge about how things got to be that way.

4. Some phenomena, such as achievement orientation, modern attitudes, and acculturative stress now have such a large literature that it is perhaps time to think through it rather than add to the research, and to integrate rather than generate new data. These variables are in danger of swamping the field.

5. In contrast, many other phenomena remain largely undeveloped in the literature. Specifically, there are questions about the depth of perceptual and cognitive changes, and about the dynamics of reaffirmation that require research attention. Moreover, the whole area of race and ethnic relations, although well developed in its own right, has not been brought into the arena of social and cultural change. Finally, *comparative* studies of social change are rare; case studies (in single cultures) do not permit the systematic examination of covariation or cause among the numerous variables.

6. A great deal of the psychological research is based upon populations of convenience; studies in North America predominate, with substantial material also available from Africa and Oceania; very little is available on Asia (particularly that massive and apparently successful social change experiment—China) and almost none at all from Latin and South America (Escovar, 1974). Even the cross-cultural psychology movement can be charged with cultural bias!

7. Interactions are also present between these cultural areas with inadequate information and some of the variables in the preliminary analysis. For example, most studies dealing with psychological antecedents of change are based upon indigenous populations that are the majority in their societies (e.g., in Africa, India); in contrast, most studies dealing with consequents of change are based upon either indigenous or migrant populations where they constitute the minority (e.g., in North America and Australia). With this interaction, it is difficult to pinpoint the variables that are operating in situations of social and cultural change.

8. Finally, the conceptualizations of most of the social and cultural change issues are rooted in Western science, and change is often subtly and covertly defined in terms of Westernization. Until theoretical approaches, and not just empirical examples, become culturally more diffuse and representative, the whole study of social and cultural change (whether by psychologists or by other social scientists) will be suspect by those very populations whom researchers seek to aid (see Sinha, 1973; Jahoda, 1975; Zaidi, 1975).

Notes

1. This chapter was prepared while the author was a Fellow at the Netherlands Institute for Advanced Study in the Humanities and Social Sciences, Wassenaar, The Netherlands (1974–75). The support of the Institute and of the library facilities of the Institute for Social Study (The Hague) are gratefully acknowledged. A number of individuals provided critical commentary on the draft manuscript; for their assistance, I thank Lutz Eckensberger, Angela Ginorio, Alex Inkeles, Rich Brislin, and Harry Triandis.

2. One other integrated statement was made at about the same time: Kushner, Gibson, Gulick, Honigmann and Nonas (1962) assembled a comprehensive propositional inventory, from an anthropological perspective, on "what accounts for sociocultural change?"

3. This provocative term appears to have been used deliberately by Doob, since he devotes the first paragraph in his book to his choice of words. He explains: "I am not using the word 'civilization' either in a snobbish or a derogatory sense. We need some kind of concept to call attention to the differences between people who unwittingly live next to one another in the bush and those who wittingly live on top of one another in modern apartment houses. If 'civilization' suggests the possibility of a variation not only in the dwelling places but also in the values of the two groups, then the term is satisfactorily discharging its function. Whether one set of values is better or worse than the other is not proclaimed. In addition the title of the book proposes a continuum rather than a sharp distinction: not civilized and uncivilized, but more and less civilized people are compared" (p. ix). What is intended is a term to "refer to the culture, or way of life, possessed by modern literate and industrial nations in Europe and America" (p. 2), and the transition to this state, which he equates with "modernization" (p. 2). Perhaps Doob selected this term as a shock cure for the complex value issue.

4. "Achievement motivation" is most often defined as a personal characteristic that drives an individual to persistently compete with a standard of excellence. In nontechnical language, it has been simplified to "the urge to improve" (McClelland & Winter, 1969, p. 10), and its usual designation is "nAch" (for "need for achievement").

5. An important reinterpretation of these group differences by Heckhausen (1971) suggests that actual behavior may change even when achievement scores change very little. He further suggests that training reduces the "fear of failure" more than it increases achievement striving.

6. Hagen excludes hunting and gathering societies on the grounds that "so far in the world's history, economic growth has begun only in agricultural societies . . . it seems unlikely that it can begin in societies that have not reached the state of settled agriculture" (p. 20).

7. The Rorschach Inkblot test is regarded by many cross-cultural psychologists as an unsatisfactory tool (see Holtzman, Volume 2). However, sensitive ethnographers like Hallowell have used it to advantage, as an adjunct to standard field observation techniques.

8. Reactive movements that are often also referred to as reaffirmation, revitalization, or millenarian movements (see e.g., Burridge, 1969; Linton, 1943; and Wallace, 1956), are sociocultural level phenomena that selectively return the life style of a group to a quasi-traditional form. They almost certainly involve individual psychological reorientation as well, including identity, attitudes, beliefs, and emotional stress reactions. Such a reaffirmation was envisaged by Storequist (1935, p. 12) who suggested that one possible course for "marginal man" was to "swing about and identify themselves" again with the traditional life.

9. Those countries that have recently faced the task of forging a nation from a variety of continuing immigrant peoples, and a variety of indigenous peoples (e.g. Australia, New Zealand, South Africa, and all of North and South America) have pursued a variety of policies. The three most common are *assimilation* (where groups are encouraged to enter into the central culture), *integration* (where groups maintain their cultural integrity, but are encouraged to pull together for national goals) and *segregation* (where groups are kept out, or keep themselves out of a central cultural life). A study of national attitudes toward such cultural policy options in Canada has indicated greater support for the *integration* option in a culturally plural society. (Berry, Kalin, & Taylor, 1977).

References

APTER, D. E., & MUSHI, S. S. Political science. *International Social Science Journal,* 1972, *24,* 44–68.

BALANDIER, G. Sociology. *International Social Science Journal,* 1972, *24,* 69–79.

BARBICHON, G. La diffusion des connaissances scientifiques et techniques dans le public: ses conditions dans les pays en voie de dévelopement. *Journal of Social Issues,* 1968, *24,* 135–56.

BARRY, H., CHILD, I., & BACON, M. Relation of child training to subsistence economy. *American Anthropologist,* 1959, *61,* 51–63.

BEAGLEHOLE, E. *Social change in the south pacific.* New York: MacMillan, 1957.

BELSHAW, C. S. Anthropology. *International Social Science Journal,* 1972, *24,* 80–94.

BERRY, J. W. Temne and Eskimo perceptual skills. *International Journal of Psychology,* 1966, *1,* 207–29.

―――. Independence and conformity in subsistence level societies. *Journal of Personality and Social Psychology,* 1967, *7,* 415–18.

―――. Ecology, perceptual development and the Muller-Lyer illusion. *British Journal of Psychology,* 1968, *59,* 205–10.

————. Marginality, stress and ethnic identification in an acculturated aboriginal community. *Journal of Cross-Cultural Psychology*, 1970, *1*, 239–52.

————. Ecological and cultural factors in spatial perceptual development. *Canadian Journal of Behavioural Science*, 1971a, *3*, 324–26.

————. Psychological research in the north. *Anthropologica*, 1971b, *13*, 143–57.

————. Radical cultural relativism and the concept of intelligence. In L. J. Cronbach & P. Drenth (Eds.), *Mental tests and cultural adaptation*. The Hague: Mouton, 1972, pp. 77–88.

————. Differentiation across cultures: cognitive style and affective style. In J. L. M. Dawson & W. J. Lonner (Eds.), *Readings in cross-cultural psychology*. Hong Kong: University of Hong Kong Press, 1974a, pp. 167–75.

————. Psychological aspects of cultural pluralism: unity and identity reconsidered. *Topics in Culture Learning*, 1974b, *2*, 17–22.

————. Amerindian attitudes toward assimilation: multicultural policy and reality in Canada. Paper presented to 34th Annual Meeting, Society for Applied Anthropology, Amsterdam, 1975.

————. *Human ecology and cognitive style: comparative studies in cultural and psychological adaptation*. Beverly Hills, Calif.: Sage/Halsted, 1976.

BERRY, J. W. & ANNIS, R. C. Acculturative stress: the role of ecology, culture and differentiation. *Journal of Cross-Cultural Psychology*, 1974, *5*, 382–406.

BERRY, J. W. & DASEN, P. (Eds.), *Culture and cognition*. London: Methuen, 1974.

BERRY, J. W. & KALIN, R., & TAYLOR, D. M. *Multiculturalism and ethnic attitudes in Canada*. Ottawa: Government of Canada, 1977.

BERRY, J. W. & LONNER, W. J. (Eds.), *Applied cross-cultural psychology*. Amsterdam: Swets and Zeitlinger, 1975.

BIANCHI, G. N., CAWTE, J. E., & KILOH, L. G. Cultural identity and the mental health of Australian Aborigines. *Social Science and Medicine*, 1970, *3*, 371–87.

BOWD, A. Practical abilities of Indians and Eskimos. *Canadian Psychologist*, 1974, *15*, 281–90.

BRISLIN, R., & VAN BUREN, H. Can they go home again? *International Educational and Cultural Exchange*, 1974, *9*, 19–24.

BRODMAN, K., ERDMAN, A. J., LORGE, I., GERSHENSON, C. P., & WOLFF, H. G. The Cornell medical index health questionnaire: the evaluation of emotional disturbances. *Journal of Clinical Psychology*, 1952, *8*, 119–24.

BRUNER, J. S. The perfectibility of the intellect. In A. R. Desai (Ed.), *Essays on modernization of underdeveloped societies*, Vol. 1. Bombay: Thacker, 1971, pp. 523–35.

BURRIDGE, K. *New heaven, new earth: a study of Millenarian activities*. New York: Schocken, 1969.

CAMPBELL, A., & CONVERSE, P. (Eds.), *The human meaning of social change*. New York: Russell Sage Foundation, 1972.

CAUDILL, W. Psychological characteristics of acculturated Ojibway children. *American Anthropologist*, 1949, *51*, 409–27.

————. Social change and cultural continuity in modern Japan. In G. de Vos (Ed.), *Responses to change: society, culture and personality*. New York: Van Nostrand, 1976, pp. 18–44.

CAWTE, J. E. *Cruel, poor and brutal nations*. Honolulu: University of Hawaii Press, 1973.

CAWTE, J. E., BIANCHI, G. N., & KILOH, L. G. Personal discomfort in Australian Aborigines. *Australian and New Zealand Journal of Psychiatry*, 1968, *2*, 69–79.

CHANCE, N. A. Culture change and integration: an Eskimo example. *American Anthropologist*, 1960, *62*, 1028–44.

———. Acculturation, self-identification and personality adjustment. *American Anthropologist*, 1965, *67*, 372–93.

———, (Ed.). *Conflict in culture: problems of developmental change among the Cree.* Ottawa, Canada: Canadian Research Centre for Anthropology, 1968.

———. Directed change and northern peoples. In G. W. Rogers (Ed.), *Change in Alaska: people, petroleum and politics.* University of Alaska Press, 1973, pp. 180–94.

CHILD, I. L., STORM, T., & VEROFF, J. Achievement themes in folk tales related to socialization practice. In J. W. Atkinson (Ed.), *Motives in fantasy, action and society.* New York: Van Nostrand, 1958, pp. 479–92.

COHEN, R. *Modernization in Africa: a social and psychological model of analysis.* Seventh Herskovits Memorial Lecture, Centre for African Studies, University of Edinburgh, 1968.

COLE, M., & SCRIBNER, S. *Culture and thought.* New York: Wiley, 1974.

DASEN, P. R. Cross-cultural Piagetian research: a summary. *Journal of Cross-Cultural Psychology*, 1972, *3*, 23–39.

———. Concrete operational development in three cultures. *Journal of Cross-Cultural Psychology*, 1975, *6*, 156–72.

DAWSON, J. L. M. Traditional values and work efficiency in a West African mine labour force. *Occupational Psychology*, 1963, *3*, 209–18.

———. Traditional versus Western attitudes in West Africa: the construction, validation and application of a measuring device. *British Journal of Social and Clinical Psychology*, 1967a, *6*, 81–96.

———. Cultural and physiological influences on spatial-perceptual processes in West Africa. Part I. *International Journal of Psychology*, 1967b, *2*, 115–25.

———. Attitudinal consistency and conflict in West Africa. *International Journal of Psychology*, 1969a, *4*, 39–53.

———. Attitude change and conflict among Australian Aborigines. *Australian Journal of Psychology*, 1969b, *21*, 101–16.

———. Exchange theory and comparison level changes among Australian Aborigines. *British Journal of Social and Clinical Psychology*, 1969c, *8*, 133–40.

———. Effects of ecology and subjective culture on individual traditional-modern attitude change, achievement motivation, and potential for economic development in the Japanese and Eskimo societies. *International Journal of Psychology*, 1973a, *8*, 215–25.

———. Adjustment problems encountered by individuals in the process of modernization in the resolution of traditional-modern attitudinal conflict. Paper presented at East-West Centre Culture Learning Institute, Hawaii, January, 1973b.

DAWSON, J. L. M., LAW, H., LEUNG. A., & WHITNEY, R. E. Scaling Chinese traditional-modern attitudes and the GSR measurement of "important" versus "un-important" Chinese concepts. *Journal of Cross-Cultural Psychology*, 1971, *2*, 1–27.

DAWSON, J. L. M., WHITNEY, R. E., & LAW, R. T-S. Attitude conflict, GSR, and traditional-modern attitude change among Hong Kong Chinese. *Journal of Social Psychology*, 1972, *88*, 163–76.

DEREGOWSKI, J. B. Industrialization of developing countries: problem of simple skills. *International Review of Applied Psychology*, 1973, *22*, 77–84.

———. Teaching African children pictorial depth perception: in search of a method. *Perception*, 1974, *3*, 309–12.

DESAI, A. R. (Ed.), *Essays on modernization of underdeveloped societies* (2 vols.). Bombay: Thacker, 1971.

DEUTSCH, K. W. *Nationalism and its alternatives*. New York: Knopf, 1969.

DEVELOPMENT STUDIES. *International Social Science Journal*, 1972, *24*, no. 1.

DE VOS, G. Achievement orientation, social self-identity and Japanese economic development. *Asian Survey*, 1965, *5*, 575–89.

———. Achievement and innovation in culture and personality. In E. Norbeck, D. Price-Williams, & W. McCord (Eds.), *The study of personality: an interdisciplinary appraisal*. New York: Holt, Rinehart and Winston, 1968, pp. 348–70.

———. Introduction: change as a social science problem. In G. de Vos (Ed.), *Responses to change: society, culture and personality*. New York: Van Nostrand, 1976, pp. 1–11.

DE VOS, G., & ROMANUCCI-ROSS, L. (Eds.), *Ethnic identity: cultural continuities and change*. Palo Alto, Calif.: Mayfield, 1975.

DIAZ-GUERRERO, R. Interpreting coping styles across nations. *International Journal of Psychology*, 1973, *8*, 193–203.

DOOB, L. *Becoming more civilized*. New Haven: Yale University Press, 1960.

———. Scales for assaying psychological modernization in Africa. *Public Opinion Quarterly*, 1967, *31*, 414–21.

———. Psychological aspects of planned developmental change. In A. Gallaher (Ed.), *Perspectives in developmental change*. Lexington: University of Kentucky Press, 1968, pp. 36–78.

ECKENSBERGER, L. On types of social change: a theoretical and empirical investigation. *Die Dritte Welt*, 1972, *1*, 372–97.

EISENSTADT, S. N. *Tradition, change and modernity*. New York: Wiley, 1973.

ESCOVAR, L. A. Consideraciones teoricas necesarias en la aplicación de los principios del conductismo al cambio social. *Revista Interamericana de Psicologia*, 1974, *8*, 309–23.

FEIERABEND, I. Social change and political violence. In H. Graham (Ed.), *Violence in America: historical and comparative perspectives*. New York: Praeger, 1969.

FINISON, L. J. The application of McClelland's national development model to recent data. *Journal of Social Psychology*, 1976, *98*, 55–59.

FISHMAN, J. *Language loyalty in the United States*. The Hague: Mouton, 1966.

———. *The sociology of language*. Rowley, Mass.: Newbury House, 1972.

FRIED, M. Effects of social change on mental health. *American Journal of Orthopsychiatry*, 1964, *34*, 3–28.

———. Chinese culture, society and personality in transition. In G. de Vos (Ed.), *Responses to change: society, culture and personality*. New York: Van Nostrand, 1976, pp. 45–73.

GLASER, D. Dynamics of ethnic identification. *American Sociological Review*, 1958, 23, 31–40.

GLAZER, N., & MOYNIHAN, D. P. (Eds.), *Ethnicity: theory and experience.* Cambridge, Mass.: Harvard University Press, 1975.

GOLD, D. Psychological changes associated with acculturation of Saskatchewan Indians. *Journal of Social Psychology*, 1967, 71, 177–84.

GOODENOUGH, W. *Cooperation in change.* New York: Russell Sage Foundation, 1963.

GORDON, M. *Assimilation in American life.* London: Oxford University Press, 1964.

GOUGH, H. *Manual: California Psychological Inventory.* Palo Alto, Calif.: Consulting Psychologists Press, 1969.

GRAVES, T. D. Psychological acculturation in a tri-ethnic community. *Southwestern Journal of Anthropology*, 1967, 23, 337–50.

GREENFIELD, P. M. On culture and conservation. In J. S. Bruner, R. R. Olver, & P. M. Greenfield (Eds.), *Studies in cognitive growth.* New York: Wiley, 1966, pp. 225–56.

GREENFIELD, P. M., & BRUNER, J. S. Culture and cognitive growth. In D. A. Goslin (Ed.), *Handbook of socialization theory and research.* New York: Rand McNally, 1969.

GREGOR, A. J., & MCPHERSON, D. A. A study of susceptibility to geometric illusion among cultural subgroups of Australian Aborigines. *Psychologica Africana*, 1965, 11, 1–13.

GUSFIELD, J. R. Tradition and modernity: misplaced polarities in the study of social change. *American Journal of Sociology*, 1967, 72, 351–62.

GUTHRIE, G. *The psychology of modernization in the rural Philippines.* Quezon City: Ateneo de Manila University Press, 1970.

HAGEN, E. *On the theory of social change.* Homewood, Ill.: Dorsey Press, 1962.

HALLOWELL, A. I. Sociopsychological aspects of acculturation. In A. I. Hallowell, *Culture and experience* (Chapter 17), 1955. (Originally published in R. Linton (Ed.), *The science of man in the world crisis.* New York: Columbia University Press, 1945.)

————. *Culture and experience.* Philadelphia: University of Pennsylvania Press, 1955.

HECKHAUSEN, H. Trainingskurse zur Erhohung der Leistungsmotivation and der unternehmerischen Aktivitat in einem Entwicklungsland: Eine nachtragliche Analyse des eizielten Motivwandels. *Zeitschrift für Entwicklungspsychologie*, 1971, 3, 253–68.

HERSKOVITS, M. I. *Acculturation: the study of culture contact.* New York: Augustin, 1938.

HIMMELSTRAND, U., & OKEDIJI, F. O. Social structure and motivational tuning in social and economic development. *Journal of Social Issues*, 1968, 24, 25–42.

HIPPLER, A. Some alternative viewpoints of the negative results of Euro-American contact with non-Western groups. *American Anthropologist*, 1974, 76, 334–37.

HOFFMAN, H. Culture change and personality modification among the James Bay Cree. *Anthropological Papers of University of Alaska*, 1961, 9, 81–91.

HUDSON, W. Pictorial depth perception and educational adaptation in Africa. *Psychologia Africana*, 1962, 9, 226–39.

INKELES, A. Continuity and change in the interaction of the personal and the sociocultural systems. In B. Barber & A. Inkeles (Eds.), *Stability and social change.* Boston: Little, Brown, 1971.

————. The modernization of man in socialist and non-socialist countries. In M. Field (Ed.), *Social consequences of modernization.* Baltimore: Johns Hopkins Press, 1976.

————. Understanding and misunderstanding individual modernity. *Journal of Cross-Cultural Psychology,* 1977, *8,* 135–76.

INKELES, A., & SMITH, D. The fate of personal adjustment in the process of modernization. *International Journal of Comparative Sociology,* 1970, *11,* 81–114.

————. *Becoming modern.* Cambridge, Mass.: Harvard University Press, 1974.

JAHODA, G. Aspects of westernization, I. *British Journal of Sociology,* 1961, *12,* 375–86.

————. Aspects of westernization, II. *British Journal of Sociology,* 1962, *13,* 43–56.

————. Some research problems in African education. *Journal of Social Issues,* 1968, *24,* 161–75.

————. Supernatural beliefs and changing cognitive structures among Ghanaian university students. *Journal of Cross-Cultural Psychology,* 1970, *1,* 115–30.

————. Applying cross-cultural psychology to the Third World. In J. W. Berry & W. J. Lonner (Eds.), *Applied cross-cultural psychology.* Amsterdam: Swets and Zeitlinger, 1975, pp. 3–7.

JONES, P. The validity of traditional-modern attitude measures. *Journal of Cross-Cultural Psychology,* 1977, *8,* 207–40.

KAHL, J. *The measurement of modernism: a study of values in Brazil and Mexico.* Austin, Texas: University of Texas Press, 1968.

KAVOLIS, V. Post-modern man: psychocultural responses to social trends. *Social Problems,* 1970, *17,* 435–48.

KELMAN, H. C., & WARWICK, D. P. Bridging micro and macro approaches to social change: a social psychological perspective. In G. Zaltman (Ed.), *Processes and phenomena of social change.* New York: Wiley, 1973, pp. 13–449.

KILBRIDE, P. L., ROBBINS, M. C., & FREEMAN, R. B. Pictorial depth perception and education among Baganda school children. *Perceptual and Motor Skills,* 1968, *26,* 116–18.

KUBANY, E. S., GALLIMORE, R., & BUELL, J. The effects of extrinsic factors on achievement-oriented behavior: a non-western case. *Journal of Cross-Cultural Psychology,* 1970, *1,* 77–84.

KUNKEL, J. *Society and economic growth: a behavioral perspective of social change.* London: Oxford University Press, 1966.

KUSHNER, G., GIBSON, M., GULICK, J., HONIGMANN, J. J., & NONAS, R. *What accounts for sociocultural change? a propositional inventory.* Chapel Hill, N.C.: Institute for Research in Social Science, 1962.

FISHMAN, J., FERGUSON, C., & DAS GUPTA, J. (Eds.). *Language problems of developing nations.* New York: Wiley, 1968.

LEIGHTON, A. H. Mental illness and acculturation. In I. Galdston (Ed.), *Medicine and anthropology.* New York: International Universities Press, 1959.

LEVINE, R. *Dreams and deeds: achievement motivation in Nigeria.* Chicago: University of Chicago Press, 1966.

LIEBERSON, S. *Language and ethnic relations in Canada.* New York: Wiley, 1970.

LIJPHART, A. Ethnic conflict in the First World: theoretical speculations. Paper presented at conference on Ethnic Pluralism and Conflict in Contemporary Western Europe & Canada. Cornell University, May, 1975.

LINTON, R. Nativistic movements. *American Anthropologist*, 1943, 45, 230–40.

MAZRUI, A. A. From social Darwinism to current theories of modernization: a tradition of analysis. *World Politics*, 1968, 21, 69–83.

MACARTHUR, R. S. Some ability patterns: Central Eskimos and Nsenga Africans. *International Journal of Psychology*, 1973, 8, 239–47.

———. Differential ability patterns: Inuit, Nsenga and Canadian whites. In J. W. Berry & W. J. Lonner (Eds.), *Applied cross-cultural psychology*. Amsterdam: Swets and Zeitlinger, 1975.

MCCLELLAND, D. C. *The achieving society*. Princeton, N.J.: Van Nostrand, 1961.

———. NAch and entrepreneurship: a longitudinal study. *Journal of Personality and Social Psychology*, 1965, 1, 389–92.

———. Some themes in the culture of India. In A. R. Desai (Ed.), *Essays on modernization of underdeveloped societies*, Vol. 2. Bombay: Thacker, 1971, pp. 254–93.

MCCLELLAND, D. C., ATKINSON, J. W., CLARK, R. A., & LOWELL, E. L. *The achievement motive*. New York: Appleton-Century-Crofts, 1953.

MCCLELLAND, D. C., & WINTER, D. *Motivating economic achievement*. New York: Free Press, 1969.

MCGURK, H., & JAHODA, G. Pictorial depth perception by children in Scotland and Ghana. *Journal of Cross-Cultural Psychology*, 1975, 6, 279–96.

MEAD, M. (Ed.), *Cultural patterns and technical change*. Paris: UNESCO, 1953.

———. *New lives for old*. New York: Morrow, 1956a.

———. The implications of culture change for personality development. In D. G. Haring (Ed.), *Personal character and cultural milieu*. Syracuse, N.Y.: University of Syracuse Press, 1956b.

MILLER, R. J. Cross-cultural research in the perception of pictorial materials. *Psychological Bulletin*, 1973, 80, 135–50.

MURDOCK, G. P., & PROVOST, C. Measurement of cultural complexity. *Ethnology*, 1973, 12, 379–92.

MURPHY, H. B. M. Social change and mental health. *Milbank Memorial Fund Quarterly*. 1961, 39, 385–445.

———. Migration and the major mental disorders: a reappraisal. In M. B. Kantor (Ed.), *Mobility and mental health*. Springfield, Ill.: Thomas, 1965, pp. 5–29.

———. Psychiatric concomitants of fusion in plural societies. Paper presented at Conference "Social Change and Cultural Factors in Mental Health in Asia and the Pacific," Honolulu, 1969.

———. The low rate of mental hospitalization shown by immigrants to Canada. Unpublished paper, McGill University, 1974.

NISBET, R. Ethnocentrism and the comparative method. In A. R. Desai (Ed.), *Essays on modernization of underdeveloped societies*, Vol. 1. Bombay: Thacker, 1971, pp. 95–114.

O'BRYAN, K., REITZ, G., & KUPLOWSKA, O. *Non-official language study*. Ottawa: Government of Canada, 1975.

OMVEDT, G. Modernization theories: the ideology of empire? In A. R. Desai (Ed.),

Essays on modernization of underdeveloped societies, Vol. 1. Bombay: Thacker, 1971, pp. 119–37.

PAREEK, U. A motivational paradigm of development. *Journal of Social Issues*, 1968, 24, 115–22.

PARK, R. E. Human migration and the marginal man. *American Journal of Sociology*, 1928, 33, 881–93.

POGGIE, J., & LYNCH, R. (Eds.), *Rethinking modernization*. New York: Greenwood Press, 1974.

RIN, H. The synthesizing mind in Chinese ethno-cultural adjustment. In G. de Vos & L. Romanucci-Ross (Eds.), *Ethnic identity: cultural continuities and change*. Palo Alto, Calif.: Mayfield, 1975, pp. 137–55.

ROBBINS, R. H. Alcohol and the identity struggle. *American Anthropologist*, 1973a, 75, 99–122.

————. Identity, culture and behaviour. In J. J. Honigmann (Ed.), *Handbook of social and cultural anthropology*. Chicago: Rand McNally, 1973b.

ROGERS, E. M. Social structure and social change. In G. Zaltman (Ed.), *Processes and phenomena of social change*. New York: Wiley, 1973, pp. 75–87.

ROSEN, B. C. Race, ethnicity and the achievement syndrome. *American Sociological Review*, 1959, 24, 47–60.

SACHS, I. The logic of development. *International Social Science Journal*. 1972, 24, 37–43.

SANUA, V. D. Immigration, migration and mental illness. In E. Brody (Ed.), *Behavior in new environments*. Beverly Hills, Calif.: Sage, 1970, pp. 291–352.

SCRIBNER, S., & COLE, M. Cognitive consequences of formal and informal education. *Science*, 1973, 182, 553–59.

SEGALL, M., CAMPBELL, D. T., & HERSKOVITS, M. J. *The influence of culture on visual perception*. Indianapolis: Bobbs-Merrill, 1966.

SEGALL, M., DOORNBOS, M., & DAVIS, C. *Political identity: a case study from Uganda*. Syracuse, N.Y.: Foreign and Comparative Studies/East Africa XXIV, 1976.

SINGER, M. The modernization of religious beliefs. In M. Weiner (Ed.), *Modernization*. New York: Basic Books, 1966.

SINHA, D. Psychology and the problems of developing countries. *International Review of Applied Psychology*, 1973, 22, 5–27.

SLOGGETT, B., GALLIMORE, R., & KUBANY, E. A comparative analysis of fantasy need achievement among high and low achieving Hawaiian-Americans. *Journal of Cross-Cultural Psychology*, 1970, 1, 53–61.

SMITH, D., & INKELES, A. The OM Scale: a comparative socio-psychological measure of individual modernity. *Sociometry*, 1966, 29, 353–77.

SOCIAL PSYCHOLOGICAL RESEARCH IN DEVELOPING COUNTRIES. *Journal of Social Issues*, 1968, 24, no. 2.

SOCIAL SCIENCE RESEARCH COUNCIL (US). Acculturation: an exploratory formulation. *American Anthropologist*, 1954, 56, 973–1002.

SOMMERLAD, E., & BERRY, J. W. The role of ethnic identification in distinguishing between attitudes towards assimilation and integration of a minority racial group. *Human Relations*, 1970, 23, 23–29.

SPINDLER, G. Psychocultural adaptation. In E. Norbeck, D. Price-Williams, &

W. McCord (Eds.), *The study of personality: an interdisciplinary appraisal.* New York: Holt, Rinehart and Winston, 1968, pp. 326–47.

SPINDLER, L., & SPINDLER, G. Male and female adaptation in culture change. *American Anthropologist,* 1958, *60,* 217–33.

SPRADLEY, J. P., & PHILLIPS, M. Culture and stress: a quantitative analysis. *American Anthropologist,* 1972, *74,* 518–29.

SRINIVAS, M. N. Modernization: a few queries. In A. R. Desai (Ed.), *Essays on modernization of underdeveloped societies,* Vol. 1. Bombay: Thacker, 1971, pp. 149–58.

STEPHENSON, J. Is everyone going modern? a critique and a suggestion for measuring modernism. *American Journal of Sociology,* 1968, *74,* 265–75.

STOREQUIST, E. V. The problem of the marginal man. *American Journal of Sociology,* 1935, *41,* 1–12.

TAFT, R. *From stranger to citizen.* London: Tavistock, 1966.

———. Coping with unfamiliar cultures. In N. Warren (Ed.), *Studies in cross-cultural psychology.* London: Academic Press, 1977.

TANAKA, Y. Toward a multi-level, multi-stage model of modernization. *International Journal of Psychology,* 1973, *8,* 205–14.

TRIANDIS, A. C. Subjective culture and economic development. *International Journal of Psychology,* 1973, *8,* 163–80.

VALLEE, F. Stresses of change and mental health among the Canadian Eskimos. *Archives of Environmental Health,* 1968, *17,* 565–70.

VERNON, P. E. *Intelligence and cultural environment.* London: Methuen, 1969.

WAGATSUMA, H. Problems of cultural identity in modern Japan. In G. de Vos & L. Romanucci-Ross (Eds.), *Ethnic identity: cultural continuities and change.* Palo Alto, Calif.: Mayfield, 1975, pp. 307–34.

WALLACE, A. F. C. Some psychological determinants of culture change in an Iroquoian community. In W. N. Fenton (Ed.), *Symposium on local diversity in Iroquois culture.* Washington, D.C.: Bureau of American Ethnology, Bulletin 149, 1951.

———. Revitalization movements: some theoretical considerations for their comparative study. *American Anthropologist,* 1956, *58,* 264–81.

WEBER, M. *The Protestant ethnic and the spirit of capitalism* (transl. T. Parsons). New York: Scribner, 1930.

WEINER, M. (Ed.), *Modernization: the dynamics of growth.* New York: Basic 1966.

WINTROB, R. M. Acculturation, identification and psychopathology among Cree Indian youth. In N. A. Chance (Ed.), *Conflict in culture: problems of developmental change among the Cree.* Ottawa: Canadian Research Centre for Anthropology, 1968, pp. 93–104.

WINTROB, R. M., & SINDELL, P. Culture change and psychopathology: the case of Cree adolescent students in Quebec. In J. W. Berry & G. J. S. Wilde (Eds.), *Social psychology: the Canadian context.* Toronto: McClelland and Stewart, 1972, pp. 259–71.

WITKIN, H. A., & BERRY, J. W. Psychological differentiation in cross-cultural perspective. *Journal of Cross-Cultural Psychology,* 1975, *6,* 4–87.

WOBER, M. Adapting Dawson's traditional versus western attitudes scale, and presenting some new information from Africa. *British Journal of Social and Clinical Psychology,* 1971, *10,* 101–13.

————. Personality and identity in Africa: a review. Makerere University, Department of Sociology, Occasional Paper No. 19, 1973.

ZAIDI, H. Psychological research on social change. In H. Zaidi (Ed.), *Frontiers of psychological research in Pakistan*. Karachi: Karachi University, 1975, pp. 43–59.

7

Organizational Psychology[1]

Arnold S. Tannenbaum

Contents

Abstract

In modern societies, people are exposed to a wide range of organizations.
Recruitment into organizations depends on the persons entering the orga-

nization having appropriate skills, and social behavior habits that are rare in less developed societies. People also differ in their needs for achievement, affiliation, security, and self-actualization, and this has relevance for behavior in organizations, Societies differ not only in the motivational patterns that are frequent in them, but also in norms, and attitudes of people toward authority. Thus, subordinates react differently to supervisors in various societies. Societies prescribe rules about how organizations are to be owned and governed and what rights and prerogatives apply to members.

The research reviewed in this chapter is concerned with the similarities as well as the differences between cultures relevant to these issues, and some of this research hints at principles that may transcend culture. The ways in which these principles manifest themselves, however, are different in different places and attempts to apply these principles appear to require techniques that are culture-specific. For example, data suggest that people who have or feel that they have influence in their work situation will feel a corresponding sense of responsibility and will be motivated to perform well in the organization. But it does not follow that the organizational arrangements that enhance the influence of members or that contribute to their feeling of influence in one culture will do so in another culture. Thus people in traditional societies may differ from middle class Americans not so much in their reaction to being influential, but in what it takes to make them influential.

Some research by organizational psychologists such as that on job enlargement, sociotechnical systems, and autonomous groups in a number of countries illustrates the effort to translate general principles into practical procedures. Those who attempt to transfer the experience with these procedures in one society to another society, however, would do well to distinguish between the principles that are general to these societies and the techniques that are specific to each society. The effort of psychologists who are studying organizations cross-culturally can be viewed in part as an attempt to provide a basis for making this distinction.

Introduction

Organizational psychology has an international heritage. The important theories of organization that are relevant to the psychology of members, their motivation, reactions, and adjustments, have been developed by people from a variety of countries. In fact, organizations and conceptions about organizations have existed in many places during the course of written history. As early as 4000 B.C. the Egyptians, and subsequently the ancient Hebrews, Chinese, and Greeks, offered conceptions about organizations that are as meaningful today as they were in former years. The notions of specialization, chain of command, centralization-decentralization, the need for written records, for planning and controlling, and even the desirability of a minimum wage were proposed long before these ideas were incorporated into modern approaches to organizing (George, 1968; Dale, 1973).

Thus, organizations in all cultures, ancient and modern, share common features. All organizations are concerned with converting inputs of energy and materials into services or products through the coordinated effort of people who play specialized roles. The coordination and order that are essential to organizations do not occur spontaneously; they must be created and maintained. Hence there is the need in all organizations for a system of authority and the means to recruit, socialize, and motivate members so that their behavior is appropriate to the pattern of actions and interactions that defines the organization (Katz & Kahn, 1978).

All organizations share common features, yet the problem of organizing human effort differs from one society to another since societies themselves differ in ways that are especially relevant to organizations. For one thing, societies differ in their prevalence of complex organizations—one criterion of the so-called modern society (Inkeles & Smith, 1974). In the "modern society" people, starting at a very early age, are exposed to many different organizations—hospitals, schools, factories, businesses and various governmental agencies. In such a society, people who are recruited into organizations are likely to have the habits, skills and cognitive styles appropriate to organization; they are already socialized in ways that members of less developed societies are not. Societies also differ in the people's prevailing needs that have direct relevance to their behavior in organizations, such as the needs for achievement, affiliation, security, and self-actualization. Hence the motivation of members to belong, to work, and to advance in the organization may be different in different places, and the problem of motivating members will differ from one society to another. Societies differ too in norms about social control and in the attitudes of people toward authority. Hence, reactions of members to supervision and to the social control that are inherent in organizations can be expected to differ from place to place. Furthermore, some of these norms may be expressed as official ideologies and even as laws. Many societies prescribe rules about organizations: how organizations are to be owned and governed, and what rights and prerogatives apply to members. Thus socialist and capitalist societies imply differences, not only in the character of ownership of work organizations but also in their systems of authority and decision making and in the way rewards are distributed within them (Tannenbaum, Kavcic, Rosner, Vianello, & Weiser, 1974).

These differences in ideologies, laws, norms, attitudes, skills, cognitions and needs, and in the prevalence of organizations themselves provide a basis for expecting differences between societies in the character of organizations and in the nature of the adjustment of members. Such differences, to the extent that they occur, do not, however, minimize the importance of similarities that are also apparent among all organizations. Differences between cultures may be interesting, but these differences become important for the science of organizations only when they are understood relative to principles that have some generality. Therefore, this chapter will present the results of research that indicate similarities as well as differences between countries and that are relevant to general propositions about the social psychology of organizations. (For two earlier reviews see Barrett & Bass, 1972; and Roberts, 1970.)

Plan of Chapter

The remainder of this chapter is composed of six main sections. The first briefly summarizes several classic theories of organization. Much of the research reported in the remaining sections has some bearing on these theories from an international perspective. The second section focuses on managers, their general attitudes and values that have implications for their approach to organizing. The third concerns supervisors and factors that have been studied by researchers in a search to explain supervisory effectiveness. The fourth concerns organization members, their reaction to their work and their attitude toward their organization. The fifth reviews research about schemes of job and organizational design that attempt to apply principles of social psychology to the work setting. A final section summarizes the implications of the foregoing for organizational psychology.

Theories of Organization

Near the turn of the century, the German sociologist Weber (1947, 1952) formulated the concept of bureaucracy as the most efficient possible way to organize human effort. The key to bureaucracy was to be its rationality, and for Weber that meant its impersonality. Weber reacted in part to what he saw as the highly personalized and organizationally dysfunctional control in many organizations of traditional societies, in feudalism and in the family-type business where leadership is inherited. In some of these organizations the subordinate owes allegiance to the superior as a servant does a master. Obedience is demanded as a personal service in many areas of life—not just within the narrowly defined limits of the job. Superiors can exercise arbitrary power based on whim or personal taste, practicing nepotism or exhibiting favoritism toward those they like while discriminating against those they don't like.

Weber assumed that bureaucracy, by eliminating personal and nonrational emotional considerations, would achieve a rationality and therefore an efficiency superior to that of all other organizations. Furthermore, Weber's intent was to make organizations culture-free, to create a universal system of organization that would be the most efficient system anywhere. Hence, bureaucracy is a system of law, more than of man; a system in which rules cover all contingencies and where obedience is assured through the appointment of technically expert supervisors who administer law with precise and cold impartiality. The bureaucratic system is autocratic, since it has a rigid chain of command in which people at the top give orders and those at the bottom unquestioningly obey. But the superior does not exploit subordinates and the latter do not subjugate themselves to the superior (as in the kinds of organizations to which Weber was reacting) since the superior's orders are always within the framework of the law that restricts the superior's prerogatives within legitimate, job-essential bounds, guaranteeing equal treatment for all. Furthermore, objective criteria, such as seniority or tested competence—not personal preference by a superior—are, theoretically, the bases for advancement in the organization.

Weber's model is an idealization, yet most complex organizations today resemble Weber's model in significant ways (Perrow, 1972). Theories of administrative science that were developed in France, England, and the United States, like Weber's model, also illustrate features that are found widely in organizations of contemporary societies (Fayol, 1949; Gulick & Urwick, 1937). These theories are similar to Weber's in the effort to achieve an impersonal rationality and they add specific guidelines to help make leadership more rational in organizations. For example, one such guideline, *unity of command*, asserts that a subordinate should have one and only one immediate superior, since a subordinate with more than one superior might get conflicting orders from them, or the superiors themselves might be unclear about who is responsible for the subordinate's performance. The *scaler principle*, a second proposition, limits communications to people in a direct hierarchical relationship. A person under one supervisor may not communicate to a person under another supervisor except by going through his or her own supervisor; otherwise communications get out of hand and create confusion.

These classical theories of bureaucracy and administration, because of their preoccupation with "rationality," have little to say directly about the psychology of members, although these theories do have serious, if unintended, implications for members. Theories of human relations, to which psychologists have contributed substantially, grew up in part as a reaction to these implications. Mayo (1945), an Australian and an early proponent of human relations in industry, argued that many of the problems of organizations, including inefficiency, conflict, and alienation, occur because organizations do not take into account the attitudes and feelings of members. To Mayo, the results of the famous Hawthorne experiment seemed to demonstrate that considerate supervision and attention to the personal needs of workers can help eliminate these problems. The Hawthorne experiment seemed also to demonstrate that group and social forces more than financial incentives and physical conditions of work are important determinants of worker productivity. Thus psychologists began to formulate a social psychology of organizations that challenged the rationality of earlier, classical theories. Psychologists proposed a conception of the organization member as a person with social needs and needs for self-actualization in addition to the simple need for economic security. Furthermore, some psychologists questioned the assumptions that seemed implicit in earlier theories, that members prefer to avoid work and that they have only a limited capacity for initiative and self-direction. On the contrary, members are capable of initiative and they seek to use their abilities. Psychologists therefore asserted that organization members represent an untapped reserve of technical and intellectual skills that might contribute substantially to the organization effort, if only members are given the opportunity to use their relevant abilities (Miles, 1965). Hence traditional concepts of authority and of leadership were modified to include participative procedures and leadership by peers in groups as means of fostering self-direction and of tapping the latent human resources available in every organization. In the United States, research contributed to a conception of the considerate and supportive leader and the leader with social skills in addition to the task leader and the technical expert (Halpin & Winer, 1957; Likert, 1961; Blake & Mouton, 1964). In England, Norway, and Sweden *sociotechnical systems* and *autonomous groups* were offered as means of modifying the rigid, unilateral chain of command of the classical models by assigning responsibility for a job to teams of workers and by having those workers decide themselves how their job is to be done (Emery & Trist, 1969; Thorsrud, 1972; Rubenowitz, 1974). In Britain as well as in the United States the *organic organization* (Burns & Stalker, 1961; Lawrence & Lorsch, 1967) and the so-called *temporary system* (Bennis & Slater, 1968) illustrate participative models that were proposed, by way of contrast with the bureaucratic, *mechanistic* organization, as the more effective approaches to coping with a dynamic and changing environment. According to the proponents of these models, organizations that must react to a turbulent environment must continually create task forces composed of members who possess as a group the mix of skills needed to cope with the problem of the moment. Such groups bring together people of different ranks from different parts of the organization—and a member's influence in the group depends not on his or her formal position but on his or her expertise. With the problem solved, the group disbands and members move to other groups and other problems. Hierarchy in such a system lacks the stability and rigid authoritarian character of the classical model.

The recent, growing concern among students of organization with the adaptability of organizations to changing conditions and the need felt by organizational psychologists for more general conceptions of organization than those of earlier models has lead some psychologists to turn to *open system* theory, and to a redefinition of some of the issues that are important for understanding organizations (Katz & Kahn, 1978). Open system theory assumes a continuous exchange between the organization and its environment, which classical theories of organization, including traditional human relations theories, ignore. According to these classical theories, organizations do not have to accommodate the vicissitudes of an external world. As a result, each of these theories postulates relatively simple and fixed relations between members, and a fairly constant mode of operation as the one best way to achieve organizational effectiveness. Open system theory asserts a more complex and potentially fluid set of interdependencies; consequently, it presumes a "law of equifinality": an organization can achieve a given result in any of a variety of ways. There need not be only one best way to organize (Katz & Kahn, 1978).

Psychologists in a number of countries have conducted research concerning issues raised by these theories and the results of this research is summarized in the following sections. Most of the research in this field has been done in business and industrial organizations although some of it was conducted in other types of organizations and in the laboratory. The data come largely from questionnaires or personal interviews administered through survey methods, but some data are based on experimental treatments and on observational procedures. Very few comparative studies of organizational behavior employ representative samples; consequently, there are questions about the generality of the findings in each study. Taken together, however, they do suggest some important facts and principles about organizations and their members in different societies.

Values of Managers

Organizational leaders in many countries endorse the ideal of participative decision making. This, at least, is the implication of a study by Haire, Ghiselli and Porter (1966) of 3,500 managers in fourteen countries. Tannenbaum and Cooke (1979) reach essentially the same conclusion on the basis of a review of studies in fourteen countries including communist, socialist, and capitalist ones. Yet, according to Haire et al., most managers are not consistent in their support of participation since they also maintain that organization members are incapable of leadership and that they prefer to be directed and to avoid responsibility. This conclusion from the Haire data applies broadly to managers, regardless of culture. Nonetheless, managers do differ from one another in the extent to which they endorse participation and in their belief about the capacity of members to participate effectively.

Country Groupings

Haire et al. found four clusters of countries on the basis of a factor analysis of their survey data: Nordic-European (Norway, Denmark, Germany, and Sweden); Latin-European (France, Spain, Italy, and Belgium); Anglo-American (Britain and the United States); and developing countries (Argentina, Chile, and India). Japan, the fourteenth country, stood alone, managers here endorsing group goal setting and mutual influence more than managers in any of the other countries.

Studies by other researchers provide support for some of the conclusions suggested by Haire et al. The Japanese emphasis on group decision making and mutual influence between superior and subordinate has been noted by a number of observers (Abegglen, 1958; Cole, 1971). Such emphasis is all the more intriguing because it seems contrary to some distinctly authoritarian features of organizations in Japan including the importance attached to hierarchy and to formal status that is associated with rank. The Japanese have a term, *ringi system*, that refers to the custom of using groups in decision making, and Cole, who worked as a participant observer in two Japanese plants, notes the common practice of foremen in these factories consulting with workers on changes in work methods or on worker complaints. Cole (1971) sees

> a parallel to the Japanese family where the father, as head of the household, holds decision power, but in practice consults extensively with the rest of the family to determine their wishes (pp. 186–87).

The unusual emphasis on the group in Japan is consistent with the finding of Hesseling and Konnen (1969) that Japanese managers shared information with one another more than did Dutch managers during a decision-making exercise. It is consistent also with Abegglen's (1958) and Ouchi and Jaeger's (1978) observation that *group* performance (rather than individual performance) is more likely to be accepted as a measure of success in Japan than in the United States. Pascale (1978), however, does not find a difference between Japanese and American managers in the extent to which they employ a consultative approach in decision making.

While Japanese managers stand out among the respondents in the study by Haire et al. (1966) in their endorsement of group decision making and mutual influence, managers from the developing countries scored relatively low. Italian managers, however, fall at the lowest end of the scale while Anglo-American and Nordic-European managers fall between the extremes. The uniqueness of the Italian managers suggested by Haire et al., like that of the Japanese managers, is also substantiated by the work of others. Ferrarotti (1959) explains the attitudes of Italian managers in terms of the family structure in Italy, and the prevalence of family owner-ship of businesses in that country.

> In general, Italian enterprise authority is highly centralized and personalized and reflects the paternalistic orientation of the patrimonial business elite. This means that Italian managers are reluctant to delegate authority and they tend to think of their authority in terms of personal [rather than impersonal, bureaucratic] power. . . . The enterprise is seen as some sort of private king-dom. . . . In Italian industry, the manager who feels hurt if anything has been done without his direct knowledge and participation is a familiar character (pp. 239–40).

Similarly, Harbison and Burgess (1954) contrast the character of manage-ment in France, Belgium and Italy (which belong to Haire's Latin-Euro-pean cluster) with that in the United States and they find greater social distance between managers and workers in the former group than in the latter. Employing quite a different methodology, Tannenbaum et al. (1974) compared questionnaire responses of members at all hierarchical levels in ten Italian factories with those of a matched set of respondents in ten American factories and found that members in the Italian plants are much less likely to report that their superiors are responsive to their ideas and suggestions than the American members are likely to report. Trust in their managers felt by the Italian workers is also lower than that felt by the American workers according to these data.

Haire, Ghiselli, & Porter (1963) report that American managers more than managers in other groups endorse a belief in the capacity of individu-als to exercise initiative and leadership. These authors assert that this be-lief is an important underpinning of real participation (even though American managers are very close to average in their endorsement of par-ticipation). Clark and McCabe (1970) also report a relatively positive atti-tude of American managers in this regard compared to British and Australian managers, who fit Haire's Anglo-American cluster. Maier and Hoffman (1962) present data that indicate American personnel are less in-clined to authoritarian decision making than are British personnel. These latter data are based on experiments involving college students who were asked to solve industrial personnel problems through group decision making. Bennis and Slater (1968), who agree that there is in the United States a predisposition for participative approaches, attribute this predisposition to a tradition that goes back to the early days of American history. The American pioneer family depended on its younger members, many of whom were more adept than their elders in coping with life in the wilderness. A certain respect and authority were therefore tendered to the young, who in other societies were required to observe the traditional authority of more senior and established people.

Developing Societies and Norms Concerning Authority

The relatively low level of support by managers for participative approaches in developing countries suggested by the Haire data is also reported in the work of others. Bass and his associates have collected data through questionnaires from managers in a large number of countries and while these managers are undoubtedly a highly select group (all of them were participants in an international training program), the results are consistent with those obtained employing other methods and samples. These researchers report that managers in "traditional" countries like Greece and India prefer passive subordinates while American and British managers prefer more active and involved subordinates (Barrett & Bass, 1970; Bass, 1968; Thiagarajan & Deep, 1970). Barrett and Franke (1969) report that managers in seven countries prefer two-way communication to one-way communication. In general, these managers perform better in simulated organizational problems under conditions of two-way communication, but this preference for two-way communication is correlated (.75) with level of economic development. "The relative preference for the more authoritarian communication mode is associated with lower economic growth" (p. 598). Similarly, Cascio (1974), drawing from the above data bank, found that between 50 and 64.7 percent of managers from five groups of countries prefer a participative superior. India, however, stood alone with only 29.4 percent of the managers there preferring such a superior. Negandhi (1973) suggests on the basis of a study of management practices in Taiwan that Taiwanese managers are more authoritarian and paternalistic compared to Japanese and American managers, consistent with the contention that such leadership is more characteristic in developing societies than in modern societies.

Questionnaire data from organization members in Yugoslavia, another developing nation, also provide evidence of a leadership style that is relatively nonparticipative compared to that in matched plants in the United States, Austria, and Israeli kibbutzim (Tannenbaum et al., 1974). Only in Italian plants of this study do members indicate a lower degree of participativeness on the part of their superior. The relatively low rating in

Yugoslav plants occurs despite the acknowledgement by members in these plants of *formal* participation that may occur through workers' councils and other decision making bodies that are part of the system of workers' self-management in that country. Tannenbaum et al. explain in terms of culture, broadly defined, the lack of interpersonal participativeness despite the highly participative formal system in Yugoslavia and these authors illustrate some of the difficulties imposed by "tradition" and other social conditions in actualizing the formal plan.

> Formal participativeness is subject to legislation, and such participativeness has been mandated in Yugoslav plants. These plants are therefore participative formally. But informal [interpersonal] participativeness [in the day to day interactions of superior and subordinate] cannot be determined directly by law. It is subject to culture and tradition, to the habits, norms, and skills of members.... Modern industry in Yugoslavia has grown out of a tradition based on hierarchy at least as extreme as that in Italy. Authoritarian hierarchical relations in prewar Yugoslavia were fostered by persistent unemployment, which led many persons to accept work under the harshest of conditions.... [Consequently] workers regarded authority figures with a mixture of hatred, fear, and reverence. The peasants too, many of whom were moving into industry, were in conflict with the ideology of self-management by reason of their traditions.... Individualistic and distrustful of strangers, the peasant had little regard for the social orientation of self management—or for any management for that matter (pp. 221–23).

An unusual study by Negandhi and Prasad (1971) provides further evidence concerning the difference in managerial attitudes between developed and underdeveloped countries, and it illustrates as well the possible impact of one culture on managerial practice in a second culture. These researchers compared American subsidiaries in Argentina, Brazil, India, the Philippines, and Uruguay with matched locally owned firms in order to explore how managerial philosophy and environmental factors affect management practice. In general, managers in the American subsidiaries are more likely to use delegation than are managers in the locally owned firms, and managers in the former are more likely to express confidence and trust in the capacities of members, consistent with a "human resources" (Miles, 1965) view of organization. For example, the chief executive is likely to make policy decisions entirely on his own in thirteen of seventeen Indian companies compared to only six out of seventeen American subsidiaries. Similarly, top executives of local firms in Argentina, Brazil, Uruguay, and the Philippines were less likely than executives in American subsidiaries to share decision making with others. In these countries twenty-three of the forty-seven subsidiaries, as compared to thirteen of the forty-five local companies, used relatively "democratic" forms of leadership. But the difference in managerial practice between the American subsidiaries and local firms is not entirely attributable to differences in the nationality of the executives. Eighty percent of the executives in the United States subsidiaries were local nationals. No differences in the measure of managerial practice were found between American managers and native managers within the subsidiaries. Native managers were trained in the subsidiaries and they may have acquired the skills and attitudes that were compatible with the subsidiary's philosophy of management. It is also possible that native managers were selected in the first place on the basis of their compatibility with the organization's norms. There is evidence in this research of a possible impact through organization of one culture on another and, in the cases presented by Negandhi and Prasad, this effect introduces or supports participative managerial attitudes.

In fact Inkeles and Smith (1974) argue that the factory itself, whether a subsidiary or a locally owned plant, is a "school of modernity" and that the difference in the character of human relationships between developed and underdeveloped societies is attributable in part to the modernizing effect of the factory. Their research, based on data collected from factory workers and cultivators (peasants) in Argentina, Chile, East Pakistan, India, Israel, and Nigeria, serves to contradict the commonly accepted notion that the factory creates alienation and conflict in contrast to the idyllic harmony fostered by village life. On the contrary, people with factory experience show better psychological adjustment than their counterparts in the villages, and Inkeles and Smith argue that this is attributable in part to "the norm of treatment in the factory [that] emphasizes just, humane, respectful treatment of subordinates, at least compared to what goes on in many other settings in underdeveloped countries" (Inkeles & Smith, 1974, p. 160). Also, a more supportive and participative managerial approach might be expected in most developed countries compared to most underdeveloped countries—which is what the available data suggest.

Differences between countries in the managers' endorsement of participative approaches that have been noted presumably reflect differences between cultures in prevailing values concerning authority. Studies of authoritarianism suggest that cultures differ in this regard. Meade and Whittaker (1967), for example, administered the California F scale to college students in the United States and in a number of developing countries in Asia, Africa, and South America. Authoritarianism measured in this way was significantly lower among the Americans than among any other group. The highest score was found among the Indian students who were not significantly different from college students in Rhodesia whose society until recently was based on "a tribal system in which elders made nearly all decisions" (p. 4). Students from Arabia were also substantially higher in authoritarianism than were the American students, a result that agrees with that of Prothro and Melikian (1953) and Melikian (1956, 1959). And Kagitchibasi (1970) reports higher scores on authoritarianism among Turkish students compared to American students. Hagen (1962, p. 97) concludes on the basis of an extensive review that the struggle for survival under harsh and unpredictable conditions in many traditional societies fosters in the member of such a society "a perception of the world as arbitrary, capricious, not amenable to analysis . . . (and the need to rely) on the judgment or will of individuals superior to him in authority or power."

The preponderance of data support the generalization implied above, but some data do not. For example, in a study of personal and interpersonal values held by managers in fourteen countries, Hofstede (1976) finds that Swedish managers cluster with American and British managers rather than with Danish, Norwegian, and German managers; the latter clustering is reported by Haire et al. (Hofstede also notes that German-speaking Swiss managers are like German and Dutch managers while French-speaking Swiss managers are like other managers from Latin countries.) Sirota (1968) found Brazilian employees preferred democratic-participative leadership more than Japanese employees did; Farris and Butterfield (1972) found a relatively equalized distribution of influence within Brazilian development banks, contrary to the image of authoritarian management in organizations of less developed lands. Although Italian managers in the Haire et al. (1966) study were low in their support of participation, other managers in the Latin-European cluster were not low. Inconsistencies such as these undoubtedly reflect:

1. The statistical character of the relationships being studied; differences between groups are to be understood as implying *probable* differences, not *certain* differences. A number of "inconsistencies" are therefore to be expected.
2. "Samples" are usually very select, and a good deal of error can be expected when generalizing about countries from "samples" within them. For example, the Brazilian banks studied by Farris and Butterfield are composed of highly educated bankers (80 percent of the respondents were either lawyers, economists, engineers, or accountants, whose work entails evaluating applications for loans).
3. Measures may differ from one study to another and differences in results may be attributable to the different variables actually being measured.

Norms Concerning Bureaucratic Values

Differences in attitude toward authority between developed and developing countries have led some researchers to conclude that participative procedures that might be effective in the developed countries would be inappropriate and ineffective in the developing countries. But participation is not the only possible feature of organization that conflicts with cultural norms in traditional countries. All forms of complex organization entail inconsistencies with prevailing norms and values in traditional societies more than in modern ones. Bureaucratic values, for example, that are normal and therefore taken for granted in modern societies, like the United States, deviate sharply from norms in many traditional societies (Weber, 1958).

An insight into this difference in norms between cultures can be seen when people from one culture are exposed to people from another culture. Thus, Triandis (1967) administered questionnaires to thirty-one American workers in Athens and to sixteen of their Greek coworkers in order to study the perceptions that they had of the respective groups. These perceptions, according to Triandis, reflect mutual negative stereotypes that are likely to apply where high-status foreign visitors work in a low-status culture. To the Greek respondents, "American behavior in organizations appears 'inhumanly' legalistic, rigid, cold, and overconcerned with efficiency (p. 51)." Americans "show extraordinary emotional control, social distance, and lack of emotional involvement in social relations . . . [They are] too hardheaded in personnel decisions, i.e., give overwhelming weight to competence and not enough weight to human factors" (p. 41). This stereotype of the Americans fits remarkably well the image of the bureaucratic employee proposed as an ideal by Weber. But it is not a positive image in Greece. Thus Triandis points out that while the Greek civil service is a very complex bureaucracy, "decisions are often taken on the basis of friendship and following strictly personal norms . . . [Contrary to the Western ideal] Greeks cannot understand the distinction between 'work behavior' and 'friendship behavior'" (p. 51). Triandis and Vassiliou (1972) found that Greeks will give greater weight to recommendations by friends and relatives than will Americans when hiring a new employee and these authors suggest that the importance of friendship in Greece illustrates the general inclination of people in traditional societies to rely on members in their ingroup for support and to feel some distrust of others. Similarly, Zurcher (1968) found that Mexican bank employees attach substantially more importance to the obligations of friendship in an institutional setting than do American bank employees. Effective organization according to Weber (and most organization theorists), however, requires a more universalistic and impersonal basis for cooperation. Organization members have to work with many people whether they are friends or not.

Need for Achievement

The hardheaded concern for efficiency that Greeks attribute to Americans undoubtedly reflects the strong need for achievement that distinguishes Americans from people in many other societies; McClelland (1961) argues that effective organization requires managers with such a need. People in underdeveloped societies tend to have relatively little need for achievement and organizations in such societies therefore lack this vital ingredient. Thus McClelland found that the level of need for achievement in a society coded from a sample of children's stories correlates .53 with the rate of economic growth of the society as measured by the consumption of electric power. LeVine (1966) showed that the Ibo of Nigeria, who are noted for their entrepreneurial spirit and effectiveness, are higher than the Hausa in their need for achievement. The Ibo, more than the Hausa, have pursued "Western-type economic activity with the changes in ways of life that were required for it" (p. 84). Furthermore, managers differ in need for achievement from nonmanagers within the same society. For example, McClelland used a thematic apperception test to measure the need for achievement of managers and of nonmanagerial professionals in the United States, Italy, Poland, and Turkey. In each of these countries, except Turkey, managers were more achievement motivated than nonmanagers. In Turkey the nonmanagerial group included teachers who as young boys had left home by the age of fourteen, freeing themselves from very authoritarian fathers. A study by Bradburn (1963) is consistent with this explanation of the exceptional finding in Turkey. In Bradburn's study young Turkish executives showed less need for achievement than did a comparable group of Americans, but those Turkish executives who had grown up away from their fathers had a greater need for achievement than their more "normal" cohorts.

Managing a business organization requires "drive" that apparently is measured by need for achievement. McClelland followed the careers of people in the United States who were tested for achievement motivation as college students in 1947; he found fifteen years later that 85 percent of the students who had gone into sales or into managing a business were those high in need for achievement compared to 21 percent who had gone into credit, traffic, personnel, or who had become office managers. Andrews (1967) found that executives of a rapidly expanding firm in Mexico City scored higher on need for achievement than did executives of a firm that was expanding slowly. McClelland and Winter (1969) describe the research of Koch (1965) in a number of small firms in Finland in which need for achievement on the part of decision makers in these firms correlated .41 (p < .10) with growth in work force during the period 1954 to 1961, .39 (p < .10) with gross value of output, .63 (p < .05) with gross investments, and .46 (p < .05) with turnover. Wainer and Rubin (1969) provide substantiating evidence from a study of fifty-one people who founded their own companies in the United States.

Aronoff and Litwin (1971) and McClelland and Winter (1969) have attempted with some success, through training, to raise the level of achievement motivation of organization leaders. McClelland and Winter, for example, found after a two-year period that community leaders in

India who had gone through the training "work longer hours . . . start more [new business] ventures . . . [and] employ more workers" (p. 230). They note, however, that

> opportunity plays a major role in determining whether increase in n achievement leads to greater activity. For the men who were not in charge of their business, the nAch increase had no significant effect. . . . There is even a suggestion . . . that increasing nAch when no opportunities exist will actually lead to less activity" (p. 334).

The apparent success of this training program did not, however, lead to the adoption of such training in India. On the contrary, the program was abandoned because of "power conflicts" that were created by it.

Cognitive Style

The relatively low level of need for achievement and the authoritarian attitudes among people in developing societies may be accompanied by a cognitive style that is inimical to the adaptation of these people to the complexities that modern societies and organizations require. All societies are characterized by a differentiation and integration of roles, but the differentiae in traditional societies are relatively few and the problem of integration is correspondingly simple. Modern societies are more complex, in part because bureaucracies, which form a component of all such societies, are characterized by a high degree of differentiation and coordination. An added complexity in many modern societies is introduced by "organic" organizations that, unlike bureaucratic-mechanistic organizations, have the capacity to change adaptively to turbulent conditions (Burns & Stalker, 1961; Lawrence & Lorsch, 1967; Emery & Trist, 1969). Thus modern societies are more complex than traditional ones, not only because they contain more organizations, but because many of these organizations are more dynamic and complex than those of traditional societies.

The complexity that distinguishes modern societies and organizations from less modern ones may require appropriate cognitive skills and a corresponding cognitive differentiation on the part of members, if these societies and organizations are to function effectively (Tannenbaum, 1968, Ch. 21; Triandis, 1973). The cognitive style known as field-independence or field articulation (Witkin, Dyk, Faterson, Goodenough, & Karp, 1962; Witkin & Berry, 1975; Witkin, 1967; Gruenfeld & MacEachron, 1975) has been proposed as a way of defining the ability of people to cope with such complexity, and evidence suggests that this ability is likely to be more prevalent among people in economically advanced countries than in less advanced ones.

Field-independent people are analytic and differentiated rather than global and diffuse in their thinking. According to Witkin et al. (1962),

Field-dependent people take a rather long time to locate a familiar figure hidden in a complex design. Because they are less likely to attempt to structure ambiguous stimuli, as Rorschach inkblots, they usually experience such stimuli as vague and indefinite. They often find difficulty with the block-design, picture-completion, and object assembly parts of standard intelligence tests (p. 2).

Witkin et al. (1962) suggest on the basis of their research that field-dependent people are more likely than field-independent people to be conformist to authority figures, to show relatively little interest in achievement, to form impressions of people on the basis of their physical characteristics, to express ideas and feelings of aggression in response to TAT pictures that portray an aggressive act, and to have difficulty seeing new or different ways of using items that have served a familiar function. Field-dependent people may also be more personal and attentive rather than impersonal in their approach to others (Witkin & Berry, 1975, p. 63). Furthermore, adults are typically more field-independent than children.

Gruenfeld and MacEachron (1975) are explicit in connecting this cognitive style to the functioning of industrial organization.

The cognitive strategy most adaptive to scientific and western technological behavior in industrial organizations usually involves the inhibition of global [field-dependent] responses in favor of a conceptual analytic [field-independent] response. The essence of this conceptual strategy requires the imposing of structure on unstructured fields or the restructuring of previously structured fields (p. 27).

Gruenfeld and MacEachron undertook a substantial review of research that shows a positive relationship between measures of field articulation and (a) scores on officer selection tests in the Israeli Defense Forces (Preale, Amir, & Sharan (Singer), 1970), (b) productivity, use of deferred judgment and conceptual analysis in problem solving among Civil Service administrators in simulated problem solving exercises (Frederiksen, Jensen, & Beaton, 1972), (c) exposure to technical education among African technical school students (McFie, 1961), (d) acculturation of African and Jamaicans (Doob, 1960), (e) travel by South African natives outside of their rural area (Du Preez, 1968), and (f) cultures and ethnic groups that have childrearing practices "which stress self-reliance, autonomy, individualism, and ingenuity, and are permissive" rather than those which "stress obedience, conformity, and authoritarianism and are very strict" (Wober, 1967, p. 32) (see also Berry, 1966; Dawson, 1967; Dershowitz, 1971; Siann, 1972; Witkin, 1967, 1969). MacEachron (1977) also finds a positive relationship between field independence and job level among a group of nurses in an American hospital.

Gruenfeld and MacEachron hypothesize on the basis of their review (and very much in line with the analyses of Hagen, 1962, see above) that the economically adverse conditions of underdeveloped countries contribute to "feelings of fatalism, reliance on magic and tradition to reduce uncertainty, and extensive obedience and dependence on kin for protection in a hazardous environment" (p. 18). These conditions result in the development of a global rather than an analytic, field-articulate cognitive style.

To test their hypothesis, Gruenfeld and MacEachron measured the degree of field articulation of 329 managers and technicians from twenty-two countries in South and Central America, Africa, Asia, and the Middle East. They also measured the level of economic development of each country by such indexes as per capita income, GNP, energy consumption, newspaper circulation, radios, doctors, hospital beds, protein consumption, and caloric intake. The results indicate that managers from countries that are relatively developed economically are likely to have a more field-articulated cognitive style than managers from less developed countries. This relationship between economic development and cognitive style illustrates the obstacles faced by undeveloped societies in achieving economic advancement. Conditions of impoverishment contribute to a cognitive style that is inconsistent with effective organizational management; this inconsistency in turn serves to perpetuate the impoverishment through impeding the growth of complex organizations. There is some evidence, however, that education serves to increase field articulation (McFie, 1961).

Supervisory Leadership

In a series of studies launched in 1945, social scientists at the Ohio State University distinguished between two dimensions of supervisory leadership, *initiating structure* and *consideration* (Halpin & Winer, 1957; Hemphill & Coons, 1957). This distinction was revealed by factor analyses of data from questionnaires administered to large numbers of organization members; in a number of respects, it is similar to the distinction between traditional bureaucratic or administrative science approaches to leadership and human relations approaches. Consideration, for example, reflects "the extent to which the leader has established rapport, two-way communication, mutual respect, and consideration of the feelings of those under him" (Fleishman, 1974, p. 185). Initiating structure, on the other hand, reflects the

> extent to which the supervisor defines or facilitates group interactions toward *goal attainment* (italics in original). He does this by planning, scheduling, criticizing, initiating ideas, organizing the work, and so forth (Fleishman, 1974, p. 185).

This distinction, in one form or another, has been the basis of a good deal of research by psychologists in a number of countries.

Tscheulin (1973), in an attempt to understand the extent to which these factors apply in Germany as they apparently do in the United States, administered a translation of the questionnaire developed by Fleishman to 183 employees in two German firms and found that the factor loadings were similar to those in the American research. Furthermore, Tscheulin reviewed several other studies in Germany, each of which employed a different method of factor analysis, but all of which provided results consistent with the distinction between consideration and initiating structure (Fittkau-Garthe, 1970; Hoefert, 1971; Luck, 1970; Nachreiner & Luck, 1971). Tscheulin concludes that "the similarity of results across almost 20 years with different cultures and different methods of analysis can be considered remarkable " (p. 20). Measures of these factors have also been employed in Holland, Sweden, Norway, Finland, Japan, Poland, Turkey, and Israel (Fleishman, 1973; Fleishman & Simmons, 1970; Matsui, Osawa, & Terai, 1975; Misumi & Tasaki, 1965; Shirakashi, 1968a, b; Mannheim, Rim & Grinberg, 1967; Lennerlöf, 1968).

Supervisory Effectiveness

The results of studies designed to test the effectiveness of these approaches to supervision are not entirely consistent within a country, much less among them. Korman (1966), for example, reviews studies exploring the Ohio State University measures in the United States during the period 1953–1964. Some of this research was conducted in hospitals and academic institutions, as well as in military, business, and industrial organizations. Correlations between measures of consideration and initiating structure on the one hand and a variety of criteria of effectiveness such as worker productivity, satisfaction, absences, grievances, and turnover fail to yield consistent results with the exception that "consideration might have some relation to a 'pleasantly affective' work situation as it is rated both by . . . [the supervisor himself or herself] (Oaklander & Fleishman, 1964) and by subordinates (Parker, 1963)" (Korman, 1966, p. 351).

A good deal of research that has grown out of the human relations movement and that has employed measures that are conceptually akin (if not operationally identical) to consideration and initiation structure—e.g., supportive versus punitive supervision, employee versus production centered supervision, general versus close supervision—yield results in a number of countries that are consistent with the above quotation from Korman (Likert, 1961). For example, a national survey in the United States shows that of nineteen aspects of a job, the single highest correlate of job satisfaction ($r \, ¿ \, .37$) is having a "nurturant supervisor" such as "one who takes a personal interest in those he supervises and goes out of his way to praise good work" (U.S. Department of Labor, 1971, p. 432). The lowest correlate is income from the job ($r \, ¿ \, .16$). Thiagarajan and Deep (1970) show positive relationships between participative supervision and satisfaction with supervision in Belgium, Italy, the United Kingdom, and the United States. Similar findings are reported by Bartoelke (unpublished) in Germany. This positive relationship between morale and consideration undoubtedly reflects the general preference that organization members have for psychologically supportive (employee centered, general supervision, participative) treatment. Yet even with respect to such treatment, qualifications are suggested—and some of these qualifications are cultural.

Cultural relativity.   For one thing, the meaning of support may be different in different places and Likert (1961) argued that supervisory techniques that are effective because they imply support in one culture may not be effective in another culture simply because they do not imply support in that culture. Thus Whyte and Williams (1963) reported different correlations among workers in a Peruvian company and among workers in an American company between the emphasis that supervisors place on production (as reported by workers) and the satisfaction felt by these workers with their supervisor. Among the Americans the correlation was negative, but among Peruvians it was positive. Similarly, the Peruvian workers were satisfied with their superiors to the extent that they perceive them to exercise close rather than general supervision, contrary to the results among the American workers. Furthermore, group meetings in which workers could discuss matters with their supervisors were strongly related to satisfaction with the supervisor among the American workers but not among the Peruvian workers.

These results illustrate differences between the reactions of workers to supervision in Peru and the United States. But similarities also occur. For example, the American and Peruvian workers responded in much the same way to the supervisor "who is thought to understand the problems and needs of his people, who stands up for them before his superiors, and who gives a good deal of emphasis to their training" (p. 5). Consideration and support measured relative to *these* criteria have positive implications in both places.

A study of bank employees in Brazil by Farris and Butterfield (1972) also shows results that agree in some respects but not in others with results that are often found in American studies. Employees in these banks (like the Peruvian workers described above) reacted positively to superiors whom they saw exercising close (rather than general) supervision, contrary to the prevailing result in the United States. But these Brazilian employees reacted negatively to supervisors who behaved sarcastically toward them or who belittled them—a result that is entirely predictable from American research. Thus this negative effect of punitive (low consideration) supervision in Brazil is consistent with the assertion that subordinates in general prefer and are more satisfied with superiors who behave (or are perceived to behave) supportively rather than nonsupportively.

However, while this generalization may have applicability in such divergent cultures as those in Peru, Brazil, and the United States, it says little about what behaviors may constitute support or consideration in a given culture. Close supervision and pressure for production may imply lack of support in the United States, but not in Peru. Communication between supervisors and subordinates in a group may be a setting through which support occurs in the United States, but not in Peru.

Trust as a condition.   The existence of such differences between cultures is interesting, but not entirely satisfying from a theoretical standpoint. Cross-national research in organizations is only beginning to define such differences and it has made little progress in explaining these differences beyond attributing them to "culture" in general. Several authors, however, offer explanations that do have general theoretical implications although none of these explanations have been adequately tested or documented internationally. For example, Williams, Whyte, and Green (1966) note an absence of interpersonal trust among workers in Peru (which fits the general notion that people in traditional societies are less likely than people in modern ones to trust others); these researchers take lack of trust as a basis for explaining why Peruvian workers do not react as positively to the supportive behaviors that American workers react positively to. In pursuing this issue, Williams et al. performed separate analyses of Peruvian workers high in trust and those low in trust and they found that the former workers do in fact react positively to leadership that would be defined as supportive in American society while the latter do not. Farris, Senner, and Butterfield (1973), however, find no such conditioning effect of trust among their group of bank employees in Brazil. However, Farris et al. are dealing with an unusual group of professional employees—75 percent of them having fifteen years or more of formal education. Trust among these employees is substantially higher than that among the group of white collar workers in Peru and is not very different from a group of university students in the United States.

Maslow's need hierarchy as a condition.   Maslow (1954) offers another possible explanation in the thesis that higher order needs such as the need for autonomy or for self-actualization are unimportant when lower order needs such as the need for physical security are unmet. If so, "psychological" support would be irrelevant in economically disadvantaged societies where lower level needs are not fulfilled; support in such places would have meaning only in terms of actions that contribute directly to the economic and physical well being of organization members. Research by Greenwood (1971) involving IBM personnel does suggest that the need for job security is prepotent in economically poor countries and that in the more wealthy countries the need for autonomy and for challenging work is relatively more important. Singh and Wherry (1963) suggest a similar conclusion on the basis of their research in India. On the other hand, Orpen and Ndlovu (1977) find that black clerical workers in South Africa have stronger higher order needs than do white workers even though "blacks in South Africa form a disadvantaged caste ... [whose] lower order needs for food and shelter and for security are only occasionally met ..." (p. 32). Similarly, the study of managers by Haire et al. (1966) is not entirely consistent with the Maslow thesis. For example, managers in the Anglo-American cluster compared to managers in the other clusters indicate relatively low fulfillment of all of the needs in the Maslow hierarchy, yet they attach relatively low importance to these needs. According to Maslow's thesis, managers should attach moderately high importance to needs that are not fulfilled very well. On the other hand, Japanese managers attach a relatively high degree of importance to these needs even though Japanese managers experience a high degree of fulfillment. Only among the Nordic-European group do managers attach low importance to needs that they report as highly fulfilled. Thus, the evidence relative to a possible explanation of differences between countries in reactions of people to supervision is mixed.

"Contingency theories."   Inconsistencies among studies concerning leadership even within a culture have led researchers to look beyond the simple linear relationship between a variable like consideration and an effect like worker satisfaction or productivity. Fiedler (1966), for example, proposes a "contingency theory" that considers aspects of the situation along with the personality of the leader as determinants of the leader's effectiveness. According to this theory, leaders differ from one another in a personality attribute (called LPC) that reflects their motivation to be related socially to others. On the basis of experiments conducted in Holland (Fiedler, Meuwese, & Oonk, 1961) and Belgium (Fiedler, 1966) as well as experiments in the United States (e.g., Meuwese & Fiedler, 1965), Fiedler argues that leaders high in this attribute will react with consideration only when their work situation is unfavorable for them as, for example, when they have little power and influence or when they do not feel accepted. When the situation is favorable, however, such people will be task oriented. Thus the same leader will behave differently with respect to consideration and initiating structure depending on the favorableness of the situation.

Furthermore, a leader's effectiveness according to Fiedler's theory (1971) will depend on the relationship between the leader's style—whether "task-oriented" or "relationship-oriented"—and the favorableness of the situation. For example, the task-oriented leader would perform more effectively in situations that are either very favorable or very unfavorable, while the relationship-oriented leader would do better in situations that are moderate in favorableness. Inconsistencies between leadership studies therefore occur because these studies view consideration and initiating structure as simple causes rather than as effects, and they do not take into account the interactive effect of personality and situation that underlie a leader's behavior and effectiveness.

The notion of a contingency theory is appealing in principle. Human behavior is complicated, and an attempt to explain subordinates' reactions by a single variable like supervisory consideration or initiating structure would seem to be an oversimplification. Introducing contingencies into a model provides the basis for a more complex and presumably more sophisticated explanation. The importance of contingencies is especially apparent in cross-national comparison; theories that may have some applicability in one culture are suspect in another because "conditions" are manifestly so different in the two places. Thus, Bennett (1977) found that high performing bank managers in the Philippines are low on Fiedler's LPC scale while such managers in Hong Kong are high on Fiedler's scale; he surmises that the different "contingencies" in the two cultures explain the different relationships between LPC scores and performances, consistent with Fiedler's hypotheses. Similarly, Heller (1971, 1973) questions, on the basis of his experience with several pilot projects in South America, that participative leadership style has universal applicability. On the contrary, quite different styles are appropriate, depending on the situation. But Heller (1973) questions the adequacy of Fiedler's model because it too, like the "universalistic" theories of leadership, does not take into account the many contingencies that are important; Fiedler considers only three conditions that define the favorableness of the situation for a leader. The important contingencies according to Heller include a larger number of factors such as characteristics of the manager, technology, microstructural and macrostructural characteristics (like span of control and size of organization), and ecological variables (such as the "cultural environment" or the level of economic development). Studies by Heller (1971) in the United States, and by Wilpert & Heller (1972) in Germany, indicate that managers select a leadership style depending on some of these conditions. For example, Heller (1973) used job functions as an indication of sociotechnical factors, and he found that American managers in finance and production employ a more autocratic style than managers in personnel and unspecialized managerial jobs. Managers in purchasing and sales were intermediate in their style. The results in Britain, however, do not correspond to those in the United States and Heller continues to analyze his data in search of an explanation.

Personality, values, and expectations as condition.   Several authors have suggested that differences in personality or in personal values and expectations on the part of subordinates may explain differences between them in their reactions to leadership practices (Tannenbaum & Allport, 1956;

Vroom, 1965), although studies in the United States have not been consistent in supporting this notion (Abdel-Halim & Rowland, 1976). Virtually nothing has been done to test this idea internationally in organizations. The research by Lewin, Lippitt, and White (White & Lippitt, 1960) in children's groups has been replicated in India and in Japan, and the results of these replications fit the notion that differences between cultures in reaction to leadership occur because of differences in prevailing attitudes toward authority. For example, the replication in India by Meade (1967) yielded results that contrast with those from the original American research. In the Indian case, members of the democratic groups were absent more often, preferred their leaders less, and turned out poorer quality work compared to members in the autocratic groups. On the other hand, Misumi (1974) summarized the results of a number of studies in Japan that were designed to replicate the Lewin research, and he concluded that the results in Japan were essentially like those in the United States.

French, Israel, and As (1960) attempted to replicate in a Norwegian factory the earlier experiment by Coch and French (1948) in the United States where workers responded positively to participative procedures. The response of the Norwegian workers, however, was not positive and the authors explained the lack of success partly by the experimental manipulation that created only a very weak form of participation that did not meet the values and expectations of the workers. Hence this experiment too might be taken to illustrate the importance of values as a condition affecting the workability of participative procedures, although in this case the problem may have been too little participation rather than too much.

Joint effects of consideration and initiating structure. Other researchers have also attempted to understand the effects of leadership by considering more than one variable at a time. Halpin and Winer (1957) suggested on the basis of their early analyses of consideration and initiation that leadership effectiveness could be maximized not under one or another of these leadership styles, but under a combination of the two. Similarly, Likert's (1961) theory of management specified a combination of conditions that have to be met if an organization is to perform effectively. Among these are high standards of performance set by the superior, together with strong psychological support. Blake and Mouton (1964), too, argued that the combination of concern by superiors for production along with a concern for people is the key to organizational success. Support or consideration alone is not likely to explain performance, according to these arguments.

Misumi in Japan has come to a similar conclusion. Misumi and Tasaki (1965) defined a distinction between the production-oriented supervisor (measured by questions such as, "Is your [supervisor] a stickler for the rules?" and "Does your [supervisor] urge you to finish your daily norm by the specified time?") and the human relations-oriented supervisor (measured by questions such as "Does your [supervisor] tend to ask your opinion about important matters concerning the work?" and "Can you easily speak to your [supervisor] about your work?"). Misumi and Tasaki sought to learn how these different styles of supervision would affect the morale and productivity of work groups. Contrary to the implications of some earlier research in the United States, Misumi (1960a, 1960b) found that high producing work groups were led by production-oriented supervisors while low producing groups were led by human relations-oriented supervisors. However, the high producing groups were more likely than the low producing groups to have second line supervisors who were human relations-oriented. Consequently, Misumi sought to understand how the *combination* of production and human relations orientations relate to the reactions of subordinates; therefore, he defined four categories of supervisors depending on whether the supervisors were high or low on each of the two orientations. His results in a study of 500 coal getters showed that productivity was likely to be higher in groups where the first or second line supervisor expressed *both* production and human relations concerns. On the other hand, most of the low producing work groups were likely to have first and second line supervisors who emphasized production exclusively (a result similar to that found in some American studies). In the remaining low producing groups first and second line supervisors expressed neither production nor human relations concerns. These latter supervisors followed a laissez-faire style.

These results, like most results based on survey research, do not distinguish cause from effect. Misumi and Shirakashi (1966) therefore undertook an experimental simulation of a hierarchical organization in which people supervised "workers" engaged in the simple task of counting holes in IBM cards. The results of this experimental manipulation of supervisory style again showed that high performance by "workers" is associated with concern by "supervisors" for *both* production and human relations. Thus Misumi and his colleagues conclude that the most effective supervisory style combines a concern for both production and human relations, a conclusion that corresponds with that drawn by a number of researchers in the United States (Anderson, 1966; Fleishman, 1969; Fleishman & Harris, 1962; Fleishman & Ko, 1962; Sergiovanni, Metzcus, & Burden, 1969).

Two studies in Israel yield results that lead to similar conclusions (Fleishman & Simmons, 1970; Rim, 1965). One of these studies is especially interesting because of the variation in method that it employs. Twenty-seven head nurses and thirty-nine industrial supervisors participated in an experiment in which they responded individually to problems that were designed to measure their willingness to take risks. Each participant also completed a questionnaire designed to measure his or her supervisory style. They were then formed into groups of four or five where they were asked to arrive at a consensus concerning the risk-taking problems. Rim found that some individuals were more influential than others in bringing the group to a final decision, and that the most influential people, those whose initial decision was adopted (or came closest to being adopted) as the final group decision, were people high in both structure and consideration. Thus influence, as a criterion of supervisory effectiveness, is associated in this study with a combination of the two leadership factors.

The Organization Member

Social critics from Marx to Mayo have cited the factory as a source of frustration and alienation for workers. Contemporary expressions of this indictment against the factory include the assertation that workers are becoming increasingly frustrated. There is little research documentation, however, to substantiate the contention that frustration and alienation have increased over the years. In a thorough analysis of data based on national samples during the past fifteen years in the United States, Quinn, Staines and McCullough (1974) concluded that there has been no decline in job satisfaction. In Germany, Katona, Strumpel, and Zahn (1971) undertook a longitudinal analysis of national survey data during the period 1951 to 1962 and they found, on the contrary, a substantial increase in reported satisfaction. Work is described in negative terms (e.g., as a heavy burden or as a necessary evil) by 51 percent, 46 percent, and 38 percent of the work force in 1951, 1957, and 1962, respectively. On the other hand, it is referred to as a satisfactory activity implying an inner commitment by 47 percent, 50 percent, and 60 percent and as wholly satisfactory by 50 percent, 55 percent, and 59 percent during these years. The economic progress and rising standard of living in Germany during this period may have contributed to the improvement in attitudes toward work, but this improvement nonetheless contradicts the argument that dissatisfaction is inevitably increasing.

Furthermore, there is little evidence that machinery per se is a growing source of frustration—although some machines may be more frustrating than others. Mueller, Schmiedeskamp, Hybels, Sonquist, and Staelin (1969) reported, on the basis of a national sample survey in the United States, that 58 percent of workers who indicate having experienced a change in machines in their work report that they are more satisfied with their work than they were five years earlier. On the other hand, only 40 percent of the workers who experienced no change in machines report that they are more satisfied than they were five years earlier. Modern machines may be better from the workers' standpoint than are the older machines that are being replaced.

Inkeles and Smith (1974) conducted a longitudinal study of people who moved from farm to factory in Argentina, Chile, East Pakistan, India, Israel, and Nigeria. These researchers found better psychological adjustment on the part of factory workers compared to peasants, but more significantly they found that positive adjustment increased with years of factory experience. Using an index that included measures of feeling of personal efficacy, aspirations, openness to new experiences, a belief in the calculability of the world, and trust in people to meet their obligations, Inkeles and Smith (1974) stated that

> Through the reinterviews we could prove that the very same individuals steadily and vigorously increased their scores in the intervening years of factory work. Some part of the change observed over the reinterview period had properly to be attributed to the usual accompaniments of increased factory experience, such as exposure to the mass media and larger incomes. But after we took that into account, it was still clear that the qualities inherent in industrial employment consistently exerted a significant [positive] influence on workers' scores (p. 174).

Inkeles and Smith illustrated the sense of personal efficacy that might be engendered by factory work through the words of a Nigerian worker who was asked how his work made him feel: "Sometimes like nine feet tall with arms a yard wide. Here in the factory I alone with my machine can twist any way I want a piece of steel all the men in my home village together could not begin to bend at all" (p. 158). The research of Eden & Leviatan (1974) that compares the adjustment of agricultural and factory workers in Israeli kibbutzim suggests that it is not simply the difference between working on the land and working in a factory that explains the difference in adjustment between peasant and urban workers. Where agricultural workers employ modern technology as on the kibbutz farms, and where they are exposed to essentially the same larger social environment as are factory workers, they do not differ from factory workers on criteria of alienation, mental health, and job satisfaction.

Factors Affecting Reaction to Work and Organization

Numerous studies suggest that workers performing unskilled, repetitive, machine-paced work report less satisfaction with their job than do workers performing skilled work that involves variety and self-pacing (Caplan, Cobb, French, Van Harrison, & Pinneau, 1975; Hulin & Blood, 1968; Rousseau, 1977; and Srivastva, 1975). Hulin and Blood (1968), however, argue that this widely accepted generalization must be qualified by the cultural background of the workers. These authors note that unskilled, machine-paced work is not frustrating to *all* groups of workers. They cite, for example, the work of Turner and Lawrence (1959) who found that while workers from small towns in the United States reacted positively to and were more satisfied with complex and varied than with simple, repetitive jobs, workers from cities showed no such reaction. Birchall & Wild (1977) found that most female manual workers in a British electronics company were actually more satisfied with repetitive jobs that required little skill and responsibility than with jobs that were varied and that required high skill and responsibility. Blood and Hulin (1967) inferred that people from cultures imbued with the Protestant ethic, typified in the American small town community, would react positively to job enlargement, but that people from cultures without such an ethic, typified in the big city and especially in the inner city, would not react positively to job enlargement. Hulin and Blood (1968) cite a number of studies in the United States to support their cultural hypothesis. Little has been done, however, to test this idea internationally, although data from studies in a number of countries do have some indirect bearing.

Rank and attitude. Research generally demonstrates that measures of positive adjustment in the work situation increase statistically with hierarchical ascent; people at higher levels in an organization feel more satisfied with their job, express greater interest in their work, and have a more favorable attitude toward their organization than do people at lower levels. Evidence for this effect of hierarchy has been found in studies involving more than 5,000 people in 130 industrial organizations of thirteen countries that differ widely from one another in culture and political system: Austria, Brazil, Bulgaria, Germany, Hungary, Ireland, Israel, Italy, Mexico, Poland, Romania, the United States and Yugoslavia (Tannenbaum, Kavcic, Rosner, Vianello & Weiser, 1974; Tannenbaum & Kozgonyi, submitted for publication). An unusual set of data collected from displaced persons from the Soviet Union after World War II and reported by Inkeles (1960) is entirely consistent with the results found in other countries. Among unskilled and semiskilled workers (workers who are likely to be at the very bottom of the organizational hierarchy) only 23 percent and 45 percent respectively respond affirmatively to the question, "Did you like the job you held in 1940?" On the other hand, 77 percent of administrative and professional people (people who are likely to hold positions of relatively high rank) respond affirmatively. Countries may differ in the magnitude of relationships between rank and measures of adjustment, and exceptions to the rule that defines this relationship are occasionally found (Mozina, 1969), but this nearly universal relationship suggests that there is something about hierarchy or about the correlates of hierarchical rank that is general to organization and that is general also in its implications for human adjustment. Several researchers have explored some of these correlates in a number of countries in an attempt to explain job satisfaction and reaction to the work situation.

Education and attitude.   Education is one such correlate of rank; people at upper levels on the average have had more years of formal education than people at lower levels. One exception to this generalization has been found in the factories of Israeli kibbutzim; managers and supervisors there do not have more formal schooling than do the workers (Tannenbaum et al., 1974). But, education per se does not explain the greater job satisfaction or the more favorable attitude toward the company felt by people at upper levels compared to those at lower levels. On the contrary, regression analyses of data in ten plants each of Austria, Italy, the United States, Yugoslavia, and Israeli kibbutzim (Tannenbaum et al., 1974), Brazil (de Souza & de Souza), Bulgaria (Staikov, et al.), Germany (Bartoelke), and Hungary (Gyenes & Rozgonyi), [the latter four of which will be published by Tannenbaum and Rozgonyi (submitted for publication)] indicate that education has a *negative* impact on job satisfaction or on attitude toward the company. Other things being equal (including hierarchical rank and characteristics of the job), more educated people (in a number of countries at least) are less satisfied with their job or with their company than less educated people, probably because education creates skills that are not utilized in some jobs and because it creates expectations that are not met. The negative relationship between education and job satisfaction in these countries is in accord with the findings of other studies in the United States (Mann, 1953; Morse, 1953; Lawler, 1971).

The educational level of the work force has risen over the years in many countries, which might be expected to have had a depressing effect on job satisfaction. But this predicted effect has not occurred, in so far as available data indicate, which suggests that the character of work is also changing along with the rise in education and in a manner that compensates for the rising skills and expectations of workers.

Age, seniority, and attitude.   Age and seniority form a second set of correlates of hierarchical position. People at upper levels in the plants of each of the countries studied on the average were older and had more seniority than people at lower levels. Regression analyses on data from the international set of plants discussed indicate that age (but not seniority) does have a positive effect on attitude toward the company and, in at least some of these plants, on job satisfaction. Blunt (1972), however, found no such relationship in a study of English-speaking South African middle managers.

The positive attitude of older people toward their enterprise that is found in nearly all of the countries studied fits the notion that older people are more conservative than younger people, even if the former earn the same salary, have the same seniority, and are at the same hierarchical level as the latter (factors controlled in the regression analyses). This relatively "favorable adjustment" of older workers occurs despite their less happy adjustment in certain aspects of nonwork life (in the United States at least) (Gurin, Veroff, & Feld, 1960; Morse, 1953), which emphasizes the special importance of work for them. Crozier (1971) and Marenco (1959) noted a similar relationship between age and job satisfaction in France that they explain in terms of a "classic pattern": younger workers enter a job with some enthusiasm but they are soon disillusioned and their attitude declines sharply. In time, however, they accommodate to the realities of organizational life, learn how to cope with some of the difficulties of the job, and develop a tolerance for the frustrating aspects of organization that younger people find disturbing. Hence there is a steady growth of positive attitude with age following an initial decline.

Pay and attitude.   Pay is a further correlate of hierarchy (in all but the kibbutz plants) that might, in principle, explain the more positive reaction of people at upper levels. But regression analyses of data in the plants of Austria, Italy, the United States, and Yugoslavia (Tannenbaum et al., 1974); Germany (Bartoelke, in press); Hungary (Gyenes & Rozgonyi, in press); and Ireland (O'Broin & Hurley, in press), indicate that level of pay has no bearing on attitude toward the company in any of these countries and that it may have some impact on job satisfaction only in the plants in Ireland. Obviously pay cannot explain why kibbutz managers are more satisfied with their jobs and are more favorable toward their organization than are rank and file workers, since kibbutz managers are not paid more than workers; all people in the kibbutz factory receive the same nominal allowance regardless of position. Zdravomyslov and Iadov (1964), in a study of over 2,550 young Soviet workers, found that while many of these workers attach importance to wages, level of pay per se does not affect satisfaction with work. For example, unskilled manual workers earn relatively high wages compared to other workers, but they are the least satisfied with their jobs. In the United States, a survey employing a national sample of over 1,000 workers shows that of nineteen characteristics of the work situation the lowest correlate ($r = .16$) of job satisfaction is income from the job (U.S. Department of Labor, 1971). Reasonably enough, however, pay does have implications for satisfaction with pay in most of the above countries if not for satisfaction with job. An interesting exception occurs among the young Soviet workers studied by Zdravomyslov and Iadov (1964). Unskilled manual workers whose jobs are routine and monotonous are more dissatisfied with their wages than are skilled workers, even though their earnings are actually higher than those of the skilled workers. This result is in accord with the finding of Tannenbaum et al. (1974) that the character of the job has a bearing on satisfaction with pay (even though pay does not affect satisfaction with job) in Italy, Yugoslavia, and the United States. A person's satisfaction with pay is determined in part by the person's standing relative to others on a number of dimensions (such as qualities of the job) relevant to pay (Patchen, 1961; Lawler, 1971).

Authority and attitude.   People at upper levels of an organizational hierarchy in general have more authority and influence over important decisions in their organization than do people at lower levels; this hierarchical distribution of control represents a further possible explanation for differences in job satisfaction and favorable attitude that accompany differences in rank. Bureaucratic and administrative science theories prescribe such a distribution, and members themselves report that this is the way control in fact is distributed. Tannenbaum and Cooke (1978), in a review of studies in fourteen countries, find that this characterization by members occurs in organizations in developed and developing countries as well as in capitalist, communist, and socialist societies. It is found in businesses, industrial and military organizations, cooperatives, municipal agencies, schools, colleges, religious institutions and even, with some exceptions, in voluntary organizations. Furthermore, while officers and rank and file members may differ from one another in their perception of details about how much authority and influence different groups exercise in their organization, they do not disagree about the hierarchical character of control: both groups report that upper levels have more authority and exercise more influence than do lower levels. In this one respect at least, work organizations would seem universally to fit the bureaucratic model.

People in general want or at least say they want to exercise control or influence in their work situation. Individual differences may occur in this expressed desire for more influence, but for most people having some say in the work situation is preferred to being powerless. When this preference is operationalized by questions in which members are asked about the amount of authority and influence they have and the amount they would like to have, the preponderant result is what Porter (1962) refers to as a perceived need deficiency; people want more than they see themselves as having. Furthermore, the deficiency is greater near the bottom of the organization than near the top. This result occurs in countries with a prevailing Protestant ethic like the United States and Germany (Katz, 1954; Porter, 1962; Bartoelke), and in predominately Catholic countries like Italy and Ireland (Tannenbaum et al., 1974; O'Broin & Hurley). It also occurs in developing countries like Brazil and Mexico (de Souza & de Souza; Otolora Bay), as well as in communist countries like Yugoslavia, Hungary, Bulgaria, and Romania (Tannenbaum et al., 1974; Gyenes & Rozgonyi; Staikov, Dragan et al.); all of the studies mentioned without dates will be published by Tannenbaum & Rozgonyi. Workers (but not managers) in the factories of Israeli kibbutzim report the same discrepancy; they too want or say they want to have more influence than they see themselves as having in their work situation (Tannenbaum et al., 1974).

It seems reasonable to expect that the exercise of influence or the perception of such influence is a source of satisfaction in most if not all cultures. Thus, analyses by Tannenbaum et al. (1974) of data from Austria, Israeli kibbutzim, Italy, the United States, and Yugoslavia; by Bartoelke in Germany; by O'Broin & Hurley in Ireland; and by Dragan et al., in Romania show positive relationships between measures of job satisfaction or of favorable attitude toward the company and self-reports of influence even when rank, age, and some other possible determinants of these reactions are partialed out. Even the Peruvian workers who, in the study by Whyte and Williams (1963), expressed distrust and who did not react positively to American-style human relations techniques of supervision nonetheless reported satisfaction with their supervisor to the extent that they saw themselves and their coworkers as having influence "about how things are done in [their] work group" (p. 5). Similarly, black clerical workers in South Africa ". . . who are the object of legalized and social discrimination which forces them to occupy inferior positions in society," report satisfaction with their jobs to the extent that they feel that they have influence over decisions that affect their work (Orpen & Ndlovu, 1977, p. 32). An exception is the kibbutz organization where influence does not relate to job satisfaction, but even in these organizations, as in the organizations of other places, influence does correlate with the sense of responsibility that members report in their work situation (Tannenbaum et al., 1974). Egalitarian norms in the kibbutz may create ambivalence on the part of some members toward the authority and influence that they inevitably must exercise over others. Consequently, exercising influence may not make kibbutzniks happy, but it does seem to make them responsible. The more positive reaction of people near the top of a hierarchy than of those near the bottom, which seems universal in organizations, appears therefore to be explained in part by another underlying universality: the hierarchical distribution of control in organizations.

Social status and attitude.   Social status or prestige represents a further correlate of rank that would seem to explain the more positive reaction of members at upper levels compared to those at lower levels. The respect and recognition that are accorded to people in prestigious positions undoubtedly contribute to a sense of self-esteem and satisfaction and therefore to a positive adjustment in the work situation. Porter (1962), for example, in a study of 2,000 American managers found that managers at higher levels feel less deprived in their sense of self-esteem than do those below them, and Weaver (1977) concluded on the basis of data from a national survey in the United States that occupational prestige is a more important determinant of job satisfaction than is working autonomy, authority, or income.

The ranking of occupations according to their social status is remarkably similar in many societies even though the societies differ in culture and political system. Inkeles and Rossi (1956) report correlations mainly above .90 among rankings of occupations in Japan, Britain, New Zealand, the United States, and the Soviet Union. The lowest correlation, that between the USSR and Japan, is .74. Sarapata and Wesolowski (1961) found essentially the same magnitude of correlations between the rankings from Poland, England, Germany, and the United States. The lowest correlation, .86, occurred between Poland and England. Furthermore, Sarapata (1974) found, in a longitudinal analysis, that the status structure has remained fairly stable in Poland although he detected a slight flattening that entailed a small increase in prestige accorded occupations at the lower end accompanied by a very slight decrease at the upper end (personal communication). The occupational status hierarchy in industrial societies is apparently determined largely by features of the industrial system that all industrial societies have in common, rather than by idiosyncratic features of culture (Inkeles & Rossi, 1956).

In all of the countries, according to these studies, factory managers (and other people, such as engineers) who are at relatively high levels in an organizational hierarchy enjoy substantially greater prestige than do workers who are placed at the bottom of the hierarchy. Prestige may be more important to people in some societies such as the Italian than in others such as the American (Tannenbaum et al., 1974), but the prestige structure is similar in these societies and prestige therefore seems to be another reasonable explanation for the relatively favorable reaction of people at upper levels to their job and their work situation that is found in all countries.

Character of work and attitude.   The nature of work also varies as a function of hierarchical position. Work near the bottom of the hierarchy in industrial plants is likely to be more repetitious, routinized, fractionated, physically tiring, dangerous, and dirty than work near the top, and jobs at lower levels are likely to allow less discretion and less opportunity to learn and to use one's ideas and skills (Argyris, 1964). Such differences between ranks are documented through the responses of members themselves in the plants of all of the countries, regardless of culture or political system, where research on this subject has been undertaken. Analyses that have been performed in Austria, Israeli kibbutzim, Italy, the United States, Yugoslavia (Tannenbaum et al., 1974), Brazil (de Souza & de Souza, in press), Bulgaria (Staikov et al., in press), Germany (Bartoelke, in press), Hungary (Gyenes & Rozgonyi, in press), Ireland (O'Broin & Hurley, in press) and

Romania (Dragan et al., in press) indicate that these characteristics relate to members' satisfaction with their jobs or to their attitude toward the organization even when rank, perceived authority, age, and education are controlled through regression procedures. People who report opportunities to set their own work pace, to use their skills, to learn new things on the job or who report that their jobs are not repetitious, dirty, heavy, dangerous, or physically tiring are in general relatively satisfied with their work and they are relatively favorable toward their organization. Rousseau (1977) reviewed research in the United States concerned with job design and found support for the notion that jobs are satisfying to the extent that they have characteristics (which are more likely at the top of the hierarchy than at the bottom) such as providing the incumbent with the opportunity to use a number of different skills or to make decisions related to the work process (see also Rousseau, 1978; Srivastva, 1975). A national sample survey in the United States showed that in the work force as a whole people who reported that their job allowed them autonomy in matters that affected their work or who reported that their job had "enriching" demands (e.g., a job that demanded that one learn new things, have a high level of skills, be creative and do a variety of different things) were likely to be more satisfied with their jobs than people who did not report such characteristics—although the correlations, .28 and .38, are not large (U.S. Government, 1971; see also Friend & Burns, 1977). Emery and Phillips (1976) compared skilled workers with unskilled, urban workers in Australia, and showed that the unskilled perceive themselves to have little freedom, variety, or opportunity to learn on their jobs, and felt correspondingly little satisfaction with and enthusiasm for their jobs. Administrative and professional personnel, on the other hand, reported substantially more "positive" reactions than did either of the other groups. Zdravomyslov and Iadov (1964), agreeing essentially with Herzberg's (1966) theory, concluded from their study of young Soviet workers that the most important determinant of job satisfaction is the job's content. Jobs that are routine and monotonous are less satisfying than jobs that are complex and that require some discretion and decision making on the part of workers. Such characteristics of work, it would seem, help to define the advantage experienced by people at the top compared to those at the bottom and they help to explain the more favorable attitudes and feelings of satisfaction associated with high rank in many cultures.

Methodological and Substantive Implications of Research Concerning Attitudes

Many of the correlations upon which this description was based have been computed from questionnaire measures and these correlations might therefore be interpreted to reflect response biases more than to indicate genuine relationships between variables. Therefore, some consideration should be given to the possible implications of this methodological limitation. Job satisfaction in a number of the studies discussed was measured through questionnaire items that employed scales opposite in direction to that of most of the other scales with which they were correlated. Hence the index of job satisfaction in which component scores were reversed implies a negative rather than a positive response set relative to most of the other measures with which it was correlated and the effect should be to create negative rather than positive correlations. Responses that reflect "social desirability" (Orpen, 1974) or an affective "halo," however, could conceivably explain some of these correlations. If such biases are in fact operating, they seem to be the "middle class" biases defined as a condition in the Hulin and Blood (1968) hypothesis; for example, the bias that job satisfaction, personal influence, opportunity to learn and to use one's skills are all "good," or socially desirable, or socially expected. (It is unlikely that respondents view them all as "bad" since respondents on the average indicate that they would like to have more of these qualities than they perceive themselves to have in their jobs.)

Hulin and Blood argue that only workers who accept middle class values and who are imbued with the Protestant ethic will react positively to job enlargement and to other features of work prescribed by the human relations school. The data do not provide a direct test of this hypothesis, but if the data are to fit the hypothesis they require the assumption that people in each of the countries studied have responded in terms of middle class, Protestant ethic values. Supervisory and managerial people are included among the respondents in many of these studies and it is conceivable that on the average respondents in each of the studies do behave in accordance with middle class norms. In any event, the similarity of the results among countries suggests that the dynamics and/or the methodologically biasing social values that underlie these correlations have some cross-cultural generality.

The relationships suggested in these studies appear consistent, on the surface at least, with aspects of a "human relations" or "human resources" view broadly defined. Jobs that allow people some authority and influence and that provide people with the opportunity to use their skills, to learn new things, and to set their own work pace seem, according to these correlations, to be more satisfying than jobs that do not have these qualities. The amount of authority that people have or perceive themselves to have in their work appears especially to relate to their feeling of responsibility on the job. Having some authority or influence in the work situation is therefore more than merely satisfying; it is motivating—if the correlations are accepted on their face value. The correlations are not always large and in some cases they are negative (Birchall & Wild, 1977) which suggests that conditions similar to those proposed by Hulin and Blood (1968),

Fiedler (1971), Heller (1973), MacEachron (1977), Oldham, Hackman, & Pearce (1976), and Tannenbaum & Kuleck (1978) may affect outcomes. But whatever the "adverse" conditions may be, they do not appear to be the conditions that are dominant where most of these studies have been undertaken. It is possible, therefore, that these relationships imply principles that have broad applicability.

Job and Organizational Design

A variety of schemes of job and organizational design—job enlargement, job enrichment, participation, autonomous groups, and sociotechnical systems—assume the validity of these principles. Published research and case studies illustrate a number of successes and several failures in efforts to expedite these schemes in organizations.

Davis (1972) reviews research concerning several such schemes, including the work of Trist and Bamforth (1951; Trist, Higgin, Murray, & Pollock, 1963) in British coal mines and Rice (1953) in an Indian textile mill; he concludes that improved performance in small organizational units or work groups is achieved when these units incorporate a number of features (which illustrate aspects of the autonomous group and the sociotechnical system):

> a) group composition that permits self-regulation of the group's functioning, b) group composition that deliberately provides for the full range of skills required to carry out all the tasks in an activity cycle, c) delegation of authority, formal or informal, to the group for self-assignment of tasks and roles to group members, d) group structure that permits internal communication, and e) a group reward system for joint output (Davis, 1972, p. 326).

The W. E. Upjohn Institute for Employment Research (1973) presents a review of thirty-four case studies of programs that

> entail some combination of features, such as delegating responsibility for the production process to the work group, having the group set its own production standards and goals, and providing the group with more information [for purposes of self-regulation] concerning costs and terms of the government contract on which it was working (p. 190).

The results of these programs, twenty-three in the United States, three in Norway, two in Yugoslavia, three in Britain, two in Holland, and one in Mexico, indicate that organizational design incorporating features of the autonomous group and of job enlargement lead to improved morale and/or increased productivity. Some also indicate a negative effect on absenteeism, tardiness, grievance, and waste.

Walton (1974) and Srivastva (1975) reviewed experiments in Australia, Britain, Canada, France, Holland, India, Ireland, Norway, Sweden, and the United States that incorporate features of self-managing work teams, enlarged tasks, and flexibility in work assignments. Most of these experiments showed positive effects on productivity, quality control, or quality of working life, although some people did not react positively to such participation. In a subsequent article (Walton, 1977) described the failure of eight firms from the same countries to adopt successfully the model of work design that the earlier research had shown to be effective. Thus, these countries were similar to one another in providing examples that demonstrated the effectiveness of the participative restructuring of work, and also examples that demonstrate failure to adopt the presumably more effective system.

Engelstad (1972) reported the results of one of four experiments carried out as part of the Industrial Democracy Project in Norway (Thorsrud & Emery, 1970). These experiments were formulated with attention to principles of open systems that have a number of implications. For example, the primary task of the manager according to Engelstad is to control the boundary conditions of his unit rather than to control internal processes. Furthermore, the basic regulation of open systems is self-regulation, and this self-regulation requires that every production system include a subunit to convert inputs to outputs, a set of standards and measures for the evaluation of output, and some means of regulating performance so that standards are maintained. The implication for members is to allow them more discretion in their work situation and to give them more control over and responsibility for their department's operations. Specific procedures to help translate these principles and their implications into a workable plan of action included: (a) training to broaden the skills of workers so that each could perform most tasks within their department, (b) an information center that provided quick feedback about performance, (c) facilities for group meetings, and (d) a bonus plan that puts some emphasis on group performance.

The outcome of this experiment included substantial reduction in costs and improvements in quality of product. Furthermore, members participated effectively as problem solvers and decision makers, and a significant number of suggestions for improving work and working conditions were activated. Qvale (1976), evaluating the results of the Norwegian Industrial Democracy Program, in general considers it a "moderate success" on the basis of the number of Norwegian companies that have become involved since its inception in 1962. In addition, Qvale refers to "spin-offs" from the Norwegian project in Sweden, where as many as 300–500 companies have been working toward the adoption of the principles of the program. Davis and Cherns (1975) reported a similar development in Australia, Holland, Italy, and the United States.

Rubenowitz (1974) summarizes the results of four experiments on "industrial democracy" in Sweden that have been influenced by the Norwegian work and that emphasize, in addition to the usual features of the autonomous group, a wage plan that is tied to the productivity of the group. (See also Aguren, Hansson, & Karlsson, 1976; Norstedt & Aguren, 1973; Agervold, 1975; Hammarstrom, 1975). Rubenowitz offers several arguments for emphasis on the group, including that complex production systems make it difficult to draw the line between tasks performed by one individual and another, and difficult therefore to set specific production targets for individuals.

Two of the experiments reported by Rubenowitz have taken place in the Saab company. In the first experiment in a truck manufacturing plant, one or two production groups were established under each foreman in the plant to decide about aspects of the work performed by the group. In addition, each foreman chaired a planning group composed of several workers, a productivity technician and other specialists who might be brought in for consultation. A total of 1,500 persons were involved in this program, and the data indicate an increase in production (which Rubenowitz attributes partly to changes in methods of work initiated by the development groups) and a decline in turnover, unplanned stoppages, and time necessary to make corrections for quality control. Problems are also noted, including the feeling on the part of some members that the system is chaotic and that some members of the group do not do their best.

The manifest success of this project led to a second and highly unique "experiment" in which an entire manufacturing plant was designed to incorporate sociotechnical principles. Thus the Saab engine factory built in 1972 at Sodertalje included the following features:

1. assembly groups rather than assembly lines
2. assembly of a *whole* engine by a group
3. determination by group members of how work is to be allocated within the group
4. a cycle time of thirty minutes rather than one and eight-tenths minutes that is typical of the assembly line
5. selection of workmates by team members

Systematic research documentation is not available, but Rubenowitz concluded on the basis of interviews and observations that both managers and workers reacted favorably to this system.

An attempt by French, Israel, and As (1960) to replicate in Norway the Coch and French experiment (1948), in which participative procedures resulted in favorable attitudes and increased productivity in an American plant, did not result in higher morale and productivity. The experimenters surmised that the rather weak version of participation introduced in the experiment did not meet the expectations of the workers. Marrow (1964) attempted a similar replication in Puerto Rico and here again the outcome was not favorable. According to Marrow these Puerto Rican workers had been "conditioned to blind obedience" and they interpreted the "sudden change in the emphasis in authority as a sign of weakness in the management" (p. 16). Many of them left to seek jobs in better run companies where management knew enough to tell the workers what to do. A further replication by Juralewicz (1974) in a Puerto Rican textile company yields results that are not inconsistent with Marrow's conclusions. Juralewicz found, contrary to the Coch and French results, that a "moderate" degree of participation through representatives or no participation at all, rather than a "high" degree of direct participation, resulted in improved performance.

Misumi (1974) reported a number of programs in a Japanese shipyard where participative, group discussion methods were employed. One such program was established to cope with a conflict between older supervisors who were committed to traditional values and younger workers who were brought up in postwar Japan and who had more formal education than their foremen. (See Whitehill & Takezawa, 1961, 1968, for research concerning changing values in Japan.) Weekly meetings were arranged in which workers and their foremen could discuss and decide about personnel assignments. This system of discussion groups involved 2,000 workers and a total of 85,000 man hours per year but despite this "loss" of time, production increased substantially. The system of group meetings at the time of Misumi's report had been going on for twelve years.

A second program was established to improve safety in the hull construction department. This program involved 4,000 workers divided into small groups that met weekly to evaluate their performance in reducing accidents during the past week and to establish plans for the following week. The discussion in these groups treats a very specific topic—one that is defined more narrowly than those subject to discussion and decision in the Swedish and Norwegian experiments. Yet it is a topic that is the basis for decisions that are important and engaging for the participants. The experiment illustrates the Japanese penchant for group action and it illustrates a very Japanese reaction in these meetings. Imagine Western workers, for example, offering suggestions like: "Whole hearted greetings should be exchanged during the three-minute morning meeting," "Everyone should yell 'Go!' at the time they start working in the morning," "A meeting should be held after the end of each day's work to do soul searching about safety!" (p. 8). These meetings consumed 160,000 man hours a year, a cost that was justified by a 60 percent drop in accidents during the course of three years.

According to Strauss (1976) the available reports concerning experiments on job redesign and organizational development in the United States and abroad generally indicated a decrease in turnover and absenteeism and an increase in job satisfaction as a result of the experimental procedure. Strauss nonetheless expressed skepticism about the generalizability of these studies because of the highly select organizations in which many of them have taken place and because of the likelihood that successful experiments are more widely publicized than unsuccessful ones. Accordingly Mirvis and Berg (1977) presented a set of case studies illustrating failure in attempts to introduce schemes of work redesign and organizational development; some of these failures might be explained in terms of "culture." Steele (1977) suggested on the basis of his experience with organizational development programs in Britain how culture may be "hostile" to such programs. For example, societies with a deeply rooted class structure, with a strong strain of fatalism, with values that emphasize tradition, continuity, and "security and stability" versus the unknown risks of "rocking the boat" are not likely to take well to participative, job redesign and organizational development programs. Yet it is in England where Trist and others developed the sociotechnical approach to organizational design, and early, successful attempts to employ this approach took place in a British coal mine (Trist & Bamforth, 1951) and in an Indian textile company (Rice, 1958; Miller, 1975). De (1977a, 1977b) notes the opposition by Indian culture to participative approaches to work redesign. Nonetheless, several recent participative, action research programs that he describes proved successful in three large Indian organizations. De suggests that although the "socio-cultural stereotypes" held by Indian workers may be in conflict with organizational development efforts the stereotypes may change as a result of the programs. Thus, the application of sociotechnical and related approaches to job and organizational redesign may be more difficult in some countries than in others because of the "hostility" of culture, but successful as well as unsuccessful applications of such approaches apparently have occurred in a variety of countries.

Workers' Control

The impetus for participation in industry does not come exclusively or even primarily from psychologists. The demand for workers' participation is being expressed widely throughout the industrial world. In many socialist countries, workers' participation is a matter of political doctrine and in Western Europe participation is endorsed by groups that span a broad range of the political spectrum. In many places the law requires that workers have the opportunity to influence decisions in their enterprise through a council of elected representatives and/or through a directorial board that includes representatives of management and labor, although the issues subject to such joint decision may not be very broad, and, in the case of directorial boards where workers' representatives join management in decisions about policy, workers' representatives are usually a minority (Tannenbaum, 1976). Such systems are found in Austria, France,

Spain, the Netherlands, Germany, Norway, the United Kingdom, Ireland, the United Arab Republic, Belgium, Italy, Mexico, Switzerland and other countries (Schregle, 1970). Little comparative research has been undertaken on these systems, although the limited evidence available suggests that participation through elected representatives does not have many positive psychological effects on the mass of workers who do not sit in the council or vote on the board (Holter, 1965; Lammers, 1967; Thorsrud & Emery, 1970). Nonetheless, in Germany workers are found through surveys to support the idea of codetermination (Fuerstenburg, 1969).

Two systems of participation, that in the industrial plants of Yugoslavia and of the kibbutzim of Israel, go as far as any in giving control to workers, and some research documentation is available concerning the psychological implications of these Marxist approaches to organization. The Yugoslav system provides to all employees, through an elected workers' council and through other assemblies and referendum procedures, ultimate authority over basic policy, personnel, and technical issues of the firm (SFR of Yugoslavia Assembly, 1977). The kibbutz plants too provide workers with ultimate control over a wide range of basic issues through their electoral power and through their membership in a Workers' Assembly. Workers in kibbutz plants also elect their supervisors.

Tannenbaum et al. (1974) administered questionnaires to people at all levels in ten industrial plants each of Yugoslavia, Israeli kibbutzim, Italy, Austria, and the United States in order to understand how organizations based on socialist principles might differ from organizations of capitalist societies in their effects on members. These researchers found that all of the plants, socialist and capitalist alike, are characterized by hierarchical gradients; people at upper levels have more authority and influence than do people at lower levels, according to members, and people at upper levels also report more satisfaction with their job, a feeling of responsibility, and a favorable attitude toward the enterprise than do people at lower levels. Given the diversity of these systems, and the extent to which the kibbutz and Yugoslav organizations are structured formally to achieve an egalitarian ideal, Tannenbaum et al. conclude that hierarchical gradients of authority and reward and of the psychological reactions of members are probably universal in the work organization. However, gradients are a matter of degree and these gradients are less steep in the socialist plants than they are in the capitalist ones, consistent with the hypothesis that the socialist model of organization is the more egalitarian.

Tannenbaum et al. (1974) note that the plants of the five countries differ not only in gradient but also in average level of reaction and adjustment. Members in the Italian plants, for example, when compared to members in other plants, were dissatisfied with their jobs and with the company and they felt little sense of responsibility, motivation, or initiative. This relatively "poor" adjustment of members in the Italian plants fits well the hypothesis that conflict and frustration will be greater in the nonparticipative system than in the formally participative one. The highly participative kibbutz plants, too, conformed to the hypothesis; members here generally responded positively to questions concerning the above reactions and adjustments. But members of the American plants also ranked high on these items, while members in the Yugoslav plants do less well, as do those in the Austrian plants. Thus, while the hierarchical gradients of reactions and adjustment are relatively flat in the Yugoslav and kibbutz plants compared to others, the *average level* of reaction and adjustment is not consistently higher (or lower) in the socialist plants than in the capitalist plants. Tannenbaum et al., (1974) therefore suggest that "workers' control" based on socialist principles is probably a better predictor of the *distribution* than of the average level of adjustment in an organization.

Conclusion

Roberts (1970), in a review of cross-cultural research related to organizations, concluded pessimistically that "[t]he increment in knowledge seems minimal and possibly not worth all the effort thus far placed in cross-cultural work" (p. 345). The frustration that Roberts expressed is understandable. The cross-cultural study of organizations is itself not well organized. Therefore, the field has a large number of individual studies contributing to a whole that may be less than the sum of its parts. One might imagine on the other hand a model of cross-cultural research in which a concerted set of studies concerning a limited, but central, set of issues is undertaken in carefully selected countries with standardized instruments and common research designs. Such a model of organization for cross-cultural organizational research might not be the one-best-model but it helps to illustrate a need and to define a pole at the other end of the continuum from the current research. There is value, nonetheless, in what has been done, and there is ample justification for continuing the effort, albeit in a more organized fashion.

Cultures, nations, and political systems differ from one another in ways that are crucial to organization. Each model of organization, from the bureaucratic to the organic, assumes its own conception of human nature. Bureaucratic theory assumes members to be imbued with a Protestant-ethic rationality and a commitment to "duty"; human relations assumes "middle class" values and "higher order" needs; organic organization assumes "resources" and cognitive skills on the part of members; and all theories assume that members are motivated by the rewards and incentives dispensed by the organization whether they be money, social approval, or promotion in the hierarchy.

It must be assumed, however, that societies differ from one another in the appropriateness of each of the assumptions and therefore in the appropriateness of one or another approach to organization. Psychologists and other behavioral scientists are beginning, through research, to define these differences between cultures and, ironically, the data seem to suggest that in some societies (like traditional ones) *none* of the above assumptions fit very well. Hence, organizations themselves do not fit very well in some societies—at least organizations as they are defined in the United States.

Organizational psychologists have long been interested in the fit between the individual and the organization. Cross-cultural research adds perspective to the study of this issue by making of it more than a study of individual differences. Whole societies differ from one another in this fit, and the problem of the individual in the organization can therefore be seen as part of a larger issue. The growing interest in system theory adds to the theoretical appeal of a cross-cultural perspective since this perspective calls attention to the organization within a larger social context. There may even be justification for the cross-cultural perspective in the concern of psychologists with practical problems. The gap between the have and have-not nations is partly a problem of individual-organization fit, on a grand scale.

These theoretical and practical problems would certainly be more difficult to resolve if each culture were completely unique. But common denominators do exist among all societies in the character of organizations and in the reaction of members. Furthermore, the data of cross-cultural organizational psychology hint at principles that may transcend culture. The way in which these principles manifest themselves, however, may be different in different places, and attempts to apply these principles may require culture-specific techniques. For example, data suggest that people who have or feel that they have influence in their work situation will feel a corresponding sense of responsibility and will be motivated to perform well in the organization. But it does not follow that the organizational arrangements that enhance the influence of members or that contribute to their feeling of influence in one culture will do so in another culture. Thus people in the inner city or in Peru may differ from middle class Americans, not in their reaction to being influential, but in what it takes to make them influential. General versus close supervision and other techniques of human relations may be culture specific in this sense—effective in some places but not in others. It is conceivable that in some societies practicable techniques cannot easily be developed. But if the underlying *principle* is valid in these societies, then a search for techniques might ultimately prove fruitful even though many attempts will fail.

Some research by organizational psychologists such as that on job enlargement, sociotechnical systems, and autonomous groups in a number of countries illustrates the effort to translate principles into techniques. Those who attempt to transfer the experience with these techniques in one society to another society, however, would do well to distinguish between the principles that are general to these societies and the procedures that are specific to each society. Hopefully, cross-cultural psychology will provide some help in making this distinction.

Notes

1. I would like to thank Klaus Bartoelke, Richard Brislin, Robert Cole, Leopold Gruenfeld, Daniel Katz, Sigvard Rubenowitz, Stanley Seashore, Krishna Swaminathan, and Harry Triandis for their helpful suggestions.

References

ABDEL-HALIM, A. A., & ROWLAND, K. M. Some personality determinants of the effects of participation: a further investigation. *Personnel Psychology*, 1976, *29*, 41–55.

ABEGGLEN, J. C. *The Japanese factory*. Glencoe, Ill.: Free Press, 1958.

AGERVOLD, M. Swedish experiments in industrial democracy. In E. L. Davis & A. Cherns (Eds.), *The quality of working life*, Vol. 2. New York: Free Press, 1975.

AGUREN, S., HANSSON, R., & KARLSSON, K. G. *The impact of new design on work organization*. Stockholm: The Rationalization Council SAF-LO, 1976.

ANDERSON, L. R. Leader behavior, member attitudes, and task performance of intercultural discussion groups. *Journal of Social Psychology*, 1966, *69*, 305–19.

ANDREWS, J. D. W. The achievement motive and advancement in two types of organizations. *Journal of Personality and Social Psychology*, 1967, *6*, 163–68.

ARGYRIS, C. *Integrating the individual and the organization*. New York: Wiley, 1964.

ARONOFF, J., & LITWIN, G. Achievement motivation training and executive advancement. *Journal of Applied Behavioral Science*, 1971, *7*(12), 215–29.

BARRETT, G. V., & BASS, B. M. Comparative surveys of managerial attitudes and behavior. In J. Bradburn (Ed.), *Comparative management: teaching, training and research*. New York: Graduate School of Business Administration, New York University, 1970.

————. Cross-cultural issues in industrial and organizational psychology. Technical report 45, Management Research Center, Graduate School of Management, University of Rochester, August 1972.

BARRETT, G. V., & FRANKE, R. H. Communication preference and performance: a cross-cultural comparison. *Proceedings of the 77th Annual American Psychological Association Convention*, 1969, 597–98.

BARTOELKE, K. The importance of membership in top, middle and bottom groups in selected plants in the FRG. In A. S. Tannenbaum & T. Rozgonyi (Eds.), *Au-*

thority and reward in organizations: an international study. New York: Pergamon, in press.

BASS, B. M. A preliminary report on manifest preferences in six cultures for participative management. Technical report 21, Management Research Center, Graduate School of Management, University of Rochester, June 1968.

BENNETT, M. Testing management theories cross-culturally. *Journal of Applied Psychology,* 1977, *62* (5), 578–81.

BENNIS, W. G., & SLATER, P. E. *The temporary society.* New York: Harper & Row, 1968.

BERRY, J. W. Temne and Eskimo perceptual skills. *International Journal of Psychology,* 1966, *1,* 207–29.

BIRCHALL, D., & WILD, R. Job characteristics and the attitudes of female manual workers: a research note. *Human Relations,* 1977, 30 (4), 335–42.

BLAKE, R. R., & MOUTON, J. S. *The managerial grid.* Houston, Texas: Gulf Publishing Co., 1964.

BLUNT, P. Age and need satisfaction amongst middle management in South Africa. *Journal of Behavioral Science,* 1972, 2, 229–35.

BLOOD, M. R., & HULIN, C. L. Alienation, environmental characteristics, and worker responses. *Journal of Applied Psychology,* 1967, *51,* 284–90.

BRADBURN, N. M. N-achievement and father dominance in Turkey. *Journal of Abnormal and Social Psychology,* 1963, 67(5), 464–68.

BURNS, T., & STALKER, G. M. *The management of innovation.* London: Tavistock Publications, 1961.

CAPLAN, R. D., COBB, S., FRENCH, J. R. P., Jr., VANHARRISON, R., & PINNEAU, S. R., Jr. *Job demands and worker health, main effects and occupational differences.* HEW Publication No. (NIOSH) 75–160, Washington, D.C.: U. S. Government Printing Office, 1975.

CASCIO, W. F. Functional specialization, culture, and preference for participative management. *Personnel Psychology,* 1974, 27(4), 593–603.

CLARK, A. W., & McCABE, S. Leadership beliefs of Australian managers. *Journal of Applied Psychology,* 1970, 54, 1–6.

COCH, L., & FRENCH, J. R. P. Overcoming resistance to change. *Human Relations,* 1948, 4(1), 512–33.

COLE, R. E. *Japanese blue collar: the changing tradition.* Berkeley: University of California Press, 1971.

CROZIER, M. *The world of the office worker.* Chicago: University of Chicago Press, 1971.

DALE, E. *Management: theory and practice* (3rd ed.). New York: McGraw-Hill, 1973.

DAVIS, L. E. The design of jobs. In L. E. Davis & J. C. Taylor (Eds.), *Design of jobs.* Baltimore: Penguin Books, 1972.

DAVIS, L. E., & CHERNS, A. *The quality of working life,* Vol. 2. New York: Free Press, 1975.

DAWSON, J. L. M. Cultural and physiological influences upon spatial-perceptual processes in West Africa—part I. *International Journal of Psychology,* 1967, 2, 115–28.

DERSHOWITZ, Z. Jewish subcultural patterns and psychological differentiation. *International Journal of Psychology,* 1971, 6(3), 223–31.

DE, N. R. Participative redesign of work system and enrichment of the quality of work life. *National Labour Institute Bulletin*, 1977a, *3* (5), 184–200.

———. Participative redesign of work system and enrichment of the quality of work life. *National Labour Institute Bulletin*, 1977b, *3* (6), 237–53.

DE SOUZA, F., & DE SOUZA, E. *Brazil*. In A. S. Tannenbaum, & T. Rozgonyi (Eds.), *Authority and reward in organizations: an international study*. New York: Pergamon, in press.

DOOB, L. W. *Becoming more civilized*. New Haven, Conn.: Yale University Press, 1960.

DRAGAN, I., GIGORESCU, P., CRISTEA, P., CHELSEA, S., STEFANESCU, S., & ZAMFIR, C. *Romania*. In A. S. Tannenbaum, & T. Rozgonyi (Eds.), *Authority and reward in organizations: an international study*. New York: Pergamon, in press.

DUPREEZ, P. D. Social change and field dependence in South Africa. *Journal of Social Psychology*, 1968, *76*, 265–66.

EDEN, D., & LEVIATAN, U. Farm and factory in the kibbutz: a study in agrico-industrial psychology. *Journal of Applied Psychology*, 1974, *59* (5), 596–602.

EMERY, F. E., & PHILLIPS, C. *Living at work*. Canberra: Australian Government Publishing Service, 1976.

EMERY, F. E., & THORSRUD, E. *Form and content in industrial democracy*. London: Tavistock-Assen, Van Gorcum, 1969.

EMERY, F. E., & TRIST, E. L. Socio-technical systems. In F. E. Emery (Ed.), *Systems thinking*. Baltimore: Penguin Books, 1969.

ENGELSTAD, P. H. Socio-technical approach to problems of process. In L. E. Davis & J. C. Taylor (Eds.), *Design of jobs*. Baltimore: Penguin Books, 1972.

FARRIS, G. F., & BUTTERFIELD, D. A. Control theory in Brazilian organizations. *Administrative Science Quarterly*, 1972, *17*(4), 574–85.

FARRIS, G. F., SENNER, E. E., & BUTTERFIELD, D. A. Trust, culture, and organizational behavior. *Industrial Relations*, 1973, *12*(2), 144–57.

FAYOL, H. *General and industrial management*. London: Pitman, 1949.

FERRAROTTI, F. Management in Italy. In F. Harbison & C. A. Myers (Eds.), *Management in the industrial world*. New York: McGraw-Hill, 1959.

FIEDLER, F. E. The effect of leadership and cultural heterogeneity on group performance: a test of the contingency model. *Journal of Experimental Social Psychology*, 1966, *2*, 237–64.

———. Validation and extension of the contingency model of leadership effectiveness: a review of empirical findings. *Psychological Bulletin*, 1971, *76*, 128–148.

FIEDLER, F. E., MEUWESE, W., & OONK, S. An exploratory study of group creativity in laboratory tasks. *Acta Psychologica*, 1961, *18*, 100–19.

FITTKAU-GARTHE, H. Die Dimensionen des Vorgesetztenverhaltens und ihre Bedeutung fur die emotionalen Einstellungsreaktionen der unterstellten Mitarbeiter. Unpublished dissertation, Universitat Hamburg, 1970.

FLEISHMAN, E. A. *Manual for leadership opinion questionnaire* (rev. ed.). Chicago: Science Research Associates, 1969.

———. Leadership climate, human relations training, and supervisory behavior. In E. A. Fleishman, & A. R. Bass (Eds.), *Studies in personnel and industrial psychology* (3rd ed). Homewood, Ill.: Dorsey Press, 1974, pp. 183–96.

FLEISHMAN, E. A., & HARRIS, E. Patterns of leadership behavior related to employee grievance and turnover. *Personnel Psychology,* 1962, *15,* 43–56.

FLEISHMAN, E. A., & KO, I. Leadership patterns associated with managerial evaluation of effectiveness. Unpublished report, Yale University, 1962.

FLEISHMAN, E. A., & SIMMONS, J. Relationship between leadership patterns and effectiveness ratings among Israeli foremen. *Personnel Psychology,* 1970, *23,* 169–72.

FREDERIKSEN, N., JENSEN, O., & BEATON, A. E. *Prediction of organizational behavior.* New York: Pergamon, 1972.

FRENCH, J. R. P., ISRAEL, J., & AS, D. An experiment on participation in a Norwegian factory: interpersonal dimensions of decision-making. *Human Relations,* 1960, *13*(1), 3–19.

FRIEND, E. K., & BURNS, L. R., Sources of variation in job satisfaction: job size effects in a sample of the U. S. Labor Force. *Personnel Psychology,* 1977, *30,* 589–605.

FUERSTENBURG, F. Workers' participation in management in the Federal Republic of Germany, No. 4. *International Institute for Labor Studies Bulletin,* 1969, *6,* 94–148.

GEORGE, C. S. *The history of management through 1968.* Englewood Cliffs, N.J.: Prentice-Hall, 1968.

GREENWOOD, J. M. Group attitudes and organizational performance. Paper presented at the 78th annual American Psychological Association convention, Miami, September 1971.

GRUENFELD, L. W., & MACEACHRON, A. E. A cross-national study of cognitive style among managers and technicians. *International Journal of Psychology,* 1975, *10*(1), 27–55.

GULICK, L., & URWICK, L. (Eds.), *Papers on the science of administration.* New York: Columbia University Institute of Public Administration, 1937.

GURIN, G., VEROFF, J., & FELD, S. *Americans view their mental health.* New York: Basic Books, 1960.

GYENES, A., & ROZGONYI, T. Hierarchical structures in Hungarian plants. In A. S. Tannenbaum & T. Rozgonyi (Eds.), *Authority and reward in organizations: an international study.* New York: Pergamon, in press.

HACKMAN, J. R., & LAWLER, E. E. Employee reactions to job characteristics. *Journal of Applied Psychology,* 1971, *55,* 259–86.

HAGEN, E. E. *On the theory of social change.* Homewood, Ill.: Dorsey Press, 1962.

HAIRE, M., GHISELLI, E., & PORTER, L. W. An international study of management attitudes and democratic leadership. In *Proceedings CIOS XII, International Management Conference.* New York: Council for International Progress (U.S.A.), 1963, 101–14.

HAIRE, M., GHISELLI, E. E., & PORTER, L. W. *Managerial thinking: an international study.* New York: Wiley, 1966.

HALPIN, A., & WINER, B. A factorial study of the leaders behavior descriptions. In R. Stogdill & A. Coons (Eds.), *Leader behavior: its description and measurement.* Columbus, Ohio: Bureau of Business Research, Ohio State University, 1957.

HAMMARSTRÖM, O. Joint worker-management consultation: the case of LKAB, Sweden. In E. L. Davis & A. Cherns (Eds.), *The quality of working life,* Vol. 2. New York: Free Press, 1975.

HARBISON, F. H., & BURGESS, E. W. Modern management in Western Europe. *American Journal of Sociology*, 1954, *60*(1), 15–23.

HELLER, F. A. *Managerial decision-making: a study of leadership styles and power-sharing among senior managers.* London: Tavistock, 1971.

————. Leadership, decision-making and contingency theory. *Industrial Relations*, 1973, *12*(2), 183–99.

HEMPHILL, J., & COONS, A. Development of the leader behavior description questionnaire. In R. Stogdill & A. Coons (Eds.), *Leader behavior: its description and measurement.* Columbus, Ohio: Bureau of Business Research, Ohio State University, 1957.

HERZBERG, F. *Work and the nature of man.* Cleveland, Ohio: World, 1966.

HESSELING, P., & KONNEN, E. Culture and subculture in a decision-making exercise. *Human Relations*, 1969, *22*(1), 31–51.

HOEFERT, H. W. Darstellung einer Untersuchung uber die Anwendbarkeit von Fragebogen zur Beurteilung des Borgesetztenverhaltens im Industriebereich. Unpublished paper, Institute für Psychologie (FU), 1971.

HOLTER, H. Attitudes toward employee participation in company decision-making processes. *Human Relations*, 1965, *18*, 297–321.

HOFSTEDE, G. Nationality and espoused values of managers. *Journal of Applied Psychology*, 1976, *61*(2), 148–55.

HULIN, C. J., & BLOOD, M. R. Job enlargement, individual differences, and worker responses. *Psychological Bulletin*, 1968, *69*(1), 41–55.

INKELES, A. Industrial man: the relation of status to experience, perception, and value. *American Journal of Sociology*, 1960, *66*, 1–31.

INKELES, A., & ROSSI, P. H. National comparisons of occupational prestige. *American Journal of Sociology*, 1956, *61*, 329–39.

INKELES, A., & SMITH, D. H. *Becoming modern: individual change in six developing countries.* Cambridge, Mass.: Harvard University Press, 1974.

JURALEWICZ, R. S. An experiment in participation in a Latin American factory. *Human Relations*, 1974, *27*(7), 627–37.

KAGITCIBASI, C. Social norms and authoritarianism: a Turkish-American comparison. *Journal of Personality and Social Psychology*, 1970, *16* (3), 444–51.

KATONA, G., STRUMPEL, B., & ZAHN, E. *Aspirations and affluence.* New York: McGraw-Hill, 1971.

KATZ, D. Satisfactions and deprivations in industrial life. In A. Kornhauser, R. Dubin, & A. M. Ross (Eds.), *Industrial conflict.* New York: McGraw-Hill, 1954.

KATZ, D, & KAHN, R. L. *The social psychology of organizations* (2nd ed.). New York: Wiley, 1978.

KOCH, S. E. *Management and motivation.* Helsingfors: Affaersekonomisk Foerlagsfoerning, 1965.

KORMAN, A. K. "Consideration," "initiating structure" and organizational criteria—a review. *Personnel Psychology*, 1966, *19*, 349–61.

LAMMERS, C. J. Power and participation in decision-making in formal organizations. *American Journal of Sociology*, 1967, *73*(2), 201–16.

LAWLER, E. E. *Pay and organizational effectiveness: a psychological view.* New York: McGraw-Hill, 1971.

LAWRENCE, P. R., & LORSCH, J. W. *Organization and environment: managing differentiation and integration.* Cambridge, Mass.: Harvard University, 1967.

LENNERLÖF, L. *Supervision.* The Swedish Council for Personnel Administration. 1968.

LEVINE, R. *Dreams and deeds: achievement motivation in Nigeria.* Chicago: University of Chicago Press, 1966.

LIKERT, R. *New patterns of management.* New York: McGraw-Hill, 1961.

LUCK, H. E. Einige Determinanten und Dimensionen des Fuhrungsverhaltens. *Gruppendynamik,* 1970, *1,* 63–69.

LUND, R. *Employees' influence on management's decisions within municipal institutions of the city of Copenhagen.* Copenhagen: The Danish National Institute of Social Research, Publication 52, 1972.

MACEACHRON, A. E. Two interactive perspectives on the relationship between job level and job satisfaction. *Organizational Behavior and Human Performance,* 1977, *19,* 226–46.

MAIER, N. R. F., & HOFFMAN, L. R. Group decision in England and the United States. *Personnel Psychology,* 1962, *15,* 75–87.

MANN, F. C. A study of work satisfactions as a function of the discrepancy between inferred aspirations and achievement. Unpublished dissertation, The University of Michigan, 1953.

MANNHEIM, B. F., RIM, Y., & GRINBERG, G. Instrumental status of supervisors as related to workers' perceptions and expectations. *Human Relations,* 1967, *20,* 387–97.

MARENCO, C. *Employes de Banque.* Paris: Counseil Superior de la Recherche Scientifique, 1959.

MARROW, A. J. Risks and uncertainties in action research. *Journal of Social Issues,* 1964, *20* (3), 5–20.

MASLOW, A. H. *Motivation and personality.* New York: Harper and Brothers, 1954.

MATSUI, T., OSAWA, T., & TERAI, T. Relations between supervisory motivation and the consideration and structure aspects of supervisory behavior. *Journal of Applied Psychology,* 1975, *60*(4), 451–54.

MAYO, E. *The social problems of an industrial civilization.* Cambridge, Mass.: Harvard University, 1945.

MCCLELLAND, D. C. *The achieving society.* New York: Van Nostrand, 1961.

MCCLELLAND, D. C., & WINTER, D. G. *Motivating economic achievement.* New York: Free Press, 1969.

MCFIE, J. The effect of education on African performance on a group of intellectual tests. *British Journal of Educational Psychology,* 1961, *31,* 232–40.

MEADE, R. D. An experimental study of leadership in India. *Journal of Social Psychology,* 1967, *72,* 35–43.

MEADE, R. D., & WHITTAKER, J. D. A cross-cultural study of authoritarianism. *Journal of Social Psychology,* 1967, *72,* 3–7.

MELIKIAN, L. Some correlates of authoritarianism in two cultural groups. *Journal of Psychology,* 1956, *42,* 237–48.

———. Authoritarianism and its correlates in Egyptian culture and in the United States. *Journal of Social Issues,* 1959, *15,* 58–68.

MEUWESE, W., & FIEDLER, F. E. *Leadership and group creativity under varying conditions of stress.* Urbana, Ill.: Group Effectiveness Research Laboratory, University of Illinois, 1965.

MILES, R. E. Human relations or human resources? *Harvard Business Review,* 1965, *43*(4), 148–54.

MILLER, E. J. Socio-technical systems in weaving, 1953–1970: A follow-up study. *Human Relations,* 1975, *28,* 349–86.

MIRVIS, P. H., & BERG, D. N. (Eds.), *Failures in organization development and change.* New York: Wiley, 1977.

MISUMI, J. A field study of human relations in Japanese small sized enterprises, I. *Industrial Training,* 1960a, *6*(3), 2–12.

————. A field study of human relations in Japanese small sized enterprises, II. *Industrial Training,* 1960b, *6*(4), 2–13.

————. Action research on the development of leadership, decision-making processes and organizational performance in a Japanese shipyard. Paper presented at the 18th International Congress of Applied Psychology, Montreal, 1974.

MISUMI, J, & SHIRAKASHI, S. An experimental study of the effects of supervisory behavior on productivity and morale in a hierarchical organization. *Human Relations,* 1966, *19*(3), 297–307.

MISUMI, J., & TASAKI, T. A study of the effectiveness of supervisory patterns in a Japanese hierarchical organization. *Japanese Psychological Research,* 1965, *7,* 151–62.

MORSE, N. C. *Satisfaction in the white-collar job.* Ann Arbor, Mich.: The University of Michigan Press, 1953.

MOZINA, S. Management opinions on satisfaction and importance of psychosocial needs in their jobs. *Proceedings 16th International Congress of Applied Psychology,* 1969, 788–94.

MOZINA, S., JEROVSEK, J., TANNENBAUM, A. S., & LIKERT, R. Testing a management style. *European Business,* Autumn 1970, *27,* 60–68.

MUELLER, E., SCHMIEDESKAMP, J., HYBELS, J., SONQUIST, J., & STAELIN, C. *Technological advance in an expanding economy: its impact on a cross-section of the labor force.* Ann Arbor, Mich.: Institute for Social Research, 1969.

NACHREINER, F., & LUCK, H. E. Experiences with a German translation of Fleishman's Ohio leadership questionnaire. Paper presented at the NATO Symposium on Leadership and Management Appraisal, Brussels, August 1971.

NEGANDHI, A. R. *Management and economic development: the case of Taiwan.* The Hague: Martinus Nijhoff, 1973.

NEGANDHI, A. R., & PRASAD, S. B. *Comparative management.* New York: Appleton-Century-Crofts, 1971.

NORSTEDT, J. P., & AGUREN, S. The Saab-Scania report. Stockholm: Swedish Employers' Confederation, 1973.

OAKLANDER, H., & FLEISHMAN, E. A. Patterns of leadership related to organizational stress in hospital settings. *Administrative Science Quarterly,* 1964, *8,* 520–32.

O'BROIN, N., & HURLEY, J. Ireland. In A. S. Tannenbaum & T. Rozgonyi (Eds.), *Authority and reward in organizations: an international study.* New York: Pergamon, in press.

OLDHAM, G. R., HACKMAN, J. R., & PEARCE, J. L. Conditions under which employees respond positively to enriched work. *Journal of Applied Psychology*, 1976, *61*, (4), 395–403.

ORPEN, C. Social desirability as a moderator of the relationship between job satisfaction and personal adjustment. *Personnel Psychology*, 1974, *34*, 103–08.

ORPEN, C., & NDLOVU, J. Participation, individual differences, and job satisfaction among black and white employees in South Africa. *International Journal of Psychology*, 1977, *12*(1), 31–38.

OTOLORA BAY, G., Hierarchy and its effects in selected Mexican plants. In A. S. Tannenbaum, & T. Rozgonyi (Eds.), *Authority and reward in organizations: an international study*. New York: Pergamon, in press.

PARKER, T. C. Relationships among measures of supervisory behavior, group behavior, and situational characteristics. *Personnel Psychology*, 1963, *16*, 319–34.

PASCALE, R. T. Communication and decision making across cultures: Japanese and American companies. *Administrative Science Quarterly*, 1978, *23*, 91–110.

PATCHEN, M. *The choice of wage comparisons*. Englewood Cliffs, N.J.: Prentice-Hall, 1961.

PERROW, C. *Complex organizations: a critical essay*. Glenview, Ill.: Scott, Foresman, 1972.

PORTER, L. W. Job attitudes in management: perceived deficiencies in need fulfillment as a function of job level, I. *Journal of Applied Psychology*, 1962, *64*(1), 23–51.

PREALE, I., AMIR, Y., & SHARAN (Singer), S. S. Perceptual articulation and task effectiveness in several Israel subcultures. *Journal of Personality and Social Psychology*, 1970, *15*, 190–95.

PROTHRO, E., & MELIKIAN, L. The California Public Opinion Scale in an authoritarian culture. *Public Opinion Quarterly*, 1953, *17*, 353–62.

QUINN, R. P., STAINES, G. L., & McCULLOUGH, M. R. Job satisfaction: is there a trend? Manpower Research Monograph No. 30, U. S. Department of Labor, 1974.

QVALE, T. U. A Norwegian strategy for democratization of industry. *Human Relations*, 1976, *29*, 453–69.

RICE, A. K. Productivity and social organization in an Indian weaving shed. *Human Relations*, 1953, *6*, 297.

———. *Productivity and social organizations: the Ahmedabad experiment*. London, Tavistock, 1958.

RIM, Y. Leadership attitudes and decisions involving risk. *Personnel Psychology*, 1965, *18*, 423–30.

ROBERTS, K. H. On looking at an elephant: an evaluation of cross-cultural research related to organizations. *Psychological Bulletin*, 1970, *74*, 327–50.

ROUSSEAU, D. M. Technological differences in job characteristics, employee satisfaction, and motivation: a synthesis of job design research and sociotechnical systems theory. *Organizational Behavior and Human Performance*, 1977, *19*, 18–42.

———. Measures of technology as predictors of employee attitudes. *Journal of Applied Psychology*, 1978, *63* (2), 213–18.

ROZGONYI, T., & GYENES, A. *Hierarchia a gazdasagi szervezetekben*. Budapest: Magyar Tudomanyos Akademia, Szociologiai Kutato Intezetenek Kiadvanyai, 1974.

RUBENOWITZ, S. Experiences in industrial democracy and changes in work organizations in Sweden. *Psykologiska Institutionen*, Goteborgs Universitet, 1974, *2*(1).

SARAPATA, A. Occupational prestige hierarchy studies in Poland. Paper presented at the 8th World Congress of Sociology, Toronto, 1974.

SARAPATA, A., & WESOLOWSKI, W. The evaluation of occupations by Warsaw inhabitants. *American Journal of Sociology*, 1961, *66*, 581–91.

SCHREGLE, J. Forms of participation in management. *Industrial Relations*, 1970, *9*, 117–22.

SERGIOVANNI, T. J., METZCUS, R., & BURDEN, L. Toward a particularistic approach to leadership style: some findings. *American Educational Research Journal*, 1969, *6*, 62–79.

SFR OF YUGOSLAVIA ASSEMBLY. *The Associated Labour Act*. Novi Sad: Provesta, 1977.

SHIRAKASHI, S. Leadership in the forestry workers' group. *Shogaku Ronshu*. Seinan Gakuin University, 1968a, *14*(2), 25–64.

————. Leadership in the forestry workers' group. *Shogaku Ronshu*. Seinan Gakuin University, 1968b, *15*(2), 83–100.

SIANN, G. Measuring field dependence in Zambia: a cross-cultural study. *International Journal of Psychology*, 1972, *7*, 87–96.

SINGH, P. N., & WHERRY, R. J. Ranking of job factors by factory workers in India. *Personnel Psychology*, 1963, *16*, 29–33.

SIROTA, D. International survey of job goals and beliefs. Paper presented at the 16th International Congress of Applied Psychology, Amsterdam, 1968.

SRIVASTVA, S., SALIPANTE, P. F., JR., CUMMINGS, T. G., NOTZ, W. W., BIGELOW, J. D., & WATERS, J. A. *Job satisfaction and productivity*. Dept. of Organizational Behavior, Case Western Reserve University, Cleveland, 1975.

STAIKOV, Z., TODOROVA, S., & PETKOV, K. Bulgaria. In A. S. Tannenbaum & T. Rozgonyi (Eds.), *Authority and reward in organizations: an international study*. New York: Pergamon, in press.

STEELE, F. Is the culture hostile to organizational development? The U. K. example. In P. H. Mirvis & D. N. Berg (Eds.), *Failures in organization development and change*. New York: Wiley, 1977.

STRAUSS, G. Job Satisfaction, motivation and job redesign. In G. Strauss, R. Miles, C. Snow, & A. S. Tannenbaum (Eds.), *Organizational behavior: research and issues*. Belmont, Calif.: Wadsworth, 1976.

STRAUSS, G., MILES, R., SNOW, C., & TANNENBAUM, A. S. (Eds.), *Organizational behavior: research and issues*. Belmont, Calif.: Wadsworth, 1976.

TAKAGI, K. A social psychological approach to the Ringi-system. *International Review of Applied Psychology*, 1969, *18*(1), 53–57.

TANNENBAUM, A. S. *Social psychology of the work organization*. Monterey, Calif.: Brooks-Cole, 1966.

————. *Control in organizations*. New York: McGraw-Hill, 1968.

————. Systems of formal participation. In G. Strauss, R. Miles, C. Snow & A. S. Tannenbaum (Eds.), *Organization behavior: research and issues*. Belmont, Calif.: Wadsworth, 1976.

TANNENBAUM, A. S., & ALLPORT, F. H. Personality structure and group structure: an interpretative study of their relationship through an event-structure hypothesis. *Journal of Abnormal and Social Psychology*, 1956, *54*(3), 272–80.

TANNENBAUM, A. S., & COOKE, R. A. Organizational control: a review of research employing the control graph method. In C. J. Lammers & D. Hickson (Eds.), *Organizations alike and unlike*. London: Routledge & Kegan Paul, 1978.

TANNENBAUM, A. S., KAVCIC, B., ROSNER, M., VIANELLO, M. & WEISER, G. *Hierarchy in organizations*. San Francisco: Jossey-Bass, 1974.

TANNENBAUM, A. S. & KULECK, W. The effect on organization members of discrepancy between perceived and preferred rewards implicit in work. *Human Relations*, 1978, *31*, 809–22.

TANNENBAUM, A. S., & ROZGONYI, T. (Eds.), *Authority and reward in organizations: an international study*. New York: Pergamon, in press.

THIAGARAJAN, J. M., & DEEP, S. D. A study of supervisor-subordinate influence and satisfaction in four cultures. *Journal of Social Psychology*, 1970, *82*, 173–80.

THORSRUD, E. Job design in the wider context. In L. E. Davis & J. C. Taylor (Eds.), *Design of jobs*. Baltimore: Penguin Books, 1972.

THORSRUD, E., & EMERY, F. E. Industrial democracy in Norway. *Industrial Relations*, 1970, *9*(2), 187–96.

TRIANDIS, H. C. Interpersonal relations in international organizations. *Journal of Organizational Behavior and Human Performance*, 1967, *7*, 316–28.

⸻. Subjective culture and economic development. *International Journal of Psychology*, 1973, *8*, 163–82.

TRIANDIS, H. C., & VASSILIOU, V. Interpersonal influence and employee selection in two cultures. *Journal of Applied Psychology*, 1972, *56*(2), 140–45.

TRIST, E. L., & BAMFORTH, K. W. Some social and psychological consequences of the longwall method of coal-getting. *Human Relations*, 1951, *4*, 3–38.

TRIST, E. L., HIGGIN, G. W., MURRAY, H., & POLLOCK, A. B. *Organizational choice*. London: Tavistock, 1963.

TSCHEULIN, D. Leader behavior measurement in German industry. *Journal of Applied Psychology*, 1973, *57*(1), 28–31.

TURNER, A. N., & LAWRENCE, P. R. *Industrial jobs and the worker*. Boston: Harvard University School of Business Administration, 1959.

U. S. GOVERNMENT PRINTING OFFICE. Document No. 2916-0001. *Survey of working conditions: Final report of univariate and bivariate tables*, 1971.

VROOM, V. *Motivation in management*. New York: American Foundation for Management Research, 1965.

W. E. UPJOHN INSTITUTE FOR EMPLOYMENT RESEARCH. *Work in America*. Cambridge, Mass.: MIT Press, 1973.

WAINER, H. A., & RUBIN, I. M. Motivation of research and development entrepreneurs: determinants of company success. *Journal of Applied Psychology*, 1969, *53*, 178–84.

WALTON, R. E. Innovative restructuring of work. In J. E. Rosow (Ed.), *The Worker and the job*. New York: Columbia University, 1974.

⸻. The differences of new work structures: explaining why success didn't take. In P. Mirvis & D. N. Berg, *Failures in organizational development and change*. New York: Wiley, 1978.

WEAVER, C. N. Occupational prestige as a factor in the net relationships between occupation and job satisfaction. *Personnel Psychology*, 1977, *30*, 607–12.

WEBER, M. *The theory of social and economic organization*. New York: Free Press, 1947.

————. The essentials of bureaucratic organization: an ideal-type construction. In R. K. Merton, A. P. Gray, B. Hockey, & H. C. Selvin (Eds.), *Reader in bureaucracy.* Glencoe, Ill.: Free Press, 1952.

————. The religions of India: the sociology of Hinduism and Buddhism. Glencoe, Ill.: Free Press, 1958.

WHITE, R., & LIPPITT, R. *Autocracy and democracy: an experimental inquiry.* New York: Harper & Row, 1960.

WHITEHILL, A. M., & TAKEZAWA, S. Cultural values in management-worker relations, Japan: Gimu in transition. Chapel Hill, N.C.: University of North Carolina School of Business Administration, Research paper 5, March 1961.

————. *The other worker.* Honolulu: East-West Center Press, 1968.

WHYTE, W. F., & WILLIAMS, L. K. Supervisory leadership: an international comparison. Symposium B3, paper B3c, CIOS XIII, 1963.

WILLIAMS, L. K., WHYTE, W. F., & GREEN, C. S. Do cultural differences affect workers' attitudes? *Industrial Relations,* 1966, 5(3), 105–17.

WILPERT, B., & HELLER, F. A. Power-sharing and perceived skill reservoirs at senior management levels. Mimeographed report from International Institute of Management, West Berlin, 1972.

WITKIN, H. A. A cognitive-style approach to cross-cultural research. *International Journal of Psychology,* 1967, 2(4), 233–50.

————. Social influences in the development of cognitive style. In D. A. Goslin (Ed.), *Handbook of socialization, theory, and research.* Chicago: Rand McNally, 1969.

WITKIN, H. A., & BERRY, J. W. Psychological differentiation in cross-cultural perspective. *Journal of Cross-Cultural Psychology,* 1975, 6(1), 4–87.

WITKIN, H. A., DYK, R. B., FATERSON, H. F., GOODENOUGH, D. R., & KARP, S. A. *Psychological differentiation.* New York: Wiley, 1962.

WOBER, M. Adapting Witkin's field independence theory to accommodate new information from Africa. *British Journal of Psychology,* 1967, 58, 29–38.

ZDRAVOMYSLOV, A. G., & IADOV, V. A. An attempt at a concrete study of attitude toward work. *Soviet Sociology,* 1964, 3, 3–15.

ZURCHER, L. A. Particularism and organizational position: a cross-cultural analysis. *Journal of Applied Psychology,* 1968, 52, 139–44.

8

Cultural Aspects of Environment-Behavior Relationships[1]

Irwin Altman and
Martin M. Chemers

Contents

Abstract

This chapter examines cultural factors associated with the physical environment. Specifically, the chapter considers (1) how contemporary and historical societies viewed the relationship of people to the physical environment and to nature, (2) cultural differences and similarities in environmental cognition and perception, (3) cultural factors in relation to a variety of environmental behaviors and processes, such as privacy, personal space, territory, and crowding, and (4) the built environment, including cities, communities, houses, and interiors.

An underlying theme of the chapter is that cultural and environmental phenomena are best viewed from a "systems" perspective and involve interdependency and multicausal relationships, with environment and culture operating on one another in a reciprocal fashion.

Introduction

This chapter examines cultural factors in relation to the physical environment. The environment refers to (1) physical aspects of natural environments, such as landscape, wilderness and other geographic features, and (2) the built or man-made environment of cities, communities, homes and other places.

Several broad assumptions will guide the presentation. First, a range of environments will be examined from small-scale to large-scale ones. These will include the microenvironment of a person or social group, such as personal space and person proximity; moderate-scale environments of homes and neighborhoods; large-scale environments of communities, cities, regions, and nations. Second, social and interpersonal processes in relation to the environment will be emphasized. Physical factors such as illumination, lighting and color will be dealt with only insofar as they bear on social processes. Third, a social systems approach to environment-behavior relationships will be adopted that states that culture, environment, and behavior are linked in multidirection cause-effect bonds. Changes in one part of the system can affect other parts of the system, so that environment can produce behavioral changes, and vice versa. Similarly, culture and environment can have reciprocal effects on one another. Fourth, the chapter will search out both similarities and differences across cultures in relation to environmental phenomena. Finally, the possibility that many apparent cultural differences have underlying genetic similarities will be explored. For example, processes such as privacy may involve different phenotypic mechanisms across cultures, but may also operate according to similar genotypic principles. Thus, similarities and differences across cultures may exist simultaneously, depending upon the level of analysis.

Because the study of environment and behavior is intrinsically multidisciplinary, and because disciplines take varying perspectives and present materials in many forms and places, it is not possible to grasp all the relevant literature in the area. Thus, a representative but not comprehensive review of research and theory on culture and environment will be presented.

Organization of the Chapter

The first section of the chapter is an historical overview of the environment-behavior field and provides a context for understanding cross-cultural phenomena. The next section presents a conceptual framework whose key elements include cultural and environmental factors, environmental cognition and perception, social behaviors and processes, and environmental outcomes. Successive sections treat each of these parts of the framework.

Historical Background

Historians, theologians, philosophers, and poets have mused about peoples' relationship to the physical environment for centuries, as have scientists and professionals from geography, anthropology, sociology, psychology, architecture, planning, and other disciplines. However, in the past dozen years there has evolved, for the first time, a unique *multidisciplinary* orientation to environment and behavior that has several features: (1) communication across social and behavioral science disciplines such as psychology, sociology, anthropology, political science, geography, (2) contact between action-oriented, problem-solving professions of architecture and planning and research-oriented social and behavioral sciences, and (3) recognition that environment-behavior relationships are complex and approachable from many perspectives.

Momentum to study environment-behavior relationships began in the late 1950s and early 1960s. Impetus came from several sources. Barker (1968) had been following the philosophical approach of Lewin for many years and developed a "behavioral ecology" orientation. This approach, descriptive in strategy, analyzed the behavior of people in natural environments, beyond the laboratory, to determine the fit of behavior-environment relationships. Although outside the mainstream of social psychology, Barker's work gained momentum in the 1960s as researchers became concerned with the narrowness of the laboratory orientation, and as practitioners sought out behavioral scientists. A second major influence came from the work of Hall (1959, 1966), an anthropologist, who proposed the study of "proxemics" or use of space in social settings. Hall's work, reviewed later, highlighted the importance of cultural differences in use of space, and he offered a general framework for examining such differences.

Another influence on the field came from the work of cultural ecologists in sociology, anthropology, and cross-cultural psychology who emphasized the role of the physical environment as a powerful and often direct determinant of differences in culture and behavior. Cultural ecology provides many perspectives and a rich vein of data on the way in which such factors as climate, natural resources, geography, and other features of the environment affect and perhaps determine cultural practices and institutions (see Berry, 1975, and Chapter 6 of this volume for further information about this orientation). These and other broad approaches were complemented by the work of researchers such as Sommer (1958, 1961, 1962, 1969), who examined the impact of changes in the environment on social interaction and who demonstrated that such work could be done experimentally and descriptively in naturalistic situations.

At the same time, in the early 1960s, there was increased contact among researchers and practitioners in the form of interdisciplinary conferences, organizations, and newsletters (Altman, 1973). These activities had several origins. On one side, discontent had been mounting among some professional practitioners, e.g., architects and urban planners, who claimed that traditionalists in applied environmental design fields had neglected people and social problems in the design process, and that aesthetics had been overly emphasized at the expense of human needs. Those who felt alienated sought out social scientists who presumably could incorporate knowledge of human behavior into the design process. At about the same time, seeds of discontent had grown in psychology, focusing on the typical laboratory-oriented study that seemed to neglect the role of the environment in social behavior. Discontented psychologists turned toward the "real world" and toward the environmentally oriented disciplines of architecture and planning. The result was a mushrooming of interest in the so-called fields of "environmental psychology," "environmental sociology," "man-environment relations," as well as an exchange of methodologies and concepts across fields.

The study of culture in relation to the environment has benefited from this multidisciplinary contact. For example, our analysis of environmental perception and cognition will depend heavily on the contributions of geographers and psychologists. And, when concepts such as privacy, territory, and crowding are discussed, the work of sociologists, psychologists, anthropologists, and political scientists will provide a rounded picture of knowledge in the area. Also the discussion of housing and community design in relation to culture will draw on the work of anthropologists, planners, and sociologists, each of whom has looked at the area from a different perspective.

A Conceptual Framework

The analysis of environment-behavior relationships in a cross-cultural context is complicated in terms of the number and interrelationships of variables. A formal theory will not be proposed, only a framework of relevant variables and their approximate relationships, which will then serve as a way to organize the chapter.

In general, a "social systems" orientation will be adopted that has several features. First, it suggests that several classes of variables are relevant to the issue of culture and environment, such as those in the inner ring of Figure 8-1: physical environment, culture, environmental orientations and representations, environmental behaviors and processes, and out-

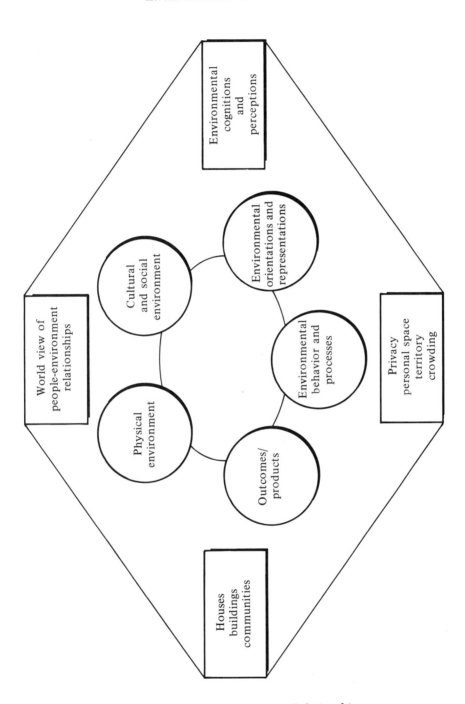

Figure 8-1. A Framework of Culture-Environment Relationships.

comes/products of behavior. The *physical environment* refers to features of the natural environment such as temperature, rainfall, climate, terrain and geographic features, and flora and fauna. The *cultural/social environment* refers to all aspects of culture such as socialization processes, norms, customs, and values. *Environmental orientations and representations* refer to perceptual and cognitive beliefs and differentiations people have about environments. *Environmental behavior and processes* (e.g., personal space, territorial behavior, privacy) include how people use the environment in the course of social relationships. *Outcomes/products* of behavior include the results of peoples' actions, such as the built environment of homes, communities, cities, and modifications of the natural environment such as farms, dams, and climate changes.

The outer ring of Figure 8-1 contains extensions of the inner ring, and provides the basis of organization for the remainder of this chapter. The outer ring variables are hypothesized to result from the action of various combinations of inner ring variables. Thus, physical environment and culture can affect differences in *world views* or general approaches to the physical environment. For example, several writers have contrasted philosophical and value orientations to the environment in different cultures that derive from a complex set of variables. Another result of the operation of various combinations of inner ring variables concerns *cognitions and perceptions about environments* in different cultures. Another area of relevant work concerns ways in which *privacy, territory, personal space,* and *crowding* occur across cultures. In addition, cultures differ in *environmental products*— homes, cities, and communities—which result from complex combinations of inner and outer ring variables.

Another feature of a social systems approach is that simple linear cause-effect relationships are not always clearly discernible, since every variable can theoretically serve in both an independent and dependent role. For example, it is often implied that the physical environment is primarily an independent variable that affects culture or other variables in a one-way, linear fashion. While it is true that environmental factors such as terrain, climate, and temperature may play an important role, the reverse can also occur, e.g., cultural practices and establishment of cities can alter the environment drastically. So it is with almost any part of the figure, resulting in multiple directions of causation. The presentation of variables in a circular format, without arrows of directionality, suggests that antecedents and consequents can occur almost anywhere. This fact does not rule out the need to track specific causal relationships between variables. But, in formulating general principles it can easily be forgotten that a specific directional relationship is not necessarily the universe of all possible relationships.

A related feature of a systems orientation is that interventions in any part can reverberate throughout the system. Thus, cultural factors can theoretically affect any other set of variables and vice versa. Also any location on the circle can be an accumulation of effects from other variables. Thus, environmental behaviors and processes (privacy, personal space, and territory) may be a cumulative result of perceptions and cognitions, cultural factors, environmental factors, and outcomes of earlier behaviors, which is analogous to Lewin's (1951) notion of life space that is a contemporary integration of the history of prior experiences.

The social systems orientation that will guide this analysis has roots in the literature of cultural ecology. As discussed earlier, cultural ecology is concerned with the impact of the physical environment on cultural adaptation and group-shared behavior. Historically, there have been both "strong" and "weak" principles of cultural determinism (Berry, 1975). The "strong" position holds that aspects of the physical environment dramatically limit and define cultural processes. Whiting's (1964) classic paper on the effects of climate on cultural practices is an example of the strong determinist position. He reasoned that circumcision performed at puberty serves to enhance male role definition, that it occurs in cultures where children are reared close to the mother, and where they are physically removed from extensive contact with male family heads. Furthermore, this practice often occurs in polygamist societies; Whiting (1964) states that polygamy in turn is common in cultures that have a long prohibition on sexual relations following the birth of a child. Presumably, such prohibitions are necessary to insure adequate supplies of protein-rich mother's milk in geographical areas where other foods are low in protein. Thus, Whiting presents a causal chain in which certain climates that have low protein production necessitate late weaning that is protected by sex taboos that, in turn, leads to polygamy. Polygamy itself frequently requires male initiation rites at puberty to insure appropriate identification of males with their sex-related roles. Whiting argues that since cultural features cannot affect climatic variables, the causal chain must flow from climate and environment to culture.

In Berry's terms (see Chapter 6 in this volume), this chapter offers a "weak" version of an ecological perspective on cross-cultural issues, in that functional interdependencies among physical, cultural, and other variables are emphasized without attempting to account for specific cause-effect relationships. As an example, consider the role of the physical environment in the determination of house forms. Rapoport (1969) and others indicate that, while the physical environment may play a large part in determining some aspects of house form, e.g., building materials, ventilation, etc., many other aspects of home and community design may also be culturally determined and often vary dramatically across groups within a comparable ecological environment. Thus, strongly deterministic approaches do not easily account for all the variations seen in culture-environment relations.

At another level of analysis, Berry (1975) described a more pervasive and complex form of ecosystem influence. For example, he noted that climatic and geographical considerations may help contribute to acceptable forms of food production, e.g., farming versus hunting and gathering, which in turn may contribute, along with other factors, to cultural adaptations such as family structure, socialization and personality. But, such relationship links do not operate, according to the framework in Figure 8–1 and Berry's framework, in a simple one-to-one monotonic fashion. Rather, they result from a complex interplay of a variety of factors.

Also, no presumptions are made about cultural advances in the sense of progress toward some more sophisticated state (Berry, 1975) as a result of cultural adaptation. Or, as Herskovits (1952) pointed out, all cultures have been, are, and will continue to be in the process of development and change along myriad dimensions. Thus, it is inappropriate to compare different cultures on a single continuum of development, be it technological, social, political, or any other.

World Views of the Environment

Although scientific research on environment and behavior is relatively recent, there is no lack of history, philosophy, and mythology concerning the relationship of people to nature. From the time of recorded history and earlier, people have been concerned with the physical environment, sometimes viewing it as hostile, sometimes as nurturant, sometimes seeing themselves as part of the environment, and sometimes believing themselves to be separate from (and often above) nature. And, views of nature have been part and parcel of various cultures, woven directly into the fabric of their social structures.

Kluckhohn (1953), an anthropologist, noted that cultures can be characterized in terms of whether they believe that (1) *people are subjugated to nature*, where they live at the whim of a powerful and uncompromising nature, a kind of grin-and-bear-it situation, (2) *people are an inherent part of nature*, like animals, trees and rivers, where they try to live in harmony with their environment, and (3) *people are over nature, dominating the environment*. According to this last view, people are separate from nature and have the power (and sometimes the right) to act on, alter, and control the natural world.

Ittelson, Proshansky, Rivlin, and Winkel (1974) examined these and related approaches in an historical perspective. They suggested that nature worship was an early part of man's history and that some cultures, historically as now, viewed nature as imbued with a life spirit. Fairly often, nature was perceived as a powerful and uncontrollable force, greater than people, to which they had to bend and be subjugated, as in Kluckhohn's first approach to the environment. Even later, in Biblical times and at certain periods in recent history, the environment and nature were viewed as wild, powerful, threatening, and dangerous—something to be avoided or dealt with in a subordinate and submissive fashion. Thus, Ittelson et al. (1974) observed how, in Western fairy tales, the natural landscape, such as the dark forest where dangerous figures lived often took on a menacing character, to be avoided as much as possible. And, when one had to be in contact with the wilderness, it was to be done in a cautious fashion.

Beginning with the early Greeks, Ittelson et al. (1974) described somewhat different views of nature, akin to Kluckhohn's second orientation. For them, the natural world was orderly and functioned in a cyclical and purposive fashion, with seasons, days and nights, and natural events repeating themselves in a harmonious and clocklike fashion. People were part of this process, albeit central, and the whole system operated in a unified way.

The third orientation described by Kluckhohn (1953) fits with Ittelson et al.'s (1974) analysis of Western, Judeo-Christian world views of the environment. The idea of God as the creator of the universe and people's special place in the scheme of things led to a dualism between people and nature. Man was not just another object in the world, but a special being of divine origin who was put on earth to do God's will. In Western religions' artistic and poetic works, the duality of people and nature became even stronger over the years. Furthermore, this way of thinking eventually emphasized the rational, mechanistic quality of nature. In addition, a cause and effect perspective grew that emphasized a chain of events. This approach, coupled with the scientific revolution, generated a further separation between people and the environment, and the philosophical perspective of people as *above* nature. Their role (and right) was to control, alter, shape, and change nature by means of technology, buildings, radical agriculture, and the like. These values still predominate in Western cultures, although the ecology movement has sensitized people to the systemlike quality of people and the environment.

A different line of philosophical thinking appears in Eastern religions (although Eastern and Western thinking are by no means internally homogeneous). In ancient Chinese philosophy people were viewed as being at one with nature. Contrary to more egocentric Western philosophy the Chinese viewed people as an intrinsic element in nature, in harmony with it. Moreover, people achieved understanding by treating themselves as part of nature, in the same sense as animals, plants, and trees. According to this perspective, nature does not operate in a linear step-by-step fashion, but often follows a process of ebb and flow, of force and counterforce, of cyclical and progressive growth. It is a kind of general pattern, but one without a fixed form (Ittelson et al., 1974). The emphasis in this way of thinking is on process—knowing, seeing, and becoming—not on end products such as knowledge, having seen, and being. People and environments are viewed as one, as changing together, and as in a timeless mutual relationship. A vivid example of this type of world view appears in Turnbull's (1961) description of the Pygmies of Zaire, Africa. This communal hunting and gathering group resides in a heavily vegetated rain forest that is so dense that they can rarely see more than a few hundred yards in any direction, including up toward the sky. The Pygmies view themselves as an intrinsic part of the forest and they see the forest as a living thing with which they interact on a personal basis. One Pygmy said,

> The forest is a father and a mother to us, and like a father and mother it gives us everything we need, food, clothing, shelter, warmth . . . and affection. Normally everything goes well, because the forest is good to its children. But when things go wrong, there must be a reason (p. 92).

When misfortune happens, the Pygmies believe that the forest must have been sleeping and was therefore not able to take care of them, its children. So they seek its help: "We wake it up by singing to it, and we do this because we want it to awaken happy. Then everything will be well and good again" (p. 92).

Tuan (1971, 1974, 1977), a geographer, provided a complementary description of how different cultures and civilizations have related to the environment. Adopting a dialectic mode of analysis, Tuan noted how people often have conflicting attitudes toward nature, which reside side by side. Thus, nature is sometimes seen to be in control of people and sometimes under their control; sometimes positive and sometimes negative; sometimes beneficial and sometimes hostile. These oppositional conceptions have often existed within and between periods of history, e.g., there are characteristic good and bad seasons within a year, the farmer's love and appreciation of the soil is often mingled with fear and concern about weather.

In a larger historical vein Tuan (1971, 1974) discussed how different periods in history and different cultures had alternative feelings about the *wilderness* or natural environment, the *garden* or cultivated part of nature, and the *city* or totally man-made part of the environment. For example, the so-called "Edenic ideal" is a simplified view of people-environment relationships. Here the rural garden-village is positive and sacred, but the wilderness is undesirable. A more complex world view is portrayed in what Tuan called the Jeffersonian middle landscape, where both the wilderness and city were more negative than the garden and rural landscape. As Tuan observed, these world views are also reflected early in the Bible, where the cultivation of land and the form of the Garden of Eden were treated as ideal. Somewhat later in the Bible, however, the concept of the city as a positive place developed, partly because it represented man's control over nature and partly because the city served as a center for religious, political, and economic life.

Tuan indicated that in the nineteenth and twentieth centuries matters were seen somewhat differently. Cities were treated as a new kind of wilderness because of their uncontrolled growth and almost ungovernable character. Presently, wilderness is viewed as ideal, to be protected and preserved, and a new form of "garden" is emerging in the shape of planned communities and towns. These are to have a blend of rural and city quality, reasonable access to wilderness, and a return to a more harmonious balance between the city, the garden, and the natural wilderness. The conflicting forces of the built and natural environment, and people as controllers versus components of nature seem all tangled up in this latest world view. It will be interesting to see what balance of forces emerges in the last quarter of the century.

From this cursory treatment of philosophical, religious, and historical world views of environment-people relationships, the discussion proceeds to how people and cultures perceive and acquire knowledge about the environment.

Environmental Perception and Cognition

Lewin (1951) and Heider (1958) emphasized the idea that environmental and social factors are important insofar as they are represented in a person's perceptual and cognitive fields, thereby making these processes central to the study of environmental psychology. Likewise, differences in perceptual and cognitive processes, such as perceptual illusions (Allport & Pettigrew, 1957; Segall, Campbell, & Herskovits, 1966; see Deregowski's chapter in Volume 3 of this *Handbook* for a detailed review of this work), or "subjective culture" (Triandis, 1971) are of utmost importance in the study of cross-cultural psychology.

As was discussed earlier, culture and environment are inextricably linked. Cultures develop strategies for adaptation that have limits and directions that are partially influenced by the physical environment. The cognitive and perceptual processes that filter, organize, and give meaning to the environment are central to such strategies. From the earlier work on differences in perception of illusions across cultures to recent attempts to place environmental cognition in the nexus of a culture's adaptation (Berry, 1975; Rapoport, 1974), researchers have recognized the close interrelationship of culture, environment, and subjective beliefs and reactions.

According to this chapter's framework, the question of whether perception and cognition "creates" the environment or vice versa is oversimplified. Wohlwill (1973) stated that the environment is not only "in the head," but that it exists physically, independent of the organism. It is certainly true, however, that what people select, attend to, store and use will determine how they behave in relation to the environment. Thus, if a culture such as the Sioux Indian values and is dependent on wilderness areas for religious and economic reasons, their cognitive and perceptual representations of those areas are likely to be articulated and affectively positive. And, the fact that Eskimos will not enter certain areas believed to be inhabited by evil spirits, and that European tourists will not enter certain areas of United States cities because of perceived dangers, makes it clear that spatial perceptions influence spatial behavior. Likewise, ancient Greeks, whose cosmology stressed symmetry, composed maps in which natural phenomena (e.g., the rivers Danube and Nile) were arranged symmetrically (Ittelson et al., 1974), and subjective maps drawn by residents of a Venezualan city contained railroad tracks and thoroughfares where culturally based experience suggested they should be (Appleyard, 1970).

Simon (1957) provided a useful analysis of the relationship between features of physical stimuli and their perception and cognition in the context of the objectivity versus irrationality of man. His concept of "bounded rationality" holds that people behave rationally with respect to the information that is at their disposal. Since, however, the amount of information in the environment almost always exceeds processing capacity, information must be selected, ordered, and truncated. How this is done is heavily influenced by culture. The work of Bruner (1957) on cultural influences on categorization and meaning provides an illustration of this process. The central notion is that needs, values, and previous socialization help to determine the perceptual categories that an individual employs to give meaning to the environment. Cultural variables, of course, have profound effects in these spheres.

Definitional Aspects of Cognitive and Perceptual Processes

What subjective representational systems are used to deal with the spatial environment? This question, which forms the core of the study of environmental perception and cognition, has its historical roots in the place learning of Tolman (1932) and in the early Gestalt concepts of perception (Koffka, 1935). Although there is considerable divergence in goals, methods, and theorizing, the thread that links various phenomenological approaches to behavior is the common belief that specialized cognitive perceptual processes operate to form, store, and use information about the spatial environment.

This heritage is evident in recent work on environmental cognition. Researchers from the different disciplines of psychology, anthropology, geography, architecture, and urban planning attack problems of environmental cognition and perception with approaches, methods, and theoretical orientations unique to their particular goals and backgrounds. Thus, environmental perceptions and cognition is a growing, multidisciplinary area of study where theory and integration lag behind the generation of new research. While this state is not unusual for a young discipline, nor necessarily an undesirable one, it makes a coherent review a difficult task.

A central notion in the study of environmental cognition and perception is the idea that "... human spatial behavior is dependent on the individual's cognitive map of the spatial environment" (Downs & Stea, 1973, p. 9). Even this general statement must be qualified, however; the use of the term *cognitive map* is partly a result of the field's history. The pioneer work on perception of cities by Lynch (1960) and on preferences for geographical areas by Gould (1973a, 1973b) and Gould & White (1974) depended heavily on the notion of subjective maps and employed modified cartographic representations as an end product. Obviously, there is no reason to believe that environmental information is subjectively represented in the form of a map, and the term "cognitive map" is often used, therefore, to include more than simple cartographic representation.

Image is another popular term but it is too closely tied to visual aspects of a multimodal phenomenon. Thus, when precision of meaning is required, the terms *cognitive* or *perceptual representation* are most frequently used and are sufficiently devoid of any particularistic referent to make them acceptable to almost everyone. The more common term, however, remains *cognitive map*, with the reader properly warned that it may not be a map at all, and if it is, it is certainly quite different than a typical two-dimensional cartographic map. Downs and Stea (1973) stated that:

> Cognitive mapping is a process composed of a series of psychological transformations by which an individual acquires, codes, stores, recalls, and decodes information about the relative locations and attributes of phenomena in his everyday environment (p. 9).

This definition highlights the adaptive focus of environmental cognition; specifically, a complex physical environment emits stimuli that must be processed by an individual so that he or she can behave adaptively with respect to that environment. Moreover, the term *cognition* is preferred by Downs and Stea (1973) to the term *perception* since cognition is thought to encompass perception as well as learning, memory, and thinking, all of which are basic to people's relationship with the environment.

At this point one might wonder why environmental cognition is not wholly subsumed under the general study of cognition or perception. Although researchers of environmental cognition acknowledge its close relationship to basic analyses of cognition and perception, they also maintain that environmental cognition has some special features. For example Ittelson (1973) identified several unique characteristics of the physical environment as a perceptual-cognitive object:

1. *The environment surrounds.* There is and can be no subject-object distinction in the perception of the environment. While this can be said of any object, its import and appearance is much greater for the environment.
2. Because the environment surrounds, because it is simultaneously proximal and distal, central and peripheral, it cannot be apprehended at a single point in time. *Environmental perception requires action and movement* and has, therefore, a unique temporal quality.
3. *The environment is multimodal* and impinges on all the senses simultaneously.
4. Environments, more than most perceptual objects, are characterized by *sensory stimulus overloads.* The various perceptual processes that limit and organize the sensory field become especially important in environmental perception.
5. *Environments always have an atmosphere,* difficult to define, but of overriding importance.

Thus, while environmental cognition need not disassociate itself from cognitive and perceptual psychology, it does require specialized approaches and methods of study. To these unique characteristics another one may be added, namely, that accurate perception of the environment has considerable significance to the organism's survival, both immediately and in terms of evolutionary processes. Kaplan (1973) reasoned, for example, that the ability to form rapid and highly articulated cognitive representations is a result of long-term evolutionary adaptation, originating when a survival premium was placed on speed and accuracy of reaction.

Approaches to the Analysis of Environmental Cognition

Several approaches have been used to study environmental cognition in relation to culture. In a useful taxonomy, Ittelson (1973) proposed five levels of analysis at which people relate to the environment: (1) affect or feeling towards the environment, (2) spatial orientation within the environment, (3) categorization or grouping of environmental phenomena, (4) systematization of environmental features in terms of relationships, causal and otherwise, and (5) manipulation of the environment. These five levels are not independent of one another but they do provide a reasonable framework within which to examine different approaches to the study of environmental cognition.

Gould's (1973b) and Gould & White's (1974) work on geographical preferences is partially an affect-oriented approach in that it deals with positive and negative feelings about the environment. For example, Gould asked people to rate a variety of geographical locations in the United States and elsewhere on several dimensions, such as desire to visit or live in the place, and degree of social, cultural, economic, or political attractiveness. Summaries of preferences were then presented in the form of topographical maps in which isobars (similar to those typically used to represent altitude) reflected attractiveness and desirability of various places. As another example, Saarinen (1973b) and Kates (1962, 1963) examined perceptions of natural hazard areas through the use of projective techniques designed to tap affective components of perception and cognition. Rather than asking for a quantifiable rating of the environment on some linear dimension, as in Gould's procedure, Saarinen sought more global affective reactions. Midwestern farmers were shown a picture of a farmer standing in a wind-blown, drought-decimated field and were asked to describe the scene in their own words. Responses were then content analyzed in terms of several affective features, such as optimism, attitudes toward the land, etc.

Probably the largest body of research on environmental cognition has been concerned with Ittelson's second level of analysis—how people perceive the environment in terms of spatial orientation. In these studies, individuals describe a geographical configuration such as a city, neighborhood, or region and often orient themselves in the environment in terms of direction or distance. For example, Orleans (1973) asked residents to draw a map of Los Angeles. The maps of white, black and Mexican-American residents were then compared for scope, completeness, and detail, e.g., presence or absence of particular areas or buildings, the orientation of maps, psychologically relevant distortions, inclusions, and omissions.

Other studies that focus on orientation and related factors include analyses of perceptions of societies in different parts of the world (Appleyard, 1970; DeJonge, 1962; Lynch, 1960; Milgram, 1976), perceptions of neighborhoods (Ladd, 1970; Lee, 1973; Maurer & Baxter, 1972), and perceptions of distance from one place to another (Lowry, 1973). Also included here are studies of the development and learning of spatial orientations by children (Blaut, McCleary, & Blaut, 1970; Hart & Moore, 1973; Stea & Blaut, 1973a, 1973b). These latter studies generally involved examination of the ability of children of various ages to understand and use spatial concepts and cognitive mapping procedures.

Research on the manner in which people group and categorize aspects of the environment, Ittelson's third level of analysis, includes studies on how neighborhoods are subjectively defined (Lee, 1973) and student views of the world (Saarinen, 1973a). Research on Ittelson's fourth level of analysis is concerned with identification of generic dimensions of environmental cognition, especially through the use of multivariate techniques such as factor analysis (Cox & Zannaras, 1973; Golledge & Zannaras, 1975;

Gould, 1973a, 1973b). For example, Cox and Zannaras found that rankings of similarities of United States cities yielded several dimensions, one being a provincial-cosmopolitan factor. In a more theoretical vein, Hart and Moore (1973) used the approaches of Bruner and Piaget to understand the social development of maps in terms of such conceptual dimensions as assimilation-accommodation, egocentric-geocentric orientations, integration-differentiation. Finally, several psychological and anthropological studies have been directed at how cultures manipulate their environment, the fifth level of analysis, and a later section of the chapter will describe this process in detail.

Methods for Studying Environmental Cognition

Rapoport (1975) recently discussed the different emphases of psychology and anthropology in the study of environmental cognition. The psychologist generally stresses people's knowledge and understanding of the environment whereas the anthropologist views cognition processes in terms of how they help make the world meaningful. However, both approaches proceed from the assumption that what is known and how knowledge is organized reflects what is important to the perceiver. Given the obvious statement that researchers wish to understand the nature and organization of cognitive representations, the question is "What response modes are most valid for expressing these cognitions?"

A wide variety of methods have been used to address this issue, ranging from open-ended techniques such as projective responses to picture stimuli (Saarinen, 1973a, 1973b), individual descriptions of what is seen on a casual walk (Lynch & Rivlin, 1959), factor analysis of rankings of cities or other areas in terms of various descriptive dimensions (Gould, 1973b), and perceived similarities and differences in environments (Cox & Zannaras, 1973). It is difficult to generate a simple typology of research methods in environmental cognition. Researchers often use similar tools to answer different questions; at other times, different techniques are used to answer the same question. For purposes of exposition, methods can be grouped as follows: maps, rankings and ratings, judgments, free responses and projective techniques, illusions, and cultural descriptions. Space restrictions permit only a sampling of contemporary methodological approaches here. For a fuller discussion of methodology in cross-cultural research, including environmental research, see Volume 2 of this Handbook.

Maps. A variety of techniques involve the use or generation of maps as stimuli, responses, or representations of collective responses. The most common use of mapping procedures is to have subjects draw a freehand sketch map of a geographical area. Following Lynch (1960), many researchers employed freehand sketch maps of cities including Ciudad Guayana, Venezuela (Appleyard, 1970), Los Angeles (Orleans, 1973), Houston (Maurer & Baxter, 1972), and Rome and Milan (Francescato & Mebane, 1973). Other studies obtained maps of neighborhoods (Ladd, 1970; Maurer & Baxter, 1972), or even of the world (Saarinen, 1973a, 1973b). Typically, individual sketch maps are distilled into a composite using either mathematical or subjective criteria. Freehand sketch techniques have been criticized by Francescato and Mebane (1973) on the grounds that not all cultures or social classes are equally familiar with the use of maps, nor are they equally likely to offer free expression of what they are familiar with. In their studies of perceptions of Rome and Milan, Francescato and Mebane found social class and age differences in people's willingness to draw such maps. Thus, findings such as those obtained by Orleans (1973) on the restricted nature of maps of Los Angeles drawn by blacks and Mexican-Americans may be due to their lack of knowledge of the city, their unfamiliarity with cartographic representation, or with their unwillingness to comply with an experimenter's request.

Maps have also been used as stimuli. For example, Lee (1973) showed subjects maps of their home city and asked them to draw a line representing the boundaries of their neighborhood. Using a different technique, Stea and Blaut (1973a) and Blaut et al. (1970) studied the development of map use in children. They showed children aerial photographs and asked them to identify objects in the photograph. They also had children trace maps to be used in solving spatial problems. For Gould and White (1974) maplike charts resulted from a data gathering process in which subjects rated or ranked their preferences for geographical areas in Sweden, England, Tanzania, and the United States. These rankings were mathematically combined to yield collective preferences that were then represented as preference contours and surfaces on a map.

Rankings and ratings. Another common technique requires people to group, rank, or rate a set of standard geographical or spatial stimuli. One such method used by Gould and White (1974), partially described above, involves a standard set of stimuli, such as cities or areas within a country that are rated for residential preference or for such dimensions as social, political, economic, or cultural potential.

Sophisticated mathematical techniques have also been used to discern underlying dimensions of geographic perception. For example, Cox and Zannaras (1973) had people rank a city or nation in terms of similarity to a cue stimulus. After all stimuli served as the cue stimulus, the resultant rankings were factor analyzed.

Judgments.   Several studies examined the estimation of geographical distances using a technique patterned on psychophysical scaling procedures (Briggs, 1973; Howard, Chase, & Rothman, 1973; Lowrey, 1973). Typically, subjects are presented with a standard stimulus such as the distance from their home or campus to some known location. Then they are asked to choose other locations relative to the standard. Accuracy of estimation was then related to such factors as sex or socioeconomic status, or to environmental variables such as direction towards or away from urban centers, degree of directness, or routes, etc.

Free responding and projective techniques.   Projective techniques depend on immediate and open-ended responses such as word associations, TAT pictures, sentence completion tests, choice, or ordering techniques. For example, Saarinen (1973b) investigated farmers' perceptions using TAT-like pictures, many of which depicted drought scenes; Appleyard (1969) used recall of buildings or landmarks in the environment to assess the salience of various environmental stimuli; Golledge and Zannaras (1973) collected route maps and diaries of trips to work or to shopping areas to gain information about how routes were learned.

Brislin, Lonner, and Thorndike (1973) provide a fuller description of the problems associated with the use of projective techniques in cross-cultural research. Control and reliability generally may be sacrificed in the interest of a rich and unfettered data flow. And, when specific response guidelines are absent, subjects usually supply their own idiosyncratic sets, an especially serious problem in cross-cultural research. That is, response styles are likely to vary across cultures, confounding the true nature of differences in perception. Nevertheless, projective techniques may play an important role in the early stages of research, when the richness of data may offset problems of interpretation.

Illusions.   Early cross-cultural research on perception was not directed specifically at environmental cognitions. Instead investigators were interested in knowing if differences in the physical environment and cultural adaptations influenced the perception of standard stimuli. Generally, visual illusions were chosen as stimuli since their ambiguous nature often allows perceptual differences to become more readily apparent. Allport and Pettigrew (1957), for example, found Zulus to be less susceptible than Europeans to the trapezoidal window illusion that appears to be dependent upon experience with rectangular and straight edge structures. (Deregowski presents a comprehensive discussion on research of this type in Volume 3 of this *Handbook*.)

Cultural and historical descriptions.   While they do not represent a specific research methodology, anthropological studies provide an extremely rich source of information about attitudes and perceptions of the environment. Some of this work is reviewed in other parts of this chapter.

Cross-Cultural Factors in Environmental Cognition

Few studies qualify as comparative tests of cultural patterns in cognition. Rather, there are a number of studies of different cultures and subcultures taken singly, and only a few instances of cross-cultural comparisons. However, just as diversities in values, norms, and cognitive patterns are likely to create differences in environmental perceptions, so pressures un-doubtedly exist that foster certain similarities across cultures. Therefore, it may be possible to identify common features along with differences in environmental cognition among and within cultures in spite of a lack of very many comparative studies.

As Wohlwill (1973) noted, the environment is not entirely subjective. That is, there are physical aspects of the environment that, while subject to some perceptual distortion, are not totally transmutable. That Wohlwill need even remind us of such factors is testimony to the tremendous swing towards cultural and psychological explanations and away from the rigid environmental determinism of earlier days. Recognizing the cogency of the argument, Rapoport (1969) pointed out that, while cultural factors are critical determinants of environmental perception, it is also the case that physical environments making comparable demands on different cultures may generate similar patterns of adaptation. Therefore, it is important to be sensitive to the interplay of cultural and environmental factors on per-ceptions and cognitions.

The development of environmental cognitions.   Some research indicates that children form utilitarian cognitions about the environment at an early age. Several researchers (Blaut et al., 1970; Hart & Moore, 1973; Stea & Blaut, 1973a, 1973b) demonstrated that the ability to understand and use aerial photographs and cartographic representations appear to be fully devel-oped by about seven to eight years of age. While the universality of the development of this ability had not been unequivocally established, their studies indicated no great differences across cultural or class groups. As a possible genetic mechanism, Kaplan (1973) argued that certain cognitive processes are of such high survival value that they have been evolution-arily selected, and spatial perception may be such an example. Without the ability to orient in space and to form and store cognitions, the accu-mulation of food and flight from predators would be almost impossible.

There has been relatively little comparison of the development of en-vironmental cognitions across cultures. However, a study by Blaut et al. (1970) found few differences between Massachusetts and Puerto Rican urban and rural school children in their ability to use aerial photographs and maps. The importance of the development of spatial cognition and the relative similarity of basic demands on human beings in widely divergent physical environments suggests that its development might be roughly similar in all cultures.

In an earlier section it was noted that the environment is an extremely complex perceptual object. Forming cognitive representations requires selection and restriction of incoming stimuli, and organization of resultant perceptions into meaningful cognitions that can be stored, recalled, and used. The "structures" that underlie the selection and organization of environmental stimuli have been thought by some theorists to be akin to Bruner's (1957) categories or to Piaget's schemata. (For a fuller discussion of the development of spatial cognitions, see Hart & Moore, 1973). Culture, through socialization processes, helps to determine which aspects of perceptual objects are to be attended to and how the percepts are to be organized. A question central to the cross-cultural study of cognition is whether the process and structure of cognition varies across cultures or if it is only content that varies (Cole & Scribner, 1974). The discussion of the interplay of environment, perception, and behavior is relevant here. If an individual has reason to travel in a particular area frequently, he or she probably develops a fairly well-articulated perception of the area. For example, Orleans (1973) found that Jewish senior citizens had highly accurate and detailed cognitive maps of the area where they lived in Los Angeles and also of the San Fernando Valley, an area with a high concentration of Jewish people. While the content of their cognitions may differ from those of other people, the possibility of genetic similarity of acquisition processes across cultures remains.

Knowledge and differentiation.   The question of what people notice and remember about their environment has been widely researched with a variety of different nationalities, ethnic groups, and social classes. Differences between various populations tend to be small and do not seem attributable to important differences in underlying cognitive processes. For example, Orleans (1973) found that black and Mexican-American subjects drew less sophisticated maps of the Los Angeles area than did middle class white subjects. The most parsimonious explanation for these results is differential familiarity with the areas, since blacks and Mexican-Americans traveled less. Similar findings were reported by Ladd (1970) and Maurer and Baxter (1972) in other locales. From such research can it be concluded that cultures vary in the genetic way in which they encode, store, and retrieve spatial information, or do they simply differ in which information they choose to deal with? For example, when modern college students are asked to draw a map of the world they generally attend to the political entities of geography such as nations or cities rather than natural landmarks like rivers or seas. On the other hand, environmental descriptions of American Indians tend to stress natural phenomena such as rivers, mountains, and mesas. While such substantive differences may be attributable to cultural and functional factors, the question remains as to whether cultures are similar in terms of underlying processes or schemata.

In comparing the maps of residents of Ciudad Guayana, Venezuela, Appleyard (1970) found differences among social classes in the type and frequency of errors. Subjects who rode the bus had more inaccurate maps than those who drove cars. This finding highlights the difficulties of interpretation of the literature. The two groups of subjects (drivers and bus riders) differed not only in terms of social class, but also in terms of freedom of movement and need to know, as well as in their different roles as active and passive learners.

Or, consider studies that examined perceptions of cities in different countries, including Boston, Los Angeles, Ciudad Guayana, Amsterdam, and Paris. Some studies, such as those by DeJonge (1962) of Amsterdam and Rotterdam, and by Francescato and Mebane of Rome and Milan (1973), involved perceptions of different cities within the same nation and point to an important difficulty in making culturally based inferences. While residents of different cities often show striking variations in their verbal reports or maps, there are also dramatic physical differences between the cities. Thus, there are differences in both stimuli and cultures of the respondents. Culture is not, therefore, a wholly singular explanation for such differences, which was Wohlwill's point in stressing the objective import of physical differences on the perception of the environment.

The same point can be made about cross-cultural similarities. Lynch (1960) used five elements to describe features of urban environments—paths, nodes, landmarks, districts, and edges. While these elements have been useful in analyzing responses to cities throughout the world, does this mean that there are no cultural differences in perception? No, only that cities throughout the world may share perceptual similarities because they share many of the same functions, i.e., the very notion of a city is a cultural adaptation.

What can generally be said about knowledge of environments is that the crucial variables are access and need, which are closely related. People tend to know about places they have had experience with, either direct or vicarious, and they tend to have experience with those areas that are important or necessary to them. Gould and White (1974) found that the amount of information that subjects have about a place is roughly a function of the population of the place multiplied by the distance. This equation represents a simple information flow effect. That is, populous areas emit more people who carry information. The flow of people, and thus of information, is diffused over distance. The qualifiers to this general equation are that more will be known about places that are distinctive because of some especially desirable or undesirable characteristics, e.g., southern

California, Las Vegas, Death Valley, Acapulco, or Alaska, or because they are associated with some distinctive event in the news, e.g., an earthquake, revolution, or nude beauty pageant.

Several researchers (Gould & White, 1974; Ladd, 1970; Orleans, 1973; Saarinen, 1973a, 1973b) found that people have the most differentiated and accurate representations of their home range and areas proximate to it; this occurs in a variety of cultures—Asians, Africans, Scandinavians (Gould & White, 1974). In a study typical of many in this area, Saarinen (1973a) asked college students to draw freehand maps of the world. He found that people knew a lot about their own geographical area and major industrial areas, e.g., United States, western Europe, and about areas that were important to them for some reason, e.g., southeast Asia for American college students of the Vietnam period. Thus, functional factors also have a strong influence on which geographical areas are considered important and cognitively differentiated.

The literature on estimation of physical distances also points to the role of cultural variables, though not in a cross-cultural context. For example, Briggs (1973) found that locations in the direction of an urban center were perceived as more distant than those in directions away from the city. The important question is why does this distortion occur and is it universal? One explanation might be that density of traffic is greater around an urban center, making movement more difficult and enhancing subjective feelings of distance. Another possible explanation is that urban centers in the Western world, and especially in the United States, have come to be associated with a host of negative factors by some people, e.g., danger, filth, and congestion.

Both of these explanations are susceptible to cultural interpretations. Do all people perceive cities as negative? Do some cultures perceive aspects of urban centers as more positive than other cultures? Tuan (1971) pointed out that cultures have generally used a sacred-profane dimension in classifying environmental categories. In different cultures and at different times, cities, suburbs, and wilderness areas have been alternately classified as sacred or profane. Such value-laden classifications of the environment would most certainly be affected by perceptions of and knowledge about different environmental features.

A classic work on geographical preferences and a major stimulant to the general field of environmental cognition comes from the work of Gould and his associates who obtained residential preference data in Europe (Gould, 1973a), America (Gould, 1973b), and Africa (Gould & White, 1974). Gould's findings show considerable comparability within and across national samples. For example, children begin to form stable preferences for particular geographical areas at age eight or nine. By middle teens preferences are quite comprehensive, articulated, and stable, and agree with the preferences of the local adult population. These findings point towards a learning process, influenced possibly by adult socialization or perhaps simply by the gathering of geographical information.

The most consistent finding in this research is that people show the greatest preference for their home areas and its environs, as well as for areas associated with good climate (e.g., southern California in the United States, the Brighton area in England, the southern portion of Sweden) and areas noted for natural beauty and/or pleasant pursuits (e.g., Rocky Mountains).

The structure and form of these preference patterns are quite similar for Americans and Europeans, each evaluating their own countries. An interesting difference between Western cultures and such African nations as Ghana, Nigeria, and Tanzania relates to perceptions of urban areas. Swedish and English samples had, at best, an ambivalent attitude towards the major cities of their countries. However, some African college students showed extremely high preferences for urban areas. Gould (1973b) pointed out that African cities represent the focal points of excitement and opportunity in the countries studied and, likewise, these cities may not have reached the size or density that brings with it the adverse characteristics that many Westerners find in their own megalopolis.

To summarize, the literature on environmental cognition has not yet lent itself well to cross-cultural analysis. Rarely have studies of a truly cross-cultural nature been done in which comparable questions were investigated by similar methods in more than one cultural sample. Perhaps only Gould's work of residential preference comes closest to this goal. Furthermore, while studies have been done in a variety of locales, the interrelatedness of culture and environment makes it difficult to separate these two factors and to compare their mutual effects.

As stated earlier, the relationship of culture and environment is a complex, reciprocal network in which environment can influence cultural patterns of adaptation, and vice versa, which in turn can act on perception of the environment. The existing data suggest that cultures are simultaneously similar and different in processes of environmental cognition and perception, a theme that seems to pervade the literature on environment and behavior.

Environmental Behaviors

This section considers overt social behaviors in relation to the environment. The discussion will be keyed around four basic processes: privacy, personal space, territory, and crowding. Figure 8-2, adapted from Altman (1975), presents some relationships between these processes.

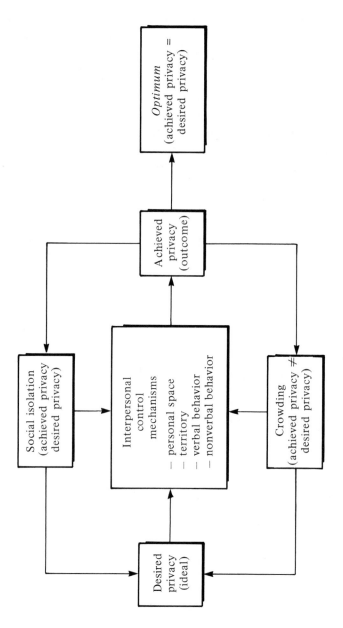

Figure 8–2. Overview of Relationships between Privacy, Personal Space, Territory, and Crowding.

Privacy is the central organizing concept and is defined as *selective control over access to the self* (Altman, 1975). Thus, privacy is a process by which people regulate social interaction, such that they sometimes make themselves accessible to others and sometimes close themselves off from others. *Desired privacy* (or what level of stimulation a person or group would like to have) is distinguished from *achieved privacy* (the actual level of stimulation received). To the extent that achieved and desired privacy match one another one can speak of successful control over interaction. A poorly operated privacy system exists when achieved and desired privacy do not match.

The framework also suggests that a series of behavioral mechanisms are used to help meet a momentary desired level of privacy. These mechanisms include *verbal behavior* (telling someone to "keep out" or "come in"), *paraverbal behavior* (voice intonation, tone, interruptions, and pauses), *nonverbal behavior* (gestures, body postures, head positions, and movements), and *personal space, territorial behavior,* and *cultural styles* of responding. Emphasis will be placed on the latter behaviors since they bear most closely on environmental issues.

Personal space refers to the "invisible boundary" surrounding a person or group, intrusion into which often produces discomfort (Altman, 1975; Hall, 1966; Sommer, 1969). It is commonly studied in terms of distance and/or angle of orientation among people. *Territorial behavior* refers to ownership and control of environmental areas and objects (Altman, 1975). *Cultural styles* include norms, customs, and rules of interaction, such as visiting or not visiting neighbors, rules for using other's property and space, styles of probing others, or avoiding intrusion.

Privacy mechanisms can function in different combinations within and between cultures, yielding a complex system of responses. That is, in one situation verbal and personal space behaviors may predominate, whereas in another situation people may rely more on territorial and nonverbal behavior. So it may be that one culture uses one set of mechanisms to regulate privacy and another culture may rely on a different behavioral mix.

The figure also suggests that privacy regulation may be successful and yield a good match between desired and achieved levels of privacy. However, the system may overshoot and produce more privacy than desired, i.e., a person or group may be more socially isolated than desired. Or, the system may undershoot and yield less privacy than desired, i.e., a person may be crowded or intruded upon. Naturally, crowding and privacy also have a heavy perceptual component, so that the earlier discussion of the impact of cultural variables on perception and cognition applies here as well. Within the framework of Figure 8–2, emphasis is on the concepts of *privacy, personal space, territory,* and *crowding* in the context of cross-cultural processes.

Privacy

Whereas there are about three hundred studies on personal space and numerous studies on crowding and territorial behavior, empirical research on privacy is almost nonexistent. However, privacy has been discussed at a conceptual level by sociologists, political scientists, and philosophers. From the perspective of cross-cultural analysis, the concept has several important features. First, privacy is viewed as a dialectic process. A traditional conception is that privacy is strictly an exclusionary process, a shutting off of interaction. But privacy is better conceptualized as an interplay of opposing forces—being out of contact versus interacting with others. Sometimes a person or group wishes to be alone; at other times, they desire social stimulation. Thus, privacy is a dynamic and changing process, with openness-closedness varying over time and with circumstances. A related property is that privacy is a boundary control process, whereby individuals or groups make themselves more or less accessible to others. Thus, privacy regulation is analogous to the shifting permeability of a cell membrane that becomes more or less open depending upon the external and internal environment. Another feature is the optimizing quality of privacy. That is, at any point in time there is an optimal level of openness-closedness of the self to others. Deviation from this optimum in either a "too much" or "too little" direction is undesirable. Other properties are that privacy can involve different sized social units: single people, pairs, families, and other groups, and that privacy is managed by a series of behavioral mechanisms discussed earlier that include verbal behavior, nonverbal behavior, personal space, territory, and cultural styles.

Some of these aspects of privacy have been addressed by others, although most writers emphasize a one-way, exclusionist approach. For example, Westin (1970) identified four privacy states: (1) *solitude*, where a person is alone and free from observation by others, (2) *intimacy*, where a small group separates themselves in order to be alone, (3) *anonymity*, where a person is "lost in a crowd," in a public place and does not expect to be recognized, and (4) *reserve*, where others are "tuned out" in a psychological sense. Although Westin emphasized the exclusionist quality of privacy in this analysis, he noted elsewhere that people and groups seek an optimum balance between being open and being closed. Similarly, Proshansky, Ittelson, and Rivlin (1970) stated that privacy involves an attempt to maximize freedom of choice, to achieve a range of behavioral options in dealing with others. In so doing, territory, personal space, and other behavioral mechanisms are employed. Several other writers (Kelvin, 1973; Laufer, Proshansky, & Wolfe, 1973; Wolfe & Laufer, 1974) proposed similar lines of thinking.

How do these features of privacy bear on cross-cultural processes? There is implicit in the preceding the idea that privacy management may be a "cultural universal." (See Lonner's chapter in Volume 1 of this *Handbook* for a discussion of the issue of cultural universals.) A hypothesis that the process of privacy regulation, as defined above, occurs in *all* cultures is proposed here. People and groups in diverse societies all seem to regulate their accessibility to others, sometimes and in some ways being open and at other times and in other ways being closed to social contact. In spite of the fact that some cultures may appear to be highly private and others may appear to be without any privacy, the thesis is that if cultures are carefully analyzed, different mechanisms for regulating interaction will be uncovered from culture to culture. Thus, while the process of privacy regulation is hypothesized to be universal, specific behavioral mechanisms used to regulate privacy may differ among cultures (see Altman, 1977, for a fuller treatment of this question). Consider several anthropological examples, with two cautions in mind: (1) such cases must be considered in light of the etic-emic issues discussed throughout this *Handbook*, especially in Brislin's chapter (in Volume 2 of this *Handbook*), and (2) one must be sensitive to the dangers of choosing cases that support a hypothesis and ignoring those that do not. The ethnographic examples in this section are only illustrative of a line of reasoning and not definitive confirmations of a hypothesis.

The Mehinacu culture of Brazil.   (Gregor, 1970, 1974; Roberts & Gregor, 1971). The Mehinacu are a small tribal group who live in an isolated tropical forest region in central Brazil. They reside in small villages and, on the face of it, seem to have little privacy. Homes are shared by several families; the thatched walls of the dwellings do not mask noises very well; almost anyone can listen in on others' conversations. Moreover, the huts are built around a small open plaza and everyone in the village is visible, since people often sit in their doorways working, resting, or talking. Also, people are easily seen as they leave and approach the village since paths are wide, long, and straight. In fact, Roberts and Gregor (1971) noted that people can be seen some fifteen minutes before they arrive in the village area. Also, the paths are sandy and people come to recognize one another's footprints, so that a person's whereabouts are often known even if he is not seen directly. Furthermore, agricultural fields around the village are contiguous with one another, making for easy observation of others.

Can we conclude that the Mehinacu have no ability to regulate their social contacts? No, not if one views privacy as involving a complex repertoire of several levels of behavior. Roberts and Gregor identified a number of practices whereby the Mehinacu, do, in fact, regulate their contact with others. For example, there are specific rules against intrusion—women are not permitted access to a men's building in the center of the village, a kind of social club and religious place; people do not intrude into one another's residences; and those who share the same hut do not go into one another's parts. Furthermore, the Mehinacu have a childrearing process that fosters seclusion. When a boy reaches nine years of age he enters a period of social isolation that lasts for several years—he stays inside the home during the day, learns various social and religious rituals, is taught to conceal strong emotions and to speak quietly, and the like. Furthermore, throughout life, periods of isolation occur; at the birth of a man's first child, on the death of a spouse, and when a man trains to become a religious leader. There is also a strong norm of discretion, so that people do not expose other's failings and do not probe one another about intimate or embarassing topics. Thus, the Mehinacu culture fits the thesis; in spite of an apparent lack of privacy, a series of behavioral mechanisms are available to facilitate the regulation of social interaction. These mechanisms include verbal, nonverbal, and environmental behaviors, as well as various cultural practices. Moreover, the Mehinacu culture is a simultaneous blend of accessibility and inaccessibility of people to one another, in line with the dialectic, changing quality of privacy described earlier.

Two Indonesian societies: Bali and Java.   Geertz (cited in Westin, 1970) described how Balinese and Javanese societies differ in terms of privacy regulation:

> In Java people live in small, bamboo walled houses, each of which almost always contains a single nuclear family—i.e. mother, father, and unmarried children . . . The houses face the street with a cleared front yard in front of them. There are no walls or fences around them, the house walls are thinly and loosely wove, and there are commonly not even doors. Within the house people wander freely just about any place any time, and even outsiders wander in fairly freely almost any time during the day and early evening. In brief, privacy in our terms is about as close to nonexistent as it can get. You may walk freely into a room where a man or woman is stretched out (clothed, of course) sleeping. You may enter from the rear of the house as well as from the front with hardly more warning than a greeting announcing your presence. . . .
>
> Now in Bali people live in house yards surrounded by high stone walls into which you enter by a narrow, half blocked-off doorway. Inside such a yard lives some form of what anthropologists call a patrilineal extended family. Such a family may consist of from one to a dozen or so nuclear families of the Javanese sort whose heads are related patrilinearly: i.e., father, his two married sons, his two married brothers, *his* father. . . .
>
> In contrast to Java, nonkinsmen almost never enter one's houseyard. . . . Within the yard one is in one's castle and other people know better than to push their way in. . . . Other patrilineal relatives of yours may come around in the early evening to gossip and in some cases a close friend or two may do so, but except for these when you are in your houseyard you are free of the public. Only your immediate family is around (pp. 16–17).

Once again the interplay of forces toward openness and closedness, accessibility and nonaccessibility existing side by side in each society is seen. And, equally important, although one society seems totally open and the other totally closed, if matters are more closely examined there are elements of both in each society. Thus, while the particular mechanisms used to regulate interaction vary across cultures, there is an underlying communality of processes of privacy management.

It is also easy to point to ways in which Western cultures regulate social interaction. For example, Schwartz (1968) and Kira (1970) noted how bathrooms occupy a sacred place in American culture, where people can be assured of not being intruded upon when the door is closed. In another study, Altman, Nelson, and Lett (1972) found that Americans usually knock on closed bathroom doors rather than barge in, and more intimate activities, e.g., using the toilet, are usually done alone, with others not permitted entry. Thus, Western culture emphasizes closed doors in such places as bathrooms, where an occupant has considerable control over access by others. Yet, other parts of the home—the kitchen and family room—are quite accessible to visitors, whereas in some cases, such as certain subgroups of Puerto Ricans (Zeisel, 1973), the living room is an off-limits area to other than good friends, because religious and other treasured items are kept there. Or as Canter and Canter (1971) observed, the Japanese home is an interesting blend of openness-closedness. The home itself has high walls around the outside and a location that prevents visual access by outsiders. Yet, within the home, space is used flexibly, with walls taken down or put up to serve different functions and to achieve different degrees of privacy. (For a detailed analysis of the social and cultural significance of American home design, see Altman and Chemers, in press.)

Furthermore, as discussed earlier, it is important to note that the regulation of privacy does not always involve physical and environmental controls; general behavioral styles are also important. Thus, in Java there are few physical symbols of privacy, but people use psychological and behavioral techniques—relationships are polite, etiquette and decorum are important, and people speak softly. Or, as Hall (1966) noted, the English do not often possess private offices but use reserve, aloofness, nonverbal, and verbal means to regulate their openness-closedness to one another. And, the Navajo Indians do not rely extensively on physical means to achieve privacy but have clear norms concerning individual autonomy and nonintrusion (Lee, 1959).

To summarize, the sampling from different cultures illustrates the theme that privacy regulation is a dialectic, dynamic, and shifting process that changes over time and involves the interplay of a variety of behavioral mechanisms. There are both similarities and differences among culures in privacy management. The differences between cultures seem to come from the particular blend and repertoire of behavioral mechanisms used to regulate privacy. The universality among cultures derives from the idea that all cultures appear to have some type of mechanism, however different, to regulate and pace interaction, and to permit individuals and groups to be in contact with others on some occasions and to be inaccessible or closed off at other times. The following sections will examine two of these privacy regulation mechanisms—personal space and territorial behavior.

Personal Space

The concept of personal space has its roots in ethology, where it was observed that many animals had fight, flight, and social distances from one another (Hediger, 1950). According to Hall (1966) and Sommer (1969) personal space in humans refers to an invisible boundary, a kind of personal bubble that surrounds a person, and intrusion into it sometimes leads to discomfort or tension.

The study of personal space has blossomed in the past fifteen years, with well over two hundred studies in the literature. Research methods for studying personal space include *simulation methods, laboratory methods* and *field methods.* Simulation methods involve placements by subjects of symbolic representations of people, such as dolls, stick figures, and line drawings, under different conditions of sex composition (e.g., male-male; male-female), friendship, etc. Laboratory methods ask people to approach or be approached by others in various experimental conditions, with distance and/or angle of orientation used to reflect personal space. Finally, field methods are used in naturalistic settings, with distance measurements done in an unobtrusive fashion.

The major impetus to work in personal space, especially in a cross-cultural context, stemmed from the writings of Edward Hall, an anthropologist, who proposed the study of "proxemics," or how people use space to communicate (Hall, 1966).

Hall proposed four spatial zones involved in social relations: (1) *intimate distance,* 0–18 inches, is usually maintained only with intimates or close associates, and not often in public. At this distance a rich array of cues can be exchanged—heat, smell, fine visual details, touch; (2) *personal distance,* 1.5–4 feet, is a transitional distance where rich communication possibilities still exist; (3) *social distance,* 4–12 feet, is the distance of business and general public contact. Office desks, furniture arrangements in public settings, and chair locations in homes generally put people somewhat in this zone. One can still gain a fair amount of communication cues, but they are not fine grained; and (4) *public distance,* 12–25 feet, is usually reserved for formal occasions, public speakers, or high status figures. Here only gross cues are available and such cues as smell, heat, and fine visual details are lost.

An analysis of over one hundred studies indicated general support for Hall's spatial zone hypotheses (Altman & Vinsel, 1977). People who interacted in standing arrangements typically used the far edge of the intimate zone (about 18 inches) or the near end of the personal zone (18–30 inches). People in seated arrangements typically were separated by about 2.5–4 feet, the upper boundary of the personal zone, or they used the lower boundary of the social zone (4–7 feet). These findings were stable across a range of conditions, gender differences, personal factors, degrees of attraction between people, and so on. Thus, Hall's ideas about spatial zones are well supported by empirical data.

In relation to culture, Hall observed, qualitatively, that different groups used space and furniture arrangements in different ways. For example, people from certain "contact cultures" (Arabs, Latin Americans, and southern Europeans) maintained close distances to one another and were highly sensory in their communications. Hall observed that they often were nose to nose, touched one another, and breathed in one another's faces. On the other hand, northern Europeans seemed more physically distant in social settings. According to Hall, Germans, for example, are more sensitive to spatial intrusion than Americans, and both Germans and English are rather "private" people. Germans rely on physical separation, such as doors and physical objects, whereas the English, Hall stated, employ verbal reserve and reticence, nonverbal behavior such as reduced eye contact and formal body postures, to maintain personal space. While these may or may not be accurate characterizations, Hall's anecdotal observations set the stage for a modest account of cross-cultural research on personal space.

The earliest empirical test of Hall's idea was a comparison among Arabs and Americans in a discussion task (Watson & Graves, 1966). As expected Arabs showed more direct face-to-face orientation, maintained less distance from one another, touched more, had more direct visual contact, and spoke louder than Americans. A later study by Forston and Larson (1968) found no comparable differences between North and South Americans.

These studies compared the spatial behavior of actual people whereas other investigations used simulation techniques. For example, Little (1968) compared subjects from the United States, Sweden, southern Italy, Scotland, and Greece on a doll placement task. As predicted, those from Mediterranean cultures placed dolls closest together, followed by Americans and then by so-called "noncontact cultures" (Sweden and Scotland). In another study, Sommer (1968) had college students from the United States, England, Sweden, Netherlands, and Pakistan rate the intimacy of various seating arrangements, e.g., corner to corner, side by side, opposite. Everyone rated side by side as most intimate, and opposite and other distant arrangements as least personal. Beyond this, American, Swedish, and English students were similar in their ratings; the Dutch viewed corner seating as less intimate than Americans; and the Pakistanis saw opposite seating as quite distant. In another study, Ziller, Long, Ramana, and Reddy (1968) reported that Asian Indian students had higher self-esteem, identification with their parents, and self-centeredness than Americans, based on their placement of symbols representing themselves and others. Finally, Engebretson and Fullmer (1970) obtained few differences in use of personal space by native Japanese, Hawaiian-Japanese, and Caucasian-Americans.

From these few studies there is some, but not consistent, support for Hall's thesis. Therefore, more research is necessary to unravel how and under what circumstances cultural similarities and differences operate. Hall's ideas about cross-cultural differences in personal space are plausible, but not yet fully documented.

There have also been several studies of personal space among ethnic groups in the United States, although their theoretical underpinnings are not always linked to Hall's ideas. For example, in an early field study, Willis (1966) found a tendency for blacks to maintain greater conversational distances than whites. Later, Baxter (1970) observed pairs of people watching exhibits in a zoo and found that Mexican-Americans stood closest, whites were intermediate, and blacks kept the greatest distances from one another. But there were many qualifying factors. For example, sex composition made a difference, e.g., in mixed sex groups, whites and blacks were closest whereas, among Mexican-Americans, female pairs were closest and males were most distant. Also, Mexican-Americans were closest in outdoor settings, whereas blacks were closest at indoor exhibits. In another field study in a hospital canteen and at a high school, Thompson and Baxter (1973) found that blacks tended to move backwards and away from a person of another ethnic group as they conversed, whereas Mexican-Americans moved forward (white Americans were intermediate).

However, other studies do not always corroborate these findings, suggesting that cultural differences are not as simple as one might think. In one study Jones (1971) photographed interacting pairs of blacks, Puerto Ricans, Italians, and Chinese on the streets of New York. No differences were obtained in distance or angular orientation among groups. Then, Aiello and Jones (1971) observed first- and second-grade black, Puerto Rican, and white children in school yards. They found that middle-class white children stood further apart than lower class blacks and Puerto Ricans, with no differences among the latter groups. But, blacks faced one another less directly than the other groups. However, these results may be confounded by differences in socioeconomic status and age levels of the different groups, factors that have been treated more carefully in recent studies. For example, Jones and Aiello (1973) compared upper-lower class blacks and middle-middle class white children from the first, third and fifth grades in a free discussion situation. The results were complex but indicated that blacks stood closer in the first grade but were not different from whites in the third grade (and even may have reversed the trend in later grades). There were also complicated sex differences, e.g., black females stood closest and white females were furthest apart. And, angular facing entered in, with black children in all grades facing one another less directly than whites.

Hall (1974) recently undertook a photographic proxemics (touching, looking, body distances, etc.) analysis of working class blacks, Puerto Ricans, and middle class whites in naturalistic settings in Chicago. Using two raters he found that whites faced one another more directly than did Puerto Ricans, with mixed results for blacks. On measures of distance he found that whites and Puerto Ricans were not different from one another but blacks positioned themselves closer than whites.

In summary, this series of studies on ethnic minorities in the United States does not lead to any compelling conclusions about personal space differences as a function of cultural factors. Rather the mixed results probably are due to many factors, including within-culture variance and cultural interactions with age, sex, social class and other variables. For example, one potentially important variable is socioeconomic status, which was largely uncontrolled in the studies cited above. Scherer (1974) did two studies that examined the role of this factor. First, he observed black and white first- to fourth-grade children in a schoolyard where all children were from lower socioeconomic groups. There were no differences among ethnic groups. In a second study, he compared black and white children from lower and middle class socioeconomic levels. Here middle class children were further apart than lower class children for both ethnic groups, although the results were reliable only for whites. There were no differences between white and black middle class children or between white and black lower class children. This is an important study for it is the first to clearly separate ethnic and socioeconomic factors, and the first to suggest that previous differences among blacks and whites may have been a function of socioeconomic factors, not ethnic ones.

What conclusions can be drawn from this array of studies? Frankly, no simple conclusions are possible. While Hall's thesis of culture differences remains plausible, the few studies available reflect some uncertainty about the relationship between culture and personal space. Some evidence points to differences, but several studies suggest interactions of culture with sex, socioeconomic status, age, and setting factors. Thus the precise contribution of cultural factors to personal spacing has not been yet identified in the research. While the tendency is to seek differences among cultures in space usage, it must also be recognized that spacing is probably a basic feature of human behavior and may show as many cross-cultural similarities as differences.

What are some promising directions for research on cross-cultural aspects of personal space? Research to date has demonstrated that (1) personal space relates to interpersonal relationships and degree of acquaintance, i.e., people who are friendly maintain closer distances, people at closer distances are perceived as friendlier and so on. It is likely that such a relationship exists in some form across cultures and might be worthy of cross-cultural study; (2) personal space is a learned process, and children demonstrate appropriate mechanisms fairly early in their lives. How does culture interact with social development processes? Do some cultures foster nonactive personal space usage early or late, or differentially for boys and girls? and (3) personal space varies with situations, with greater distance maintained in formal versus informal settings. How does this operate cross-culturally? Do the same settings elicit similar behaviors cross-culturally, or are there complex interactions of culture and setting?

Territory

The concept of territory is a pervasive one in everyday vernacular—"my turf," "keep off, private property," "members and guests only." People fence their yards, use name plates and signs, build walls around homes and communities, and have guards at national frontiers. In the language of this framework, territorial behavior, or the ownership, control, and personalizing of areas and objects, is a vehicle to regulate social contact.

In psychology the investigation of human territorial behavior lagged until the last dozen years; even now, only a small number of studies are available, and none of these are cross-cultural. Within sociology and anthropology, however, there are traditions for studying human territorial behavior. For example, sociological analyses of urban life begun in the 1920s (Park, Burgess, & McKenzie, 1925; Thrasher, 1927; and others) consistently observed the presence of territories in urban settings, often demarcated by streets, sides of streets, and other boundaries. Sommer (1969) described a popularized account of a neighborhood in Chicago where one street was populated by blacks and the other street was occupied by Irish. Each street had its own ethnic stores and facilities and neither was ever used by the other group. Boal (1969) described a similar situation in Belfast, Ireland, where a single street was a dividing line between Roman Catholics and Protestants, with the whole fabric of life totally different on each side of the street.

Early sociologists also portrayed gang territories in urban areas that were "owned" by the occupants and were vigorously defended against intrusion. But these and other forms of human territory are not always rigid; they shift with circumstances. For example, Suttles (1968) described an overlapping territory in a Chicago neighborhood where residents were black, Italian, Puerto Rican and Mexican-American. While each group had its own territory, they also shared certain spaces in a mutually consensual arrangement. They literally took turns using a restaurant, each group avoiding entry when another group was present. Anthropologists have also treated territorial behavior in different cultures, but it is difficult to locate these materials since they are often embedded in detailed accounts of a culture's total life. Unfortunately, there are few direct comparisons across cultures.

Types of territories.   Territories can be grouped into three categories: primary, secondary, and public territories (Altman, 1975; Altman & Chemers, in press). *Primary* territories are owned and exclusively used by individuals or groups, are clearly identified as theirs, and are important in the day-to-day lives of the occupants. In addition, primary territories are usually under the long-term control of occupants. For example, a home and a bedroom are usually strongly identified with an occupant, and the owner generally has unquestioned control over use by others. Primary territories are not often entered by outsiders without permission, and reactions to intrusion are often extreme, perhaps because primary territories are closely linked to a person's or a group's self-identity.

The idea of primary territory seems widespread across cultures. Most people, families, or close kinship groups have places identified solely with them—a tent, hut, or other dwelling. Entry is often restricted and under the control of occupants. Even communal living arrangements, like the Mehinacu (Roberts & Gregor, 1971), have primary territories, such that families do not use other than their own parts of the dwelling place. Consider the Ngadju Dayaks of Borneo, who live in villages and farm hamlets along a river bank (Miles, 1970). Families sometimes reside in long houses that contain twenty to thirty families or, more often, they reside in smaller dwellings with two to three families. Yet, even though people live together in communal arrangements, territorial behavior is prevalent. For example, everyone has their own sleeping mats and sleeping areas, families have their own storage areas and dine at different times, people leave if a husband and wife are arguing, and others do not interfere in the child rearing of other families. And, in crowded tenements in Mexico, Lewis (1959, 1961) observed that families were careful not to enter inappropriately others' homes. Furthermore, the concept of primary territory is not necessarily restricted to family versus nonfamily members; it can occur within families. For example, in Western culture a person's bedroom can be a primary territory in that a long-term occupant has almost complete control. Among the Fulani of west Africa, Prussin (1974) noted that the woman is proprietor of the interior furnishings of a hut, such as decorations and utensils, whereas the male is responsible for the outside walls and hut itself. In earlier times, when these people were nomads, the woman was sole proprietor of the tent, bed, and family possessions. Similar practices occur in many societies, where men often have religious and social buildings (such as the American Indian kiva) from which women and young children are barred. Such distinctions within families and between families and outsiders are not unusual across cultures. What may distinguish cultures is not so much the absence or presence of territorial behavior, but which parts of the environment are associated with which owners or controllers.

Primary territories can also involve larger groups such as communities or nations. For example, Australian Aborigines (Peterson, 1975; Rapoport, 1974) have fairly strict rules about outsiders being admitted into their camps. Typically, messengers or visitors remained at the fringes of an encampment or community until an escort was sent out to receive them. In some instances, the escort presented the visitors with a fire stick to symbolize a welcome, or there was a brief symbolic feinting and clash of shields and weapons to welcome the visitor. And, national borders are typically seen as under the sole control of occupants, with invasions usually resisted vigorously.

Secondary territories are less central, pervasive, and exclusive, and occupants do not have total control over them. For example, Cavan (1963, 1966) studied neighborhood bars as secondary territories. She identified regular users who often had specific seats and who used the bar for a variety of away-from-home functions, such as check cashing, obtaining messages, etc. But bar users did not have absolute control since it was a public place and others had entry rights. Secondary territories have, therefore, a simultaneous blend of public availability and some control by occupants. Because of the mixed quality of access, confusion may occur regarding use of secondary territories, probably increasing the possibility of conflict. For example, Fahim (1974) described the impact of nomadic groups settling alongside the newly relocated (from the Aswan Dam site in Egypt) Halfan people in northern Sudan. Among a multitude of social and political issues, the Halfan people were unhappy when the nomads settled within their new village boundaries, and were also upset when nomads herded their animals in the area. Because these new lands were semipublic or secondary territories, there was a mixture of public and private use that led to overlapping and somewhat unclear control by occupants. Another example of the potential for conflict in secondary territories is provided by Newman's (1972) analysis of "defensible space." He reported higher crime rates in low-cost urban housing developments when semipublic areas, such as hallways, entranceways, and street areas around homes were not easily watched by occupants, when they were not visibly designed to be under the control of occupants, or when they did not have clear boundaries. By creating sharper boundaries and markers through use of walls, semiprivate entrance ways, hedges, fences, and lighting configurations, Newman felt that territories would be under greater control of the occupants.

An example of strict regulation of secondary territories appears among the Woleia people, who live on a small atoll in the South Pacific (Alkire, 1968). In this communal society male-female contacts were minimized or heavily ritualized in a variety of ways, including use of secondary territories. For example, in the cleaning of villages, areas were separately assigned to men and women so that they never worked together. Areas near the canoes and the beach were off-limits to women, whereas interior paths on the island were considered women's areas.

Unfortunately, there is little systematic knowledge about the nature and dynamics of use of secondary territories across cultures. Because of their potentially ambiguous character and the associated likelihood of conflict, the study of secondary territories across cultures is a fruitful area of study.

Public territories have a temporary quality and almost anyone has access and occupancy rights as long as certain social rules are observed, e.g., parks, public beaches, seats on a bus or in a movie, or restaurant tables. One is an occupant of public territories only temporarily and only so long as one is physically present or leaves a marker, e.g., a reserved sign or a coat on a chair in a library. No matter how small a cultural group, it is likely that some parts of their environment are available to large numbers of people, e.g., a plaza or central city area, a street, shopping area, or market place. And, if different cultural groups occupy adjacent areas and have some contact, then cross-cultural public territories may exist.

It would be interesting to examine how different cultures create a blend of primary, secondary, and public territories. For example, Alexander (1969) noted that certain low income families in Peru systematically arranged their homes in order to regulate who had access to different parts of the residence. The front porch and door was used as the boundary for relative strangers; casual acquaintances could come into the formal parlor which was just beyond the door; close friends could come further into the home, to the informal living room and kitchen. Zeisel (1973) described how selected Puerto Rican families in New York treated their living room as a sacred place, with entry restricted to close friends and family. It contained expensive furniture, pictures of political heroes and family members, as well as religious objects. Once again, however, there is little systematic research on cross-cultural analysis of public territories; it is an area in need of future investigation.

Territorial markers.   Research on territorial behavior has been especially concerned with the role of "markers," or devices used to label and personalize environments. Several studies demonstrate that markers do preserve territories, even public ones. For example, Sommer and Becker (1969) found that personal markers, such as a sweater, were more effective in protecting a seat in a library than were less personal markers, such as a book or a newspaper. Becker (1973) reported that sheer number of markers also made a difference, and that markers were effective in protecting table space in a cafeteria. In another study, Edney (1972) found that longer term residents of homes had more distinctive markers such as fences, hedges and signs, than did shorter term occupants. Ley and Cybriwsky (1974) recently analyzed graffiti on public buildings and places in Philadelphia and suggested that one function of slogans, names, epithets, taunts, and aggressive markings that appear in graffiti often serve to mark off gang turfs in different neighborhoods of the city.

While markers may demarcate territories as a signal to outsiders, personalization may also serve as a form of self-expression and identification of a place with an occupant. For example, Hansen and Altman (1976) observed that college dormitory residents almost universally decorated their rooms with a variety of materials reflecting personal interests, values, and types of entertainment pursued. People from many cultures decorate their homes, places of worship, and other areas with art, pottery, and crafts. Even primitive cavemen personalized their places with materials that portrayed aspects of their lives. Of course, the function of decorations and markers can vary quite a bit within and between cultures. Fences and walls are widely used around the world to keep outsiders out or to signal that a place is not accessible (see Rapoport, 1969, and Tuan, 1971, for an analysis of housing and community design around the world and throughout history). Thus, decorations and markers are often used to signal ownership, to personalize and beautify, and sometimes to protect owners from disease, bad luck, and other malevolent forces. Once again, systematic analyses of similarities and differences across cultures in decorating/marking processes would be valuable.

Territory and social regulation.   A consistent theme in animal and human literature is that territories help stabilize and regulate social systems (Dubos, 1965, 1968). If everyone has his "place" to eat, mate, rear young, and perform other life functions, then social friction and conflict may be reduced. And, this can operate at all levels—individual, group, community, and national (Edney, 1976). This stabilizing process is evident even in the day-to-day lives of families. For example, people who share bedrooms—brothers, sisters, parents—are generally territorial about space in that each person has his own drawers, bureaus, and sides of a closet; people have regular seats at family tables, etc. (Altman et al., 1972). With everyone having a "place," daily activities are smoother and do not have to be negotiated continually. People respect other's territories, e.g., they are careful to knock on closed doors of bathrooms and bedrooms (Altman et al., 1972); only infrequently do strangers enter other's homes without permission; national borders are not continuously violated; neighborhood residents and groups do not repeatedly intrude on other's territories, etc.

The notion of territorial boundaries as a regulatory process even exists in some legal codes. For example, Prussin (1974) described the fourteenth century basis of Moslem building codes in north Africa that dealt with intrusion of privacy and territories, even by visual means. The code stated than any new opening in a wall between residences was illegal if it gave visual access to a neighbor; a building could not be made higher if it permitted observation by others; entranceways of different homes could not be directly across from one another. Walls surrounding Japanese homes (Canter & Canter, 1971), street boundaries separating neighborhood groups (Suttles, 1968), fences and hedges in American culture (Edney, 1972), hedgerows of France (Hall, 1966), and a myriad of other examples all suggest how territorial behavior plays a role in stabilizing social systems, by informing people where spatial and territorial boundaries exist. Stilgoe (1976) offers an historical analysis of the important role that boundary markers have played in European history.

In summary, a modest body of research and theory on territoriality suggests its role as a boundary regulation process. Relatively little cross-cultural research exists, however, and it would be especially profitable if information were developed on the following: (1) the nature of primary, secondary, and public territories in different cultures. How are they similar and different across cultures for individuals, families, communities, and larger social groups? (2) the nature and operation of markers and boundaries as signaling devices. Again, what similarities and differences occur across cultures and in various groups within cultures? and (3) territorial behavior as a reflection of social system viability. Where, when, and how does territorial behavior act to stabilize social interaction within and between groups?

Crowding

Crowding is a popular social issue and is receiving increased attention in the social and behavioral sciences. Before reviewing research in relationship to cross-cultural issues, the meaning of crowding needs to be addressed, especially the difference between "crowding" and "density." Stokols (1972a, 1972b) termed density a strictly physical indicator of population concentration—number of people per acre, per neighborhood, or per census tract. As such, density has no direct psychological meaning. Crowding, on the other hand, Stokols defined as an experiential, motivational state, a subjective feeling of stress often associated with too little space. Thus, density is not equivalent to crowding, although it can be an important antecedent.

It is also important to dimensionalize the concept of density, to include distinctions between actual and perceived density (Rapoport, 1975) and between inside dwelling density and outside dwelling density, e.g., a crowded urban ghetto often involves high inside and high outside density; a poor rural farm can involve high dwelling density and low outside density.

According to the framework of this chapter, crowding occurs when a privacy regulation system malfunctions, such that more social contact occurs than was originally desired. Density may play a role in this process by increasing the probability of social interaction, by blocking access to desired resources, or by facilitating various types of intrusion. When more interaction occurs than desired, the model hypothesizes the generation of psychological stress that motivates a person or group to make renewed attempts at achieving a desired level of interaction. As this happens certain "costs" may occur. These can take various forms: *physical,* such as energy expenditure, *physiological,* such as heightened adrenal and cardiovascular functioning, disease, and illness, or *psychological* such as stress, conflict, and social disorganization. Thus, as people handle situations of crowding, negative outcomes may occur if coping requires extensive mobilization of personal and group resources. Before exploring these ideas in a cross-cultural context, a word is in order about the history of crowding research.

Status of crowding research.   Research on crowding began in the 1920s as sociologists explored relationships between population density and indicators of social pathology, such as disease, mental health, crime, and mortality (see Altman, 1975, for a summary of this literature). Although moderate relationships were found between density and social pathology, these studies were criticized on several grounds: lack of analysis of different levels of density, nonpartialing out of confounding variables such as ethnicity and socioeconomic status, the presence of alternative explanations, and the emphasis on outcomes rather than associated social processes. Recently, more sophisticated sociological studies of crowding and density have emerged. For example, a prototype study by Galle, Gove, and McPherson (1972) examined different types of density: (1) number of persons per room in apartment dwellings, an interpersonal level of density, (2) number of rooms per housing unit, (3) number of housing units per apartment house, and (4) number of residential structures per acre—a macromeasure of density. Also, statistical adjustments were made for differences in ethnicity and socioeconomic status. They found the highest correlations between people per room measures of density and social pathology, and the lowest correlations between pathology and the number of residential structures per acre. Galle et al. interpreted their results in terms of ongoing social processes that might have occurred in densely populated homes. That is, ill people may have not obtained the seclusion they needed, resulting in higher mortality rates, or children may have received less attention and supervision, eventually leading to more juvenile delinquency. Thus, they demonstrated the feasibility of viewing crowding at a microinterpersonal level, and in terms of management of social interaction.

A second stream of research is laboratory oriented and uses strangers who are placed in short-term settings under various experimental conditions (see the reviews of this literature by Altman, 1975; Baum & Epstein, 1978). This research has focused on social processes, such as feelings of stress, task performance, and social behavior. More recent studies in this stream have been sensitive to density differences such as social density (variations in number of people in the same size space) and spatial density (variations in amount of space for the same size groups). In addition, a few studies have begun to examine delayed impacts of density as well as short-term effects.

Cross-cultural responses to crowding. This section examines three aspects of crowding in relation to culture: psychological and social feelings, coping responses, outcomes and costs. It should be noted that there are few direct cultural comparisons in existing research; most are single-culture studies from which some qualitative comparisons can be made.

Psychological and social feelings. A few laboratory studies demonstrated mixed or mild stress reactions to density in laboratory settings (Altman, 1975). The relatively weak stress responses in the studies may have occurred because crowding was short term, people were with strangers and had no long-term commitment to one another, and they were in relatively small groups. Research by Sundstrom (1975) also suggests that, over the length of an experiment, people can successfully cope with the discomfort of crowding by verbal withdrawal or nonverbal avoidance behaviors such as turning away, or blocking out the other person. In studies by Baum and Valins (1977) students in crowded living arrangements reduced feelings of discomfort by socially withdrawing from contact with others.

On the other hand, longer-term studies often found greater levels of stress, although not universally. For example, in a study of Filipino families, Marsella, Escudero, and Gordon (1970) found more anxiety, nervousness, potentially eruptive violence, and physical symptoms among those in crowded family living environments. However, Mitchell (1971), in a survey of four thousand families in Hong Kong, an extremely high density area, found some complaints about lack of space and privacy and some feelings of strain in crowded homes, but no severe psychological stress or symptomatology. Thus, within Western and other cultures there is some evidence for stress reactions to population density, especially in crowded families. However, there is also variability in reactions that may be due to different cultural coping styles.

Coping responses and behavioral reactions. It has been hypothesized that social interaction is managed by a variety of behavioral mechanisms and that crowding occurs when these mechanisms do not operate effectively, resulting in more social interaction than desired. Such an imbalance was said to trip off a variety of coping behaviors designed to establish a better balance between desires and outcomes. Cross-cultural data sheds some light on this process.

Several writers have observed that Japanese society exemplifies skillful coping in crowded living conditions (Canter & Canter, 1971; Hall, 1966; Michelson, 1970). Use of movable walls and separators within the home illustrates how the same area can serve several functions, for example, eating, recreation, and sleeping. Thus, volume and configuration of space changes with social needs, unlike the American tradition where rooms often have singular functions. In addition, the Japanese have been said to cope with limited space by miniaturizing parts of their environment and by an attitude of pride in perfection of detail, as in art and Bonsai gardening practices. They also deal with outside noise and density by erecting walls around their homes, and by careful arrangement of interior spaces. Similarly, in Hong Kong, Michelson (1970) and Mitchell (1971) reasoned that styles of family functioning, social organization, and other cultural mechanisms evolved in order to cope with population concentration. As another example, Anderson (1972) did a case study of Chinese families in Malaysia who lived in communal dwellings. While there was considerable contact and occasional tensions, families maintained separation from one another by means of several cultural practices. These included taboos for entering or looking into others' sleeping areas, separate family storage areas and family stoves in various parts of the communal kitchen, clear status relationships among the elderly and young, and between men and women, freedom for anyone to discipline children, and the maintenance of neutral and unemotional relationships with people from other families. The role of cultural coping mechanisms in the presence of population density was also substantiated by Biderman, Louria, and Bacchus (1963), who did a case study analysis of historical incidents of overcrowding on slave ships, in prisoner-of-war camps, and on immigrant ships. They concluded that disease and social pathology were low where groups had some social organization and cultural practices for coping with the situation.

The same theme emerges in analyses of crowding in Latin American and Mexican slums. Rogler (1967) examined squatter families in city slums in Colombia and Peru. Many such communities evolved their own methods for coping with high population density, such as norms of privacy, strong reactions to intrusion, secluding children, and rejection of newcomers. Lewis (1959) described a similar situation in a Mexican slum, where people did not visit one another's homes—perhaps because they were crowded, perhaps because they were not well furnished, or perhaps as a vehicle to cope with high population density.

Consider one of the few cross-cultural analyses of responses to crowding. Munroe and Munroe (1972) and Munroe, Munroe, Nurlove, and Daniels (1969) compared several African societies that differed in population concentration. The Logali had about 1,400 people per square mile, the Gusii had 700 people per square mile, and the Kissigis had only 250 people per square mile. They observed that the most densely populated groups were different in several ways from the least concentrated group. They had norms against holding hands with friends, they had the worst recall for interpersonal affiliation words, and they evaluated other family members less favorably. Perhaps the more densely populated groups gradually developed withdrawal practices to cope with population concentration.

From these and other studies, it may be that withdrawal is a widespread response to density, not only in the laboratory but also in a variety of cultural settings. This is further illustrated in a study by Draper (1973) of the !Kung Bushmen of southwest Africa. This hunting and gathering group lives in villages of about 150 people, where huts are extremely close together and where neighbors can literally touch one another as they sit around. During a typical day most of the people remain in the village and social contact is high, generating a very dense situation. But the !Kung seem to enjoy the close contact and engage in extensive interaction. They do not seem to suffer physically or psychologically. Draper described a !Kung norm that may permit coping with such high levels of population concentration, to the effect that individuals or families can leave the village at any time and relocate somewhere else. Because of their extensive family networks with other groups, coming and going is an easy and undramatic event. Thus, when social conflicts begin to mount a person or group can simply leave and go somewhere else—again a form of social withdrawal.

Various forms of social withdrawal have also been used to characterize urban dwellers (Milgram, 1970; Simmel, 1950). City residents are often described as aloof, detached, and uninterested in others, perhaps because of the stimulus overload quality of their situation. In fact, Milgram described a series of regulatory mechanisms, including allocation of less time to others, curt contacts, disregard of all but the most intense inputs, and the use of physical and electronic barriers such as doormen and unlisted phone numbers.

Withdrawal is also evident in laboratory studies of crowding in children (Hutt & Vaizey, 1966; Loo, 1973; McGrew, 1970). Ittelson, Proshansky, and Rivlin (1970) observed a similar pattern among patients in a densely populated psychiatric ward; Valins and Baum (1973) and Baum and Valins (1973) found comparable results in college dormitory students; Sundstrom (1975) reported nonverbal withdrawal behaviors in a laboratory study of crowding, including looking away and fidgeting. Also, married couples who lived in close quarters while in Peace Corps training (McDonald & Oden, 1973) developed explicit norms not to "peek" while others dressed and undressed, avoided intrusion into other's conversations and the like.

But withdrawal is not the only response to crowding. Some studies report conflict and aggression in dense conditions (Hutt & Vaizey, 1966; Rohe & Patterson, 1974). The latter study demonstrated that a combination of density and lack of sufficient resources tripped off aggression in children, whereas high density and high resources did not. Thus, when children had to compete for toys in a dense situation, they were more aggressive, whereas density alone was not sufficient to generate aggression.

Outcomes of crowding. The fact that coping with population density is widespread does not mean that it is always successful or that it is accomplished without any costs—psychological, physical, or physiological. As suggested earlier recent work has clarified the impact of population density on some aspects of social pathology, such as crime and delinquency, mortality, and disease. In addition to the study by Galle et al. (1972) and others, a study by Booth and Welch (1973) illustrates the nature of outcomes or costs in a cross-cultural context. They examined the relationship between levels of density (in homes and out of homes) on aggressive crimes of homicide and civil strife in sixty-five nations. Their data indicated stronger relationships between homicide, civil riots, and person-per-room measures of density than with more molar indicators of population correlation. Thus, across cultures crowded homes were associated with social upheaval, perhaps because of disruptions in peoples' ability to regulate interaction with one another. (Obviously, broader political, social, and economic issues also interact with such factors.)

Other outcomes of long-term population density include mental and physical illness, and heightened mortality rates (Altman, 1975). Yet, there are also examples where this is not the case, as in Hong Kong (Mitchell, 1971) and the !Kung bushmen (Draper, 1973); the latter group exhibits few biological stress symptoms such as high blood pressure or high blood cholesterol.

From this array of research it seems reasonable to hypothesize that population concentration is an important, though not exclusive, determinant of crowding reactions, and also that different cultures have evolved mechanisms to cope with such circumstances. These coping mechanisms include norms and styles of social withdrawal, culturally approved practices and behaviors, and the like. While there is a modest amount of research on the topic, it is also clear that few direct cross-cultural studies exist and that considerably more research is needed.

Environmental Outcomes and Products

The framework of this chapter hypothesized systemlike relationships between several classes of variables: physical environment, cultural and social environment, environmental cognitions and perceptions, environmental behaviors and processes, and outcomes or products of behavior. The present section discusses the last class of variables.

Environmental outcomes or products refer to what people create in the form of cities, communities, homes, and other modifications of the natural environment. Subjective perceptions, world views and philosophies of the environment, as well as behavioral processes in relationship to the environment have already been discussed. Oftentimes these psychological and social processes contribute to the design of homes and communities, and variations in such products as they relate to cultural factors will be examined. But, as emphasized earlier, a simple linear deterministic view is not assumed; rather environmental products are seen as a result of several factors. The products themselves can have an impact on perceptions, culture, and the environment.

There are many different scales of environmental outcomes. For example, communities can vary from metropolitan areas or regions to towns and villages. At another level differences in home design can be examined, including their relationship to culture, fit with climate, and other factors. Even more specific aspects of design can be investigated, such as entrance-ways, position and orientation of homes, room configurations, bathroom design, standards for lighting, space, and heat. Another direction of analysis is in terms of special places, such as hospitals, courtrooms and other locales, especially in technologically advanced societies. In subsequent sections several of these levels of analysis will be touched upon.

Community and Home Design

Tuan (1971, 1974) and Rapoport (1969, 1977) observed how broad cultural and world views of nature are associated with the design of cities and communities, indicating that culture orientations to nature are often translated into environmental design outcomes. For example, Tuan (1971, 1974) observed that many cultures make "vertical" distinctions about the environment, in terms of an earth, a sky, heaven and stars, and an underworld. Yet other people, like certain Pygmy groups (Turnbull, 1961) do not do this, since they reside in dense undergrowth and only see the sky and stars in a scattered fashion. More critical, however, are distinctions made along a horizontal dimension, where the notion of "center" is important, as are differences in how space is organized around the center. For some cultures, such as the agricultural Zuni Indians, the universe is organized into zones for religious purposes, with the outer zones always oriented toward the pueblo as the center (Tuan, 1971). On the other hand, the Navajo, who are sheepherders, organize their world around their huts or Hogans, which can be quite dispersed and even movable. For the ancient Greeks, Mount Olympus and Delphi were the cosmological centers, and communities were often built around these religious places. In many ancient Greek cities Acropolis temples were built on the highest ground and at the center of the communities. Tuan (1971, 1974) also observed that in ancient China the earth was conceived of as a square divided into concentric belts, with the imperial world at the center and successively less sophisticated and more barbaric groups at peripheral layers. Thus, the spatial idea of center as sacred dominates community designs in a variety of cultures.

Another interesting dimension relates to a square versus circular conception of nature. According to Tuan (1971, 1974), the Oglala Sioux have a circular conception of the world that is directly translated into the design of their homes and communities:

> The sky is round . . . the wind . . . whirls. Birds make their nests in circles, for theirs is the same religion as ours. The sun comes forth and goes down again in a circle. The moon does the same. Even the seasons . . . always come back again to where they were. The life of a man is a circle from childhood to childhood, and so it is in everything where power moves. Our teepees were round like the nests of birds, and these were always set in a circle, the nation's hoop, a nest of many nests, where the great spirit meant for us to hatch our children (Neihardt, cited in Tuan, 1971, p. 24).

Tuan observed that certain other cultures also historically adopted a circular concept of community design. For example, the neo-Hittite capitol in Anatolia (first millennium B.C.) was built on a circular concept (as were other cities in earlier times) even though the topography was not especially suited to such a design. And Howard, a designer of an idealized garden city in the 1880s, conceived of a series of circularly related large and small urban areas, connected by railroads and concentrically designed cities. As another example, African Hottentot villages are laid out in a circular arrangement that coincides with their view of the perfect form of heaven (Rapoport, 1969).

Yet in other cultures, for example, Eastern cities of ancient times, Tuan reported rectangular arrangements, or combinations of rectangular and circular designs. Thus, several Chinese cities from 600–1600 A.D. were rectangular and were oriented to cardinal directions of north, south, east, and west. This was also true of certain Middle Eastern cities, e.g., Barsippa (604–561 B.C.) which was laid out in a square with the angles oriented towards the cardinal positions. This format carries through in many Western cities today. One notable example that incorporates American pioneer pragmatism and religious values is exemplified by Salt Lake City, Utah and other Mormon communities in the western United States. The temple or religious house is at the center of the community in a Cartesian coordinate system, i.e., the church represents O,O coordinates and the streets are organized on a north, south, east, and west coordinate system. Variants of this basic design are quite common in the United States.

Rapoport (1969, 1977) related home and community design to cultural factors (see also Bochner, 1975). At the level of the city he explicitly noted the compatibility between cultural values and architectural and community design. For example, in the Dogon and Bambara culture of Mali, villages are built in pairs to represent heaven and earth; agricultural fields are arranged in spirals because the people believe that the world is created spirally; villages are laid out in the relationship of parts of the body, etc. Pawnee Indian villages are oriented toward one another as certain stars are in the sky. Also, Rapoport noted that village design in certain Baltic countries is related to heavenly bodies, especially to the path of the sun, with streets facing north-south and doors and facades facing east-west (getting either sun position during the day).

Even at a less cosmic level, community design reflects cultural values. For example, some cultures emphasize privacy in the traditional sense of reducing stimulation, perhaps because of population concentration or for other reasons, and this value is often reflected in community design. Rapoport observed that in certain Eastern and Middle Eastern countries (Iran, India, and Japan) homes are often surrounded by walls. This arrangement also appears in several African communities where a family or group of families builds walls around their residences or cluster of homes.

Rapoport also compared several African societies in terms of housing and village arrangements. For example, the Masai enclose a circular or oval compound arrangement of homes with a thorn fence. Houses are located around the inner side of the fence, with sheep and cattle at the center. Because livestock are important for economic and religious reasons, the animals are located at the center. A similar arrangement occurs for the Moundang group in the Cameroons, Africa, except that granaries are located at the center of the compound, again reflecting their importance in the culture. In another context Rapoport noted that the Foulbe, a polygamous group in the Cameroons, have circular living arrangements, with the male residing in a central hut surrounded by his wives' huts.

There are numerous other examples illustrating how cultural values are reflected in community design, whether it is a modern or ancient city, or a village, farm, or small compound. More important than the anthropological details, however, is the question of how cultural factors are reflected in environmental design. Rapoport (1969) hypothesized that housing and community design is a complex result of many factors—cultural, physical, economic, and religious. He rejected a single variable causation approach, and argued that cultural variables are central, and that physical factors such as climate and available technology are modifiers of cultural influences.

Rapoport also noted that cultures can be distinguished in terms of their environmental design process. For example, he pointed to the difference between *folk architecture* that is often a direct and unconscious translation of culture into design and *grand design architecture,* such as monuments and temples where there is a conscious and deliberate effort to convey a set of values. Within folk architecture Rapoport pointed to two approaches: primitive and vernacular construction. In primitive building, members of a society are capable of building their own structure without assistance from specialists, such as carpenters. In vernacular construction specialists are often used; there is a separation between the consumer and the builder and in technologically advanced societies plans and specialized procedures are typically employed.

Another dimension by which cultures can be compared is degree of differentiation of buildings. In many less technologically developed societies all buildings are similar in design and function; there is little specialization. In more complex societies there are often specialized places for work and living, for eating and sleeping. And, in many societies religion and status are often associated with greater size, more decorations, and prime locations. For example, Rapoport observed that certain Polynesian island cultures are similar to Eastern and Western cultures in that leaders' homes are more elaborate, as are religious places. Rapoport also noted that a culture often works up to its technological and artistic limits in such places, and special buildings can symbolize the level of technological development of the culture as a whole.

Thus, cultures often impose their religious and social values on the design of their communities, and these values often are similar in different parts of the world, e.g., square versus circular orientations. Furthermore, what is important to a culture is often reflected in the design of communities, whether they are cities, villages, or compounds. According to Hertzberg (1966) the League of the Iroquois, an American Indian Confederacy with a complex political and social system, repeated the concept of the Longhouse, their dwelling, throughout many levels of the culture, even conceiving of their collective national territory as having the form of a great longhouse.

There are numerous cultural and related factors that also bear on the designs of homes and living spaces. For example, Rapoport (1969) noted that in Fiji the east wall of a home is for chiefs; in China the most sacred part of the home is the northwest corner; among the Tuareg nomads of northern Africa the entry to the tent is on the south, with men located on the east and women on the west. Or, the home among certain groups in Madagascar is subdivided according to the twelve lunar months, with each section of the home having different use according to religious values. And, furniture is arranged in accord with such values, e.g., the bed is located in the east and faces the north.

Rapoport also described how sex roles are reflected in home designs. Societies with extended kinship arrangements often live under the same roof or in separate but proximate quarters. In polygamous societies wives often have separate houses with the husband nearby, often in the center. Some other societies provide separate space within the home for men and women.

In another domain, some societies achieve privacy by environmental design. For example, in India, Iran, and Latin America, Rapoport observed that buildings traditionally face inward. Roberts and Gregor (1971) analyzed a number of societies and found a definite relationship between level of political integration, agriculture, animal husbandry, technological development, and use of environmental privacy mechanisms. Thus, use of doors, windows, and partitions occured in technologically complex societies, whereas other cultures did not employ such mechanisms. More environmentally private societies also had more differentiated religious systems and marriage customs, suggesting that the type of privacy mechanism not only varies with the culture, but also with its technological features.

While Rapoport (1969) emphasized the role of cultural factors, he readily acknowledged how factors such as temperature, humidity, wind, rain, and availability of construction materials played a central role in affecting the form of housing. For example, among the Paiute Indians, winter homes were conically shaped, had a central fire pit and roof smoke hole, were constructed of juniper, and were covered with mattings of bark, reeds, and grass. In warmer weather they lived in walled, square, flat-roofed dwellings with screens. Or, in humid environments one often sees roofs designed to shed rain water, high-domed dwellings with roof overhangs, and raised floors and high ceilings that maximize air flow. In cold climates one often sees igloo shapes that minimize surface exposure to the outside, offer little wind resistance, and provide maximum interior space. As other examples, nomadic life is associated with tents and other movable residences, e.g., Mongolian Yurts use portable, folding frame structures; some American Indians had movable tents and transport systems. Also, various cultures have developed unique solutions to gravitational, compression, and vertical load problems in terms of their available technology.

While adaptive responses to the physical environment are widespread, Rapoport (1969) observed that they do not always occur, and that cultural and other factors can play an overriding role. For example, there are numerous instances in which home designs are simply not compatible with the environment. Certain peoples in the Amazon use large, communal houses with heavily thatched roofs and walls, with no cross ventilation—a design clearly not well suited for a humid tropical climate. In some cultures the terrain is sometimes ignored. For example, in India, some homes are oriented to the east because of religious reasons and entrance-ways often face uphill, even on steep hillsides. So, while physical features of the environment are important, cultural and idealized factors can play an even more important role.

Interior Design

The mix of cultural, social, and other values is often translated into detailed features of the interiors of homes and other places. This is nicely illustrated in Hazard's (1962) analysis of courtroom designs in different cultures. His basic theme is that courtrooms reflect the culturally defined role of the participants, whether they are judges, prosecutors, defendants, or juries. For example, in the Soviet Union prior to 1917 the judge sat at the same level as participants; the intention was to reinforce his role as conciliator and wise person in the village. In modern Russia, however, the judge sits on a platform and everyone stands as he enters the room, reflecting a higher and different status than before. This is also true in American and British courtrooms, where the judge is a high status person, a robed and remote figure at the center of the courtroom. The physical location of the judge clearly indicates a powerful position and controlling role in legal affairs. The relationship of the jury box, the witness, and the judge is also interesting. In English and American courtrooms, the jury box is located to the side, and the witness chair is between the judge and jury, facing outward, which lends a sense of importance to the roles of judge and jury, although it also indicates their separate roles in the judicial system. In Swiss courts, however, the judge and jury share the same physical location, sitting side-by-side at a long table. In some cases, they also share mutually in the decision making of guilt or innocence. Thus, their joint role in judicial decisions is reflected in their physical location near one another. In summary, the physical position of the judge and jury vis-à-vis one another is an example of the fit between cultural roles and environmental design.

The location of the prosecutor in different societies also fits with cultural roles. In the American courtroom, the prosecutor is at the same level of equality as the defense attorney and has no special chair or table compared to the defense. Both face the judge and jury, and both are equal advocates of their positions in the eyes of the law. However, in Switzerland, the judge, jury and prosecutor all sit at a large semicircular bench, with the judge in the middle and all three parties above the other participants. Here, the prosecutor is viewed as a closer part of the magistrate system than in American courts and this is reflected in physical location in the courtroom. Thus, the examination of special places and their interior arrangements often reveals how cultural values are represented in environmental design.

As another example of interior design, Altman et al. (1972) reported that a sample of lower middle class homes in the northeastern and midwestern United States had common facilities in kitchens and similar layouts of living and family rooms. For example, there often was a design unit consisting of a sofa, coffee table, and adjacent end tables and lamps in a cohesive unit in living rooms, along with either separate dining rooms or dining areas. An interesting example of cultural assimilation was reported by Canter (undated manuscript), who examined present-day Japanese homes. Beyond the well-known flexible arrangements of furniture and space, Canter observed the gradual inclusion of Western furniture in Japanese homes. It will be interesting to track the future impact of this gradual westernization process on home use and design, and on social interaction processes.

This theme can be extended down to the level of codes, regulations, and minimal standards for health (Rapoport and Watson, 1972). For example, the acceptable temperature comfort zone in Great Britain is 63 degrees, whereas in the United States 70–72 degrees is seen as minimally acceptable (in the energy crisis of 1974, Americans were asked to sacrifice and voluntarily lower their thermostats to 68 degrees!). Furthermore, Rapoport and Watson observed that United States standards for tables in restaurants are larger than in India; double beds in India are smaller than those in England; sizes of kitchen counters vary across cultures; in the United States fewer walk-up flights are permitted in buildings than in other cultures; and American standards for office and school lighting are much higher than in many other countries.

A Concluding Comment

Whether cultures are viewed at the broad level of their world view and the design of cities and communities, or at the level of homes or interior spaces, it is clear that culture and the environment are closely linked. And, as the general framework of this chapter posits, these linkages are not one-way or simply deterministic. The environmental products of our cognitions, behaviors, and cultural and environmental forces are also the bases for changes in such factors; each of these contribute to changes in one another in a complex and dynamic system. Furthermore, while it is clear that cultures differ in many aspects of their relationship to the environment, it is also true that there are many similarities among societies. Systematic work in this area has just begun and requires the efforts of many disciplines and perspectives. At this stage of knowledge, only the most elementary relationships between culture and the physical environment have been tapped, and there are as yet no firm principles, laws, or theories. In fact, the field also lacks a firm empirical data base in several areas. However, the integration of concepts from diverse areas and the analysis of cultural similarities and differences in relationship to the physical environment is an exciting and potentially important route to the understanding of human behavior.

Note

1. We appreciate the comments made on earlier drafts of this chapter by Amos Rapoport, Marshall Segall, Harry Triandis, John Berry, David Stea, and Richard Brislin. We are also indebted to the fellows of the East-West Center who provided detailed comments on the chapter, and particularly to Brian Bishop, Betty Drinkwater, and Angela Ginorio, who were responsible for integrating reactions to our chapter.

References

AIELLO, J. R., & JONES, S. E. Field study of the proxemic behavior of young school children in three subcultural groups. *Journal of Personality and Social Psychology,* 1971, *19,* 351–56.

ALEXANDER, C. Houses generated by patterns. Center for Environmental Structure, Berkeley, 1969.

ALKIRE, W. H. Porpoises and taro. *Ethnology,* 1968, *7*(3), 280–90.

ALLPORT, G., & PETTIGREW, T. Cultural influence on the perception of movement: the trapezoidal illusion among the Zulus. *Journal of Abnormal and Social Psychology,* 1957, *55,* 105–13.

ALTMAN, I. Some perspectives on the study of man-environment phenomena. *Representative Research in Social Psychology,* 1973, *4*(1), 109–26.

———. *Environment and social behavior: privacy, personal space, territory, and crowding.* Monterey, Calif.: Brooks-Cole, 1975.

———. Privacy regulation: culturally universal or culturally specific? *Journal of Social Issues,* 1977, *33*(3), 79–109.

ALTMAN, I., & CHEMERS, M. M. *Culture and environment.* Monterey, Calif.: Brooks-Cole, in press.

ALTMAN, I., NELSON, P. A., & LETT, E. E. The ecology of home environments. *Catalog of Selected Documents in Psychology.* Washington, D. C.: American Psychological Association, Spring, 1972.

ALTMAN, I., & VINSEL, A. M. Personal space: an analysis of E. T. Hall's proxemics framework. In I. Altman & J. Wohlwill (Eds.), *Human behavior and environment: advances in theory and research*, Vol. 2. New York: Plenum, 1977, pp. 181–259.

ANDERSON, E. N., Jr. Some Chinese methods of dealing with crowding. *Urban Anthropology*, 1972, *1*(2), 141–50.

APPLEYARD, D. Why buildings are known: a predictive tool for architects and planners. *Environment and Behavior*, 1969, *1*, 131–56.

————. Styles and methods of structuring a city. *Environment and Behavior*, 1970, *2*, 100–18.

BARKER, R. G. *Ecological psychology*. Stanford: Stanford University Press, 1968.

BAUM, A., & EPSTEIN, Y. (Eds.), *Human response to crowding*. New York: Wiley/Halsted, 1978.

BAUM, A., & VALINS, S. Residential environments, group size and crowding. *Proceedings of the 81st Annual Convention of the American Psychological Association*, 1973, *8*, 211–12.

————. *Architecture and social behavior: psychological studies in social density*. New York: Wiley/Halsted, 1977.

BAXTER, J. C. Interpersonal spacing in natural settings. *Sociometry*, 1970, *33*, 444–56.

BECKER, F. D. Study of spatial markers. *Journal of Personality and Social Psychology*, 1973, *26*(3), 439–45.

BERRY, J. W. An ecological approach to cross-cultural psychology. *Netherlands Journal of Psychology*, 1975, *30*, 51–84.

BIDERMAN, A., LOURIA, M., & BACCHUS, J. *Historical incidents of extreme overcrowding*. Washington, D. C.: Bureau of Social Science, 1963.

BLAUT, J. M., McCLEARY, G. S., Jr., & BLAUT, A. S. Environmental mapping in young children. *Environment and Behavior*, 1970, *2*(3), 335–51.

BOAL, F. Territoriality on the Shankillfaus Divide, Belfast, *Irish Georgraphy*, 1969, *6*, 30–50.

BOCHNER, S. The house form as a cornerstone of culture. In R. W. Brislin (Ed.), *Topics in Culture Learning*, Vol. 3. Honolulu, Hawaii: East-West Center, 1975, pp. 9–21.

BOOTH, A., & WELCH, S. The effects of crowding: a cross-national study. Paper presented at American Psychological Association, Montreal, 1973.

BRIGGS, R. Urban cognitive distance. In R. N. Downs & D. Stea (Eds.), *Image and environment: cognitive mapping and spatial behavior*. Chicago: Aldine, 1973, pp. 361–88.

BRISLIN, R., LONNER, W., & THORNDIKE, R. *Cross-cultural research methods*. New York: Wiley, 1973.

BRUNER, J. S. On perceptual readiness. *Psychological Review*, 1957, *64*, 123–52.

CANTER, D., & CANTER, S. Close together in Tokyo. *Design and Environment*, 1971, *2*, 60–63.

CAVAN, S. Interaction in home territories. *Berkeley Journal of Sociology*, 1963, *8*, 17–32.

————. *Liquor license*. Chicago: Aldine, 1966.

COLE, M., & SCRIBNER, S. *Culture and thought: a psychological introduction*. New York: Wiley, 1974.

Cox, D. R., & Zannaras, G. Designative perception of macro spaces: concepts, methodology, and applications. In R. N. Downs & D. Stea (Eds.), *Image and environment: cognitive mapping and spatial behavior.* Chicago: Aldine, 1973, pp. 162–78.

DeJonge, D. Images of urban areas: their structure and psychological foundations. *Journal of the American Institute of Planners,* 1962, *28*(4), 266–76.

Downs, R. N., & Stea, D. Cognitive maps and spatial behavior: process and products. In R. N. Downs & D. Stea (Eds.), *Image and environment: cognitive mapping and spatial behavior.* Chicago: Aldine, 1973, pp. 8–26.

————. (Eds.) *Image and environment: cognitive mapping and spatial behavior.* Chicago: Aldine, 1973.

Draper, P. Crowding among hunter-gatherers: the !Kung bushmen. *Science,* 1973, *182,* 301–03.

Dubos, R. *Man adapting.* New Haven, Conn.: Yale University Press, 1965.

————. *So human an animal.* New York: Charles Scribner & Sons, 1968.

Edney, J. J. Property, possession and permanence: a field study in human territoriality. *Journal of Applied Social Psychology,* 1972, *3*(3). 275–82.

————. Human territories: comment on functional properties. *Environment and Behavior,* 1976, *8*(1), 31–48.

Engebretson, D., & Fullmer, D. Cross-cultural differences in territoriality: interaction distances of native Japanese, Hawaii-Japanese, and American Caucasians. *Journal of Cross-Cultural Psychology,* 1970, *1*(3), 261–69.

Fahim, H. Nubian resettlement in the Sudan. Paper presented at conference on psychosocial consequences of sedentarism, University of California at Los Angeles, 1974.

Forston, R. F., & Larson, C. U. The dynamics of space. *Journal of Communication,* 1968, *18,* 109–16.

Francescato, D., & Mebane, W. How citizens view two great cities: Milan and Rome. In R. N. Downs & D. Stea (Eds.), *Image and environment: cognitive mapping and spatial behavior.* Chicago: Aldine, 1973, pp. 131–47.

Galle, O. R., Gove, W. R., & McPherson, J. M. Population density and pathology: what are the relationships for man? *Science,* 1972, *176,* 23–30.

Golledge, R. G., & Zannaras, G. Cognitive approaches to the analysis of human spatial behavior. In W. H. Ittleson (Ed.), *Environment and cognition.* New York: Seminar Press, 1973, pp. 59–94.

Gould, P. R. The black boxes of Jonkoping: spatial information and preference. In R. N. Downs & D. Stea (Eds.), *Image and environment: cognitive mapping and spatial behavior.* Chicago: Aldine, 1973a, pp. 235–45.

————. On mental maps. In R. N. Downs & D. Stea (Eds.), *Image and environment: cognitive mapping and spatial behavior.* Chicago: Aldine, 1973b, pp. 182–220.

Gould, P. R., & White, R. *Mental Maps.* New York: Penguin Books, 1974.

Gregor, T. A. Exposure and seclusion: a study of institutionalized isolation among the Mehinacu Indians of Brazil. *Ethnology,* 1970, *9*(3), 234–50.

————. Publicity, privacy, and Mehinacu marriage. *Ethnology,* 1974, *13*(3), 333–49.

Hall, E. T. *The silent language.* Garden City, N.Y.: Doubleday, 1959.

————. *The hidden dimension.* Garden City, N. Y.: Doubleday, 1966.

————. *Handbook for proxemic research*. Washington, D. C.: Society for the Anthropology of Visual Communication, 1974.

HANSEN, W. B., & ALTMAN, I. Decorating personal places: a descriptive analysis. *Environment and Behavior*, 1976, *21*(2), 106–08.

HART, R. A., & MOORE, G. T. The development of spatial cognition: a review. In R. N. Downs & D. Stea (Eds.), *Image and environment: cognitive mapping and spatial behavior*. Chicago: Aldine, 1973, pp. 246–88.

HAZARD, J. N. Furniture arrangement as a symbol of judicial roles. *A Review of General Semantics*, 1962, *19*(2), 181–88.

HEDIGER, H. *Wild animals in captivity*. London: Butterworth, 1950.

HEIDER, F. *The psychology of interpersonal relations*. New York: Wiley, 1958.

HERSKOVITS, M. J. *Man and his works*. New York: Knopf, 1952.

HERTZBERG,, H. W. *The great tree and the longhouse: the culture of the Iroquois*. New York: MacMillan, 1966.

HOWARD, R. B., CHASE, S. D., & ROTHMAN, M. An analysis of four measures of cognitive maps. In W. F. E. Preiser (Ed.), *Environmental design research*, Vol. 1. Stroudsburg, Pa.: Dowden, Hutchinson and Ross, 1973, pp. 254–64.

HUTT, C., & VAIZEY, M. J. Differential effects of group density on social behavior. *Nature*, 1966, *209*, 1371–72.

ITTELSON, W. H. Environment perception and contemporary perceptual theory. In W. H. Ittelson (Ed.), *Environment and cognition*. New York: Seminar Press, 1973. pp. 1–19.

ITTELSON, W. H., & PROSHANSKY, H. M., & RIVLIN, L. G. A study of bedroom use on two psychiatric wards. *Hospital and Community Psychiatry*, 1970, *21*, 177–80.

ITTELSON, W. H., & WINKEL, G. H. *Introduction to environmental psychology*. New York: Holt, Rinehart and Winston, 1974.

JONES, S. E. A comparative proxemics analysis of dyadic interaction in selected subcultures of New York City. *Journal of Social Psychology*, 1971, *84*, 35–44.

JONES, S. E., & AIELLO, J. R. Proxemic behavior of black and white first, third, and fifth grade children. *Journal of Personality and Social Psychology*, 1973, *25*(1), 21–27.

KAPLAN, S. Cognitive maps in perception and thought. In R. N. Downs & D. Stea (Eds.), *Image and environment: cognitive mapping and spatial behavior*. Chicago: Aldine, 1973, pp. 63–78.

KATES, R. W. *Hazard and choice perception in flood plain management*. Chicago: University of Chicago, Department of Geography, Research Paper No. 78, 1962.

————. Perceptual regions and regional perception in flood plain management. *Papers and Proceedings of the Regional Science Association*, 1963, *11*, 217–28.

KELVIN, P. A social psychological examination of privacy. *British Journal of Social and Clinical Psychology*, 1973, *12*, 248–61.

KIRA, A. *The bathroom*. Ithaca, N. Y.: Cornell University Center for Housing and Environmental Studies, 1966. (Reprinted in H. M. Proshansky, W. H. Ittelson, & L. G. Rivlin (Eds.), *Environmental psychology*. New York: Holt, Rinehart, and Winston, 1970. pp. 269–75.)

KLUCKHOHN, F. R. Dominant and variant value orientations. In C. Kluckhohn, H. A. Murray, & D. M. Schneider (Eds.), *Personality in nature, society and culture*. New York: Knopf, 1953.

KOFFKA, K. *Principles of Gestalt psychology*. New York: Harcourt Brace, 1935.

LADD, F. C. Black youths view their environments: neighborhood maps. *Environment and Behavior*, 1970, 2(1), 74–100.

LAUFER, R. S., PROSHANSKY, H. M., & WOLFE, M. Some analytic dimensions of privacy. Paper presented at the Third International Architectural Psychology Conference, Lund, Sweden, 1973.

LEE, D. *Freedom and culture*. Englewood Cliffs, N. J.: Prentice-Hall, 1959.

LEE, T. R. Psychology and living space. In R. N. Downs & D. Stea (Eds.), *Image and environment: cognitive mapping and spatial behavior*. Chicago: Aldine, 1973, pp. 87–108.

LEWIN, K. *Field theory in social science*. New York: Harper & Row, 1951.

LEWIS, O. *Five families*. New York: Mentor Books, 1959.

————. *The children of Sanchez*. New York: Random House, 1961.

LEY, D., & CYBRIWSKY, R. Urban graffiti as territorial markers. *Annals of the Association of American Geographies*, 1974, 64(4), 491–505.

LITTLE, K. B. Cultural variations in social schemata. *Journal of Personality and Social Psychology*, 1968, 10, 1–7.

LOO, C. M. The effects of spatial density on the social behavior of children. *Journal of Applied Social Psychology*, 1973, 2(4), 372–81.

LOWREY, R. A. A method for analyzing distance concepts of urban residents. In R. N. Downs & D. Stea (Eds.), *Image and environment: cognitive mapping and spatial behavior*. Chicago: Aldine, 1973, pp. 338–60.

LYNCH, K. *The image of the city*. Cambridge, Mass.: MIT Press, 1960.

LYNCH, K., & RIVLIN, M. A walk around the block. *Landscape*, 1959, 8, 24–34.

MCDONALD, W. S., & ODEN, C. W., Jr. Effects of extreme crowding on the performance of five married couples during twelve weeks of intensive training. *Proceedings of the 81st Annual Convention of the American Psychological Association*, 1973, 8, 209–10.

MCGREW, P. L. Social and spatial density effects on spacing behavior in preschool children. *Journal of Child Psychology and Psychiatry*, 1970, 11, 197–205.

MARSELLA, A. J., ESCUDERO, M., & GORDON, P. The effects of dwelling density on mental disorders in Filipino men. *Journal of Health and Social Behavior*, 1970, 11(4), 288–94.

MAURER, R., & BAXTER, J. C. Images of the neighborhood and city among Black, Anglo and Mexican-American children. *Environment and Behavior*, 1972, 4(4), 351–89.

MICHELSON, W. *Man and his urban environment: a sociological approach*. Reading, Mass.: Addison-Wesley, 1970.

MILES, D. The Ngadju Dayaks of Central Kalimantan, with special reference to the Upper Mentaya. *Behavior Science Notes*, 1970, 5(4), 291–319.

MILGRAM, S. The experience of living in cities. *Science*, 1970, 167, 1461–68.

————. Psychological maps of Paris. In H. Proshansky, W. H. Ittelson, & L. G. Rivlin (Eds.), *Environmental psychology* (2nd ed.). New York: Holt, Rinehart and Winston, 1976, pp. 105–24.

MITCHELL, R. Some social implications of higher density housing. *American Sociological Review*, 1971, 36, 18–29.

MUNROE, R. L., & MUNROE, R. H. Population density and affective relationships in three East African societies. *Journal of Social Psychology*, 1972, 88, 15–20.

MUNROE, R. L., MUNROE, R. H., NERLOVE, S. B., & DANIELS, R. E. Effects of population density on food concern in three East African societies. *Journal of Health and Social Behavior*, 1969, 10, 161–71.

NEWMAN, O. *Denfensible space.* New York: MacMillan, 1972.

O'NEILL, S. M., & PALUCK, R. J. Altering territoriality through reinforcement. *Proceedings of the 81st Annual Convention of the American Psychological Association*, 1973, 8, 901–02.

ORLEANS, P. Differential cognition of urban residents: effects of social scale on mapping. In R. N. Downs & D. Stea (Eds.), *Image and environment: cognitive mapping and spatial behavior.* Chicago: Aldine, 1973, pp. 115–30.

PARK, R. E., BURGESS, E. W., & MCKENZIE, R. D. *The city, Chicago.* Chicago: University of Chicago Press, 1925.

PETERSON, N. Hunter-gatherer territoriality: the perspective from Australia. *American Anthropologist*, 1975, 77(1), 53–68.

PROSHANSKY, H., ITTELSON, W. H., & RIVLIN, L. G. (Eds.), *Environmental psychology.* New York: Holt, Rinehart and Winston, 1970.

PRUSSIN, L. Fulani architectural change. Paper presented at Conference on psychosocial consequences of sedentarism, University of California at Los Angeles, 1974.

RAPOPORT, A. *House form and culture.* Englewood Cliffs, N. J.: Prentice-Hall, 1969.

———. Nomadism as a people-environment system. Paper presented at Conference on psychosocial consequences of sedentarism, University of California at Los Angeles, 1974.

———. Toward a redefinition of density. *Environment and Behavior*, 1975, 7(2), 133–59.

———. Environmental cognition in cross-cultural perspective. In G. T. Moore & R. G. Golledge (Eds.), *Environmental knowing.* Stroudsburg, Pa.: Dowden, Hutchinsin and Ross, 1976.

———. *Human aspects of urban form.* Oxford, England: Pergamon, 1977.

RAPOPORT, A., & WATSON, N. Cultural variability in physical standards. In R. Gutman (Ed.), *People and buildings.* New York: Basic Books, 1972.

ROBERTS, J. M., & GREGOR, T. Privacy: a cultural view. In J. R. Pennock & J. W. Chapman (Eds.), *Privacy.* New York: Atherton, 1971, pp. 180–225.

ROGLER, L. H. Slum neighborhoods in Latin America. *Journal of Inter-American Studies*, 1967, 9(4), 507–28.

ROHE, W., & PATTERSON, A. H. The effects of varied levels of resources and density on behavior in a day care center. Paper presented at Environmental Design Research Association, Milwaukee, Wisconsin, 1974.

SAARINEN, T. F. Student views of the world. In R. N. Downs & D. Stea (Eds.), *Image and environment: cognitive mapping and spatial behavior.* Chicago: Aldine, 1973a, pp. 148–61.

———. The use of projective techniques in geographic research. In W. H. Ittelson (Ed.), *Environment and cognition.* New York: Seminar Press, 1973b, pp. 29–52.

SCHERER, S. E. Proxemic behavior of primary school children as a function of their socioeconomic class and subculture. *Journal of Personality and Social Psychology,* 1974, *29*(6), 800–05.

SCHWARTZ, B. The social psychology of privacy. *American Journal of Sociology,* 1968, *73,* 741–52.

SEGALL, M. H., CAMPBELL, D. T., & HERSKOVITS, M. J. *The influence of culture on visual perception.* Indianapolis: Bobbs-Merrill, 1966.

SIMMEL, G. The metropolis and mental life. In K. W. Wolff (Ed.), *The sociology of Georg Simmel.* New York: Free Press, 1950.

SIMON, H. A. *Models of man.* New York: Wiley, 1957.

SOMMER, R. Studies in personal space. *Sociometry,* 1959, *22,* 247–60.

———. Leadership and group geography. *Sociometry,* 1961, *24,* 99–110.

———. The distance for comfortable conversation: a further study. *Sociometry,* 1962, *25,* 111–16.

———. Intimacy ratings in five countries. *International Journal of Psychology,* 1968, *3,* 109–14.

———. *Personal space.* Englewood Cliffs, N. J.: Prentice-Hall, 1969.

SOMMER, R., BECKER, F. D. Territorial defense and the good neighbor. *Journal of Personality and Social Psychology,* 1969, *11,* 85–92.

STEA, D., & BLAUT, J. M. Some preliminary observations on spatial learning in school children. In R. N. Downs & D. Stea (Eds.), *Image and environment: cognitive mapping and spatial behavior.* Chicago: Aldine, 1973a, pp. 226–34.

———. Toward a developmental theory of spatial mapping. In R. N. Downs & D. Stea (Eds.), *Image and environment: cognitive mapping and spatial behavior.* Chicago: Aldine, 1973b, pp. 51–62.

STILGOE, J. R. Jack-O-Lanterns to surveyors: the secularization of landscape boundaries. *Environmental Review,* 1976, *1,* 14–31.

STOKOLS, D. A social psychological model of human crowding phenomena. *American Institute of Planners Journal,* 1972a, *38,* 72–83.

———. On the distinction between density and crowding: some implications for future research. *Psychological Review,* 1972b, *79*(3), 275–78.

STOKOLS, D., RALL, M., PINNER, B., & SCHOPLER, J., Jr. Physical, social, and personal determinants of the perception of crowding. *Environment and Behavior,* 1973, *5*(1), 87–117.

SUNDSTROM, E. An experimental study of crowding: effects of room size, intrusion, and goal blocking on nonverbal behaviors, self-disclosure and self-reported stress. *Journal of Personality and Social Psychology,* 1975, *32*(4), 645–54.

SUTTLES, G. D. *The social order of the slum.* Chicago: University of Chicago Press, 1968.

THOMPSON, B. J., & BAXTER, J. C. Interpersonal spacing in two-person cross-cultural interaction. *Man-Environment Systems,* 1973, *3*(2), 115–17.

THRASHER, F. J. *The gang.* Chicago: University of Chicago Press, 1927.

TOLMAN, E. C. *Purposive behavior in animals and man.* New York: Century, 1932.

TRIANDIS, H. C., VASSILIOU, V., VASSILIOU, G., TANAKA, Y. & SHANMUGAM, A. V. *The analysis of subjective culture.* New York: Wiley, 1971.

TUAN, Y. F. *Man and nature*. Commission on College Geography Resource Paper No. 10. Association of American Geographers, Washington, D. C., 1971.

―――. *Space and place: the perspective of experience*. Minneapolis: University of Minnesota Press, 1977.

―――. *Topophilia: a study of environmental perception, attitude and values*. Englewood Cliffs, N. J.: Prentice-Hall, 1974.

TURNBULL, C. *The forest people*. New York: Simon and Schuster, 1961.

VALINS, S., & BAUM, A. Residential group size, social interaction and crowding. *Environment and Behavior*, 1973, *5* (4), 421–440.

WATSON, O. M., & GRAVES, T. D. Quantitative research in proxemic behavior. *American Anthropologist*, 1966, *68*, 971–985.

WESTIN, A. *Privacy and freedom*. New York: Atheneum Press, 1970.

WOHWILL, J. S. The environment is not in the head! In W. F. E. Preiser (Ed.), *Environmental Design Research*, Vol. II. Stroudsburg, Pa.: Dowden, Hutchinson and Ross, 1973, 166–181.

WOLFE, M., & LAUFER, R. The concept of privacy in childhood and adolescence. Paper presented at the Environmental Design Research Association, Milwaukee, Wisconsin, 1974.

ZEISEL, J. *Sociology and architectural design*. New York: Russell Sage Foundation, 1974.

ZEISEL, J. Symbolic meaning of space and the physical dimension of social relations: a case study of sociological research as the basis of architectural planning. In J. Walton & D. Carns (Eds.), *Cities in change: studies on the urban condition*. Boston: Allyn and Bacon, 1973, 252–263.

ZILLER, R. C., LONG, B. H., RAMANA, K. V., & REDDY, V. E. Self-other orientations of Indian and American adolescents. *Journal of Personality*, 1968, *36*, 315–330.

Name Index

395

Tong, W. F., 70
Tonnucci, F., 131, 151
Topichak, P. M., 49, 69
Touraine, A., 90, 120
Tozgonyi, T., 330
Triandis, H. C., 1, 8, 9, 10, 11, 21, 22, 32,
    33, 35, 38, 40, 41, 42, 52, 54, 55, 56,
    57, 62, 64, 66, 67, 70, 71, 87, 103,
    120, 136, 138, 140, 144, 148, 152,
    187, 201, 209, 246, 269, 278, 294,
    296, 324, 333, 345, 386, 392
Triandis, L. M., 8, 9, 10, 11, 21, 22, 32, 33,
    35, 38, 40, 41, 42, 52, 54, 55, 56, 57,
    62, 64, 66, 67, 70, 71
Trist, E. L., 286, 296, 316, 326, 333
Tscheulin, D., 299, 333
Tuan, Y. F., 356, 372, 379, 383
Turnbull, C., 344, 379
Turner, A. N., 307, 333
Turner, J. L., 136, 152
Turner, R., 119
Tyler, L., 51, 69
Tyler, S. A., 86, 87, 120

Ueno, Y., 207
Ugurel-Semin, R., 139, 152
Underwood, B. J., 106, 107, 120
Urwick, L., 285, 327

Vaizey, M. J., 377, 389
Valins, S., 375, 378, 387
Vallee, F., 261, 263, 278
Van Buren, H., 212, 271
Van Harrison, R., 307, 325
Van Rynefeld, J., 128, 151
Vassiliou, G., 87, 120, 392
Vassiliou, V., 40, 41, 42, 43, 51, 52, 54, 70,
    71, 120, 136, 152, 294, 333, 392
Veness, T., 94, 120
Verba, S., 59, 63, 138, 139, 147
Vernon, P. E., 101, 115, 245, 287
Vernoff, J., 235, 272, 310, 327
Vianello, M., 283, 333
Vidmar, N., 178, 209
Viet, J., 118
Villone, G., 131, 151
Vinsel, A. M., 365, 387
Vogt, E. Z., 159, 173, 202
Von Grumbkow, J., 133, 152
Vroom, V., 304, 333
Vu R., 41, 46, 49, 67

Wagatsuma, H., 212, 278
Wahl, J., 94, 116
Wainer, H. A., 333
Waldman, S. R., 152
Wallace, A. F. C., 224, 244, 278
Wallach, M., 178, 205

Walster, E., 127, 130, 141, 149, 150, 152,
    153
Walster, G., 153
Walton, R. E., 316, 317, 333
Warwick, D., 7, 8, 214, 274
Waters, J. A., 332
Watson, Q. M., 365, 385, 393
Weaver, C. N., 312, 333
Weber, M., 95, 120, 278, 284, 285, 333
Weibrod, R., 63
Weick, K. E., 153
Weigert, A. J., 60, 71
Weiner, M., 277, 278
Weinstein, E. A., 125, 151
Weiser, G., 283, 333
Weiss, W., 44
Weitz, J., 49, 69
Welch, S., 387
Wesolowski, W., 313, 332
Westie, F. R., 38, 67
Westin, A., 360, 362
Wherry, R. J., 302, 332
Whicker, A., 23
White, B. J., 179, 192, 208
White, J. H., 134, 152
White, P. E., 125, 150
White, R., 205, 304, 334, 347, 348, 351,
    355, 356, 388
Whitehill, A. M., 319, 334
Whiting, B. M., 156, 163, 170, 191, 192,
    195, 208, 209
Whiting, J. W., 6, 23, 156, 163, 170, 191,
    192, 195, 208, 209, 341
Whitney, R. E., 230, 272
Whittaker, J. D., 292, 329
Whittaker, J. O., 44, 71, 156, 164, 167, 169,
    180, 207, 209
Whyte, W. F., 300, 301, 312, 334
Wicker, A., 11, 23
Wieder, L. D., 87, 120
Wild, R., 307, 315, 325
Wilde, J. S., 278
Wilke, H., 129, 133, 152, 153
Willer, D., 29, 71
Williams, L. K., 300, 301, 312, 334
Williamson, R. C., 46, 69
Wills, R., 151
Wilpert, B., 334
Windle, C., 51, 57, 69
Winer, B., 286, 298, 304, 327
Winkel, G. H., 342, 389
Winter, D., 234, 238, 244, 269, 276
Winter, D. G., 295, 329
Winters, D. G., 143, 151
Wintrop, R. M., 263, 278
Witkin, H. A., 254, 264, 267, 278, 296, 297,
    334
Wober, M., 258, 278, 334
Wofenstein, M., 206

Subject Index